Centro de Estudios Puertorriqueños

CENTRO JOURNAL
VOLUME XXX • NUMBER III • FALL 2018

COVER ART
King of the Road (2017) by Víctor Vázquez. Instalation, variable measures.
Reprinted, by permission, from Víctor Vázquez. © Víctor Vázquez.

ISSN: 1538-6279 (Print); ISSN: 2163-2960 (Online)

ISBN: 978-1-945662-30-0 (Print); 978-1-945662-31-7 (ebook)

©2018 Centro de Estudios Puertorriqueños

Hunter College / City University of New York

695 Park Avenue, E-1429, New York, NY 10065

212.772.5690 • Fax 212.650.3673 • http://centropr.hunter.cuny.edu

CENTRO Journal is indexed or abstracted in: Academic Search Complete (EBSCO host); Alternative Press Index; America: History and Life; Cabell's Whitelist; Caribbean Abstracts; CONUCO–Consorcio Universitario de Indización; Gale; HAPI—Hispanic American Periodical Index; Historical Abstracts; Left Index; MLA International Index; OCLC PAIS; Pro Quest; Scopus; Social Services Abstracts; Social Scisearch; Sociological Abstracts; Ulrich's Periodicals Service; H.W. Wilson Humanities Abstracts; Worldwide Political Science Abstracts.

CENTRO

Journal of the Center for Puerto Rican Studies

VOLUME XXX • NUMBER III • FALL 2018

Puerto Rico Post-Hurricane Maria: Origins and Consequences of a Crisis

Guest Editors:
Edwin Meléndez and Charles R. Venator-Santiago

Introduction to Puerto Rico Post-Maria: Origins and Consequences of a Crisis

EDWIN MELÉNDEZ AND CHARLES R. VENATOR-SANTIAGO

Few Americans will forget the controversy over President Donald Trump's construction of additional sections of a wall separating the U.S. from Mexico and the closing of the federal government for a month at the end of 2018 and into 2019. Yet, few Americans will recall how Puerto Rico's recovery assistance after Hurricane Maria got entangled in that controversy. As in many times in the past, U.S. policies toward Puerto Rico are conjunctural and too often have contradictory impacts on its economy and people. As a territory of the U.S., Puerto Rico is entitled to the benefits of the Stafford Act—the *de facto* national insurance policy to support communities after natural disasters. While private insurance covers most private property, such as housing and commercial buildings, the act covers public assets and damages to community's infrastructure and other assets and aid to individuals. Consistent with this purpose, as the law has provided aid in numerous occasions in the past to other states and territories, Congress appropriated funding for Puerto Rico. With the approval of the $10 billion in

Edwin Meléndez (emele@hunter.cuny.edu) is a Professor of Urban Policy and Planning and the Director of the Center for Puerto Rican Studies at Hunter College, CUNY. In addition to numerous scientific papers and other publications, he is the author or editor of thirteen books including *State of Puerto Ricans* (Centro Press, 2017) and *Puerto Ricans at the Dawn of the New Millenium* (Centro Press, 2014). He also served as invited Editor for "Pathways to Economic Opportunity" *CENTRO Journal* 23(2), 2011.

Charles R. Venator-Santiago (charles.venator@uconn.edu) is an Associate Professor with a joint appointment in the Department of Political Science and El Instituto at the University of Connecticut. He is also the Secretariat and Vice-President/President Elect (2021-2022) of the Puerto Rican Studies Association. He is the coordinator of the Puerto Rico Citizenship Archives Project and the American Samoa Nationality and Citizenship Archives Project, and the author of *Puerto Rico and the Origins of U.S. Global Empire: The Disembodied Shade* (Routledge, 2015).

contention, aid would add to about $40 billion in funding earmarked for Puerto Rico of the estimated over $80 billion in damages caused by Hurricanes Irma and Maria. Seeking funding for the wall, the White House was intended to cut the aid package for Puerto Rico proposed by the House Appropriations Committee from $10 billion to $1.3 billion. Regardless of the reasoning for undertaking this course of action or eventual outcome of the episode, this incidence is illustrative of a much lengthier historical pattern of erratic and at times arbitrary U.S. policies toward Puerto Rico.

This special issue of *CENTRO Journal* is devoted to the Puerto Rico Crisis, its origins, and how Hurricanes Irma and Maria further muddled a dreadful situation. The articles by stellar authors included cover a broad range of topics and disciplines and constitute the most in-depth analysis of Puerto Rico's situation published to date in an academic journal. But what crisis are we referring to? The mainstream media often refers to the economic crisis as a catchall concept that is inclusive of many other causes and aspects of the crisis. It is more prudent, however, to refer to the situation using a plural tense and refer to the crises of Puerto Rico. The authors in this volume make such distinctions sharp. Several authors address the underlying economic crisis, which in turn affects public borrowing and the accumulation of debt. But how to separate Puerto Rico's debt crisis from congressional policies toward Puerto Rico or from the political ineffectiveness of local political leaders who borrowed the funds, indebted the country and ultimately contributed to a prolonged economic stagnation? Furthermore, other authors address that the crises are not victimless—vulnerable populations received the

Graphic 1. EDB Economic Activity Index

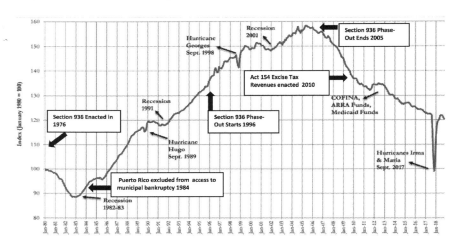

Source: The Economic Development Bank for Puerto Rico (EDB) The Puerto Rico Economic Activity Index ("EDB-EAI") November 2018.

brunt of austerity policies, while local and non-resident investors, many of them retirees living in fixed income, will probably recover a smaller share of their investment than speculative investors that bought bonds at a substantially reduced price.

This introduction provides context for the articles in this special issue. We begin with a stylized portrait of the crises. The following section addresses the origins and evolution of the economic crisis and how stagnation and political mismanagement led to the accumulation of debt. In that context, we introduce several articles that refer to the Puerto Rico Oversight, Management and Economic Stability Act (PROMESA) and the unfolding dynamics of austerity and economic recovery. These evolving dynamics of the crises have many faces. In the following section, we address core aspects of the crisis such as the evolving energy and agricultural sectors, and the exodus of Puerto Ricans and its impacts on the diaspora.

The Genesis of the Economic Crises

It is often said that one picture is worth a thousand words. Graphic 1 depicts the Puerto Rico Economic Activity Index (EAI) with a time line of key events over imposed. The EAI, published by the Economic Development Bank for Puerto Rico (EDB), correlates closely to both the level of economic activity, as measured by the Gross National Product (GNP), and to the rate of growth of the GNP. Graphic 1 summarizes Puerto Rico's economic performance since the inception of the EAI in 1980—the base year for the index (EAI=100).

In 1976, Section 936 of the Internal Revenue Code was created to support the island's economic recovery. Puerto Rico had entered in its first prolonged post-WWII

Table 1. Employment by Major Industrial Sector

Year	1995	2005	2017	95/05	05/17
Total Non Farm	912	1,053	887	15.5%	-15.7%
Mining, Logging & Construction	46	68	23	48.3%	-67.0%
Manufacturing	153	117	73	-23.3%	-37.9%
Trade, Transportation & Utilities	181	188	172	3.6%	-8.3%
Financial Industries	42	49	43	15.8%	-12.6%
Services	164	324	353	97.4%	9.1%
Government	304	308	225	1.3%	-27.1%
Federal Government	NA	15	14	NA	-3.1%
State Government	NA	230	154	NA	-32.9%
Local Government	NA	63	56	NA	-11.6%

Source: Department of Labor and Human Resources, Bureau of Labor Statistics, Establishment Survey (Non Farm Employment).

King of the Road (2017) by Víctor Vázquez. Instalation, variable measures.
Reprinted, by permission, from Víctor Vázquez. © Víctor Vázquez.

King of the Road (2017), detail. © Víctor Vázquez

recession in the 1970s when the island economy relied on processing oil imports from Arab countries after the Organization of Petroleum Exporting Countries (OPEC) imposed an embargo against the United States as President Nixon decided to support Israel during the 1973 Arab-Israeli War. The oil refinery industry collapsed, and, with it, Puerto Rico's economy went into a recession. Section 936 exempted U.S. companies from federal taxes on repatriated income earned in Puerto Rico. Section 936 worked as intended. By the early 1990s, pharmaceutical and high-tech manufacturing had become the undisputable economic anchors of the island's economy, while Controlled Foreign Corporations (CFCs) were earning billions of dollars in profits exempted from federal taxes. In 1995, President Clinton found in Section 936 federal tax exemptions a source of tax revenues to support legislation favoring U.S. small businesses. Congress began a ten-year phase out of Section 936 in 1996.

The EAI clearly shows that the economic stimulus of Section 936 to manufacturing in Puerto Rico not only led the island out of the 1970's recession but also that, during the time of federal tax exemptions for repatriation of profits, the economy grew at a steady pace up to the end of the phase out period in 2005. Table 1 summarizes employment by major industry sector for three key years: 1995, the year before Section 936's phase out began; 2005, when federal tax exemption ended; and 2017, the most recent data. The table provides a bird's-eye view of the economic restructuring of Puerto Rico over the last two decades. There are several notable patterns. First, the decline of 16 percent in the overall level of employment, from 1.05 million to 887 thousand, corresponding to a decline of an EAI from 158 to 120, a loss of 32 percent of its value, is demonstrative of the economic stagnation of the island since its peak in 2005.

The pattern of economic decline was briefly interrupted when The American Recovery and Reinvestment Act of 2009 (ARRA) funds were injected as a stimulus to overcome the financial crisis of 2008–09. A second pattern of importance is that manufacturing, state government and construction are the industrial sectors showing the greatest losses of employment. Manufacturing employment declined from 153,000 jobs in 1995 to 73,000 in 2017, a net loss of 80,000 jobs over the last two decades. This loss of total employment is followed by state government, with a loss of 76,000 jobs, and construction losing 23,000 jobs during the period.

Losses in employment in key industries are related to numerous causes. The prevalent narrative is that most of the job losses can be traced back to the elimination of Section 936 and the loss of federal tax exemption. Feliciano (2018, 32) finds empirical evidence establishing that "the elimination of Section 936 had a large negative impact on manufacturing employment." Though the change in policy played a key role, there were other important contributing factors, such as technological change and globalization affecting manufacturing more generally. However, the ruling political parties' inability to respond with effective economic development and fiscal policies to counter the phase out of Section 936 federal tax incentives and other broader factors, and their inability to restructure government to conform to a new fiscal reality were (and are) critical factors inducing the economic crisis (Caraballo-Cueto and Lara 2017; Meléndez 2018a).

After Congress enacted the phase-out of Section 936, Governor Pedro Rosselló launched a series of major infrastructure projects such as the Urban Train, a short-lived Superaqueduct, the Coliseum, the Convention Center, and numerous roads and bridges (Márquez and Carmona 2011). These projects required substantial financing through public borrowing, which resulted in over $24 billion increase in the debt. Of this total, the largest proportion of debt was accrued by public corporations for a total of over $17 billion. According to Meléndez (2018b, 79), "[i]nfrastructure development by increasing public indebtedness faster than induced economic activity, which would have expanded the commonwealth's tax base, was not an effective alternative long-term economic development strategy and set the foundation for the increased indebtedness of the country."

The mechanism to borrow beyond the Commonwealth's debt servicing capacity at the time was to create COFINA (from the Spanish name Corporación del Fondo de Interés Apremiante). COFINA introduced for the first time in modern history an island-wide 7 percent Puerto Rico Sales and Use Tax (SUT).

Graphic 2: Puerto Rico Public Dept by Sector

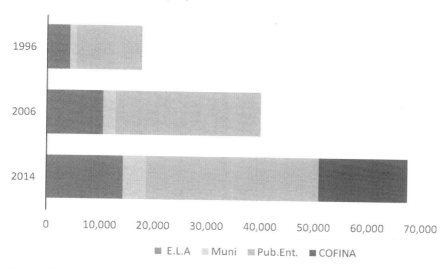

Source: Government Development Bank for Puerto Rico.
Notes: In millions of dollars, as of June 30, adjusted for inflation where 2014=0.

By 2006, when it was evident that the Commonwealth was not generating enough revenues to be able to serve future debt and maintain government operations without significant structural reforms, the political leadership's solution was to avoid dealing with the structural factors underlying the accumulation of debt by borrowing more from municipal capital markets. The mechanism to borrow beyond the Commonwealth's debt servicing capacity at the time was to create COFINA (from the Spanish name Corporación del Fondo de Interés Apremiante). COFINA introduced for the first time in modern history an island-wide 7 percent Puerto Rico Sales and Use Tax (SUT). Of the 7 percent new tax revenues, one-and-a-half percent went to municipalities, and the rest was equally divided between the central government and COFINA bondholders. In 2015, faced with declining revenues, the sales tax was increased from 7 percent to 11.5 percent. Puerto Rico now has the distinction of having the highest sales tax of any other jurisdiction in the U.S., and, by 2018, COFINA bonds accounted for the largest share (over $17 billion before restructuring) of the public debt in Puerto Rico.

After winning the 2008 elections, one of the first legislatives initiatives undertaken by Governor Luis Fortuño (2009–2012) was to declare a state of fiscal emergency. Amid massive protests, he enacted a fiscal stabilization plan that would reduce annual expenditures (at the time expected to be more than $2 billion) that eventually resulted in a 13.3 percent reduction in the Commonwealth's work force from 297,000 to 258,000

Table 2. Puerto Rican Retirement Plans, 2015 (a)

Year	Retirees	Net Pension Liability (in thousands)
ERS	124,497	33,247,795
TRS	40,601	14,994,583
JRS	430	542,583
Total	165,528	48,784,961

Source: Congressional Task Force on Economic Growth in Puerto Rico, Report to the House and Senate, 114th Congress, December 20, 2016.
Notes: Puerto Rico Retirement Plans are the Puerto Rico Teachers Retirement System (TRS), the Puerto Rico Government Employees Retirement System (ERS), and the Puerto Rico Judiciary Retirement System (JRS).

people. In addition, in October 2010, Governor Fortuño enacted one of the most significant fiscal reforms, with far reaching consequences for the manufacturing industry in Puerto Rico. The Act 154 Excise Tax Revenues enacted a 4 percent excise tax on the sales of multinational corporations (primarily pharmaceutical companies). By 2017, Act 154 revenues were estimated to be $1,924 million and accounted for 21.3 percent of total government revenues (Backdoor Bailout 2014). Perhaps because he instituted unpopular structural reforms, Governor Fortuño lost his reelection bid in the 2011 general elections. The new governor, Governor Alejandro Garcia-Padilla, inherited the height of the debt crisis when Puerto Rico bonds reached "junk" status in 2014.

The Debt Crisis
Graphic 2 depicts Puerto Rico's public debt by sectors for three critical benchmark years: 1996, when the Section 936 phaseout began; 2006, when COFINA was enacted; and 2014, the high point of accumulated public debt, when Puerto Rico bonds reached "junk" status. Infrastructure borrowing by public enterprises increased public debt about $15 billion, from $12.7 billion in 1996 to $27.2 billion in 2006—the second largest increase in debt between the selected benchmark years. By 2006 it was evident that many of the public corporations were in financial distress and many of them would have benefited from debt restructuring. A decade later, by the time that Governor Garcia-Padilla declared that Puerto Rico's public debt was "unpayable" in the summer of 2015, many public corporations were insolvent or near insolvency with mounting debt and no legal recourse to declare bankruptcy. In 1984 Congress adopted Section 903(1) of the Bankruptcy Code which excluded Puerto Rico's municipalities from access to bankruptcy—an option that was previously granted to municipal debt in Puerto Rico until the law was amended. Exclusion from bankruptcy would prove to be a critical factor later on for the enactment of PROMESA.

By 2014, Puerto Rico's total public debt reached over $74 billion. Despite the explosion of public corporations' debt in prior years, accounting for 46.8 percent of the total debt, the largest increase in public debt belongs to COFINA. Between 2006, when COFINA was enacted, and 2014, COFINA debt stood at $16.3 billion or 23.5 percent of the total debt. (Graphic 2) By 2014, the Commonwealth's (or E.L.A. for Spanish Estado Libre Asociado) debt accounted for 20.7 percent of the public debt and the municipal debt for the remaining 6 percent of the debt. According to Meléndez (2018b, 81), "If Puerto Rico had been covered by the U.S. Bankruptcy Code, the bulk of public debt carried by public authorities and municipalities accounting for over 50 percent of the total could have been restructured in federal court as the public corporations became insolvent and potentially avoided PROMESA's debt restructuring."

In addition to the public debt, the Commonwealth had nearly $49 billion in net pensions liability. As Table 2 illustrates, in 2015, Puerto Rico Retirement Plans included the Puerto Rico Government Employees Retirement System (ERS) with 124,497 retirees, by far the largest of the three systems, followed by the Puerto Rico Teachers Retirement System (TRS) with 40,601 retirees, and the Puerto Rico Judiciary Retirement System (JRS) with 430 retirees. The ERS net pension liabilities totaled $33.2 billion, the TRS $15 billion, and the JRS half a billion. Eventually, in 2017, with less than a billion in total net reserves to pay pensions, Governor Ricardo Rosselló instituted, with the consent of the Financial Oversight and Management Board for Puerto Rico (Oversight Board) and the federal court, a pay-as-you-go system in which pension benefits are paid out of the island's general fund, "to the tune of roughly $1.5 billion a year" (Valentín Ortiz 2018). Pension reform also included a defined contribution plan for active workers in which every employee will have an individual account manage by a third party and new hires will also become enrolled in social security (Bradford 2017).

In summary, when pension liabilities are added to the public debt, the actual total Commonwealth's debt and liabilities add to nearly $123 billion. The accumulation of debt was partly the result of the prolonged recession that started in 2006 and the concomitant decline in tax revenues, and partly due to the ruling political parties' inability to respond with effective economic development policies, restructure government operations and implement responsive fiscal policies. But the public debt crisis can also be attributed directly to inconsistent U.S. policies toward the island. For example, the exclusion of Puerto Rico's municipalities from access to municipal bankruptcy prevented these municipalities from being restructured and possibly sold to private investors under more favorable terms than the ongoing restructuring procedures in federal court under PROMESA Title III provisions. Despite structural reforms on governmental revenues and expenditures, by the summer of 2015 the government sector's debt crisis was uncontainable—desperate times called for desperate remedies.

Enter PROMESA

PROMESA was enacted as a rare congressional bipartisan legislation at the height of the debt crisis (Meléndez 2018a). President Barak Obama signed the legislation just hours before the Commonwealth—already strapped for cash, implementing an aggressive revenues claw back from all agencies and public corporations and facing a severe liquidity problem—faced a substantial payment to bondholders of nearly $2 billion. PROMESA's main goals are insuring a string of balanced budgets and to restore Puerto Rico's access to credit markets under favorable terms, which involves the restructuring of the debt. Modeled after International Monetary Fund (IMF)-like economic reform policies, it should be no surprise to anyone that PROMESA is working for the purpose that was intended. The Oversight Board is overseeing the administration's controlling of expenditures and boosting revenues through a series of public sector reforms. It has also proceeded to federal court to restructure the public debt and negotiate with bondholders on behalf of the commonwealth.

Restructuring the Commonwealth's public finances has led to significant austerity measures. The Fiscal Plan mandated by PROMESA, revised in 2018 after Hurricanes Irma and Maria to account for economic recovery federal funding, is severely affecting "essential" services, such as education, health, justice, the University of Puerto Rico (UPR), and police, even in the context of projections of substantial disaster recovery funding. PROMESA has a back and forth review

Table 3. Puerto Rico General Fund Budget FY 2016 and FY 2018 (In thousands)

Year	FY2016	FY2008	Change	% change
Education	1,985,496	1,498,497	-486,999	-24.5%
Health (a)	1,372,534	1,203,216	-169,318	-12.3%
Justice (b)	883,680	754,775	-128,905	-14.6%
UPR	869,696	669,713	-199,983	-23.0%
Police	804,946	710,306	-94,640	-11.8%
Pension (c)	407,219	326,188	-81,031	-19.9%
Municipalities	365,700	219,730	-145,970	-39.9%
Budget Office	304,397	2,443,116	2,138,719	702.6%
Other	1,751,640	1,458,459	-293,181	-16.7%
Public Debt	951,210	-		
Total	9,696,518	9,284,000	-412,518	-4.3%

Notes
(a) Includes: Administración de Seguros de Salud de Puerto Rico, Departamento de Salud, Administración de Servicios de Salud Mental y Contra la Adicción, Administración de Servicios Médicos de Puerto Rico, Cuerpo de Emergencias Médicas de Puerto Rico, Salud Correccional.
(b) Includes: Departamento de Corrección y Rehabilitación, Tribunal General de Justicia, Departamento de Justicia. (c) Includes: Sistema de Retiro de Maestros, Sistema de Retiro de Empleados del Gobierno y La Judicatura (Sistema Central)   .
Source: Oficina de Gerencia y Presupuesto, Gobierno de Puerto Rico, PROMESA Requirement #1A, Recommended General Fund.

process between the Oversight Board and the governor for the "development, submission, approval, and certification of fiscal plans" (2018b, 76). Table 3 summarizes Puerto Rico's general fund budget for fiscal years 2016—the last budget prior to the enactment of PROMESA and used as a baseline for comparison purposes—and 2018. The two largest budget lines are for education and health programs, accounting for about one third of the budget. Education (-24%), UPR (-23%), and municipalities (-39%) received the largest budget cuts in FY2018 as a proportion of the FY2016 baseline year. These austerity measures were implemented in the context of no debt services or payments to bondholders. In preparation for those payments, among other reasons, the Puerto Rico's government and Oversight Board have concentrated the management of funds in the budget office, which saw funding under their direct control increase 70 percent, from $304 million in FY2016 to $2.44 billion in FY2018.

The FY2018 budget (and in future budgets) assumes a significant injection of recovery related funding and other federal funding, and substantially reduced debt services. The Fiscal Plan (2018) assumes the following in their ten-year projections using FY2017 as a baseline:

- Federal funds for economic recovery are projected to exceed $100 billion over the next ten years.
- Beginning in 2018, the loss of the Affordable Care Act (ACA) Funding will amount to $32 billion.
- Federal funds for social programs and operations will increase annually from $7 billion to $8.7 billion.
- Projected annual Act 154 Revenues will decrease steadily from $2.1 billion to $1.2 billion.
- Cash flow available for debt services would be $7.87 billion, for an average of $787 million annually.

Evidently, these projections depend on whether the underlying assumptions withstand the test of time and are not significantly affected by all the intervening political processes at the local and federal levels. For instance, Community Development Block Grant (CDBG-DR) and other recovery-related expenditures greatly depend on the deployment of an infrastructure for economic recovery that Puerto Rico is currently lacking. Though it is likely that recovery efforts will pick up steam soon, at the moment this is an area that requires greater attention by local and federal authorities as much as by the private and civic sector in Puerto Rico. Similarly, ACA funding depends on Congressional action. A strong advocacy coalition in Puerto Rico and the diaspora could influence the legislative process to avoid the so-called Medicaid-cliff in the near future.

By the same token, a strong advocacy coalition could persuade Congress and the current or future administration to support core stimulus policies, which may include solving the structural disparity in Medicaid once and for all, and extending an Earned Income Tax Credit (EITC) and the full federal Child Tax Credit (CTC) to residents of Puerto Rico, among others. These are stimulus policies identified by the Congressional

Task Force on Economic Growth in Puerto Rico and subsequently endorsed by the Oversight Board that command broad support in the House of Representatives but, currently, not so much in the Senate or the White House. Finally, the 2018 Fiscal Plan projected that annual Act 154 Revenues will decrease steadily because of the CFCs adjustment in their expected future investment in Puerto Rico given the tax reforms instituted by the Tax Cuts and Jobs Act on December of 2017. This is an area where local policies, whether reforms to the taxation of CFCs or programs to support their operations, could make a difference in encouraging the continuation or expansion of CFCs operations in Puerto Rico and slowing the erosion of tax revenues.

Debt Restructuring

The assumptions and projections about debt service are dependent on the resolution of debt restructuring in federal court. Graphic 3 depicts the projections included in the Fiscal Plan. Debt services in the absence of debt restructuring through PROMESA would have amounted to $3.283 billion in 2018 and for the ten-year period picked at $3,828 in 2019, then showing a steady decline to slightly above $3 billion for the later years of the period. The sum of these payments would exceed $30 billion in the ten-year period. However, the projected debt services in the Fiscal Plan average 23 percent of the actual debt services. In other words, the accuracy of cash flows projections to meet debt services projection depend on the court settlement with bondholders. Based on these cash flows projections, the restructuring of the debt and the implicit "haircut"[1] would be substantial, probably in the 70 to 80 percent range.

Gluzmann, Guzman, and Stiglitz (2018) analyze precisely the projections made in the Fiscal Plan of 2017 (prior to the devastation caused by Hurricanes Irma and

Graphic 3: Debt Sustainability

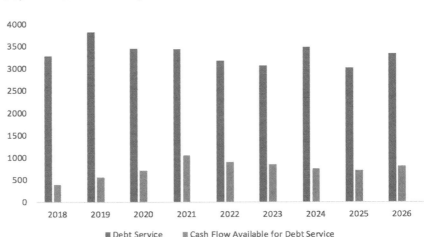

Debt Service   Cash Flow Available for Debt Service

Maria) in respect to the macroeconomic implications of debt restructuring and sustainability of debt services based on the implicit "haircut" negotiated by the Commonwealth government and the Oversight Board and then to be approved by the courts. They conclude that "the island's current debt position is unsustainable" (2018, 106), then proceed to estimate debt relief under various scenarios in order to restore sustainability. In their judgement the projections of the Fiscal Plan do not incorporate the dynamics that the plan itself will introduce in the economy—for example, a small haircut will lead to high debt service payments which in turn will induce cut in other government services, which in turn will reduce revenue collections inducing additional austerity measures, and so on. In economics, this policy feedback effect of government economic policies is referred to as a macroeconomic multiplier effect.[2] In this context, one of the core assumptions that is missing from the fiscal plan projections is exactly how much will be repaid in debt services. Debt restructuring determines debt sustainability and by implication fiscal stability and economic growth.

In addition to the endogenous feedback effects induced by the fiscal plan itself as well as debt restructuring and sustainability, the authors point to some additional key assumptions that deserve further scrutiny:

- GNP projections are based on macroeconomic multipliers that are regarded as overoptimistic;
- The proposed structural reforms focus on the supply side when "Puerto Rico's economy is a demand-constrained regime," that is, the core problem is not one of high production costs or labor constraint but, rather, one of declining employment and government expenditures that induce lower consumption;
- Migration is endogenous, to the extent that there is a decline in economic activity the exodus may increase in turn, inducing a lower aggregate demand and potentially skills shortages that further affect economic activity.

Based on the above set of assumptions, Gluzmann, Guzman, and Stiglitz (2018) construct 192 scenarios and conduct sensitivity analysis under alternative assumptions for fiscal multipliers, but maintain the same assumptions of the Fiscal Plan for real GNP growth and the annual inflation rates until 2026. Based on these projections of project real and nominal GNP for each of those 192 scenarios, they conclude:

Our projections strongly suggest that the Fiscal Plan's projections are overoptimistic. They lie on the most optimistic bound within the range of assumptions on the values of multipliers that are aligned with the empirical evidence. The magnitude of the differences between our range of projections and the projections of the Fiscal Plan is noticeably larger if we dismiss the positive effects that the structural reforms are assumed to have on GNP by the Plan.

And even under those optimistic assumptions, the plan falls into an "austerity trap": the magnitude of the targets for primary surpluses leads to a decrease in GNP over a decade that is larger than the reduction in the stock of debt, thus leading to an increase in the debt to GNP ratio by 2026. If there was no reduction in the debt principal, and if missed payments either of interest or principal were capitalized at zero interest rate, the total public debt to GNP ratio would rise from 1.09 in 2016 to 1.41 in 2026 in the scenario projected by the Fiscal Plan. (2018, 120–1)

To put the findings from Gluzmann, Guzman, and Stiglitz (2018) macroeco-nomic simulations in context, we can evaluate the implications of the COFINA restructuring approved by U.S. District Court Judge Laura Taylor Swain (Scurria 2019). COFINA debt of $17.6 billion represents 24 percent of Puerto Rico's total bonded debt and was the first debt restructuring in Puerto Rico's bankruptcy process in federal court. The restructuring reduces total COFINA debt by 32 percent, or $5.6 billion, to $12 billion. The settlement "gives senior bondholders 93 percent of the value of the original bonds and junior bondholders 55 percent" (Bradford 2019) and releases to Puerto Rico more than 46 percent of the future sales-tax revenue. It is estimated that COFINA restructuring will require debt service of $420 million per year and will gradually increase to more than $900 million per year by 2041.

"We are worried that not enough debt is being cut and that Puerto Rico's people are carrying heavy austerity burdens."

COFINA debt restructuring sets up a baseline with significant consequences for debt service sustainability. The Fiscal Plan accounts for a total annual debt services of $787, COFINA debt services of $420 to $900 billion will account for over half and up to 114 percent of the allocated average amount for debt services in the Fiscal Plan and twice the 24 percent COFINA share of Puerto Rico's total bonded debt. With a bonded debt legacy of $12 billion implied by the COFINA deal, and if the primary fiscal balance stabilized in 2026 at the value projected by the fiscal plan, then, the necessary reduction on the remaining stock of bonded public debt would have to be between 85 percent and 95 percent—an unlikely scenario—if the COFINA debt restructuring is used as a benchmark for future negotiations. Depending on Puerto Rico's economic performance and the effectiveness of structural reforms generating future cash flows for debt services, the Commonwealth's share of COFINA sales tax revenues may revert to debt payments to bondholders over time. This is the contention from Power 4 Puerto Rico, a coalition of civil rights, faith-based, labor and advocacy organizations that believe that "Puerto Rico will not generate enough revenue to comply with this agreement" (Bradford 2019). When Judge Taylor Swain approved the restructuring deal, Jubilee USA Executive Director Eric LeCompte, who monitors Puerto Rico's debt for the faith-based coalition, stated, "We are worried that not enough debt is being cut and that Puerto Rico's people are carrying heavy austerity burdens. The math isn't adding up. If plans to restructure the remaining debt fail to cut the majority of the island's debt load, Puerto Rico can't see sustained economic recovery and growth" (Puerto Rico Deal 2019).

Despite popular skepticism about the merits of the COFINA debt restructuring, the market buoyed when bondholders reached an agreement with the government and endorsed the transaction. In the days that followed, COFINA senior bonds, which were selling for less than half face value, began to trade at close to 80 cents on the dollar, while subordinated COFINA bonds began to trade at about 50 cents. An opinion piece in *The Hill* summarizes the COFINA bondholders view on the restructuring agreement:

Data shows the commonwealth has been running considerable budgetary surpluses in recent years, ranging from $1.6 billion in 2015 to $2.9 billion in 2018. The annual surplus available to pay creditors could easily rise to $4 billion or more by 2020 if reforms sought by the oversight board are expeditiously implemented. This underscores that the COFINA restructuring, which will require $420 million per year in the near-term, is a very feasible deal. Even when the escalated payment rate of more than $900 million per year is reached in 2041, the commonwealth should have ample resources to pay the restructured debt while comfortably funding other public initiatives and obligations. (Gregg 2018)

However, the COFINA debt restructuring is not yet over. Notwithstanding the final decision from Judge Swain after conducting public hearings on the matter, the Oversight Board and a group of unsecured creditors initiated legal action to declare another $6 billion of general obligation bonds issued in 2012 and 2014 as null and void as they exceed constitutional limits. In a separate filing, the creditors' committee alleged that "the debt also violates a balanced budget requirement in the constitution, because debt proceeds were used to finance deficit spending" (Bradford 2019). These legal challenges, whether completely or partially, are intertwined with COFINA and potentially can alter Judge Swain's decision in federal district court or in appeals.

The Impact of Hurricane Maria on Puerto Rico

Hurricanes Irma and Maria brought great destruction and thousands of dead to Puerto Rico. Undoubtedly, Hurricane Maria devastated the economy with losses estimated to reach and even exceed $100 billion and deepened the ongoing humanitarian crisis in the island. In this section of the introduction we examine articles included in this special issue addressing two critical areas—energy and agriculture—of the enduring economic and humanitarian crises.

The blackout that affected the whole island for weeks, and remote areas for months, was the aspect most covered by the national media after Hurricane Maria. In the immediate period following the storm efforts concentrated in repairing the affected equipment and lines and restoring electricity across the island. Yet, the disaster unleashed a broad discussion about the future of the energy system. O'Neill-Carrillo and Rivera-Quiñones examine the future of the energy sector in Puerto Rico considering the damages caused by the hurricanes, the collapse of the electrical grid, and the archaic oil-based electrical generation and distribution system in place. In the authors' opinion, "transitioning to a different, more resilient and sustainable infrastructure requires much more than just bringing technological gadgets to communities or implementing microgrids" (2018, 148). Despite the financial and physical damages caused by Hurricane María, the authors discuss the potential for true transformative actions such as "the implantation of local distributed energy resources" (2018, 148).

President Trump issued a 10-day Jones Act waiver for Puerto Rico after Hurricane Maria made landfall to help support the emergency relief effort. For many, this was too little, too late. For others it was unnecessary. Besides the fact that the same type of exemptions was granted to other states in similar circumstances, President Trump, by delaying the decision for more than a week after the storm devastated the island and limiting the waiver to ten days, revived the public discussion of an issue of great interest and controversy in Puerto Rico. Cabotage provisions in the Jones Act of 1920 were instituted to protect U.S. maritime commerce. The act requires that all goods shipped between U.S. ports (including all states and territories) be transported on ships that are built, owned, and operated by U.S. citizens. With the House of Representatives and the chairmanship of the Natural Resources Committee now in the hands of Democrats, it is likely that elements of the four bills currently pending in Congress, some that focus on disaster relief efforts, will be addressed (Lee and Cavanaugh 2017). While liner services operating as monopolies in Puerto Rico claim that the Jones Act has a positive effect on marine transportation, protecting jobs and inducing capital investments in the industry, opponents point to the harmful effects of the act on the local economy.

The importance of cabotage laws restrictions and how these induce Puerto Rico's vulnerability were highlighted after Hurricane Maria with the closure of the sea-land container shipping Horizon Lines in December 2015. Domestic firms did not have enough capacity, especially with the lack of sustainable operations on the ports of Mayagüez and Ponce, to deal with the extraordinary situation and to ensure a continuous flow of cargo to Puerto Rico. Hundreds of containers were left-behind in Florida due to lack of space on cargo vessels. In this context, Suárez (2018) examines the impact of cabotage laws on the agricultural sector in Puerto Rico. Based on a mixed method approach, the author finds that the existing cabotage laws limit local industry capacity and potential development through various regulations such as those for sanitary and phytosanitary restrictions, the weight limits on containers, and the obsolete infrastructure on their terminals for handling agricultural products. In addition, local producers and importers face other internal constraints such as the lack of volume in their market, lack of cash flow, and lack of consolidation services from abroad. As a result of these external and internal factors to the Puerto Rico market, the supply chain of local agribusinesses is affected.

Furthermore, the virtual monopoly of a few large maritime service providers precludes the analysis of impact since rates and other parameters are currently consider private transactions and data is not collected or published by the U.S. or Puerto Rico governments. According to Suarez (2018, 199), "[t]his lack of access to data only allows the shippers to allocate specific routes among themselves at predetermined rates. Those with higher volumes get the better rates and priority." Lack of data makes it difficult to estimate the real cost of cabotage laws on the agribusiness sector in Puerto Rico. Access to transaction data is a first step towards attracting more service providers and inducing a more competitive environment in the industry. The author concludes that "[s]trategic investments in commercial ports' lanes and terminals' infrastructure, automating and digitizing processes, promoting rivalry among maritime firms, strengthening the local industry firms' supporters, and manufacturers' product diversification would be the key to a healthier competitiveness environment" (2018, 200).

The Impact of Hurricane Maria on the Diaspora

La Crisis Boricua is the title of a recent book devoted to the demographic and socioeconomic connections between Puerto Rico and the diaspora—two sides of a unitary process. The recent economic crisis in Puerto Rico has driven hundreds of thousands of people to migrate to the United States, and these processes in turn have reconfigured the stateside Puerto Rican community. Mora, Dávila and Rodríguez (2018) summarize the findings of their book in an article for this special issue. Some of the most troubling aspects of the crisis that preceded the landing of Hurricanes Irma and Maria are the overrepresentation of young people, especially of child-rearing families, in the migratory outflows from the island, and the continuing dispersion to traditional and non-traditional destinations throughout the United States. Evidently, the advent of an unusually large number of Puerto Ricans increases demand in local school systems and for other social services while the potential increase in the electorate represents a challenge to local political establishments. Though destinations such as Orlando and the state of Florida, more generally, were widely covered by the media, these dynamics were unfolding in many states, whether traditional (New York, Connecticut, Pennsylvania, Texas) or new destinations (New South, *e.g.,* Virginia, the Carolinas).

While the exodus from the island brings a renewed energy and positive socioeconomic and cultural impact to local communities, in many of the traditional destinations Puerto Ricans are concentrated in impoverished areas and the advent of evacuees further accentuates the challenges posed by the exodus from the island to stateside communities. But the recent Puerto Rican population growth may actually benefit the island in terms of mobilizing support for Puerto Rico in Congress. Mora, Dávila and Rodríguez conclude:

Hurricane Maria has increased awareness about Puerto Rico's status and relationship with the mainland, which could result in support and action from Congress to help address Puerto Rico's chronic socioeconomic issues, such as its perennially weak labor market and high rates of impoverishment. This possibility is more likely now than in the past in light of the 5.6 million (and rising) Puerto Ricans on the mainland who have Congressional representation and a vote in Presidential elections. (2018, 225)

Hinojosa (2018) picks up the "Two Sides of the Coin" theme in her article for the special issue. Her focus is assessing the size and dispersion of the post-Hurricane Maria exodus. For the author, the exodus further accelerated the depopulation of Puerto Rico while inducing a revival of the diaspora stateside. Estimating the size and dispersion of the exodus is as much an art as a science. The fact is that the two conventional indicators of migration from the island—the estimates derived from the U.S. Census Bureau's American Community Survey and population estimates—have a substantial time lag before they are available to the public. A third available indicator— the Net Movement of Passenger (NMP) published by the Bureau of Transportation Statistics—has a shorter lag but greater volatility than the other two. Thus, the challenge for researchers and others concerned about the magnitude of the flow was to

Graphic 4. Estimated Migration Flows from Puerto to the U.S. 2005-2017

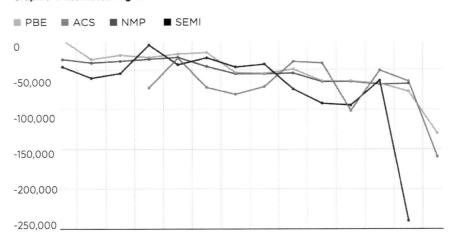

Source: 1941-2016 Department of Health and U.S. Census Bureau Population Estimates; 1991-2016 Bureau of Transportation Statistics; 2005-2018 American Community Survey; 2008-2018 Puerto Rico's Department of Education.
Note: NMP latest data available is September 2018 and PBE's vital statistics is unavailable for 2018.

identify readily available data that could serve as an indicator of the magnitude of the flow and possibly of the demographic composition and destination of migrants.

Hinojosa (2018) proposes that school enrollment data offers an acceptable migration proxy that can be used as an indicator that is readily available only a few weeks after the beginning of every semester after student enrollment is completed. The School Enrollment Migration Index (SEMI) is based on school enrollment. Given the size of the increase or decline in students registered for the semester one can then extrapolate total migrants based on historical data of the number of adults and non-school children that correspond to a given number of school-age children. Graphic 4 depicts a comparison of the four migration series available. The important observation from the historical data is that over time these indices tend to converge, yet despite relatively high volatility, NMP and SEMI are leading indicators of the level of migration in subsequent years as measured by the U.S. Census Bureau data. A key finding from these indicators is that both NMP and SEMI show a substantial exodus as a result of Hurricane Maria, ranging between 223,861 to 239,992, or three times the 2017 ACS figure of 72,521.

A second important question addressed by Hinojosa (2018) concerns the destination of migrants after Hurricane Maria. To estimate flows by state, she uses changes of addresses for FEMA claims from the victims of the hurricanes. Data for one year after Hurricane Maria reveals that Florida had the largest portion of evacuees with 8,873, followed by Northeast destinations that collectively add up to 7,470 evacuees. New York has the largest group of evacuees (2,111) in the Northeast region followed by Massachusetts (1,765), Pennsylvania (1,449), and Connecticut (1,220). These leading destinations roughly correspond to ACS 2017 states rankings for migration flows.

One of the most palpable links between Puerto Rico and the diaspora is how the exodus affects the school systems in the island through the closing of schools and the receiving stateside communities through heightened demand for bilingual education and social services support systems for parents and students. The massive exodus induced by the impact of the economic and fiscal crisis on families and children, as it has been exacerbated by the devastation caused by the hurricanes, is palpable evidence of the humanitarian crisis in Puerto Rico. Irizarry, Rolón-Dow, and Godreau (2018) focus on the impact of the exodus on stateside school systems. Immediately after the storms, many communities opened welcome centers were referrals and information about schools and housing were provided to evacuees. One of the most impressive operations was established at the Orlando, Florida airport—the gateway for the central Florida region, where tens of thousands of families relocated.

A second dimension explored by the authors was the multiple efforts of higher educational institutions inviting fellows from the island and accommodating evacuees in colleges and universities across the country. Many of these students were supported with generous financial aid and other emergency support services. The authors conclude with an examination of the restructuring of the educational system in Puerto Rico. Along with other authors in the volume, they perceive the impact of the exodus in local stateside communities as a call for action to support social reforms in Puerto Rico through Diaspora engagement in the electoral and political process. Given the direct impact of the exodus on both island and stateside communities, education is an area that could unify a common agenda among island residents and stateside Puerto Ricans.

The Crisis of Politics
For better or worse, politics are at the center of almost any issue discussed about Puerto Rico. And among the most prominent topics are the question of the political status and the recent phenomenon of declining electoral participation in regular elections and the results of recent consultations on the status question. For a context, rates of electoral participation would reach close to 90 percent percent of eligible voters just a decade back but in the last election voter turnout drop to 55 percent of registered voters. Pundits on the island quickly attributed this significant drop to the exodus since a recent court decision protected the right of voters to not be dropped after missing one electoral cycle. Vargas-Ramos (2018) examines this hypothesis using available electoral data. He concludes that "[b]ased on statistical analyses of aggregate voting and population data, results show that Puerto Rico's decline in voter participation is not attributable to emigration. Rather, an extant legitimacy crisis of the political system and its political class might be a more proximate and likely explanation for the drop in electoral participation in 2016" (2018, 279).

For the first time in the Commonwealth era, independent political candidates captured a whopping 17 percent of the vote. Considering that the difference between the elected governor and the runner up was under 3 percent of the vote, the independent vote could in theory become a major force determining electoral outcomes.

As significant as the decline in eligible voters' participation, the 2016 elections marked the advent of a new political phenomena with significant long-term implications if it continues in future elections. For the first time in the Commonwealth era, independent political candidates captured a whopping 17 percent of the vote. Considering that the difference between the elected governor and the runner up was under 3 percent of the vote, the independent vote could in theory become a major force determining electoral outcomes. Political alliances between the independent leadership and either of the contending parties may very well establish a coalition government. By the same token, a coalition of independent candidates could in theory tap into the massive discontent manifested by electoral absenteeism and redefine the electoral landscape in Puerto Rico. However, the prospects for political alliances are always muddled by the thorny issue of the political status.

The status question—whether Puerto Rico will become a state of the United Stares, evolve into some form of associated state that transcend the Commonwealth, which is widely perceived as a colonial status, or to become independent—has dominated the Puerto Rican political dynamics even prior to the U.S. invasion of the territory in 1898. In the aftermath of Hurricane Maria's devastation of the island, local and stateside politicians have renewed their call for the territorial incorporation of Puerto Rico. According to Venator-Santiago (2018), these politicians "view Puerto Rico's territorial incorporation as a pathway to both statehood and parity funding." Drawing on an analysis of the Congressional Research Index for all legislative sessions between 1898 and 2018, Venator-Santiago examines core legislative debates from the invasion to the present. He concludes:

For more than a century, the United States has relied on this racist constitutional interpretation to legitimate the separate and unequal rule of Puerto Rico. Although upwards of 134 status bills for Puerto Rico were introduced, and in some cases debated, in Congress, only eleven provide for the creation of a territorial government or the incorporation of Puerto Rico. All but one of these bills were introduced prior to the enactment of the Puerto Rican Constitution of 1952. For more than a century, Congress has refused to enact territorial legislation that expressly incorporates Puerto Rico and repudiates the racist doctrine of territorial incorporation. (2018, 313)

Given the context—a broken economic system and a lack of political consensus in Puerto Rico about status options—the odds that a divided Congress will consider, let alone enact, legislation on Puerto Rico's status question in the near future are remote, to say the least. However, changes in various of the underlying circumstances, such as the advent of a unified Congress after the 2020 presidential cycle, or an economic uptick induced by the injection of disaster recovery funding, may open a window for a congressional examination of the status question. And, as many of the authors in this special issue have suggested and in sharp contrast to past experiences, this time the diaspora is better equipped, with the experience of recent mobilizations for congressional action on debt restructuring and solidarity for disaster recovery, to affect the stateside political equation.

Conclusions: Implications of Research Findings for the Future of Puerto Rico

Paradoxically, we have seen that perhaps the only silver lining in the aftermath of the devastation caused by Hurricane Maria is the injection of recovery funding assigned to Puerto Rico. This injection of capital, though not in ideal circumstances, may serve as the additional economic stimulus that many economists and other policy analysts have touted as necessary to turn the Puerto Rico economy around and induce sustained economic recovery. Yet, based on the Fiscal Plan approved by the Oversight Board, the injection of capital is projected to have only a temporary economic impact.

Graphic 5 provides a snapshot of the economic future of Puerto Rico, it illustrates GNP projections from the FY2017 and FY2018 Fiscal Plans. The FY2017 figures were projections made prior to the injection of recovery funding and the FY2018 were made considering the injection of recovery funding. As pointed out by Gluzmann, Guzman, and Stiglitz (2018), the FY2017 GNP projections are based on overly optimistic (and actually faulty) assumptions. Based on those projections, GNP will continue to be negative until 2020 and then uptick into a positive trajectory thereafter. Yet, the post-Hurricane Maria FY2018 Fiscal Plan projects that the injection of recovery funding will have an immediate impact uplifting Puerto Rico's economy but revert to negative GNP growth rates by FY2023. In other words, official projections suggest that even with the injection of recovery funding Puerto Rico will continue to be stagnant through the near future. In this context, the prospects for ending the Oversight Board authority over the Commonwealth's finances granted by PROMESA in the next decade are uncertain.

Economic projections are not destiny. Several factors—in the hands of Congress, local authorities overseeing economic recovery, and the Puerto Rican people through their political engagement and reconstruction efforts—could affect this grim picture of the island's future. Future scenarios may include several of the following elements:

- PROMESA and the Fiscal Oversight and Management Board's policies of balanced budgets and fiscal austerity are insufficient and not likely mechanisms for overcoming the economic crisis. It is also questionable whether the federal court debt restructuring will reduce debt services to a sustainable level and provide a pathway to fiscal stability and restoring access to credit markets under favorable conditions as a precondition for and of solving the underlying problems of job creation and economic development. Even the economic pro-

Graphic 5: Fiscal Plan 2017 and 2018 GNP Growth

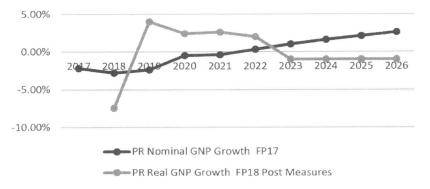

jections after the injection of recovery funding after Hurricane Maria indicate a stagnant economy in the next decade. Thus, there is a strong rationale for substantive investment of federal resources and of congressional policies that incentivize private capital investment in Puerto Rico. Congressional action on Puerto Rico's economy could support the fiscal and structural economic reforms proposed by the Oversight Board, stabilize the economy and facilitate a return to credit markets, and slowdown the population exodus. Such potential policies include the long-term or permanent renewal of Medicaid, and extending EITC and the full CTC to residents of Puerto Rico, among others.

- Civic engagement in reconstruction efforts could set up the foundation for a new economic foundation in key industries such as energy, manufacturing, housing and other infrastructure, agriculture, tourism, and restructuring critical services such as education, health and security. The advent of federal recovery funding could lay a foundation for the growth of a social entrepreneurial sector that combines the strength of the nonprofit and private sector to rebuild the economy from the ground up and in a sustainable and inclusive fashion. In addition, the extension of the Opportunity Zone and other federal programs that can be combined with CDBG-DR and other recovery funding offer a unique window for social purpose economic development. The greatest immediate challenge is to build local capacity and the alliances with stateside social purpose financial intermediaries to be able to engage a significant group of social purpose local developers in the economic recovery process and to build a long-lasting and capable civic infrastructure for social purpose enterprise development.

- The realignment of the political forces in Puerto Rico around the implementation of a common long-term recovery agenda led by the growing independent and dissatisfied electorate. This is not to suggest that the existing dominant political parties that revolve around the status question should or would disappear but rather to suggest that the ascend of the independent sector could steer the political debate to focus on issues of effective polices and government, setting the foundations for a shared vision for recovery and the economic future of Puerto Rico, and support heightened transparency and inclusiveness.

- A renewed diaspora engagement movement in solidarity with Puerto Rico and in partnership with the civic sector could be a game changer. The diaspora solidarity movement so far has largely avoided getting entangled with the thorny issue of the political status of Puerto Rico and so far has focused on the solutions to the debt restructuring and economic crisis, and the mitigation of the devastation of Hurricanes Irma and Maria and the humanitarian crisis. This minimalist common agenda has served to engage a broad stateside Puerto Rican coalition and even to spur a renewed effort to better organize the diaspora. The long-term importance of these efforts is enormous to both Puerto Rico and stateside Puerto Rican communities.

As a Puerto Rican common expression says, *"El futuro está en tus manos."*[4]

NOTES

[1] In debt restructuring agreements, a haircut is a percentage reduction of the amount that will be repaid to creditors.

[2] The multiplier effect refers to the increase in final income arising from any new injection of spending. The size of the multiplier depends upon household's marginal decisions to spend, called the marginal propensity to consume (mpc), or to save, called the marginal propensity to save (mps).

[3] Former Sen. Judd Gregg (R-N.H.) previously served as chairman and ranking member of the Senate Budget Committee. He is also the former governor of New Hampshire. He has been an advisor to the COFINA Senior Bondholders Ad Hoc Group.

[4] From Latin *Mihi cura future* ("The care of the future is mine").

REFERENCES

Backdoor Bailout Boosts Puerto Rico's Revenues. 2014. *Reuters* 10 February. <http://www.reuters.com/article/usa-puertorico-tax-idUSL2N0LF1BE20140210/>.

Bradford, Hazel. 2017. Puerto Rico Governor Signs Pension Reform Law. *Pensions & Investments* 25 August. <https://www.pionline.com/article/20170825/ONLINE/170829881/puerto-rico-governor-signs-pension-reform-law/>.

_____. 2019. Judge Considers COFINA Restructuring Deal and Is Asked to Invalidate Other Bonds. *Pensions & Investments* 17 January. <https://www.pionline.com/article/20190117/ONLINE/190119857/judge-considers-cofina-restructuring-deal-and-is-asked-to-invalidate-other-bonds/>.

Caraballo Cueto, José G. and Juan Lara. 2016. From deindustrialization to unsustainable debt: The Case of Puerto Rico. Paper presented at the University of Puerto Rico Conference. October.

Feliciano, Zadia. 2018. IRS Section 936 and the Decline of Puerto Rico's Manufacturing. *CENTRO: Journal of the Center for Puerto Rican Studies* 30(3) 30–42,.

Gluzmann, Pablo, Martin Guzman and Joseph E. Stiglitz. 2018. An Analysis of Puerto Rico's Debt Relief Needs to Restore Debt Sustainability. *CENTRO: Journal of the Center for Puerto Rican Studies* 30(3), 104–46.

Gregg, Judd. 2018. Puerto Rico Notches a Long-Awaited Win. *The Hill* 29 October. <https://thehill.com/opinion/finance/413664-puerto-rico-notches-a-long-awaited-win/>.

Irizarry, Jason G., Rosalie Rolón-Dow and Isar P. Godreau. 2019. *Después del Huracán:* Using a Diaspora Framework to Contextualize and Problematize Educational Responses Post-María. *CENTRO: Journal of the Center for Puerto Rican Studies* 30(3), 254–78.

Hinojosa, Jennifer. 2019. Two Sides of the Coin of Puerto Rican Migration: Depopulation in Puerto Rico and the Revival of the Diaspora. *CENTRO: Journal of the Center for Puerto Rican Studies* 30(3), 230–53.

Lee, Eric and J. Michael Cavanaugh. 2017. New Jones Act Legislation Pending, with Puerto Rico Focus. *Holland & Knight* 23 October. <https://www.hklaw.com/publications/

new-jones-act-legislation-pending-with-puerto-rico-focus-10-23-2017/>.

Márquez, Carlos and José Carmona. 2011.The Age of Consequences. *Caribbean Business* 28 July. <http://www.rafaelhernandezcolon.org/Comunicado/CB%20July%2028,%20 2011-%20The%20Age%20of%20Consequences.pdf/>.

Meléndez, Edwin. 2018a. The Politics of PROMESA. *CENTRO: Journal of the Center for Puerto Rican Studies* 30(3), 43–71.

_____. 2018b. The Economics of PROMESA. *CENTRO: Journal of the Center for Puerto Rican Studies* 30(3), 72–103.

Mora, Marie T., Alberto Dávila and Havidán Rodríguez. 2018. Migration, Geographic Destinations, and Socioeconomic Outcomes of Puerto Ricans during *La Crisis Boricua*: Implications for Island and Stateside Communities Post-Maria. *CENTRO: Journal of the Center for Puerto Rican Studies* 30(3), 208–29.

O'Neill-Carrillo, Efraín and Miguel A. Rivera-Quiñones. 2018. Energy Policies in Puerto Rico and their Impact on the Likelihood of a Resilient and Sustainable Electric Power Infrastructure. *CENTRO: Journal of the Center for Puerto Rican Studies* 30(3), 147–71.

Puerto Rico Debt Deal Receives Court Approval. 2019. *Jubilee USA Network* 5 February. <https://www.jubileeusa.org/pr_pr_cofina_approved/>.

Scurria, Andrew. 2019. Puerto Rico's $18 Billion Bond Restructuring Nears Completion. *Dow Jones Newswires* 19 January. <https://www.morningstar.com/news/dow-jones/lat-in-america/TDJNDN_201901192588/puerto-ricos-18-billion-bond-restructuring-nears-completion.print.html/>.

Suárez, William II. 2018. Cabotage as an External Non-tariff Measure on the Competitiveness on SIDS's Agribusinesses: The Case of Puerto Rico. *CENTRO: Journal of the Center for Puerto Rican Studies* 30(3), 172–207.

Valentín Ortiz, Luis. 2018. U.S. Judge Rules against Puerto Rico Retirement System Bond-holders. *Reuters* 17 August. <https://www.reuters.com/article/puertorico-debt-p\ensions/u-s-judge-rules-against-puerto-rico-retirement-system-bondholders-idUSL1N1V81K9/>.

Vargas-Ramos, Carlos. 2018. Political Crisis, Migration and Electoral Behavior in Puerto Rico. *CENTRO: Journal of the Center for Puerto Rican Studies* 30(3), 279–312.

Venator-Santiago, Charles R. 2018. Territorial Incorporation: A Note on the History of Territorial Incorporation Bills for Puerto Rico, 1898 -2017. *CENTRO: Journal of the Center for Puerto Rican Studies* 30(3), 313–21.

VOLUME XXX • NUMBER III • FALL 2018

IRS Section 936 and the Decline of Puerto Rico's Manufacturing

ZADIA M. FELICIANO

ABSTRACT

This paper presents new estimates on the impact of the elimination of IRS Section 936 on the manufacturing industry in Puerto Rico evaluating its effect on employment and exports. The effects on manufacturing employment are estimated using a difference-in-difference methodology where employment in service sector industries is used as the control group. The effects on Puerto Rico's manufacturing industry level exports are estimated using mainland U.S. exports as the control group. I find evidence that the elimination of Section 936 had a large negative impact on manufacturing employment but little evidence that the elimination of Section 936 caused a significant effect on Puerto Rico's manufacturing exports. [Key words: Puerto Rico, IRS Section 936, tax exemption, manufacturing, exports, employment]

The author (zadia.feliciano@qc.cuny.edu) is an Associate Professor at Queens College, CUNY, a faculty member at The Graduate Center, CUNY and a Research Economist in the Program of International Trade and Investment at the National Bureau of Economic Research. She earned her Ph.D. in Economics at Harvard University in 1995. Professor Feliciano's research is on International Trade, Foreign Direct Investment, and Labor Economics. Her most recent work is on the repeal of IRS Section 936.

1. Introduction

Several months before Hurricane Maria landed in Puerto Rico on September 20, 2017, the government of Puerto Rico filed for bankruptcy similar to Chapter 9 of the U.S. Bankruptcy Code (Scoria and Gillers 2017). Puerto Rico's government owes more than $74 billion dollars to creditors and 40 billion in pension liabilities (Farrant 2017).[1] Lack of spending in infrastructure may have contributed to the long and difficult recovery from the hurricane, responsible for thousands of deaths estimated to range from 1,400 to 3,000 (Campo-Flores 2018), and 94.4 million dollars in damages (Puerto Rico Junta de Planificación 2018). The economic crisis in Puerto Rico has resulted in large waves of Puerto Rican migrants to the mainland. Mora, Dávila and Rodríguez (2018) estimate that 646,932 people migrated from Puerto Rico to the U.S. mainland between 2006 and 2016. Edwin Meléndez and Jennifer Hinojosa (2017) projected that between 114,000 and 213,000 Puerto Ricans will leave the island every year from 2017 to 2019 due to the economic crisis and the devastation caused by Hurricane Maria.

The roots of the economic crisis in Puerto Rico have been traced in part to a large decline in the manufacturing industry, precipitated by the elimination of Internal Revenue Service (IRS) Section 936 tax exemption for U.S. corporations in 2006 (Krueger, Teja and Wolf 2015; Caraballo Cueto and Lara 2018). Under Section 936, any qualifying U.S. corporation could choose to receive a tax credit equal to the portion of its U.S. corporate income tax liability attributable to taxable income from activities outside the United States from the conduct of operations in a U.S. possession and from income generated by qualified investments in a U.S. possession. Under Section 936, Puerto Rico attracted large amounts of manufacturing investments (Alm 2006). The elimination of Section 936 may be one of the most important factors contributing to the decline of the manufacturing industry in Puerto Rico.

Research on the impact of the elimination of IRS Section 936 tax exemption program in the manufacturing sector, at the industry or firm level, has been limited. In previous research (Feliciano and Green 2017), we estimated the impact of the elimination of IRS Section 936 using a difference-in-difference methodology based on data from the US Census of manufactures, which is collected every five years, from 1982 to 2012. Our results show the elimination of Section 936 had the effect of decreasing average manufacturing wages in Puerto Rico by 16.7 percent compared to those in the mainland U.S. We did not find a significant impact of Section 936 on manufacturing employment or the number of manufacturing establishments in the island when the U.S. mainland was used as a control. However, we estimated that the number of manufacturing establishments decreased by 18.7 percent to 28.0 percent as a result of the phase-out and elimination of IRS Section 936 when the control group is composed of the states of Indiana, North Carolina and Oregon.

In this paper, I provide new estimates of the impact of the elimination of IRS Section 936 on the manufacturing industry in Puerto Rico evaluating its effect on employment and exports. I estimate the effects on manufacturing employment using a difference in difference methodology where employment in service sector industries is used as the control group. I estimate the effects on Puerto Rico's industry level manufacturing exports using mainland U.S. exports as the control group. I find evidence that the elimination of Section 936 had a large negative impact on manufacturing employment but little evidence that the elimination of Section 936 caused a significant decline on Puerto Rico's manufacturing exports.

2. IRS Section 936

U.S. corporations doing business in Puerto Rico received tax exemptions since the Revenue Act of 1921 (Holik 2009). However, over time the benefits given to U.S. corporations diminished. IRS Section 936 was created by the Tax Reform Act of 1976 to promote investments by U.S. corporations in U.S. territories, and to increase employment and economic activity in U.S. possessions. Under Section 936, U.S. corporations received full credit from income resulting from the conduct of trade or business in a U.S. possession. The Tax Equity and Fiscal Responsibility Act of 1982 and the Tax Reform Act of 1986 created restrictions on tax exemption for U.S. possessions corporations. To receive tax exemption, corporations doing business in a U.S. possession had to meet a direct labor or value-added test with respect to a specific product or service produced. The percentage of gross income that a corporation had to earn from trade or business in a U.S. possession was increased from 65 to 75 percent in 1986 (Holik 2009).

The Small Business and Job Protection Act of 1996 eliminated Section 936 tax exemption for U.S. possessions corporations beginning with tax years after December 31, 1995. U.S. corporations already conducting business in a U.S. possession were allowed to continue getting tax exemptions for years 1995 to 2005 (Holik 2009).

Congress eliminated section 936 in part due to the view that the job creating benefits of the program did not justify the loss of U.S. tax revenue. Moreover, many Section 936 corporations shifted intangible assets to the island to increase the amount of income that would qualify for tax exemption (Hexner and Jenkins 1995). The Small Business and Job Protection Act of 1996 eliminated Section 936 tax exemption for U.S. possessions corporations beginning with tax years after December 31, 1995. U.S. corporations already conducting business in a U.S. possession were allowed to continue getting tax exemptions for years 1995 to 2005 (Holik 2009).

While the benefits from Section 936 applied to all territories, most U.S. possessions corporations located in Puerto Rico. In 2005, 98.8 percent of the 0.9 billion dollars in tax credits awarded under Section 936 were given to U.S. possessions corporations located in Puerto Rico. Moreover, most of these corporations were engaged in manufacturing; 69 percent of tax credits were given to firms in the manufacturing industry (Holik 2009).

3. Data

To study the impact of the elimination of IRS Section 936 on Puerto Rico's manufacturing employment, I constructed data series on Puerto Rican employment by industry from the "Encuesta de Empleo Asalariado en el Sector No Agrícola," collected by the Puerto Rico Negociado de Estadísticas del Departamento del Trabajo y Recursos Humanos for the years 1990 to 2016. These data are compiled for the Quarterly Census of Employment and Wages which is collected and estimated for every state in mainland U.S., Puerto Rico and the Virgin Islands. Data are collected every quarter from establishments. The employment variable is the count of filled jobs, including both full-time and part-time workers. The industries included in the analysis are: manufacturing, retail trade-transportation-utilities, information services, professional services, education and health services, hotel and recreation services.

I also constructed panel data on industry level exports for Puerto Rico and the United States for the years 1991 to 2016. Export data for Puerto Rico are from the Puerto Rico Planning Board, Governor's Office, "Economic Report to the Governor." These data were reported at the two-digit Standard Industrial Classification (SIC) level from 1990 to 2000 and at the three-digit North American Industrial Classification System (NAICS) level from 2001 to 2016. Mainland U.S. exports are from the United Nations (UN) Comtrade Database, available at the SIC level through the World Integrated Trade Solution (WITS).

To create the panel, I used a concordance between SIC and NAICS to connect the industry series, which led to their consolidation into 12 industries.[2] Both employment and exports data include 15 years of tax exemption for U.S. corporations through IRS Section 936, including the ten-year phase-out period that started in 1995 and ended in 2005.

4. Methodology

I use difference-in-difference methodology to analyze the impact of the elimination of IRS Section 936 on Puerto Rico's manufacturing employment and exports. Puerto Rico is a territory of the United States and has no votes in the U.S. Congress. The phase out of IRS Section 936 was a policy change imposed on Puerto Rico by the U.S. Congress with the purpose of increasing tax revenue. Thus, the policy of eliminating IRS Section 936 was exogenous to economic conditions in Puerto Rico, and thus it represents a natural experiment on the impact of removing tax exemptions on US corporations located in the island.

I estimate a fixed effects regression equation of manufacturing employment in Puerto Rico using employment in service sector industries in Puerto Rico as a control group. The manufacturing sector benefited the most from IRS Section 936, accounting for 69 percent of tax benefits: thus, the elimination of tax exemption should have affected manufacturing employment more than any other sector in the economy. In the difference-in-difference estimation, the first difference is before IRS Section 936 was eliminated (1989 to 2005) and after its elimination (2006–2016). The second difference measures the difference in employment trends between manufacturing industries and a control group during the same period. It is difficult to find a perfect control group for Puerto Rico's manufacturing employment since Puerto Rico has significantly lower wages than all states in the U.S., employment in Puerto Rico's service sector industries is a good comparison group.

The employment difference in difference equation is:

$$Log(Employment_{it}) = \alpha + \beta_1 AfterTaxCredit_{it} + \beta_2 Manuf_{it} + \beta_3 Manuf_{it} *$$

$$AfterTaxCredit_{it} + \sum_i Ind_i + \varepsilon_{it} \ (1)$$

where *Employment* is the number of workers in industry i (manufacturing or a service sector) in year t. *AfterTaxCredit* is a dummy variable that equals 1 if the year is after the elimination of the IRS Section 936 (2006–2016) and zero otherwise. Manuf is a dummy variable that equals 1 if employment is in the manufacturing industry and zero otherwise. $\sum_i Ind_i$ is a series of industry dummies designating service sector industries: retail trade-transportation-utilities, information services, professional services, education and health services, hotel and recreation services. The variable ε_{it} is a random error with mean zero. The interaction term between the *AfterTaxCredit* variable and the manufacturing dummy variable captures the differences between employment in manufacturing and service sector industries during the period after the elimination of IRS Section 936. The coefficient β_3 is the difference-in-difference estimator and thus captures the impact of the elimination of IRS Section 936 tax exemption program on employment in manufacturing industries in Puerto Rico.

I estimate another fixed effects regression equation for manufacturing exports from Puerto Rico to the rest of the world for 12 industries from 1991 to 2016, using mainland U.S. exports to the rest of the world in the same 12 industries as the control group. While the mainland U.S. may differ in terms of importance of specific manufacturing industries in exports, trends in exports within industries should provide a good control group for changes in exports in Puerto Rico before and after the elimination of IRS Section 936.

The exports difference in difference equation is:

$$Log(Exports_{ijt}) = \alpha + \beta_1 AfterTaxCredit_{ijt} + \beta_2 PR_j + \beta_3 PR_j * AfterTaxCredit_{ijt} +$$

$$\sum_i Ind_i + \varepsilon_{ijt} \ (2)$$

where *Exports* is the value of exports in location j (PR or US) industry i and year t. *AfterTaxCredit* is a dummy variable that equals 1 if the year is after the elimination of the IRS Section 936 (after 2005) and zero otherwise. PR is a dummy variable that equals 1 if the observation is from Puerto Rico and zero otherwise. $\sum_i Ind_i$ is a series of industry dummies. The interaction term between the *AfterTaxCredit* variable and the Puerto Rico dummy variable captures the differences between exports from Puerto Rico and the U.S. exports to the rest of the world after the elimination of IRS Section 936. The coefficient β_3 is the difference in difference estimator since it cap-

Figure 2: Puerto Rico Employment by Sector

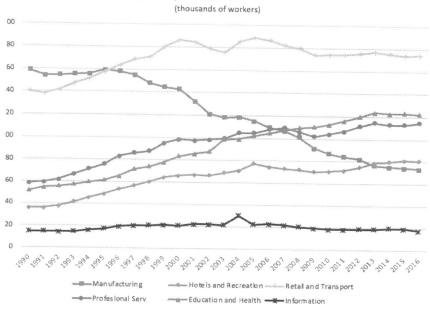

Source: US and Puerto Rico Quarterly Census of Employment and Wages.

Figure 3: Manufacturing Exports PR vs US

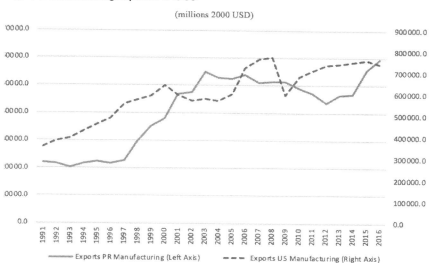

Source: Puerto Rico Planning Board, Economic Report to the Governor and United Nations Comtrade Database.

Table 2: Manufacturing Employment in Puerto Rico before and after the elimination of IRS Section 936, Puerto Rico service sector is the control group.

Independent Variables	Log Employment (1)		Log Employment (2)	
End of Tax Credit (2005-2016)	.235 (.030)	**	.484 (.031)	**
Manufacturing	.923 (.056)	**	1.263 (.066)	**
Manufacturing x End of Tax Credit	-.747 (.073)	**	-1.087 (.075)	**
Tax Credit Phase out (1995-2005)			.362 (.031)	**
Manufacturing * Tax Credit Phase-out			-.495 (.076)	**
Industry Dummy Variables	Yes		Yes	
Observations	168		168	
R-Squared	.94		.97	

Clustered standard errors. * Signfiicant at the 10 percent level, ** Significant at the 5 percent level.

interaction term of the manufacturing and end of tax credit dummies (2006–2016). The coefficient is -.747 and it is significant at the 5 percent. level. This suggests employment in manufacturing declined by 75 percent after the elimination of section 936 relative to employment in service sector industries.

Column 2 shows an alternative estimation where the manufacturing dummy is interacted with a tax credit phase-out dummy (1995–2005) and the end of the tax-credit dummy. Coefficients on the interaction terms show a negative and significant impact of the phase-out and elimination of Section 936 at the 5 percent level. The coefficient on the interaction of the manufacturing and phase-out of Section 936 dummies is estimated to be -.495 and the coefficient on the interaction of manufacturing and end of tax-credit dummies is estimated to be -1.087. This suggests the phase-out and elimination of Section 936 may be responsible for a 50 percent to 100 percent decrease in manufacturing employment relative to service sector industries. The adjusted R-square in the regression shown in column 2 is .97, which suggests that almost all the variation is explained by the model. This casts some concern about this particular regression because it may reflect trends that are not causal. Regression results in column 1 are more reliable.

Table 3: Manufacturing Exports from Puerto Rico to the rest of the world before and after the elimination of IRS Section 936, US is the control group.

Independent Variables	Log Exports (1)		Log Exports (2)	
End of Tax Credit (2005-2016)	.431 (.098)	**	.666 (.111))	**
Puerto Rico	-3.370 (.536)	**	-3.274 (.537)	**
Puerto Rico x End of Tax Credit	-.405 (.321)	**	-.501 (.459)	**
Tax Credit Phase out (1995-2005)			.320 (.043)	**
Puerto Rico * Tax Credit Phaseout			-.131 (.194)	**
Industry Dummy Variables	Yes		Yes	
Observations	636		636	
R-Squared	.80		.80	

Clustered standard errors. * Signfiicant at the 10 percent level, ** Significant at the 5 percent level.

Table 3 shows estimates of the impact of the elimination of Section 936 on Puerto Rico's manufacturing exports using mainland U.S. manufacturing exports as a control. Column (1) shows the coefficient on the interaction term between the Puerto Rico, and the end of tax-credit dummies is not significant at the 5 percent or 10 percent level. This suggests there was no significant difference in exports trends for Puerto Rico and the United States after the elimination of Section 936. Estimates in column 2 show that when the phase-out and elimination of section 936 dummies are interacted with the Puerto Rico dummy, coefficients on these terms are not significant. Thus, there is no evidence the phase-out and elimination of Section 936 had a negative impact on Puerto Rico's exports.

Conclusion

In summary, my study indicates that the elimination of Section 936 had a significant impact on the Puerto Rican labor market, accounting for the loss of 75 percent of manufacturing jobs relative to service sector industries. While technological change could have been a contributing factor in the reduction of manufacturing employment relative to service sector industries, the large magnitude and timing of reductions in manufacturing employment cannot be explained away by technological change. Many of the lost manufacturing jobs were in higher paying industries such as pharmaceuticals and electrical and electronic equipment. Thus, the elimination of Section 936 was a contributing factor to the economic crisis in Puerto Rico.

My research finds no impact of the elimination of Section 936 on manufacturing exports from Puerto Rico to the rest of the world when using United States exports as the control group. One possible explanation for this result may be that technological change in manufacturing may have increased labor productivity causing output to remain at higher levels in Puerto Rico despite the large decline in employment. The counterfactual exports from Puerto Rico without technological change are not shown here. According to the *U.S. Monthly Labor Review* (Brill, Chansky and Kim 2018), U.S. multifactor productivity in the manufacturing sector grew by an average of 2.0 percent per year from 1992 to 2004. During this period, manufacturers increased their production of goods with relatively fewer inputs. From 2004 through 2016, however, manufacturing multifactor productivity declined by an average of 0.3 percent per year. An alternative interpretation of the results is that these estimates do not capture the impact of IRS Section 936 on exports because the U.S. is not a good control for Puerto Rico's manufacturing exports due to large differences in the cost of factors of production such as labor and capital between Puerto Rico and the U.S. mainland. Thus, further evidence is needed to determine the impact of Section 936 on Puerto Rico's manufacturing exports.

ACKNOWLEDGEMENTS

Special thanks to Yilda Rivera Rosado, U.S. Bureau of Labor Statistics and Puerto Rico Department of Labor for making data available for this research project. Thanks to Luis Chacin for excellent research assistance. This paper has benefited from helpful comments from anonymous referees.

NOTES

[1] The Title III process, Puerto Rico Oversight, Management and Economic Stability Act (PROMESA), established a seven-person Oversight Board, appointed by the U.S. Congress to work with Puerto Rico's creditors to renegotiate the island's debts.

[2] The concordance is available in Appendix A.

[3] The ten-year phase-out period of IRS Section 936 began in 1995 and ended in 2005. The program was eliminated in 2006.

REFERENCES

Alm, James. 2006. Assessing Puerto Rico's Fiscal Policies. In *The Economy of Puerto Rico: Restoring Growth*, eds. Susan M. Collins, Barry P. Bosworth and Miguel A. Soto Class. San Juan: Center for the New Economy; Washington, DC: Brookings Institution.

Amadeo, Kimberly. 2018. U.S. Imports and Exports with Components and Statistics. *The Balance*. <https://www.thebalance.com/u-s-imports-and-exports-components-and-statistics-3306270/>.

Brill, Michael, Brian Chansky and Jennifer Kim. 2018. Multifactor Productivity Slowdown in U.S. Manufacturing. *Monthly Labor Review* July.

Campo-Flores, Arian. 2018. Puerto Rico: Hurricane Maria Death Toll May Have Topped 1,400. *Wall Street Journal* 24 August.

Caputo, Ibby. 2017. Hurricane Maria Devastated Puerto Rico. Then It Caused a Ripple Effect in Mainland Hospitals. *Public Radio International* 6 December. <https://www.pri.org/stories/2017-12-06/hurricane-maria-devastated-puerto-rico-then-it-caused-ripple-effect-mainland/>.

Caraballo Cueto, José and Juan Lara. 2018. Deindustrialization and Unsustainable Debt in Middle-Income Countries: The Case of Puerto Rico. *Journal of Globalization and Development* 10.1515/jg-2017-0009.

Feliciano, Zadia M. and Andrew Green. 2017. US Multinationals in Puerto Rico and the Repeal of Section 936 Tax Exemption for U.S. Corporations. NBER Working Paper 23681, August.

Farrant, Jaime. 2017. 4 Reasons Why Puerto Rico's 'Bankruptcy' Process Matters to U.S. Residents. *NBC News* 5 June. <www.nbcnews.comhttps://www.nbcnews.com/news/latino/4-reasons-why-puerto-rico-s-bankruptcy-process-matters-u-n766991/>.

Grubert, Harry and Joel Slemrod. 1998. The Effect of Taxes on Investment and Income Shifting to Puerto Rico. *The Review of Economics and Statistics* 80(3), 365–73.

Hexner, Thomas J and Glenn P. Jenkins. 1995. Puerto Rico and Section 936: A Costly Dependence. *Tax Notes International* 16 January, 235–54.

Holik, Daniel S. 2009. US Possessions Corporations, 2005. *Statistics of Income Bulletin* Spring, 92–105.

Krueger, Anne O., Ranjit Teja and Andrew Wolf. 2015. Puerto Rico – A Way Forward. Report for the Commonwealth of Puerto Rico and the Government Development Bank of Puerto Rico, 29 June.

Mora, Marie T., Alberto Dávila and Havidán Rodríguez. 2018. *Population, Migration, and Socioeconomic Outcomes among Island and Mainland Puerto Ricans: La Crisis Boricua.* Lanham, MD: Lexington Books.

Meléndez, Edwin and Jeniffer Hinojosa. 2017. Estimates of Post-Hurricane Maria Exodus from Puerto Rico. Center for Puerto Rican Studies, Centro RB2017-01, October. <https://centropr.hunter.cuny.edu/sites/default/files/RB2017-01-POST-MARIA%20EXODUS_V3.pdf/>.

Puerto Rico Planning Board, Governor's Office. 2018. Economic Report to the Governor. San Juan, Puerto Rico.

Scurria, Andrew and Heather Gillers. 2017. Puerto Rico to Square Off with Creditors. *Wall Street Journal* 4 May.

Appendix A: SIC to NAICS concordance

Industrial Groups	Description	SIC	NAICS
1	Food, beverage and tobacco	20, 21	311, 312
2	Textiles	22, 23	313, 314, 315
3	Leather and leather products	31	316
4	Lumber, wood, fabricated metal products	24, 25	321, 337
5	Paper and products, Printing and publishing	26, 27	322, 323
6	Petroleum and coal products	29	324
7	Chemicals and allied products	28	325
8	Rubber and misc. plastics products	30	326
9	Stone, clay and glass products	32	327
10	Primary metal industries	33	331
11	Fabricated metal products	34, 35, 36, 37, 38	332, 333, 334, 335, 336
12	Misc. manufacturing	39	339

The Politics of PROMESA

EDWIN MELÉNDEZ

ABSTRACT

This article provides an overview of PROMESA in the context of an erratic historical pattern of U.S. policy implementation toward Puerto Rico and offer an analysis of
the congressional political and legislative dynamics that led to the enactment of the
law. PROMESA's core components were and are contentious to various constituencies affected by the legislation, especially to those directly affected by severe austerity measures and bondholders who have lost substantial value in their investments.
PROMESA received divided support from the Puerto Rican people and its elected
officials when enacted and represents a new reality and challenge to the Puerto
Rican people both on the island and stateside. [Key words: Key words: PROMESA,
U.S. policy, debt crisis, austerity, economic development, federal funding]

The author (emele@hunter.cuny.edu) is a Professor of Urban Policy and Planning and the
Director of the Center for Puerto Rican Studies at Hunter College, CUNY. In addition to
numerous scientific papers and other publications, he is the author or editor of thirteen books
including *State of Puerto Ricans* (Centro Press, 2017) and *Puerto Ricans at the Dawn of the New
Millenium* (Centro Press, 2014). He also served as invited Editor for "Pathways to Economic
Opportunity" *CENTRO Journal* 23(2), 2011.

Governor García-Padilla's declaration that Puerto Rico's public debt was "unpayable" and the subsequent first default in August of 2015 caused widespread media attention in the U.S. to the "Puerto Rico debt crisis" and triggered the unfolding of events that led to the enactment of the Puerto Rico Oversight, Management and Economic Stability Act ("PROMESA"). At the time, Puerto Rico's public debt was over $74 billion and public pension obligations $50 billion. However, for political and financial actors it was evident that Puerto Rico was at the verge of a financial collapse when its bonds were rated as "junk bonds" in 2014 and the only credit available to the Commonwealth was offered by hedge funds and other predatory lenders. The accumulation of debt was partly the result of a prolonged recession and the concomitant decline in tax revenues. However, the ruling political parties' inability to respond with effective economic development and fiscal policies to counter the phase out of Section 936 federal tax incentives and to other broader factors such as technological change and globalization affecting manufacturing more generally, and their inability to restructure government to conform to a new fiscal reality were (and are) critical factors inducing the economic crisis. The Puerto Rico "debt crisis" called for decisive congressional action.

Enacted as a rare bipartisan legislation of the 114th Congress, PROMESA was designed to steer negotiations with creditors and lead to the restructuring of the crushing debt and pension liabilities. PROMESA, despite its flaws, provides Puerto Rico with a legal pathway for debt restructuring and greater bankruptcy protection that is available to states through Chapter 9 of the U.S. Bankruptcy Code procedures and, so far, has saved billions of dollars in payments to creditors that would have resulted in heighten austerity. PROMESA's steep cost for Puerto Rico was the imposition of a seven-member Financial Oversight and Management Board (Oversight Board) to oversee Puerto Rico's finances. The Oversight Board is comprised of seven members appointed by the U.S. President and has the authority to supersede local law in matters that affect the Commonwealth's budget and compliance with an approved fiscal plan. The Oversight Board also has the mandate to restructure the public debt, oversee the development of a long-term fiscal plan, and approve balanced budgets consistent with the approved plan. Its multimillion-dollar annual budget is paid for by the Commonwealth it oversees. In many ways, the Oversight Board resembles the authority extended to the Executive Council under the Foraker Act of 1900 where the power resided in an appointed body. Yet, the first control group under the Foraker Act was fully integrated by Puerto Ricans; PROMESA only mandates that one appointee to the Oversight Board "maintain a primary residence in the territory or have a primary place of business in the territory."

Though PROMESA was the only politically feasible policy option at the time it was enacted, there are significant tradeoffs and contradictions embedded in PROMESA that may render it insufficient as a policy framework to achieve its main goal of stabilizing Puerto Rico's economy yet exact the steep price of setting back a century of U.S.-Puerto Rico political relations. As a bipartisan legislation, especially in the context of presidential and congressional deep-rooted policy differences and the presidential electoral cycle heating up at the time, a broad coalition of Democrats and Republicans was needed to pass the legislation both in the House and the Senate. With support from the overwhelming majority of progressive Democrats, PROMESA allowed for the restructuring of the public debt inclusive of the general obligation bonds from the commonwealth, a bankruptcy procedure that exceeds what is available to states. In addition, PROMESA allowed for a stay on repayment of the debt that saved the Commonwealth and its dependencies billions of dollars in repayment of the debt since its enactment.

Yet, upon conditions imposed by the Republican majority, PROMESA installed an Oversight Board to control the island's finances by giving it authority over the budget. But as many critics have pointed out, PROMESA did not allocate federal resources to stabilize the island's economy, deal with the impending health crisis, or provide a clear mechanism for developing a comprehensive plan for job creation and economic development. The shortcomings of PROMESA are in many ways superseded by the injection of post-Hurricane Maria federal funding supporting Medicaid temporarily as well as mitigation of infrastructure and economic recovery. This funding is managed by FEMA and other federal agencies and by the Commonwealth government though the Oversight Board oversees expenses to the extent that they affect the budget.

Puerto Rico's current fiscal and political situation is as much the result of the U.S. oversight or lack thereof as it is of local political dynamics especially as it concerns mismanagement of public finances.

In this article, I provide an overview of PROMESA in the context of an erratic historical pattern of U.S. policy implementation toward Puerto Rico and offer an analysis of the congressional political and legislative dynamics that led to the enactment of the law. Puerto Rico's current fiscal and political situation is as much the result of the U.S. oversight or lack thereof as it is of local political dynamics especially as it concerns mismanagement of public finances. PROMESA represents a turning point in Puerto Rico's political and economic history. The focus of this study is the process and outcome of policy making and negotiations that led to PROMESA—the post- Hurricane Maria period is addressed here only tangentially, as are the contentious budget negotiations between the Oversight Board and Governor Rossello's administration. PROMESA's core components were and are contentious to various constituencies affected by the legislation, especially to those directly affected by severe austerity measures and bondholders who have lost substantial value in their investments. PROMESA received divided support from the Puerto Rican people and its elected officials when enacted and represents a new reality and challenge to the Puerto Rican people both on the island and stateside.

U.S. Economic Policies Toward Puerto Rico

Over time, congressional policies have provided the foundation for Puerto Rico's economy. These policies have been inconsistent, at times beneficial and at other times harmful to economic development. Puerto Rico's ability to issues triple tax-exempt bonds was granted by the Jones-Shafroth Act of 1917. Making Puerto Rico bonds earnings exempt from federal and local taxes made them very attractive to investors in municipal capital markets. Similarly, the Revenue Act of 1921 exempted corporations from taxation of all income from U.S. possessions though income was taxable on repatriation. These federal tax incentives provided needed capital for the development of infrastructure through the development of public corporations and induced industrial development in Puerto Rico through the expansion of operations of American corporations. In essence, this was Puerto Rico's postwar development model, and its foundation included access to municipal capital markets for the development of public infrastructure to support multinational corporations' investments in manufacturing and other export-oriented industries(Ayala and Bernabe 2009; Dietz 1987; Rivera Batiz and Santiago 1996).

However, business cycles and globalization have induced changes in policies that are intended to respond to the challenges facing the U.S. economy but have contradictory impacts on the island. By the 1970s the island economy relied on processing oil imports from Arab countries and then shipping them to the U.S. When the Organization of Petroleum Exporting Countries (OPEC) imposed an embargo against the United States after President Nixon decided to support Israel during the 1973 Arab-Israeli War, the oil refinery industry collapsed and with it Puerto Rico's economy went into a recession (Dietz 1982). In 1976, Section 936 of the Internal Revenue Code was created to support the island's economic recovery by exempting American companies from federal taxes on repatriated income earned in Puerto Rico (Feliciano 2018). Section 936 worked for its intended purpose. By the early 1990s, pharmaceutical and high-tech manufacturing had become the undisputable economic anchors of the island's economy. But the companies favored by Section 936 were reaping billions of dollars in profits exempted from federal taxes. A pro-statehood administration in Puerto Rico generally perceived the federal tax exemption as an impediment to statehood and a change in status (Luxner 1996). President Clinton, who had tried for years to close a perceived tax loophole, finally found token opposition from the governing party to the elimination of Section 936 and a direct source of tax revenues to support legislation favoring U.S. small businesses.

As part of the Small Business Job Protection Act of 1996, Congress approved a 10-year phase-out of Section 936 tax credit. Presumably, closing the loophole would have provided funding for business development in the United States. But in reality, multinational corporations repatriate only a small fraction, less than a quarter of their profits. Puerto Rico lost new investments in these industries, deposits were withdrawn from local banks, and Puerto Rico's economy entered into a steady decline. The program ended completely in December 2005. Though the elimination of Section 936 was not the only factor inducing the downfall of manufacturing in Puerto Rico, as globalization and technological change induced a general decline of manufacturing stateside (Feliciano 2018), Puerto Rico's most recent economic crisis began shortly after. Acrimonious local politics prevented the development of a cohesive alternative economic development strategy to counter the loss of federal tax incentives and other factors eroding Puerto Rico's industrial base, and by the end of 2007 the Great Recession further pushed the economy into a protracted recession.

President Barack Obama's stimulus policies benefitted Puerto Rico in two specific ways. First was a package of $7 billion (spent from 2009 to 2013) to inject capital to the local economy through the American Recovery and Reinvestment Act of 2009 (ARRA). These funds were disbursed primarily to cover operating expenses and a relatively small portion went to cover infrastructure investments that would have had a more direct impact on job creation or on retention (Transition Report 2013). In addition, beginning in January of 2011, the Commonwealth enacted Act 154 of 2010, which established a 4 percent Excise Tax on services transactions to foreign corporations that produced about $2 billion annually accounting for over one-fifth of the tax revenues collected by the central government. In turn, foreign corporations claimed a credit on their federal taxes for the Puerto Rico tax. Reuters referred to this arrangement as "backdoor bailout" of Puerto Rico (Bond News 2014). This arrangement became the target of the Oversight Board, which conveyed to Governor Rossello that "both the government's budget as well as any economic plan must not take into consideration the revenues generated under Act 154-2010" (Tax Alert 2017).

However, President Trump's new Tax and Jobs Act of 2017 solved Puerto Rico's government 4 percent Excise Tax conundrum. Under the new tax structure, the Global Intangible Low-Taxed Income (GILTI), the minimum tax for any U.S.-owned controlled foreign corporations (CFC) is 10.5 percent. So, CFCs would be charged an additional 6.5 percent to the local excise tax but the local tax will remain as a deductible from federal taxes (Feliciano 2018). Despite this advantage, CFCs investments in Puerto Rico are affected by both the increase in local taxes and by the lower taxation rate stateside. The net effect of the recent federal tax reform will unfold over the next few years as CFCs adjust their investment strategies to these changes. The fiscal plan approved by the Oversight Board contemplated a steady decline of this revenue source.

To this day no one has provided a consistent and credible explanation as to why Puerto Rico's exclusion [Section 903(1) of the Bankruptcy Code] was enacted as part of the law.

Borrowing through triple-tax-exempted municipal bonds in capital markets became a key element of the post-war economic development. Public borrowing made feasible the development of many public corporations that provided the country with electrical, water, roads, communications, public buildings, and all types of economic infrastructure. But when the post Section 936 recession and the impact of the financial collapse in the U.S. took a toll and many of these public corporations could not service debt payments and maintain operations, Puerto Rico could not declare bankruptcy to protect public corporations from creditors. The U.S. inattention to its territory connects directly to the debt crisis. In 1984, Congress adopted Section 903(1) of the Bankruptcy Code and introduced a new definition of "State" that excluded Puerto Rico's municipalities from legal recourse to municipal bankruptcy. To this day no one has provided a consistent and credible explanation as to why Puerto Rico's exclusion was enacted as part of the law. Even with the inclusion of Puerto Rico in the Bankruptcy Code, the general obligations of the Commonwealth would not have been covered under federal court procedures. In that sense, PROMESA bankruptcy provisions are more comprehensive and beneficial to Puerto Rico. Yet, exclusion of Puerto Rico from declaring bankruptcy led directly to the need for and the enactment of PROMESA.

With Puerto Rico crippled by public debt and pension obligations, Congress had to act to provide a legal mechanism to restructure the island's debt. PROMESA established the Oversight Board to oversee Puerto Rico's finances and budgets and provides for a court-supervised debt restructuring. PROMESA also provided for a stay in debt service of almost a year to allow the Oversight Board to examine options and possibly negotiate with creditors. For many, PROMESA offered a way out of the debt crisis and the promise of economic prosperity. But PROMESA generated a strong populist opposition from the very beginning. Over time, massive demonstrations against the policies of the Oversight Board and the populist approach of Governor Rosselló led to less favorable public opinion of PROMESA. In the future, public opinion is bound to be influenced by how the Oversight Board supports economic development, mitigate austerity and leads to the disposition of the debt. Their credibility is also tied to their audit of the debt and accountability toward financial institutions and public officials entangle in the fiscal crises and unrestrained indebtedness.

The Genesis of PROMESA

Governor García-Padilla's declaration that Puerto Rico's public debt was "unpayable" triggered the intensification of a public debate regarding options for solving the debt crisis. Though various alternatives entered the public debate about how to resolve Puerto Rico's debt crisis, PROMESA proved to be the only politically feasible policy option for the U.S. Congress and President Obama's administration. One of the first options brought to the forefront around that time was using the U.S. Treasury's Exchange Stabilization Fund (ESF) to support a restructuring of Puerto Rico's debt. Some analysts contended that the U.S. Treasury was offering advice but not considering other options that could provide debt relief. Considering that the Government Development Bank of Puerto Rico, which carried out debt-management functions similar to State Treasurers, did not have access to the fed's discount window, Puerto

Rico was at a disadvantage compared to other U.S. states and municipalities and thus justified the U.S. Treasury's consideration of other options to boost liquidity.

The U.S. Treasury's Exchange Stabilization Fund is generally seen as a policy tool used to stabilize foreign currency and, some argued, it could have been used to support Puerto Rico's restructuring of the debt. However, financial policy analysts contended that the "combination of the just-adopted 2016 Budget Resolution by Congress barring bailouts to municipalities—but not other corporations—combined with steps taken by Congress to limit Executive authority in the wake of the financial crisis of 2008, such as barring use of the Exchange Stabilization Fund, which had been used to help Mexico during the 1990s, for emergency purposes—have served to handcuff the Executive branch—even as the financial/fiscal crisis has worsened" (Puerto Rico & Federal Fiscal Policy Insolvency 2015). A year after it was first proposed, the Exchange Stabilization Fund was incorporated in a legislative proposal put forth by Senator Bernie Sanders during his presidential campaign. By all counts, ESF would not have been a viable mechanism for debt restructuring. In the case of Mexico, ESF was used as a bridge loan for liquidity purpose to a solvent government that could guarantee the repayment of the loan. In addition, whether or not statutorily available, the ESF would have lacked the cram-down provisions of Title III of PROMESA that are essential to force agreement with creditors and avoid protracted legal procedures with hedge funds and other hold-outs creditors.

A second policy option proposed at the time by various policy analysts and activists involved action by the Federal Reserve Bank. In theory, the fed had several options to intervene such as providing loans to public corporations to restructure debt, or by buying new bonds from the Commonwealth used in a Reverse Dutch Auction Process. However, the Federal Reserve Bank typically lend to commercial banks not to states or public corporations. In addition, the rationality for this intervention would have been partially based on a notion that Puerto Rico's default was a threat to the broader U.S. financial system, a standard of high order. Since the case of Puerto Rico was not perceived to be of that magnitude by policymakers, say comparable to the financial crisis of 2008, the Federal Reserve option was dismissed by Chairwoman Janet Yellen.

At the end, with proposed policy options not gaining traction with elected and other government officials, the most feasible policy pathway for restructuring Puerto Rico's debt was through congressional action. The administration, led by President Obama and Secretary Lew, proposed debt relief by extending bankruptcy procedures to the commonwealth and mitigating the impact of the crisis by maintaining funding for health programs, expanding the Child Tax Credit (CTC) and adding the Earned Income Tax Credit (EITC). In addition, Secretary of Health and Human Services Sylvia Mathews Burwell was examining options under current law through administrative regulations or executive orders to improve access to health services in Puerto Rico.

The decisive factor for the enactment of PROMESA was that the Republican congressional leadership needed democratic votes to pass a spending bill (Snell and Demirjian 2015). Puerto Rico's debt became one of the democratic leadership's demands to Speaker Paul D. Ryan (R-WI) for their support to the bill. According to House Minority Leader Nancy Pelosi (D-Calif.), Speaker Ryan "wanted to go through committee on it" and promised that "[f]irst day back [Ryan] said there would be hearings on the crisis in Puerto Rico" (Snell and Demirjian 2015). But the context for these negotiations is also important. Governor García-Padilla's declaration that the public debt was "unpayable," in addition to calling widespread attention to the depth of the ongoing recession in Puerto Rico and the scale of its financial problems, also prompted a diaspora solidarity movement with Puerto Rico. Although elected officials in Puerto Rico were actively lobbying Congress and Resident Commissioner Pedro Pierluisi had introduced and spearheaded legislation, nationwide direct action in the districts of members of congress and others advocating for Puerto Rico was a significant new phenomenon in Puerto Rican politics. Spearheaded by the leadership of Nydia Velázquez (D-NY) and José Serrano (D-NY), Leader Pelosi and Speaker Ryan were aware of the importance of the Puerto Rico issue in the upcoming presidential elections in swing states such as Florida and Pennsylvania.

The political links between Puerto Rico and the diaspora go back to the revolutionary movement of the late nineteenth century when Puerto Rican patriots saw New York as a platform to advocate for an end to Spanish colonialism in the island (Meléndez 1998). Since then, the Puerto Rican political movements have revolved around the quests for independence, greater autonomy, or annexation to the United States. The significant difference in recent years is that as a result of the millennial migration the majority of Puerto Ricans, about six of every ten now reside stateside, and of those the overwhelming majority are U.S. born, over 70 percent of them, and native English speakers (Meléndez and Vargas-Ramos 2014). While in the past political action was largely constrained to the greater New York City region, the population boom has induced significant growth of the stateside Puerto Rican community across the country. Migration is especially significant in Florida, where the political affiliation of Puerto Ricans is roughly divided between Democrats and Republicans, with a sizable share of independents, and where a significant portion of the electorate has manifested sympathy for statehood (Survey of the Puerto Rican Florida Electorate 2016). These population changes gave those advocating for congressional action a more robust presence among elected officials in both parties across the country.

The first organized effort to ascertain an articulated voice on the Puerto Rican crisis was the conference Encuentro Nacional de la Diáspora Puertorriqueña in Orlando, Florida, in October 2015 (Delgado 2015a). The summit was organized by a broad coalition of community leaders and elected officials with the stated purpose of "building a national Puerto Rican agenda." Among the over 300 participants from ten states in the conference, close to twenty national and regional Puerto Rican organizations were represented by their leaders, and close to twenty elected officials, including four members of Congress, participated. The discussions centered on the impact and effects of the economic crisis in Puerto Rico on the stateside Puerto Rican community. Besides the debt and fiscal crises, topics included the Medicaid "cliff," civic engagement, climate change, and others. Perhaps the most important outcome was the call for a national coalition and a caucus of elected officials to give continuity to the agenda and solidarity initiative.

In alliance with the Hispanic Federation of New York, Puerto Rican organizations and leaders organized the Day at the Capitol on December 2, 2015. Coalition leaders agreed to focus on the issues of extending bankruptcy to Puerto Rico, parity in health care and Child Tax Credit (CTC) programs, and the extension of the EITC to the island (Delgado 2015b). Their goal was to add these Puerto Rico-focused legislative initiatives to the Omnibus Spending Bill that was due by mid-December. With over a thousand volunteers in hand, over forty information sessions were organized with members of Congress, all of them mediated and attended by voters in their districts. Many other members of Congress were called from a telephone bank in a nearby hotel that accommodated the overflow of participants—the members of Congress offices were not large enough to accommodate all that wanted to participate nor were they able to get appointments. The end result, a clear victory for the initiative, was a commitment from Speaker Paul Ryan (R-Wis.) to take up Puerto Rico legislation by the end of March (Fuller and Barrón-López 2015). The statement about Puerto Rico was critical to persuade a significant number of Democrats to get behind the bill.

At the end, the solidarity movement was instrumental for mobilizing democratic support for a legal option for "territorial" debt restructuring and the democratic leadership in turn was able to use the vote on the spending bill to exact Speaker Ryan's commitment to a legislative process to deal with the debt crisis in Puerto Rico.

Political pressure from a broad coalition of Puerto Rican leaders from the diaspora continued. In a follow-up day of action at the capitol, led by actor Lin Manuel Miranda and congressional leaders, they pressed for the extension of bankruptcy to Puerto Rico (Escobar and Alfaro 2016). At the end, the solidarity movement was instrumental for mobilizing democratic support for a legal option for "territorial" debt restructuring and the democratic leadership in turn was able to use the vote on the spending bill to exact Speaker Ryan's commitment to a legislative process to deal with the debt crisis in Puerto Rico. Political negotiations led Speaker Ryan to ask Rep. Rob Bishop (R-Utah), Chairman of the House Natural Resources Committee, to initiate legislative procedures to consider bankruptcy for Puerto Rico. This was the genesis of what would become PROMESA.

The Enactment of PROMESA

One of the most intriguing aspects of enacting legislation were the coalitions for and against PROMESA—strange bedfellows, for sure. And, to no one's surprise, the situation of Puerto Rico got entangled in presidential politics. On the one hand, the bipartisan coalition in favor of the legislation coalesced around President Obama, Secretary Clinton, and Speaker Ryan. The opposition to the legislation was led by bondholders (no surprise) and a coalition of unions fearful of the impact of the bill on pensions advocating for protections for public retirees. Despite a majority of Republicans supporting the bill and securing the so-called "Hastert Rule" threshold, PROMESA could not have passed without Democratic support, which gave Leader Pelosi some bargaining power to shape PROMESA.

In addition to Leader Pelosi, the Obama-Ryan Coalition supporting the bill included Rep. Pierluisi and the Democratic leadership in Congress. But why were some Republicans supporting the bill? In essence, both sides realized the dire consequences of doing nothing. For the most part, Democrats saw PROMESA as the only immediate, viable alternative to gain a stay on payment of obligations in the immediate future when almost $2 billion were due July 1, 2016. And though this would not have been the first time that Puerto Rico defaulted on debt service payments, this time bondholders, led by hedge funds holding general obligation bonds, would have ensue more aggressive legal challenges and in all likelihood more severe austerity. President Obama, Treasury Secretary Jacob Lew, and others in the administration continued advocating for a legal remedy to the situation, while the diaspora solidarity movement continued highlighting Puerto Rico's situation during presidential elections.

Not all Democrats supported PROMESA. Most prominently, Senator Bernie Sanders (I-VT) running for the Democratic presidential nomination at the time squarely sided with the unions. He stated that the law did not protect pension funds, proposed a potential lowering of the minimum wage, and the authority of the control board over local government went too far. Sympathizers of this position argued that it was better to wait for a new administration to take office than to take a bad deal like PROMESA. They argued that, though a chaotic situation would surely develop in Puerto Rico after July 1, such a chaos would just put more pressure on Congress to act in favor of Puerto Rico. For context, there was the expectation among Liberals that a Donald Trump candidacy would result in a windfall for Democrats that could result in a Democratic control of Congress. However, political analysts such as David Daley argued that "redistricting post-2010 was built to withstand even a landslide loss" and such a scenario [a Democratic control of the House] was just a "fantasy."

So, a reasonable expectation at the time was that the House would be controlled by the GOP in the next Congress. This would have put bankruptcy legislation squarely back where it started—hoping for a bipartisan bill to address the fiscal crisis in Puerto Rico. However, pursuing a wait-and-hope-for-the-best strategy would have carried an enormous cost in terms of the likely legal chaos and concomitant heighten austerity in the island. In addition, part of the problem that Puerto Rico would have faced if PROMESA was not enacted was the same—finding an alternative politically feasible policy option that offered a realistic path toward restructuring of the debt. In retrospect, that option would have had a more difficult path with the election of President Trump.

Senator Sanders also proposed that "Congress should act immediately to give Puerto Rico the same authority granted to every municipality in this country to restructure its debt under the supervision of a bankruptcy court. But the Republicans in Congress continue to oppose this" (Sanders 2016). Senator Sanders was referring to extending Chapter 9, which regulates municipal bankruptcy, to Puerto Rico. Bankruptcy procedures in Detroit are an example of the implementation of this procedure. Senator Sanders' proposal was similar to Rep. Pierluisi's bill proposing to "Include Puerto Rico in Chapter 9 of the U.S. Bankruptcy Code." However, the Chapter 9 bankruptcy route for the Puerto Rico case confronted two problems. The first was that it would have been an incomplete solution to the debt problem. Chapter 9 would have excluded the Commonwealth debt, especially General Obligations bonds accounting for $12.5 billion, the second largest share of the debt. Hedge funds controlled a substantive portion of this debt and would have aggressively pursue legal remedies when the Commonwealth defaulted on upcoming payments in July. In addition, Chapter 9 procedures would have excluded another significant portion of the debt as COFINA (from the Spanish name Corporación del Fondo de Interés Apremiante) bonds, accounting for the largest share (over $17 billion) of the public debt, had enough cash flow to meet its repayment obligations and, therefore, it was not insolvent by Chapter 9 standards. In short, Chapter 9 standards would have required any Puerto Rican instrumentality to prove insolvency.

Besides the fact that Chapter 9 would have excluded general obligation and COFINA bonds, accounting for 42 percent of the total outstanding public debt at the time (excluding pension obligations), a second obstacle was that it confronted legislative hurdles in terms of having to go through various congressional committees. This is the main reason that Speaker Ryan chose to cast the Puerto Rico debt restructuring solely through the House Committee on Natural Resources, which has jurisdiction over the territories. After the markup of the revised bill, PROMESA went from the Natural Resources Committee directly to the House floor for a vote. Since the December 2, 2015, Day of Action at the Capitol the diaspora advocacy community in solidarity with Puerto Rico referred to "territorial" bankruptcy to differentiate it from Chapter 9. The strategy of channeling the legislative process through the Natural Resources Committee had the additional advantage of restricting any legislation to the "territories," thus excluding all states from legislation and, by implication, silencing the critics that raised the concern that any such legislation would establish a precedent for states with mounting debt obligations. PROMESA, with all its flaws, is inclusive of all debt, inclusive of general obligations bonds and incorporated Chapter 9-like bankruptcy procedures in federal court.

Despite attacks from the left, the most adamant opposition to PROMESA came, as to be expected given billions of dollars at stake, from the hedge funds and other bondholders. The bondholders rejected the implicit loss of value in a debt-restructuring process. They also differed in the interpretation of the way PROMESA treats pension funds obligations claiming that the law was "paving the way for the board to prioritize the Puerto Rican Government's pension liabilities over any and all classes of bondholders, including those with absolute constitutional priority" (Main Street Bondholders 2016). The issue of pensions clearly divided the opposition to PROMESA. Senator Sanders and the unions believed PROMESA would not provide protection to pensions. Hedge funds bondholders' campaign was orchestrated by the "Council for Citizens Against Government Waste" (CCAGW) that ran radio ads casting PROMESA as a bailout—a bailout with bondholders' money, to be precise. The Republican leadership framed PROMESA as necessary to avoid the use of public monies to rescue Puerto Rico. In their view, there was no alternative legislative option to provide federal funding to tackle the Puerto Rico debt crisis. Creditors took the risk when they invested in Puerto Rico financial instruments and bondholders would have to deal with the consequences as any other investor would. Despite the saturation of local markets targeting the Republican leadership in Congress, Speaker Ryan and Chairman Bishop harnessed most Republicans to support the bill.

The Commonwealth had a severe liquidity problem at the time PROMESA was enacted. For more than a year, the government had instituted emergency measures to generate operating capital such as "claw back" monies already distributed to government agencies, withhold payments to escrow accounts for payment of bonds debt, delaying income tax refunds and denying payments to pension funds. Since credit was not available and a Republican-controlled Congress was adamantly opposed to any injection of resources to mitigate the liquidity situation, schools, hospitals, and other essential services were already severely affected.

At the time PROMESA was enacted, the fiscal crisis had already evolved into severe austerity and an ensuing humanitarian crisis. For example, the budget of the island's only children's hospital had been cut by 14 percent, lacked CT and MRI machines, and has 70 vacant nursing positions; security guards for the public school system have gone unpaid for months; a town on the west coast was without its water supply for several days after a valve broke since the contractor would not fix the break due to lack of payment on prior bills; and the food supply for nearly 12,500 inmates in Puerto Rico's 37 prisons was almost interrupted after the prison system's food vendor stopped sending supplies because they were owed more than $12 million.

Under Title IV, PROMESA also provided a stay on legal action and debt repayment.

The price that Democrats paid for the stay on the debt services to provide a window for orderly negotiations with the bondholder and the restructuring of the public debt was the imposition of the Oversight Board. At first glance, PROMESA's Oversight Board appears to be a hybrid of two different models—the Oversight Board imposed by Congress to Washington, D.C., and the general bankruptcy procedure under Chapter 9 followed in Detroit. Though these models are a good approximation, there are some differences that go beyond a simple combination of these two models. The most important difference is that the Oversight Board will authorize a court procedure only after a period for voluntary negotiation would be exhausted and provided a mechanism to deal with potential holdback creditors. Under Title IV, PROMESA also provided a stay on legal action and debt repayment. At the conclusion of this period short of a year after the enactment of the Act, the Oversight Board could only initiate Title III for a court debt restructuring procedure with a super majority of five of seven members. In May 3, 2017, the Oversight Board voted unanimously to proceed with Title III and filed the case in federal court on behalf of the Commonwealth.

During the political deliberations that led to the enactment of PROMESA, several models were discussed. As in the case of DC, the Oversight Board is mandated to oversee a process that will produce balanced budgets consistent with restoring fiscal solvency. In DC the board oversaw fiscal management with far more powers to what they have in Puerto Rico but did not oversee debt restructuring. In 1997, Congress enacted the National Capital Revitalization and Self-Government Improvement Act (known as "The Revitalization Act"). The Revitalization Act provided debt and pension liability relief, ended Medicaid disparities and provided additional funding for infrastructure and economic development (Bouker 2016). But Congress also gave the Oversight Board emergency powers and authority over budget allocations and management decisions. In the case of Detroit, bankruptcy procedures respected the city's charter that gave more security to public pensions than to bondholders—which is a clear difference from the constitutional priority that was given to general obligation bonds in Puerto Rico. As it had been the case in multiple prior occasions of municipal bankruptcy, Michigan's governor appointed an emergency manager to oversee the city's finances during the bankruptcy procedures. After three consecutive balanced budgets, the state's financial oversight of Detroit's annual budgets ended in 2018, though the state-created commission "will continue to monitor Detroit's fiscal health for the next 10 years and could resume oversight if a budget deficit occurs" (Williams 2018).

In the case of Puerto Rico, one important common element with the cases of D.C. and Detroit was the issue of public employees' pensions, which at the time liabilities were closed to $50 billion. In the case of DC federal relief included pension liability relief, and in the case of Detroit pensions had statutory protection given it repayment priority over bondholders' debt. In contrast, Puerto Rico's constitution gives legal priority to bondholders over all other liabilities including pensions. Protecting public employees' pensions was the core issue for unions. PROMESA by superseding local law (including the Commonwealth's Constitution) and stating that pensions "must be adequately funded" in the fiscal plan, opened the door for pensions to be consider by the federal court proceedings on an equal footing with bondholders' debt.

Another case study that surfaced at the time was the Emergency Financial Control Board created in September 1975 to deal with New York City's $3.3 billion of debt and near bankruptcy crisis. State control of the city's finances for all practical purposes ended a decade later. However, despite the parallels with respect to the financial oversight board, a federal bailout of the city with $1.65 billion in long-term, federally guaranteed bonds represents a significance difference with the Puerto Rico case. Unlike the D.C. and New York cases, a federal bailout in any form or shape of Puerto Rico was not a politically feasible pathway. Furthermore, in contrast to D.C. and New York, in the Puerto Rico case the legislation has a clear sunset based on meeting financial targets—a sequence of balanced budgets and restoration of access to capital markets. Finally, the Oversight Board has no operational authority over the Commonwealth, only authority over the overall budget level and revenue sources to meet obligations based on the approved Fiscal Plan.

At the core of the controversy surrounding the PROMESA legislation were different interpretations of what would happen if Congress failed to approve PROMESA. The most obvious consequence was imminent legal chaos. As subsequent events showed, despite the PROMESA stay on debt service, hedge funds and other general obligation bondholders filed litigation against the Commonwealth for missed payments on the debt. General obligation bondholders contended that funds earmarked of tax revenues for COFINA bonds should be subordinated to general obligation bonds given their constitutional protections. At the time, the circuit federal court decided against them because of the stay until May 1, 2017. In the absence of the stay, the court would have had to decide the controversy between general obligation and COFINA bondholders, and they would have had to do so without a bankruptcy legal framework in the absence of PROMESA. Eventually the case went to federal Judge Taylor Swain as part of the Title III bankruptcy proceedings who, by the end of 2018, cleared the way for COFINA bondholders to vote on an agreement reached with the government and supported by the Oversight Board. The agreement restructures all $17.6 billion of COFINA debt representing 24 percent of Puerto Rico's total bonded debt (Bradford 2018).

Besides the wave of cases filed May 2, 2017, after the expiration of the stay and prior to the Oversight Board filing for Title III proceedings on May 3, another example of what would had been likely to happen when the Commonwealth missed payments to creditors in the absence of PROMESA was the case of the so-called health centers labeled 330 in reference to federally qualified health centers receiving grants under Section 330 of the Public Health Service Act. These health centers are mostly non-profit organizations that serve underserved populations. When the Commonwealth did not pay for special services for children with disability, federal judge Gustavo A. Gelpí ordered an injunction and placed the agency under a court-appointed receivership to insure payments. As this case illustrates, given the absence of a legal mechanism to enforce a restructuring of the debt, all that could be accomplished by a court procedure prior to the enactment of PROMESA, whether local or federal, would have been to enforce the contracts that defined specific financial obligations of the Commonwealth. The only clear outcome of the process would have been that the courts could only enforce existing laws and contractual obligations including payment of debt services, giving legal preference to senior general obligation bonds. Under such scenario austerity in all public services would have been more severe, and more likely to become a chaotic and arbitrary process, than those currently imposed by the Oversight Board.

In the end, the coalition led by President Obama and Speaker Ryan was able to pass self-standing legislation that satisfied the core concerns of progressive democrats that advocated for an orderly, legal mechanism to restructure the Puerto Rico debt and the core concerns of republican conservatives who advocated for tight financial controls through the Oversight Board and no federal "bail-out." The debate in Puerto Rico was as politically divided as it was in Congress. While public opinion was generally favorable to the enactment of both core elements of the legislation, the candidates of the two main political parties were divided—New Progressive Party (PNP from Spanish Partido Nuevo Progresista) candidate Ricardo Rossello aligned with the conservative position about the causes of the problem (local mismanagement) and thus supported the Oversight Board but not the debt restructuring mechanism, while Secretary of State and Popular Democratic Party (PPD, from Spanish Partido Popular Democratico) candidate David Bernier favored the progressive approach to debt restructuring but rejected the political implications of the Oversight Board.

Hope and Resistance in Puerto Rico

Prior to the enactment of PROMESA, though it was not clear what the Oversight Board really would mean for Puerto Rico, there was general support for the idea of an outside entity regulating the Commonwealth finances. In a poll conducted by a local university shortly before the enactment of the law, a majority of respondents (79%) expressed support for the Oversight Board. This support was highly correlated to support to and trust of federal institutions in Puerto Rico, such as the FBI (84% favorable) and the Supreme Court (81%). In the same opinion poll, respondents asserted distrust of Puerto Rico Political leaders: 95 percent agreed Puerto Rico was governed by a few groups that sought their own benefit. The principal investigator of the study, Professor Carlos Javier Sánchez from Universidad del Turabo, concluded that the public perceives the control board as a tool to restore sound fiscal management (Desconfían los boricuas en sus instituciones 2016). In other words, public opinion expectations prior to the passage of PROMESA were more associated with the deterioration of trust on the local political leadership to solve a problem than with the opinion of local political leaders opposing PROMESA. On this matter, public opinion in Puerto Rico shared a similar view to Republican members of Congress that demanded the imposition of the Oversight Board in the legislation.

Protests and resistance to austerity has influenced political dynamics since the beginning of the economic crisis. In 2009, massive demonstrations led by public employees came when Governor Luis Fortuño proposed Public Law 7, which declared a State of Fiscal Emergency and instituted fiscal stabilization reforms with wide impact on public employees. Thousands of government employees were laid off, causing many protests against these measures. During Governor García-Padilla's administration, on November 5, 2015, different social groups led by a coalition of all the religious denominations participated in "Unidos por la Salud," a rally that urged U.S. Congress to support equal treatment for Puerto Rico and prevent cuts in programs such as Medicare and Medicaid.

Immediately after the enactment of PROMESA, unions and other local leaders led protests including civil disobedience. For example, a group of protesters opened a camp in front of the federal court building in San Juan about a month after the enactment of PROMESA and a few weeks prior to the general elections in November. The same week, a group of protesters disrupted a Conference on PROMESA at the Hotel Condado Plaza. After a few hours of disruptions and confrontations the conference was suspended. Subsequently, in May 1, 2017, a broad coalition of unions, political leaders, and students' organizations participated in a march against austerity measures recommended by the Oversight Board, and in favor of an audit of Puerto Rico's public debt. Groups from the diaspora supported the cause by doing the same in New York.

Only three weeks prior to the elections, a poll conducted by El Nuevo Dia, *the leading newspaper in Puerto Rico, showed close to two-thirds of respondents had a favorable view of the Oversight Board.*

In the midst of a divided public opinion and a growing resistance movement, PROMESA entered the 2016 gubernatorial race in Puerto Rico. The two gubernatorial candidates representing the governing party and the main opposition party expressed opposite positions. Prior to the gubernatorial elections of November of 2016, the New Progressive Party (PNP) candidate for Governor Ricardo Rosselló expressed support for the control board but not for the debt restructuring. In essence, he argued that the debt problem was due to the bad administration of the governing party and not to a lack of funding. On the other side of the spectrum, former Secretary of State and Partido Popular Democratico (PPD) and gubernatorial candidate David Bernier

Table 1: Public Trust of Federal Institutions in Puerto Rico

Trust of Federal Institutions	
FBI	84%
Supreme Court	81%
Oversight Board	79%
Distrust of Federal Institutions	95% agree Puerto Rico is governed by a few groups that seek their own benefit

Source: Desconfían los boricuas en sus instituciones (2016).

opposed the control board but supported debt restructuring. Other leaders, such as the mayor and mayoral candidate for San Juan Carmen Yulín Cruz opposed the Oversight Board because of its colonial overtones and the granting of overarching powers to supersede democratically elected local authorities.

Despite general popular support for the control board prior to the elections and vehement opposition from unions and other political leaders, the spectrum of political opinions followed, for the most part, partisan lines. Only three weeks prior to the elections, a poll conducted by *El Nuevo Día*, the leading newspaper in Puerto Rico, showed close to two-thirds of respondents had a favorable view of the Oversight Board. Obviously, support for the Oversight Board translated into an electoral advantage to the candidate perceived to be in support of the Oversight Board (Graphic 1). Among the supporters of the Partido Nuevo Progresista (PNP) and gubernatorial candidate Rosselló, over 70 percent supported the Oversight Board, while support for the Control Board dropped to slightly more than half among those supporting candidate David Bernier of the PPD. Among independents support for the oversight Board was short of 60 percent of the respondents. But ongoing events influenced public opinion about PROMESA and the Oversight Board.

The 2016 elections results show dissatisfaction with the political parties controlling government since the late 1940's. Governor Rosselló (PNP) won the elections with 42 percent of the vote and defeated his opponent by less than 3 percent of the vote. Surprisingly, independent candidates to the governorship accumulated 17 percent of the vote—the largest percent attributed to other than the PPD and PNP candidates in decades. As significant, for a country with historically high electoral participation rates, 1.3 million registered voters did not vote. Though this number might be misleading since voters registered in prior elections were added to the electoral rosters, and the roster may include individuals who no longer are residing in Puerto Rico, there is still a marked decrease in voter participation when compare to prior elections. According to Vargas-Ramos, emigration was "not a factor in the decline of electoral participation in Puerto Rico" and the steep declined in voter participation is primarily attributed to an "extant legitimacy crisis of the political system and its political class" (Vargas-Ramos 2018).

El Nuevo Día has tracked public opinion about the Oversight Board and by implication PROMESA over time. Graphic 2 depicts the results of five different polls from the period. Public opinion was almost equally divided when PROMESA was first introduced in Congress and gained significant support immediately after its enactment on June 30, 2016. Clearly support for the Oversight Board increased after enactment, affecting the elections, and then waned in the aftermath of the 2016 elections. The decline in public support for the Oversight Board was a response to growing opposition to the austerity measures implemented by the Fiscal Plan and the approval of the first corresponding budget for FY 2018. The budget included cuts to pensions savings, public employees, furloughs, cuts in Christmas bonus, and severe to the UPR, among others. The Oversight Board's approval rating decreased from 69

Graphic 1: Support to the Oversight Board by Political Affiliation

Sentir hacia la Junta de Control Fiscal

▨ En contra   ▣ A favor

	0%	10%	20%	30%	40%	50%	60%	70%

Total

Por afiliación política	0%	10%	20%	30%	40%	50%	60%	70%

PPD

PNP

No afiliados

Source: Mayor apoyo a la Junta después de aprobada (2016).

percent in October 2016 to 43 percent in a May 2017 survey, and then dropped even further in a poll taken after Hurricane Maria devasted the island.

Despite overwhelming support prior and immediately after its enactment, by June of 2017 respondents were evenly split on whether or not they believe the Oversight Board will be beneficial for Puerto Rico—51 percent believed that the FOB would be beneficial, while 49 percent believed that it would not benefit the island at all. At the time, 44 percent of participants stated that the Oversight Board favors bondholders while only 17 percent believe that they favor the people of Puerto Rico. Both of these indicators moved toward more negative perception of the Oversight Board after the election of Governor Rosselló. Despite a more critical opinion of the Oversight Board, the majority of the respondents 41 percent were in favor of Puerto Rico filing for bankruptcy, while 32 percent were against it, and the rest were neither in favor nor against the filing. Yet, a shocking 88 percent of participants said they do not know anything or had just a bit of knowledge about the PROMESA Title III process. In a subsequent poll in November of 2018, dissatisfaction with the Oversight Board reached widespread disapproval with only 21 percent of respondents in favor while 52 percent disapproved. Other indicators, such as whether the Oversight Board favors the bondholders remain about the same at 43 percent, while 19 percent indicated that the Oversight Board was beneficial to improve the economic situation. These data suggest that public opinion over time does not favor the Oversight Board and by extension PROMESA.

After PROMESA was enacted, the act called for the congressional leadership to nominate and President Obama to appoint the Oversight Board. Amidst an intense campaign from bondholders, the President appointed four members recommended by the Republican leadership, two by the Democrats, and one of his own choosing (Mufson 2016). These appointments were made a month prior to the 2016 general elections. Since the majority of appointees were candidates nominated by the Republican congressional leadership, from its inception the Oversight Board was regarded as "favorable" to bondholders (Cornwell and Brown 2016). In particular, given their past affiliations with Puerto Rico's financial institutions, Carlos García was viewed as "an investor guy" and José González as a vote for creditor-friendly policies. Besides both of them working for the Santander Bank, one of the main brokers of Puerto Rico's debt that earned hundreds of millions in fees, García was the president of the GDB under the Fortuño administration when a substantive portion of the debt was issued, especially the COFINA bonds that became the subject of litigation in court (Meléndez and Martínez 2017).

Despite criticism of García's and González's conflict of interest, other appointees to the Oversight Board were regarded as providing expertise in the core areas of public finances and bankruptcy. In terms of public finances and government restructuring, Ana Matosantos was a former director of California's Department of Finance, and Andrew G. Biggs is an expert on state and local government pensions and public sector pay and benefits. Appointees with expertise on bankruptcy included Arthur González, a former chief judge of the United States Bankruptcy Court for the Southern District of New York who presided over three of the largest bankruptcies in history—Enron, WorldCom, and Chrysler, David Skeel Jr., a professor of corporate law at the University of Pennsylvania who specializes on bankruptcy, and José R. Carrión, an executive at an insurance brokerage firm who has served as a trustee of bankruptcy and was appointed as Chair of the Oversight Board. At the time, one of the main political concerns of the White House was that a majority of the board's appointees were Puerto Rican.

Overall, the appointees with apparent or potential conflict of interest weighted more heavily on shaping public opinion than the expertise that other appointees brought to the Oversight Board. The composition of the Oversight Board was regarded as critical because of the legal powers vested on it, especially the authority to oversee and approve a ten years fiscal plan presented by government and corresponding annual budgets and the restructuring of the debt. All in all, PROMESA supersedes local budget decisions and the Oversight Board has authority over all public finances that affect the Fiscal Plan and annual budgets. The process for the approval of budgets and debt restructuring was design as interactive, where the government will make proposals and the Oversight Board will specify amendments, until ultimately the Oversight Board will decide on the adoption of financial policies. (For more discussion on the budget process see Meléndez 2018).

Hurricane Maria Changed (Almost) Everything

Embedded in PROMESA is a back and forth process between the governor and the Oversight Board under Title II of the Act for the "submission, approval, and certification of fiscal plans and budgets for Puerto Rico" (U.S. Public Law 114-187 2016). The process, full of political acrimony and posturing, was tested during the approval of

Graphic 2: Public Opinion on the Fiscal Oversight and Management Board

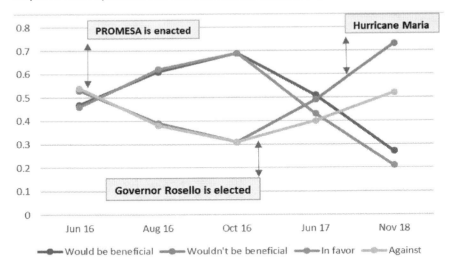

Source: *El Nuevo Dia*.
Note from the publisher: The participants for the June 2016 Pulso País was 500 eligible voters. The August and October 2016 editions of La Encuesta, and the June 2017 and November 2018 surveys polled 1,000 eligible voters.

the fiscal plan and the FY2018 budget. The Oversight Board requested that Governor Rosselló submitted a revised post Hurricane Maria fiscal plan. The post-Hurricane Maria projections for the following year contained in the fiscal plan included a drop in GDP of 11 percent and a population drop of nearly 8 percent (Coto 2018). The proposed plan did not include allocations for repayment of the debt and called for the privatization of the Puerto Rico Electric Power Authority (PREPA) (Giel 2018). A core assumption of the plan was that the federal government will provide $35 billion for the recovery of the island and thus made the overtly optimistic economic growth projections of 7.6, 2.4, 1.8 and 1.5 percent, respectively, in subsequent years despite the drop in GDP in the year immediately after the hurricane.

Disaster supplemental appropriations for Puerto Rico were part of funding requests that included Texas, California, Florida, and the U.S. Virgin Islands.

Federal disaster relief providing funding for Puerto Rico immediately after Hurricane Maria was channeled through the Federal Emergency Management Agency (FEMA), which coordinated with several federal agencies for individual and public assistance, and hazard mitigation. This type of funding covers rescue missions, shelter, clearing roads, establishing emergency and temporary medical care, distributing food and water, and providing alternate power sources for essential services. Disaster supplemental appropriations for Puerto Rico were part of funding requests that included Texas, California, Florida, and the U.S. Virgin Islands. Though these appropriations added over $50 billion, only $4.9 billion of these funds are loans (not grants) earmarking aid to Puerto Rico. Though the funds were eventually disbursed, four months after Hurricane Maria landed, the use of these funds was entangled on a dispute about the Commonwealth liquidity—the Oversight Board dismissed the administration claim that $1.7 billion in the Treasury Single Account (TSA) were restricted funds not available to the Commonwealth for disaster-related expenses and requested the completion of a forensic analysis of government bank accounts before releasing the funds (Lloréns Vélez 2018). The PREPA and the Aqueduct & Sewer Authority (PRASA) were the two public corporations most affected by insolvency.

When Governor Rosselló included $35 billion in federal aid for disaster in the fiscal plan submitted to the Oversight Board, he was considering long-term recovery and rebuilding funding such as the one provided by the Community Development Block Grant Disaster Recovery Program (CDBG-DR). Besides completing the restoration of downed power lines and the repair of damaged infrastructure long-term assistance will include the implementation of economic revitalizations strategies. For this phase of the post-hurricane rebuilding, Governor Rosselló requested $94.4 billion from Congress to rebuild the island's infrastructure, housing, schools, and hospitals. Estimates to repair the damaged caused by the storm included $31.1 billion for housing and $17.8 billion to rebuild and make more resilient the power grid (Bases 2017).

It is common for Congress to fund disaster recovery in various stages. Appropriations for Hurricanes Katrina and Sandy came only weeks after the storm, but with major disasters in Texas, Florida, California, and the Caribbean there was a backlog in producing the damage estimates that guide Congress in the appropriations process. After initial allocations for short-term disaster relief mostly disbursed through FEMA, more than $30 billion are in some way earmarked or have been distributed to Puerto Rico (Rebuild Puerto Rico 2018). In addition to a prior $1.5 billion allocation through the CDBG-DR program and the aforementioned $4.9 billion loan, earmarked funds included $4.8 billion to fund Puerto Rico's Medicaid program for two years, $2 billion for electric power restoration, and an additional $9 billion for housing and infrastructure projects.

Disaster relief funding in many ways represent the injection of capital to the island's economy that the Congressional Task Force on Economic Growth in Puerto Rico (the "Task Force") recommended but never materialized, yet in a significantly changed context after the economic devastation caused by Hurricane Maria. The Task Force made critical recommendations that have gone unattended after their final report was given to Congress. PROMESA was enacted by the 114th Congress under the premise that it was not going to be a "bailout." In many ways, Hurricane Maria opened the door for aid to Puerto Rico, yet the actions (or inaction), the track record of the 114th Congress toward the economic crisis in Puerto Rico is clear and consistent.

Pending for congresional consideration are bills addressing the Task Force recommendations on health care (Severino Pietri 2017), to extend on a permanent bases funding for Medicaid (Respaut and Brown 2017) and lift the cap for federal matching rate for Medicare; amending Section 24 of the Internal Revenue Code to include eligible families in Puerto Rico with one child or two children to claim the Child Tax Credit; support for small businesses; and, to extend the Investment Company Act of 1940 protection to investors in Puerto Rico. Betides the U.S. Territories Investor Protection Act that was approved by the House of Representatives and awaits resolution in the Senate, all of these recommendations have not been considered by Congress (Martínez 2017). Other Task Force recommendations aimed at improving the operations of federal agencies in Puerto Rico could be considered by Congress. These include recommendations to Census Bureau to improve data collection, to the Department of Commerce and Economic Development Administration for technical assistance, and to various agencies supporting the restoration of Caño Martin Peña and to conduct more studies about the impact of landfills on public health and the environment. The Task Force could not reach a consensus to recommend the extension of the Earned Income Tax Credit (EITC) to Puerto Rico as recommended by President Obama (Cornwell 2016), or other policies to support economic development.

In the end the 114th and 115th Congresses and a White House controlled by a Republican majority have implemented at best a minimalist agenda for the economic recovery of Puerto Rico. Even disbursement of a $4.9 billion federal loan for disaster relief exacted tight scrutiny by both FEMA and the Oversight Board. In this context, excluding recovery funding post Hurricane Maria, the prospect for more forceful stimulus policies similar in scope to President Barack Obama's package of $7 billion (spent from 2009 to 2013) through the American Recovery and Reinvestment Act of 2009 (ARRA) are unlikely. In part, besides the "no-bailout" conservative narrative in support of PROMESA, the perception of local fiscal mismanagement was reinforced after Hurricane Maria when a $300 million contract was extended to Whitefish, a small firm with only two employees at the time, and subsequently canceled after a public outcry and the subject of an active FBI investigation (Irfan 2017).

This perception of local fiscal mismanagement and corruption permeates members of Congress' understanding of the situation in Puerto Rico and affect the policy decision process. In a hearing of the House Committee on Natural Resources committee, former Chairman Rob Bishop (R-Utah) asserted that the government of Puerto Rico had a "credibility gap" referring to near the $95 billion request for hurricane recovering funding and the need for accountability in the disbursement of federal assistance. Chairman Bishop stated, "This lack of institutional control within Puerto Rico's largest municipal debtor raises grave concerns about PREPA's, and by association, the government of Puerto Rico's ability to competently negotiate, manage and implement infrastructure projects without significant independent oversight." He added that the island's "controversial decisions" may have made the crisis worse (Guadalupe 2017). In part as a response to these perceptions, and in part to replace some of the coordination functions that the Government Development Bank exercised before its elimination, Governor Rosselló and the legislature created the Enabling Act of the Fiscal Agency and Financial Advisory Authority (FAFAA). In addition to serving as fiscal and reporting agent for the various government agencies receiving federal funding they are tasked with serving as an intermediary with the Oversight Board. Whether the FAFAA will be able to instill operational discipline and transparency in the administration of recovery and economic development projects to overcome the entrenched perception among members of Congress of mismanagement and corruption in Puerto Rico remains an open question.

Conclusions and Discussion

PROMESA was the only politically feasible policy option at the time it was enacted, and there were significant tradeoffs and contradictions embedded in PROMESA that may render it inadequate as a policy framework to achieve its main goal of stabilizing Puerto Rico's finances. To pass the legislation supporters of the bill had to concede the installation of an Oversight Board to control the island's finances in exchange for bankruptcy procedures to allow for the orderly disposition of the debt. And, because that core political compromise to pass the legislation excluded the allocation of federal resources to deal with the impending health crisis or provided a clear mechanism for developing a comprehensive plan for job creation and economic development, PROMESA and the Oversight Board's ability to stabilize the island's economy remains an open question. Yet, it is certain that the presence of the Oversight Board itself broke the foundation of self-governance initiated more than a century ago and as reflected in the Commonwealth constitution. This is not to say that Puerto Rico somehow had autonomy or sovereign powers independent of U.S. authority, but PROMESA itself represents evidence of the ongoing contentiouness in the political relationship between Puerto Rico and the United States.

All in all, PROMESA is a continuation of an erratic historical pattern of U.S. policy implementation toward Puerto Rico. Section 936 of the Internal Revenue Code was created to support the island's recovery after the OPEC oil embargo of the mid-1970s dismantled the oil refinery industry that anchored the Puerto Rico economy at the time. When Section 936 was phased out by a coalition led by President Clinton and the pro-statehood governing party, it was a major contributing factor leading—along of global economic trends and local fiscal mismanagement—to the fiscal and economic crises of the last decade. Borrowing in U.S. municipal markets was a cornerstone of industrial development and urbanization especially during the postwar. But to understand the ongoing fiscal and debt crises, and the enactment of PROMESA as a solution to such crises, one must also consider that Congress inexplicably stripped Puerto Rico's municipalities and public corporations from legal recourse to bankruptcy in 1984.

PROMESA's core components were and are contentious to various constituencies affected by the legislation, and it received divided support from the Puerto Rican people and its elected officials when enacted. Public opinion polls at the time indicated that a majority supported federal action to restore fiscal solvency based on a core belief that U.S. institutions such as the Supreme Court or the FBI are more trustworthy than local political elites who mostly serve "their own interest." But support to the policies implemented by the Oversight Board and by implication the perceived benefits of PROMESA to Puerto Rico is contested terrain—an evolving dynamic that in part depends on the severity of ongoing austerity, the results of the audit of the debt and the accountability of those responsible for a broken government, congressional action to help with the recovery from the natural disaster and the impending health crisis, and the ability of the local political elite to transcend their own limitations in governance.

As comparable cases in New York City, Washington, D.C., and Detroit suggest, solvency and fiscal stability will be achieved eventually through the restructuring of the debt, fiscal reforms, and restoring access to capital markets—the real question is how long would it take, and by implication at what cost to the Puerto Rican people? In answering this question, we need to consider that ultimately there are three interacting actors that share responsibility in the solution to the fiscal, economic, and humanitarian crises. Whether PROMESA offers a pathway to fiscal stability in the island depends on the actions of the Puerto Rico government, the Oversight Board and Congress. First, the most responsibility falls on the Puerto Rico government. The governor and the legislature have the mandate to initiate reforms and implement the policies by engaging a broad range of local and external actors in the reconstruction project. Second, the Oversight Board, as they are empowered to approve the fiscal plans and corresponding budget and in the end, decide the balance between austerity and public services. Lastly, Congress has the responsibility to enact policies that are supportive of these efforts and not harmful to economic development.

The Oversight Board has undertaken two steps that may potentially validate the enactment of PROMESA in the near future and swing public opinion in their favor. The first was to engage the federal court in bankruptcy procedures. The debt hangs over Puerto Rico as the Sword of Damocles. PROMESA's stay on payments provided a respite to the embattled finances of the island while the filing on federal court offered an orderly way for the disposition of the debt. The outcome of the bankruptcy case will be fully known at some point in the future, and hopefully it will represent a important step toward restoring access to credit markets under competitive conditions. A second significant action undertaken by the Oversight Board is the audit of Puerto Rico's debt. The Oversight Board set up a special committee to examine the issuing of Puerto Rico's debt and appointed an independent investigator to carry out the audit. A preliminary report was issued by the end of 2018 with broad recommendations for reforms but a final report has not been issued yet. A debt auditing that is fully transparent and uncovers the individuals and financial institutions responsible for wrongdoing to Puerto Rico will go a long way in restoring public faith in governing institutions.

Ultimately, the success of PROMESA hinges on congressional action to support economic recovery. A core assumption of the revised plan submitted by the governor to the Oversight Board in the aftermath of the destruction caused by Hurricane Maria is that the federal government will provide a $35 billion appropriation for the recovery of the island. Based on the recent experiences of Katrina and Sandy, it is more likely that Congress will make several appropriations over subsequent years. And in the case of Puerto Rico, given members of Congress's perception of local fiscal mismanagement and corruption and recent experiences with disaster assistance to Puerto Rico, these appropriations are likely to depend on audited assessments of damages and costs by third parties, perceived safeguards for the management of funds and vetting by the Oversight Board, and competent implementation of reconstruction and economic development projects. In short, how much disaster recovery assistance Puerto Rico will receive and the timing of federal appropriations are unknown factors with a relatively high degree of uncertainty.

Besides disaster recovery assistance, the success of PROMESA also hinges on congressional action to implement the recommendations of the Task Force. The economic agenda recommended by the congressional Task Force was a call for action, and the main components of the policy agenda have not changed since they were originally proposed—among them, maintaining funding for health programs. Other measures such as expanding the Child Tax Credit (CTC) and adding the Earned Income Tax Credit (EITC) might be revisited by a new Congress. Whether the devastation of Hurricane Maria would persuade Congress to act on some of these or perhaps other economic stimulus policies will depend more on the composition of 115th than on policies likely to be adopted by the 114th Congress dominated by a conservative caucus that enacted PROMESA to *avoid* (emphasis added) a "bailout."

PROMESA has made apparent the contradictions of the territorial status of Puerto Rico and the congressional authority over the island. In the midst of a shifting political terrain in response to PROMESA there are two notable social movements with potential long-term implications. The first is a growing dissatisfaction with conventional political parties as illustrated paradoxically by both the support received by independent candidates to the governorship accumulating 17 percent of the popular vote, and the large number of registered voters not voting in the 2016 elections presumably because of dissatisfaction with electoral options. Any alliance of the independent or dissatisfied sectors with either of the existing political parties would have easily wiped out the small margin of votes that separated the candidates from these parties. This realignment of political forces may lead to political coalitions that support a reformist agenda with a focus on overcoming public mismanagement. The second is the ascent of a stateside diaspora solidarity movement for Puerto Rico. As a result of the millennial migration, the majority of Puerto Ricans, about six of every ten, reside now in states across the nation with concentrations in key electoral states such as Florida, Pennsylvania, and Ohio. Their actions preceding the enactment of PROMESA included nationwide direct action in the districts of members of Congress, and a more robust presence among local elected officials in both parties across the country. Potentially the diaspora could be a deciding factor in spurring congressional action in support of Puerto Rico. The historical outcome of PROMESA is still unfolding and the emergence of independent political forces in Puerto Rico and an emergent solidarity movement in the diaspora may prove to be important elements in the future of Puerto Rico.

ACKNOWLEDGEMENTS
I appreciate all the valuable comments and suggestions from anonymous referees and other colleagues. The opinions and conclusions expressed here are my own and do not represent the official opinion or standing of Centro, Hunter College, CUNY, or all others who have shared with me their comments and suggestions for this essay.

NOTES
[1] The act states: "The provisions of this Act shall prevail over any general or specific provisions of territory law, State law, or regulation that is inconsistent with this Act."
[2] Carlos García, José González, Ana Matosantos and José R. Carrión are Puerto Ricans.
[3] Congress could help the territory by simply funding its Medicaid system the way they fund the states (Newkirk 2017).

REFERENCES
Ayala, César J. and Rafael Bernabe. 2009. *Puerto Rico in the American Century: A History since 1898*. Chapel Hill: University of North Carolina Press.
Bases, Daniel. 2017. Puerto Rico requests $94.4 billion from U.S. Congress for rebuilding. *Reuters* 13 November. <https://www.reuters.com/article/us-usa-puertorico-assistance/puerto-rico-requests-94-4-billion-from-u-s-congress-for-rebuilding-idUSKBN1DD2G8/>.
Bonds News. 2014. 'Backdoor bailout' boosts Puerto Rico's revenues. *Reuters* 10 February. <https://www.reuters.com/article/usa-puertorico-tax/backdoor-bailout-boosts-puerto-ricos-revenues-idUSL2N0LF1BE20140210/>.
Bouker, Jon. 2016. The D.C. Revitalization Act: History, Provisions and Promises. *Brookings Institution* December. <https://www.brookings.edu/wp-content/uploads/2016/07/appendix-1.pdf/>.
Bradford, Hazel. 2018. Puerto Rico's COFINA bond restructuring cleared for vote by creditors. *Pensions&Investments* 21 November. <https://www.pionline.com/article/20181121/ONLINE/181129946/puerto-ricos-cofina-bond-restructuring-cleared-for-vote-by-creditors/>.
Cornwell, Susan. 2016. Obama urges doubling tax credit for low-income childless workers. *Reuters* 9 February. <https://www.reuters.com/article/obama-budget-taxcredit/obama-urges-doubling-tax-credit-for-low-income-childless-workers-idUSL2N15O0QN/>.
Cornwell, Susan and Nick Brown. 2016. Puerto Rico oversight board appointed. *Reuters* 31 August. <http://www.reuters.com/article/us-puertorico-debt-board-idUSKCN11628X/>.
Coto, Danica. 2018. Puerto Rico warns of 11 percent GDP drop in new fiscal plan. *Boston Globe* 26 January.
Delgado, José A. 2015a. Nace una coalición boricua en EE.UU. *El Nuevo Día* 15 October. <http://www.pressreader.com/puerto-rico/el-nuevo-d%C3%ADa/20151015/281479275254132/>.

_____. 2015b. The Puerto Rican Diaspora Takes On Congress: They launch the National Day of Action for Puerto Rico, demanding the help of the federal government. *El Nuevo Día* (English edition) 3 December. <https://www.elnuevodia.com/english/english/nota/thepuertoricandiasporatakesoncongress-2134228/>.

Desconfían los boricuas en sus instituciones: El Barómetro de Confianza reveló que los boricuas se fían de los organismos federales. 2016. *El Nuevo Dia* 22 May. <https://www.elnuevodia.com/noticias/locales/nota/desconfianlosboricuasensusinstituciones-2201574/>.

Dietz James L. 1982. Puerto Rico in the 1970s and 1980s: Crisis of the Development Model. *Journal of Economic Issues* 16(2), 497–506.

_____. 1987. *Economic History of Puerto Rico: Institutional Change and Capitalist Development*. Princeton, NJ: Princeton University Press

Escobar, Natalie and Mariana Alfaro. 2016. *Hamilton'* creator calls on Congress to help Puerto Rico. *Daily News* 15 March.

Feliciano, Zadia M. 2018. IRS Section 936 and the Decline of Puerto Rico's Manufacturing. *CENTRO: Journal of the Center for Puerto Rican Studies* 30(3), 30–42.

Fuller, Matt and Laura Barrón-López. 2015. House Passes $1.1 Trillion Omnibus Spending Bill: The legislation is a compromise no one liked but both parties could live with. *HuffPost* 18 December. <http://www.huffingtonpost.com/entry/house-passes-omnibus_us_5674073fe4b06fa6887cecc3/>.

Giel, Dawn. 2018. Puerto Rico unveils revised fiscal plan: No debt service payments for the next 5 years. *CNBC* 25 January. <https://www.cnbc.com/2018/01/25/puerto-rico-unveils-revised-fiscal-plan-no-debt-service-payments-for-the-next-5-years.html/>.

Guadalupe, Patricia. 2017. Congressional Committees Slam Puerto Rico Officials Over Controversial Energy Contract. *NBCNews* 14 November. <https://www.nbcnews.com/storyline/puerto-rico-crisis/congressional-committees-slam-puerto-rico-officials-over-controversial-energy-contract-n820811/>.

Irfan, Umair. 2017. The FBI is investigating Whitefish Energy's contract to rebuild Puerto Rico's grid. *Vox* 30 October. <https://www.vox.com/energy-and-environment/2017/10/30/16570684/fbi-investigating-whitefish-energy-puerto-rico-prepa/>.

Lloréns Vélez, Eva. 2018. Fiscal board: Forensic audit is key to Puerto Rico disaster loan disbursements. *Caribbean Business* 19 January. <https://caribbeanbusiness.com/fiscal-board-forensic-audit-is-key-to-puerto-rico-disaster-loan-disbursements/>.

Luxner, Larry. 1996. U.S. Law Change Shakes Island, Loss of Section 936 May Mean Drop In Puerto Rico's Standard Of Living. *JOC.com* 8 December. <https://www.joc.com/us-law-change-shakes-island-loss-section-936-may-mean-drop-puerto-ricos-standard-living_19961208/>.

Main Street Bondholders. 2016. Main Street Bondholders Calls on Congress to Reject Updated PROMESA Legislation. *PR Newswire* 19 May. <https://www.prnewswire.com/news-releases/main-street-bondholders-calls-on-congress-to-reject-updated-promesa-legislation-300272191.html/>.

Martínez, Víctor R. 2017. Congressional Task Force Present Recommendations for Puerto Rico. *Puerto Rico News* 14 April. <https://centropr.hunter.cuny.edu/events-news/puerto-rico-news/congress/congressional-task-force-present-recommendations-puerto-rico/>.

Mayor apoyo a la Junta después de aprobada. 2016. *El Nuevo Día* 18 August. <http://prdecide. elnuevodia.com/detalle/reportaje/180_mayor-apoyo-a-la-junta-despus-de-aproba-da/preview/>.

Meléndez, Edgardo. 1998. *Partidos, política pública y status en Puerto Rico*. San Juan: Ediciones Nueva Aurora.

Meléndez, Edwin. 2018. The Economics of PROMESA. *CENTRO: Journal of the Center for Puerto Rican Studies* 30(3), 72–103.

Meléndez, Edwin and Carlos Vargas-Ramos, editors. 2014. *Puerto Ricans at the Dawn of the New Millennium*. New York: Centro Press.

Meléndez, Edwin and Víctor Martínez. 2017. Conflict of Interest Shadows Members of the FOB. *Puerto Rico News* 15 April. <https://centropr.hunter.cuny.edu/events-news/puerto-rico-news/fiscal-oversight-board/conflict-interest-shadows-members-fob/>.

Mufson, Steven. 2016. White House names seven to Puerto Rico oversight board. *Washington Post* 31 August.

Newkirk, Vann R., II. 2017. The Historical Exclusion Behind the Puerto Rico Bankruptcy Crisis. *The Atlantic* 2 May. <https://www.theatlantic.com/politics/archive/2017/05/medicaid-funding-cap-puerto-rico/524973/>.

Puerto Rico & Federal Fiscal Policy Insolvency. 2015. *The GMU Municipal Sustainability Project* 7 May. <https://fiscalbankruptcy.wordpress.com/2015/05/07/puerto-rico-federal-fiscal-policy-insolvency/>.

Rebuild Puerto Rico: A Guide to Federal Policy and Advocacy. 2018. Centro PB2018-02 October. <https://centropr.hunter.cuny.edu/sites/default/files/data_briefs/CENTRO_POLICYGUIDE_PB2018-02.pdf/>.

Respaut, Robin and Nick Brown. 2017. U.S. Congress to give Puerto Rico short-term Medicaid help. *Reuters* 1 May. <https://www.reuters.com/article/us-puertorico-debt-healthcare/u-s-congress-to-give-puerto-rico-short-term-medicaid-help-idUSKBN17X285/>.

Rivera-Batiz, Francisco and Carlos E. Santiago. 1996. *Island Paradox: Puerto Rico in the 1990s*. New York: Russell Sage Foundation.

Sanders, Bernie. 2016. Sanders' Statement in Opposition to Legislation to Establish A Control Board in Puerto Rico. *Bernie Sanders U.S. Senator for Vermont* 19 May. <https://www.sanders.senate.gov/newsroom/press-releases/sanders-statement-in-opposition-to-legislation-to-establish-a-control-board-in-puerto-rico/>.

Severino Pietri, Kathya. 2017. Understanding Puerto Rico's Health Care Crisis. *Puerto Rico News* 17 April. <https://centropr.hunter.cuny.edu/events-news/puerto-rico-news/health-care/understanding-puerto-rico%E2%80%99s-health-care-crisis/>.

Snell, Kelsey and Karoun Demirjian. 2015. Congress passes budget deal and heads home for the year. *Washington Post* 18 December.

Survey of the Florida Puerto Rican Electorate. 2016. *Center for American Progress Action Fund* 3 October. <http://www.latinodecisions.com/files/1414/7568/8283/CAP_Florida_PR_Svy_Toplines.pdf/>.

Tax Alert. 2017. Proposed changes to Act 154. *Kevane Grant Thornton* 28 April. <https://www.grantthornton.pr/articles/04.07.17-tax-alert-proposed-changes-to-act-154/>.

Transition report: Gov't used ARRA funds to cover gaps. 2013. *News Is My Business* 18 February. <https://newsismybusiness.com/transition-report-govt-used-arra-funds-to-cover-gaps/>.

U.S. Public Law 114-187. 2016. Puerto Rico Oversight, Management, and Economic Stability Act or PROMESA. 114th Congress. <https://www.congress.gov/bill/114th-congress/senate-bill/2328/>.

Vargas-Ramos, Carlos. 2018. Political Crisis, Migration and Electoral Behavior in Puerto Rico. *CENTRO: Journal of the Center for Puerto Rican Studies* 30(3), 279–312.

Williams, Corey. 2018. Detroit released from state financial oversight 3 years after exiting bankruptcy. *Detroit Free Press* 30 April. <https://www.freep.com/story/news/local/michigan/detroit/2018/04/30/detroit-released-state-financial-oversight-3-years-after-exiting-bankruptcy/565500002/>.

The Economics of PROMESA

EDWIN MELÉNDEZ

ABSTRACT

In this study I examine whether PROMESA is achieving its main goal of insuring
a string of balanced budgets and to restore Puerto Rico's access to credit markets
under favorable terms that involve the restructuring of the debt, and whether
the implementation of policies consistent with achieving those goals provides a
pathway to restoring economic growth. I conclude that the Fiscal Oversight and
Management Board's policies of balanced budgets and fiscal austerity are insufficient — and based on their own ten-year Fiscal Plan projections — not likely
mechanisms for overcoming the economic crisis. Especially after the impact of
Hurricane Maria on Puerto Rico's economy and a deepening of the population exodus, achieving the stated goals is untenable in the absence of federal stimulus policies in addition to the projected disaster recovery funding. The economic effects
of PROMESA and the austerity policies currently implemented by the Oversight
Board on Puerto Rico's long-term economic development are still an open question
and critically dependent on further Congressional action. [Key words: PROMESA,
U.S. policy, debt crisis, austerity, economic development, federal funding]

The author (emele@hunter.cuny.edu) is a Professor of Urban Policy and Planning and the
Director of the Center for Puerto Rican Studies at Hunter College, CUNY. In addition to
numerous scientific papers and other publications, he is the author or editor of thirteen books
including *State of Puerto Ricans* (Centro Press, 2017) and *Puerto Ricans at the Dawn of the New
Millenium* (Centro Press, 2014). He also served as invited Editor for "Pathways to Economic
Opportunity" *CENTRO Journal* 23(2), 2011.

The Puerto Rico Oversight, Management and Economic Stability Act (PROMESA) was enacted by Congress and signed into law by President Barack Obama on June 30, 2016. At that time, Puerto Rico's public debt was over $74 billion, not including nearly $50 billion in public pension obligations, and its economy was in a prolonged recession that resulted in massive migration to the U.S. and a steady decline in the island's population. These factors in turn resulted in a sizeable decline in tax revenues and associated austerity measures. The unemployment rate in Puerto Rico remained more than double the U.S. national average, only about four of ten adults participate in the labor force, and nearly half of the population lived in poverty—a rate substantially higher than any state. In this context, Hurricane Maria landed in Puerto Rico in September 20, 2017. And, according to the 2018 Fiscal Plan, the hurricane caused an estimated "over $80 billion in damages, and is projected to cause a real decline to GNP of 7.4 percent in FY18."

The debt restructuring of Puerto Rico became the largest debt restructuring by a governmental unit in the history of the United States. From the U.S. Congress's perspective, extreme circumstances called for extreme measures. PROMESA created the Financial Oversight and Management Board for Puerto Rico (the "Oversight Board") to oversee the territory's finances "to achieve fiscal responsibility and access to the capital markets."[1] One of PROMESA's main goals, is to restore Puerto Rico's access to credit markets under favorable terms. In 2014, Puerto Rican bonds were downgraded to non-investment grade (better known as "junk status") by three bond credit rating agencies.[2] To achieve these overarching goals, PROMESA has three core policy components intended to address interrelated aspects of the fiscal and economic crisis:

- Authorizing a legal framework for the restructuring of Puerto Rico's public debt;
- The establishment of a fiscal control board to oversee public finances and establish a Fiscal Plan and corresponding annual budgets (including payment of substantial unfunded pension obligations); and,
- Enabling and expediting economic development projects, especially as they relate to energy and infrastructure.

The Oversight Board created under PROMESA is constituted by seven members appointed by the United States President and has control over Puerto Rico's finances through its budget setting authority that supersedes local law.[3] To make viable the restructuring of the debt, PROMESA granted a stay on debt services until May 1, 2017. Shortly after this deadline expired, the Oversight Board extended the debt moratorium by filing for bankruptcy on federal court on behalf of the Commonwealth of Puerto Rico. Yet, Congress acted on the premise that the legislation was not a "bailout" to bondholders or Puerto Rico and enacted a law that did not include stimulus policies or funding for the economic recovery of the island (Schroeder and Lane 2016). Considerations for federal policies to support economic development was delegated to a Congressional Task Force on Economic Growth in Puerto Rico (the "Task Force") created by PROMESA to make recommendations to Congress. To date, Congress has not acted on those recommendations.

PROMESA's promise was as simple as it was powerful: Puerto Rico's fiscal and economic house would be put in order without spending one penny of federal money—avoiding a so-called "bailout." But has PROMESA kept its promise? The main goal of this paper is to evaluate PROMESA as a policy intended to stabilize the commonwealth's finances. The analytical question examined in this study is whether the core components of the act are sufficient to achieve the act's stated goals of restructuring the government budget (and by implication operations) to achieve balanced budgets consistently, and to restore Puerto Rico's access to credit markets under favorable terms through debt restructuring. In this context, an ancillary question is whether the policies emanating from the Oversight Board— the actual implementation of PROMESA in terms of the Fiscal Plan and corre- sponding annual budgets mandated by the law, and the restructuring of the debt— are supportive of economic growth. This is not a trivial question. Contractions in government expenditures and significant population losses are a dampening force to economic activity—the more the economy contracts, the more difficult it is to balance budgets and to service the debt as revenue projections and borrowing capacity are centrally based on growth projections.

I conclude that two years after the enactment of PROMESA the policy is work- ing as intended—controlling expenditures, boosting revenues, and restructuring the debt through the federal court. But, even by the Oversight Board and the gover- nor's budget projections included in the Fiscal plan, which are inclusive of federal recovery funding and severe austerity measures, show a stagnant economy a decade after the enactment of PROMESA. Especially after the impact of Hurricane María on Puerto Rico's economy, restoring fiscal stability and access to credit markets while preserving adequate public services is untenable in the absence of substantive investment of federal resources in stabilizing public services and of other policies that incentivize private capital investment in Puerto Rico. Both the Congressional Task Force on Economic Growth in Puerto Rico and in their annual report the Oversight Board itself support stimulus measures from Congress to overcome this downward spiral dynamic. In short, though restoring economic development is not an explicit goal of the act, the effectiveness of the policies mandated by the act is interdependent with economic growth. All in all, the economic effects of PROMESA and the austerity policies currently implemented by the Oversight Board on Puerto Rico's long-term economic development are still an open question and critically dependent on further congressional action.

Infrastructure development was a strategy that required significant borrowing of public corporations in municipal markets and led directly to the accumulation of a substantial portion of debt and to the ensuing debt crisis.

I divide the paper into seven sections. The first two section provide an overview of the processes that led to the unset of the fiscal and debt crisis. The debt crisis can be attributed to global factors affecting economic development in Puerto Rico, such as the oil crisis or the impact of globalism on manufacturing, and to the interplay of federal and local politics. In the next section "Up and Down the Debt Rollercoaster," I examine how the public debt crisis can be attributed directly to inconsistent U.S. policies toward the island, such as Section 936 and other federal tax exemptions, and federal bankruptcy procedures. The following section "Local Politics and the Fiscal Crisis" examines the response of the local political elite to changing external circumstances. I demonstrate that in response to the phase-out of (or as a substitute of) Section 936, the administration of Governor Pedro Rosselló (the father of the current governor, Ricardo Rosselló) instituted a core economic development strategy of accelerating infrastructure development that required substantial borrowing for projects, such as the Urban Train, a short-lived Superaqueduct, the construction of the Coliseum and the Convention Center, and numerous roads and bridges. Infrastructure development was a strategy that required significant borrowing of public corporations in municipal markets and led directly to the accumulation of a substantial portion of debt and to the ensuing debt crisis. Yet, in 2006, the local political stalemate in response to the phase-out of Section 936 and the steady decline in manufacturing employment also affected by globalization, and the increase in debt services and declining revenues, led directly to significant additional borrowing through the enactment of an island-wide sales tax separate from the commonwealth revenues to pay for those bonds. Given a choice, politicians in both governing parties chose to "kick the can down the road" rather than compromising on structural fiscal reforms.

The following two sections examine the debt crisis and the various policies proposed or implemented to supersede the debt crisis. In the section "Debt Crisis Highpoint and Austerity," I describe the outstanding debt by public agencies and corporations as of 2017 and market indicators such as the average market value of the bonds, and whether these bonds are covered or not by the Fiscal Plan for debt services. One of the most significant fiscal reforms with far reaching consequences for the manufacturing industry in Puerto Rico was the enactment of a 4 percent excise tax on the sales of multinational corporations (primarily pharmaceutical companies). By 2017, Act 154 revenues accounted for 21.3 percent of total government revenues. In the following section, "Seeking Solutions to the Debt Crisis," I discuss how the "Krueger Report," released in June 2015, established the structural reform framework that has guided both the core policy components of PROMESA as much as the structural reforms implemented through the Fiscal Plan.

It should be no surprise to anyone that PROMESA is working as intended. For one, oversight board precedents in New York and Washington, D.C., testify to the effectiveness of fiscal oversight boards as a mechanism to control public finances. While, multiple jurisdictions across the globe that have accepted and implemented IMF-like structural reforms to accommodate debt restructuring and a limited infusion of capital to boost liquidity have experienced similar outcomes as Puerto Rico—austerity and prolonged economic stagnation. In the section "PROMESA's Ping Pong: Fiscal Plans, Budgets, and Austerity," I describe the back and forth process between the Oversight Board and the governor embedded in PROMESA for the "development, submission, approval, and certification of fiscal plans." This process, leading to significant austerity imposed by the Oversight Board, led to a legal confrontation in federal court that reiterated the Oversight Board's authority of establishing the overall budget level, while delegates the establishment of policies to achieve that level to the prerogative of the administration and the legislature.

The role and impact of structural reforms to restructure public finances and balance the budget is addressed in the section "The Simple Math of Austerity." After explaining austerity measures that affect "essential" services, such as education, health, justice, the University of Puerto Rico and police, even in the context of projections of substantial disaster recovery funding, are insufficient and not likely mechanisms for overcoming the economic crisis. The projections of the fiscal plan suggest that additional economic stimulus policies are necessary to turn the Puerto Rico economy around and induce sustained economic recovery. The next section of the study "PROMESA and Economic Development" examines the stimulus policies identified by the Congressional Task Force on Economic Growth in Puerto Rico and the Oversight Board. Core stimulus policies include solving the structural disparity in Medicaid, and extending an Earned Income Tax Credit (EITC) and the full federal Child Tax Credit (CTC) to residents of Puerto Rico, among others. In the final section of the paper "Discussion and Conclusions," I elaborate further on the findings and implications of the study.

Up and Down the Debt Rollercoaster

The history of Puerto Rico's current fiscal situation spans many decades, literally. In that span of time, congressional policies regarding Puerto Rico have been inconsistent, at times beneficial, at times harmful. And as important, U.S. policy toward Puerto Rico departed from expansionist geopolitical policies, and the interests of American corporations and political dynamics. In 1917, the Jones Act amended the Foraker Act to confer greater authority for local government and U.S. citizenship on Puerto Ricans. But the Jones Act also established triple tax-exempt bonds. Triple tax exemption served as an economic development tool and allowed the public sector—central government, municipalities and utilities—to have access to the U.S. municipal capital market. Access to municipal capital markets was an important element for the post-war expansion of state enterprises-led infrastructure development, one of the cornerstones of the government industrialization program Operation Bootstrap (Ayala and Bernabe 2007; Dietz 1987).

When enacted, access to municipal capital markets was part of a package to stimulate the economic development of U.S. territories, which also included tax benefits to companies that invested in Puerto Rico. The Revenue Act of 1921 exempted from U.S. taxation all corporations that received at least 80 percent of their income from U.S. possessions. Liquidated distributions of income from U.S. possessions were tax-free though income was taxable on repatriation. Congress expanded tax benefits to U.S corporations significantly in 1976 with Section 936 of the Internal Revenue Code that granted a foreign tax credit that exempted companies from Federal taxes on income earned in Puerto Rico and allowed for the immediate repatriation of profits (Dietz 1982; Feliciano 2018). As intended by the law, federal tax exemption induced the rapid expansion of export-oriented manufacturing especially in the pharmaceutical and technology sectors.

Prior to 1984 Puerto Rico had the option of declaring municipal bankruptcy under the Bankruptcy Code.

For reasons that elude even experts on the subject, in 1984 Congress adopted Section 903(1) of the Bankruptcy Code and introduced a new definition of "State" that excluded Puerto Rico's municipalities from access to municipal bankruptcy. Prior to 1984 Puerto Rico had the option of declaring municipal bankruptcy under the Bankruptcy Code. Exclusion from bankruptcy would prove to be critical when the economic crisis unfolded at the beginning of the twenty-first century. Though the central government would not have benefited from access to bankruptcy, the bulk of public debt carried by public authorities and municipalities would have been covered by the U.S Bankruptcy Code.

However, bonds issued by the commonwealth as general obligation bonds are of critical importance because these types of securities have constitutional guarantees that other types of bonds do not enjoy and were at the center of legal controversy in relation to debt service obligations and seniority as creditors. The July 1, 2016, presumed deadline for the enactment of PROMESA and the enactment of the stay on bond payments was driven by fears of the impact of bond payments due for close to $2 billion debt service of general obligations bonds. General obligation bonds were favorite targets of speculators who bought them often at a steep discount from face value. Hedge fund investors were betting that eventually the courts will force a substantial payout given Puerto Rico's constitutional protection of this type of bonds. The hedge funds invested substantial resources in a campaign intended on stopping the enactment of PROMESA.

In short, the accumulation of debt was partly the result of a prolonged recession and the concomitant decline in tax revenues. However, the ruling political parties' inability to respond with effective economic development and fiscal policies to counter the phase out of Section 936 federal tax incentives and to other broader factors such as technological change and globalization affecting manufacturing more generally, and their inability to restructure government to conform to a new fiscal reality were (and are) critical factors inducing the fiscal crisis. Facing the steady decline of manufacturing jobs during the phase-out period of Section 936, the local government failed to develop or implement effectively a coherent development strategy to diversify the local economy in key sectors such as the manufacturing based including the pharmaceutical and high technology sectors, service exports, tourism, and agriculture, to name just a few.

In addition, the public debt crisis can be attributed directly to inconsistent U.S. policies toward the island as much as to the local political stalemate and inability to respond with policies that circumvented, adapted, or superseded inconsistent federal tax exemption policies as cornerstone of industrial development. Industrialization through federal tax exemption, especially Section 936, had a clear impact on the development of pharmaceutical and high-tech manufacturing and these sectors pulled Puerto Rico out of stagnation and served as poles of economic growth in prior decades. Yet, when the industrialization model based on infrastructure development through borrowing in municipal capital markets collapsed and the need for restructuring of public corporations became evident, Puerto Rico lacked the legal framework for these municipalities to be restructured and possibly sold to private investors under favorable terms and better options from a public policy and interest perspective. Local political dynamics play a critical role leading to the fiscal crisis and are discussed in the next section.

Graphic 1: Puerto Rico Public Dept by Governors and Type

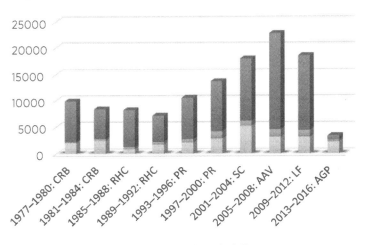

Source: Government Development Bank for Puerto Rico.
Note: In millions of dollars, as of June 30, adjusted for inflation where 2014=0.
Acronyms: Carlos Romero Barceló (CRB), Rafael Hernández Colón (RHC), Pedro Rosselló (PR), Sila María Calderón (SC), Aníbal Acevedo Vilá (AAV), Luis Fortuño (LF), Alejandro García Padilla (AGP).

Local Politics and the Fiscal Crisis

By the time Section 936 federal tax exemption were phased out (2006) and government declining revenues and mounting deficits became increasingly problematic, the question for the political elite (the governing parties and leadership in control of the legislative and executive branches) was: What type of structural reforms should be implemented to cope with the fiscal crisis? The public policy choices to cope with the crisis were not politically palatable—cuts in services and public employment, austerity, public corporations' reforms, and possibly privatization of public services and public corporations. With divided executive and legislative branches of government, other choices were less contentious and offered short-term solutions with disastrous long-term implications: use contributions to pension funds to finance deficits, borrow in municipal markets to close central government deficits and subsidize inefficient public corporations' operations, and avoid confrontations with mayors about restructuring municipal services.

Graphic 1 illustrates the relative accumulation of public debt during each of the governors from the late 1970s to 2016. Clearly the turning point for the escalation of the public debt was the borrowing during Governor Pedro Pedro Rosselló's administrations (from 1993–1996 and 1997–2000). Governor Rosselló was a fervent advocate for statehood for Puerto Rico and was a leading actor along with then Resident Commissioner Carlos Romero Barceló and President Clinton in the phasing out of Section 936. In this context, infrastructure development was partially intended to mitigate the elimination of federal tax exemption and many of the major initiatives planning begun shortly after his election. Governor Rosselló's initiatives for major infrastructure projects required substantial financing through public borrowing. These projects included the Urban Train, a short-lived Superaqueduct, the Coliseum, the Convention Center, and numerous roads and bridges (Márquez and Carmona 2011). The total public debt borrowing reached a historical low (adjusted for inflation) of about $7.1 billion during his predecessor Governor Rafael Hernández-Colón (1989–1992). By comparison, Governor Rosselló borrowed $10.5 billion during his first term and $13.7 billion during his second. By far, the largest proportion of debt was accrued by public corporations of $7.8 and $9.5 billion during the first and second terms, respectively. Infrastructure development by increasing public indebtedness faster than induced economic activity, which would have expanded the commonwealth's tax base, was not an effective alternative long-term economic development strategy and set the foundation for the increased indebtedness of the country.

Borrowing continued at an accelerated pace during the Popular Democratic Party administrations that followed Governor Pedro Rosselló. Despite initiating far fewer infrastructure projects, none of the magnitude of those under Governor Rosselló's administration, Governors Sila Calderón (2001–2004), and Aníbal Acevedo Vilá (2005–2008) increased the total debt by $17.9 billion and $22.7 billion, respectively. As was the case in all prior administrations, the largest component of the debt was of public corporations $11.8 billion and $18.2 billion, respectively. The implementation of fiscal reform was near impossible for the administration of Governor Aníbal Acevedo Vilá. After a tight electoral victory, both the House and the Senate were in control of the opposition party. This is the context in which the Puerto Rican political elite faced the end of Section 936 and the subsequent economic and fiscal crises that started in 2006 and the subsequent financial crisis that started in 2008.

The solution to this dilemma was to introduce for the first time in modern history an island-wide sales tax.

The onset of the island's debt crisis began with the phase-out of Section 936 and the acceleration of infrastructure development, events and processes that preceded the U.S. financial crisis of late 2007 and the Great Recession that followed. One of the political leadership's first steps in the avoidance of dealing with the structural factors underlying the debt crisis was to borrow from municipal capital markets. The problem faced by the rival political parties in control of the executive and legislative branches of government was how to borrow additional resources when it was evident that the commonwealth was not generating enough revenues to be able to serve future debt. The solution to this dilemma was to introduce for the first time in modern history an

Graphic 2: Puerto Rico Public Dept by Sector

Source: Government Development Bank for Puerto Rico.
Notes: In millions of dollars, as of June 30, adjusted for as of June 30, adjusted for inflation where 2014=0.

island-wide sales tax. Rival political parties could not agree on much regarding policies to cope with by then evident fiscal crisis except on increasing the debt to avoid politically difficult structural fiscal reforms. The Puerto Rico Sales Tax Financing Corporation (COFINA, from Spanish Corporación del Fondo de Interés Apremiante) was created in 2006 to issue government bonds paid for by Puerto Rico Sales and Use Tax (SUT). Originally the sale tax was of 7 percent, with one-and-a-half percent going to municipalities, and the rest equally divided between the central government and COFINA. With the deepening of the fiscal crisis, on July 1, 2015, Puerto Rico raised its sales tax from 7 percent to 11.5 percent. Puerto Rico, at 11.5 percent, has a highest sales tax than any other jurisdiction in the U.S. (Beyer 2015). COFINA bonds were paid with tax revenues set aside separate from the commonwealth revenues.

Graphic 2 depicts breakdowns the debt by type for three key benchmark years—1996 when the Section 936 phaseout began, 2006 when COFINA was enacted, and 2014 the high point of accumulated public debt when Puerto Rico bonds reached "junk" status. The second term of Governor Pedro Rosselló (1997–2000), in which his administration implemented an infrastructure development strategy to counter the phaseout of Section 936, marked the explosion of public enterprises'[4] debt. Public enterprises debt increased about $15 billion, from $12.7 billion in 1996 to $27.2 billion in 2006—the second largest increase in debt between the selected benchmark years. The following period, between 2006 and 2014, public enterprises increased their total debt about $5 billion, from $27.2 to $32.4 billion. By 2014, public enterprises share of Puerto Rico's total debt reached 46.8 percent of the total debt. The largest increase in public debt, however, belongs to COFINA. Between 2006 when COFINA was enacted to 2014, COFINA debt stood at $16.3 billion or 23.5 percent accounting for the total debt. By 2014, the Commonwealth's (or E.L.A. for Spanish Estado Libre Asociado) debt accounted for 20.7 percent of the public debt and the municipal debt for the remaining 6 percent of the debt. In this context, if Puerto Rico had been covered by the U.S. Bankruptcy Code, the bulk of public debt carried by public authorities and municipalities accounting for over 50 percent of the total could have been restructured in federal court as the public corporations became insolvent and potentially avoided PROMESA's debt restructuring.

In sum, the failure of the infrastructure development strategy to counter the loss of manufacturing employment had dire long-term consequences. For one, the continuing erosion of manufacturing jobs triggered a steady exodus of migrants relocating stateside (Mora, Dávila and Rodríguez 2018). As Puerto Rico lost population, budget restructuring became more evident and servicing the debt became more difficult. As important, local political dynamics are directly responsible for borrowing beyond repayment capacity and for instituting fiscal policies that further contributed to the debt crisis. The cumulative consequences of these erratic policies are discussed in the next section.

Debt Crisis Highpoint and Austerity

After winning the 2008 elections, one of the first legislatives initiatives undertaken by Governor Luis Fortuño (2009–2012) was to declare a state of fiscal emergency and to enact a fiscal stabilization plan. With his party in control of the legislature, Governor Fortuño proposed a Fiscal and Economic Recovery Plan that would reduce annual expenditures by more than $2 billion. Opponents to the plan suggested that up to 30,000 government employees would be laid off (Puerto Rico's Governor Says 2009). Teachers and other public employees called for massive protests. During Governor Fortuño's tenure total government employment (including municipalities) was reduced by 13.3 percent, from 297.3 to 257.7 thousand. In addition, Governor Fortuño's administration reduced expenditures of the central government modestly by slightly over $100 million, from $1,365.3 million in 2009 to $1,259.7 million in 2012 (Statistical Appendix of the Economic Report to the Governor Economic 2016).

In addition to these austerity measures, Governor Fortuño reformed the tax structure in significant ways. The first part of the reform was to impose, for the first time in Puerto Rico's history, an excise tax on the sales of multinational corporations (primarily pharmaceutical companies) of 4 percent (Valentín Ortiz 2016). Since then, this sales tax has been deducted by U.S. foreign corporations on their federal tax returns de facto becoming a federal tax business expense deduction for U.S. corporations operating in Puerto Rico (Bail-Out By The Back Door 2014). By 2017, Act 154 Excise Tax Revenues were estimated to be $1,924 million or 21.3 percent of the total General Fund Revenues of $9,045 million (Backdoor Bailout' Boosts 2014). The enactment of the Tax Cuts and Jobs Act on December of 2018, which lowers the corporate income tax rate to 21 percent and moves the United States from a worldwide to a territorial system of taxation (Preliminary Details and Analysis 2017), allows for the deduction of Puerto Rico's sale tax from federal tax liabilities as a business expense but imposes other taxes on Controlled Foreign Corporation (CFC) that could affect investments in Puerto Rico adversely (Mugabi et al. 2018).

Though García Padilla is the governor most associated with the debt crisis, he was the one with the smallest increase in debt in absolute or relative terms—simply put, the municipal market was closed to Puerto Rico and only high-risk investors such as hedge funds were willing to lend to the Commonwealth and only at excessively harsh and severe terms.

Despite cost-cutting measures taken during Governor Fortuño's first two years in office and the approval of Law 154 and other tax reforms, Puerto Rico's public debt kept mounting. Total public debt increased by $18.5 billion (in 2014 dollars, after adjusting for inflation) during Governor Fortuño's tenure. Public corporations increased the most at $14.1 billion between 2009 and 2012, while the central government debt increased by $3.1 billion during the same period.

Table 1: Puerto Rico Outstanding Debt, 2017

Agency/Corporation Total Debt ($ millions)	Principal	Interest Rate	Market Price (2016)	Maturity
Covered by Fiscal Plan				
COFINA Total	17,880	5.75%	52%	FY 2040
General Obligation Bonds	13,267	6.05%	68%	FY 2031
HTA Total	4,247	5.49%	51%	FY 2031
Public Buildings Authority	4,129	5.57%	60%	FY 2031
Government Development Bank Total	4,126	4.90%	30%	FY 2020
Employment Retirement System	3,156	6.28%	37%	FY 2040
Puerto Rico Infrastructure Financing Authority	2,207	5.08%	48%	FY 2033
Puerto Rico Public Finance Corporation	1,197	5.35%	12%	FY 2027
University of Puerto Rico	496	5.00%	41%	FY 2026
Puerto Rico Convention Center District Authority	386	4.80%	78%	FY 2029
Puerto Rico Industrial Development Company (PRIDCO)	156	5.40%	58%	FY 2025
Other Central Gov. Entities	667	NA	NA	NA
Total	51,916			
Not Covered by Fiscal Plan				
Puerto Rico Electrical Power Authority (PREPA)	8,956	5.40%	66%	FY 2030
Puero Rico Aqueduct and Sewer Company (PRASA)	4,568	5.52%	68%	FY 2035
Children Trust Fund	1,460	5.98%	77%	FY 2043
Puerto Rico Housing Finance Authority	542	4.69%	106%	FY 2023
PRIICO	98	NA	NA	NA
Municipal Debt	1,696	4.65%	44%	FY 2022
Total	17,320		55%	
Less: GDB Bonds (excl. TDF)	-3,766			
Plus: Loans from GDB/MFA Entities	8,796			
Public Sector Debt	74,268			

Source: Commonwealth of Puerto Rico Fiscal Plan to the Financial Oversight and Management Board for Puerto Rico, March 13, 2017.

The public debt crisis reached its highpoint during Governor García-Padilla's administration (2013–2016). Shortly after he took office, by 2014, Puerto Rico's debt reached $67.3 billion and obligations to pension funds added another $50 billion (see Table 1). By the end of Governor García-Padilla tenure in 2016, Puerto Rico bonds were downgraded to non-investment grade ("junk bonds,") by the "big-three" bond credit rating agencies. For the first time in decades, the overall public debt declined by $3 billion in 2014. Though García Padilla is the governor most associated with the debt crisis, he was the one with the smallest increase in debt in absolute or relative terms—simply put, the municipal market was closed to Puerto Rico and only high-risk investors such as hedge funds were willing to lend to the Commonwealth and only at excessively harsh and severe terms. In total, Puerto Rico borrowed $3.7 billion during the García-Padilla administration, with most of this debt issued as general obligations bonds. The last batch of General Obligation Bond for a total of $3.5 billion issued in March of 2014 by the Commonwealth of Puerto Rico were classified at the lowest rating of Ba2, BB+ and BB by Moody's Investors Service, Standard & Poor's and Fitch Ratings respectively, and were offered at 8 percent interest with a price of 93 prcent of face value for a yield of 8.727. By January of 2018, post-Hurricane Maria, these bonds with a 2035 maturity were selling at 27 percent of face value.

Table 1 depicts "Puerto Rico Outstanding Debt" by public agencies and corporations as of 2017. In 2016, the average market value of the bonds was 55 cents on the dollar. Prior to the enactment of PROMESA, bonds were priced way below face value—in the case of General Obligations bonds about 68 cents on the dollar, and for COFINA 52 cents on the dollar. And, because of their junk rating status, most bonds were paying substantially higher interest rates (5.43% on average versus 2% of the ten-year BAA index) than average market rates. After Hurricane María's economic devastation, bond prices were initially further eroded. For example, the newer PREPA bonds have gone from trading at 55–58 percent of face value price prior to Hurricane Maria to a 27–32 percent price post-Hurricane María, and after Congress enacted earmarks in recovery funding to Puerto Rico these bonds were trading in July of 2018 at 44.1 percent. In short, even before PROMESA was enacted and after a catastrophic natural disaster, the bond market determines a price that could be used as a benchmark for any debt-restructuring plan based on categories of bondholders. And, these benchmarks were and are clearly not nearly 100 percent of original value, though market value for bonds affected by federal recovery funding (e.g., PREPA) increased in value. Whether bonds and the public debt are restructure close to market price is an indicator of whether the proposed restructuring adjust the debt to reflect market conditions, but it is not an indicator of whether the resulting debt service is sustainable over time. Debt sustainability is primarily a function of the ability of the government to generate sufficient revenues to pay debt services over time.

Despite the complex structure of PROMESA and the fact that there was no real precedent for this type of mandate combining fiscal oversight and court bankruptcy procedures for debt restructuring, PROMESA and Title III bankruptcy procedures in federal court opened the door for public employees' pension to get in line as creditors. As depicted in Table 2, unfunded pensions liability (net of assets) total $48.8 billion. In addition, the Commonwealth owes $3.2 billion in retirement health benefits for a total of $52.2 pensions liability. For decades, the commonwealth routinely used funds designated as contributions to pension funds to cover operational deficits. As a result, the Employees Retirement System (ERS), the largest pension system servicing over 125,000 beneficiaries, had the pitiful funded ratio (assets over liabilities) of -1.77 percent. In addition, there are an almost equal number of active members' (125,671) contributing to the retirement system as of retirees' (124,497) receiving pensions. This indicated that payments to retirees would need to be made from ongoing contributions from general revenues since members' contributions are not able to support but a fraction of obligations. The other two retirement systems, accounting for an additional forty thousand retirees, had at the time a funded ratio of about 12 percent—clearly insufficient to cover upcoming obligations. By comparison, the average fund in the United States also showed unfunded pension obligations with a funded ratio of about 75 percent of obligations (State Public Pension Investments Shift 2014).

In essence, grossly unfunded pension obligations was the public employees retirees organizations and public sector union's case for including payments to existing pension systems obligations as a priority in PROMESA (Delgado 2016; Fact Sheet 2016). Though PROMESA does not give priority to pension liabilities over payments to bondholders, it mandates "adequate" funding for pension liabilities (Brannon 2017). In the absence of PROMESA, litigation in local (or federal) court over the enforcement of existing contracts would had likely given priority to General Obligation bonds as guaranteed by the Commonwealth constitution over payments to pension liabilities. Subsequently, in anticipation of a federal court-mandated pension restructuring under Title III of PROMESA, the legislature passed and Governor Ricardo Rosselló signed a pension reform law based on funding the pension system through a pay-as-you-go system and a defined contributions accounts moving forward to be managed by a third party (Bradford 2017). The Oversight Board called for an overall 10 percent cut in pensions (Oversight

Table 2: Puerto Rico Retirement Plans, 2015 (a)

($ thousands)

	ERS	TRS	JRS
Active Members	125,671	39,343	364
Retirees	124,497	40,601	430
Total Pension Liability (TPL)	32,669,162	16,307,731	585,312
Actuarial Value of Assets (net)	-578,633	1,313,148	42,729
Net Pension Liability	33,247,795	14,994,583	542,583
Net Position as % of TPL	-1.80%	8.10%	7.30%

Source: Congressional Task Force on Economic Growth in Puerto Rico, Report to the House and Senate, 114th Congress, December 20, 2016.
Notes: Puerto Rico Retirement Plans are the Puerto Rico Teachers Retirement System (TRS), the Puerto Rico Government Employees Retirement System (ERS), and the Puerto Rico Judiciary Retirement System (JRS).

Board and Puerto Rico Government 2017). With mounting pressure for covering payments on the debt and no borrowing capacity, local authorities turned to openly seeking feasible strategies for dealing with the debt crisis. In the next section I discuss the "Krueger Report" and PROMESA as the core conceptual and policy framework for solving the fiscal and debt crisis.

Seeking Solutions to the Debt Crisis

In June 29 of 2015, Governor García-Padilla declared the by-then obvious, that "The public debt...is unpayable." He also made a stark assessment of Puerto Rico's economic future and acknowledged the forgone conclusion (also at the core of his predecessor's political agenda) of the need for structural fiscal reforms and the inevitability of further austerity. With growing internal and external economic and political pressures to conceive solutions to the crisis, the government of Puerto Rico recruited Anne Krueger, IMF's former first deputy managing director, to produce a blueprint to restore economic stability and prosperity. The "Krueger Report," released in June 2015, called for structural reforms in government services, pension systems and public finances (Puerto Rico, Investors Look 2015). One of the revelations of report was that "the true fiscal deficit is much larger than assumed" and that the Commonwealth faced an imminent liquidity shortage (Krueger, Teja and Wolfe 2015).

The key recommendations package of economic reforms of the Krueger Report included (Krueger, Teja and Wolfe 2015):

- **Structural reforms.** Restoring growth requires restoring competitiveness. Key here is local and federal action to lower labor costs gradually and encourage employment (minimum wage, labor laws, and welfare reform), and to cut the very high cost of electricity and transportation (Jones Act). Local laws that raise input costs should be liberalized and obstacles to the ease of doing business removed. Public enterprise reform is also crucial.
- **Fiscal reform and public debt.** Probably the most startling finding in this report will be that the true fiscal deficit is much larger than assumed. Even a major fiscal effort leaves residual financing gaps in coming years, which can be bridged by debt restructuring (a voluntary exchange of existing bonds for new ones with a longer/lower debt service profile). Public enterprises too face financial challenges and are in discussions with their creditors. Despite legal complexities, all discussions with creditors should be coordinated.
- **Institutional credibility**. The legacy of weak budget execution and opaque data—our fiscal analysis entailed many iterations—must be overcome. Priorities include legislative approval of a multi-year fiscal adjustment plan, legislative rules on deficits, a fiscal oversight board, and more reliable and timely data.

As it was the case with Governor Fortuño's policies, the report included a package of tax increases and more spending cuts and austerity, and public employees' pension reform. But, more forcefully than the prior administration, Governor García-Padilla called for debt restructuring. Since Puerto Rico lacked a legal framework for debt restructuring since its exclusion of Chapter 9 in 1984, the Commonwealth enacted its own bankruptcy law to restructure about $26 billion of public enterprises' debt. The law was halted by the federal court and subsequently the decision was reiterated by the U.S. Supreme Court.

In many ways, the Krueger Report offered a blueprint for what would become PROMESA—with a key critical distinction. At the time the Kruger Report is released to the public, there was no legal framework allowing for debt restructuring and all the Kruger Report and the commonwealth could call for was for "a voluntary exchange of existing bonds for new ones with a longer/lower debt service profile." In principle, Puerto Rico's lenders were free to negotiate terms of a debt restructuring with the commonwealth. Yet, the prospects for a voluntary restructuring of the debt, especially for general obligation bonds guarantee by the constitutions, were minimal. Here is how *The Economist* describes the conundrum:

[ ] big mutual funds like Oppenheimer Funds and Franklin Templeton Investments — are free to negotiate terms individually. But since the island's debt lacks "collective-action clauses," which could impose the terms of a deal struck by a super-majority on all bondholders, the government cannot force recalcitrant investors to accept a loss. Any creditor who does not receive full and timely payment could file a lawsuit to obtain it, and place competing claims on the state-owned enterprises' remaining assets. Particularly aggressive bondholders might even be able to stop their conciliatory counterparts from receiving a cent until they are paid in full: last year, a group of hedge funds holding defaulted Argentine bonds persuaded American courts to block payments on Argentina's performing debt. With such strong incentives for investors to balk, Mr. García-Padilla's hope for a "transparent and consensual" restructuring looks dim. (Another Fine Debt Crisis **2015**)

Pressure was mounting. With no other viable option opened to policymakers, resolving the impasse required congressional action. The first default followed shortly after in August of 2015. For the first time in history, the Puerto Rico government default on $58 million of principal and interest due on Public Finance Corp. bonds and other so-called "moral obligation" bonds (Ismailidou 2015). Shortly after, in January of 2016, the Puerto Rico government defaults for the second time on payments of $35.9 million of non-commonwealth guaranteed Puerto Rico Infrastructure Financing Authority debt and $1.4 million of Public Finance Corp. bonds (Brown 2015). The money in an escrow account for these payments were diverted to pay investors who were owed $328.7 million of interest on general obligation debt, which were assumed to have seniority or legal priority for payment. An important element to consider in the Puerto Rico debt conundrum at the time, an important factor inducing Congress to enact PROMESA, was the staggering amount of debt forthcoming in July of 2016 in addition to the debt payments missed already in 2015. In total, Puerto Rico was scheduled to pay $5,040 million, of which $2,055 were general obligations or COFINA bonds that have first in line status from general obligations and from set-aside sales tax revenues respectively.

Puerto Rico's economic crisis pushed the commonwealth onto a fiscal crisis and ensuing humanitarian crisis, and with the first default on debt services onto a debt crisis.

Default on the debt, what many observers had predicted years earlier, forced Congress to act. Puerto Rico's economic crisis pushed the commonwealth onto a fiscal crisis and ensuing humanitarian crisis, and with the first default on debt services onto a debt crisis. Comparisons to Argentina and Greece, and to Washington, D.C., and Detroit were common. The default option and trajectory for Puerto Rico was to continue the economic downward spiral, massive defaults on general obligation and other bonds, and to eventually enter a legal entanglement in local and federal courts lacking a legal framework for debt restructuring. The default option for Congress, to do nothing, was the worst possible scenario from an economic recovery perspective and as measured by the likely humanitarian cost to be extracted by a deepening fiscal crisis.

To prevent endless litigation while the Oversight Board was established and functioning, PROMESA included a stay on debt payments. Given that Puerto Rico's lacked liquidity to make almost $2 billion in debt payments due July 1, 2016, from various branches of the Puerto Rican government, the prospect for a disorderly default were extremely likely. A glance at legal chaos ensued on Monday, May 1, 2017, at the end of PROMESA's stay on bondholders' litigations. Creditors filed multiple lawsuits against Puerto Rico the following day prompting the Oversight Board to unanimously request for court relief on Wednesday, May 3, under bankruptcy-like protection provided by Title III of PROMESA (Associated Press 2017; Walsh 2017).

PROMESA provided a concrete mechanism for restructuring the debt through federal court and provided a framework for the Oversight Board to approve the fiscal Plan and corresponding annual budgets. The process for the approval and certification of fiscal plans and budgets for Puerto Rico is the subject of the next section.

PROMESA's Ping Pong: Fiscal Plans, Budgets, and Austerity

Embedded in PROMESA is a process for the "submission, approval, and certification of fiscal plans and budgets for Puerto Rico" (U.S. Public Law 114-187 2016) that is best described as a back and forth between the Oversight Board and the governor for the "development, submission, approval, and certification of fiscal plans." The process is like table tennis or ping pong—where the rules for the back and forth are given by Title II of the Act and the federal court serves as the ultimate referee. The process starts with the governor's submission of a fiscal plan to the Oversight Board for a "period of at least five years and provide a method to achieve fiscal responsibility and access to the capital markets." Afterward each annual budget must adhere to the projections of the fiscal plan to fund essential public services, public pensions, and investments necessary to promote economic growth while balancing the budget and establish fiscal controls and accountability. If the governor fails to comply with the submission of a satisfactory fiscal plan and subsequent conforming annual budgets, the Oversight Board could develop a fiscal plan and present it directly to the legislature for approval. When the board makes recommendations to the legislature and or the governor, they are mandated to respond with recommendations whether these would be adopted or not and to provide a rationality for their action.

To date, the process has worked as intended by Congress, including the to-be-expected political acrimony about austerity measures and the implicit tradeoffs in public services and repayment of the debt. The first step in the fiscal restructuring came in October 2016 when former Governor Alejandro García-Padilla presented his fiscal and economic growth plan to the Oversight Board. Since Governor García-Padilla was not biding for reelection, the plan submitted by his administration did not include any significant fiscal reforms. Considering an annual budget hovering around $9 billion, García-Padilla's budget projected an estimated cumulative budget gap of around $59 billion dollars until 2026, which the Oversight Board changed subsequently to a budget gap estimate of $67.5 billion. Such was the starting point for newly elected Governor Ricardo Rosselló.

Shortly after Governor Rosselló's inauguration in January 2017, the Oversight Board sent a letter to the governor recommending deep cuts to the budget that included restructuring of public agencies and corporations, reductions on health care and higher education spending, and pension reform. Governor Rosselló rejected most of the FMOB recommendations and suggested various alternatives for reaching balanced budgets. Governor Rosselló's first legislative initiative, Public Law 4 (also known as Labor Transformation and Flexibility Act), did not target the government sector but was intended as an initiative for job creation (by reducing benefits to workers in the private sector). Among other provisions, the law "provides for flex-time work schedules and daily overtime rates at time-and-a-half" and "places a reduced limit on Christmas bonuses, caps the amount of damages attainable in employment discrimination cases and reduces the amount of time to file an unjust dismissal or wage claim" (Farone 2017). Despite criticisms that Public Law 4 infringed on workers' rights, Governor Rosselló defended the legislation as a necessary economic development initiative.

Governor Rosselló's first proposed ten-year Fiscal Plan was submitted to the Oversight Board on February 28, 2017. Weeks later, the Oversight Board rejected Governor Rossello's initial budget, stating that the "proposal relies on overly optimistic projections and fails to cut spending deeply enough to erase the government's chronic budget deficits" (Spalding 2017). The Oversight Board submitted amendments to the fiscal plan intended to close the projected spending gap that included additional taxes and annual cuts to pensions of $200 million beginning in 2020, $450 million cuts to the University of Puerto Rico (UPR) by the year 2021, use of furloughs to public employees to achieve liquidity, and removal of Christmas bonuses among other austerity measures.⁵ After intense negotiations and $160 million more projected in government revenue, the plan was approved. New tax revenues include higher traffic fines, an increase in an excise tax on tobacco products, a tax on insurance, and the extension of an existing tax break for manufacturers on the island (Costa 2017). The Oversight Board and the administration agreed on additional cuts if certain conditions were not satisfied, these included among others cuts in pensions, government workers' furloughs, and cuts in Christmas bonuses.

Political posturing between the Oversight Board and Governor Rosselló intensified during the 2018 budget approval process, the first one submitted under the fiscal parameters set up by the fiscal plan and under the Oversight Board supervision. The FY18 proposed budget for the government's general fund was $9.5 billion, an increase of more than $575 million from the previous year. Most of the proposed increase would come from the sale of liquid assets from the public employees' retirement system that will be used to finance a new pay-as-you-go system. In part, the budgetary negotiations gave Governor Rosselló the opportunity to come across as a populist, vowing to resist deep cutbacks to government programs that would hurt residents of an island where nearly half live below the poverty line and challenging the legal authority of an increasingly unpopular Oversight Board. The governor actively portrayed his administration as limiting the impact of austerity on public employees, education, the UPR, pension and health-care system and by extension responding to widespread protests led by unions and students.

The Oversight Board and the governor finally settled on a budget contingent on meeting specific revenue targets. Lacking evidence that the administration has reached the savings threshold called for, the Oversight Board threatened with legal action if the administration refuse to implement a budget consistent with the approved Fiscal Plan (González 2017). Specifically, the Oversight Board called for the implementation of a furlough program to close an estimated $218 million budget gap (Bernal 2017). When Governor Rosselló refused to adopt employee furloughs and pension cuts the Oversight Board sued the administration in federal court (Basas 2017). Three weeks after the filing Hurricane Maria devastated the island and the Oversight Board requested a revision of the fiscal plan from the governor, but the underlying issue of the authority of the Oversight Board to curtail specific expenditures was eventually resolved in court.

Governor Rosselló submitted revised post-Hurricane Maria fiscal plan on January 24, 2018. The projections were sobering: a drop in GDP of 11 percent and a population drop of nearly 8 percent (Associated Press 2018). The proposed plan did not include allocations for repayment of the debt setting aside the prior fiscal plan allocation of

$787 million a year on average to pay creditors. In addition, the plan called for the privatization of the Puerto Rico Electric Power Authority (PREPA) (Giel 2018). A core assumption of the plan is an injection of capital related to the recovery of the island of $35 billion from the federal government and another $22 billion from private insurance companies. Despite the drop in GDP in the year immediately after the hurricane, the plan assumed overtly optimistic economic growth projections of 7.6, 2.4, 1.8 and 1.5 percent, respectively, in subsequent years. In other words, given the uncertainty of these appropriations in Congress, the proposed fiscal plan for the recovery from Hurricane Maria were dependent upon favorable congressional action.

The process of approval of the revised Fiscal Plan eventually led to a federal court case oversee by Judge Laura Taylor Swain in charge of the bankruptcy proceedings. After the Oversight Board approved the Fiscal Plan in June 29, 2018, Governor Ricardo Rosselló challenged in court, among other provisions, the imposition of a hiring freeze, limitations on government employees' benefits (such as paid holidays, sick and vacation days, and the Christmas bonus), and the institution of automatic "efficiency savings" in agencies that were not meeting budget projections. The Retirees' Committee (Comité Oficial de Retirados) intervening in the federal bankruptcy case summarizes Judge Swain's decision as follows:

[ ] the Court explained that PROMESA permitted the Board to "make binding policy choices for the Commonwealth," but that in doing so, PROMESA did not give the Board the "power to affirmatively legislate." If a policy measure requires the Government to enact a new law or repeal an old law, the Board can only attempt to persuade the Government to take that action by imposing budget restrictions; it has no authority to mandate the legislation. Applying that understanding of PROMESA, the Court concluded that the FOMB could restrict the government from using money from prior budgets to fund current expenses or otherwise reprogramming budgeted funds, because the Board has exclusive control over the certified budget. The Court reached the opposite result with respect to the automatic budget reductions and the imposition of penalties for failure to comply with the budgets, because these provisions constituted amendments to Puerto Rico's existing legislature. (Summary of Judge Laura Taylor Swain's Orders 2018)

Clearly, Judge Swain's decision settled any dispute, short of a successful appeal to the U.S. Supreme Court, about the ultimate decision power of the Oversight Board with respect to the level of the budget, while the policies implicit or explicit as they relate to the budget are the administration and the legislature prerogative. The Oversight Board, by certifying the proposed Fiscal Plan and corresponding annual budgets, also oversees the assumptions made to estimate operating revenues and expenses. But given the reality of declining revenues and structurally sticky expenses, austerity was inevitable. The question was where the budget cuts and revenue enhancements will come from to balance the budgets. In the next section I examine the implicit tradeoffs among various budget categories, and what critical services have been most affected by austerity.

The Simple Math of Austerity

The impact of the fiscal plan and corresponding annual budgets on public services are closely related to debt services and to U.S. policies such as social transfers and reconstruction funding. With declining tax revenues, the math of austerity is simple: a dollar spent in debt services is a dollar not spent in public services or in economic reconstruction and development. Table 3 illustrates the commonwealth's budget for FY2016 (actual) to FY2018 (proposed). By far, the largest allocation in FY2016 corresponds to the Oversight Board designated "essential" services that include education, health, justice, UPR, and police. Among these, education and health accounted for $3.4 billion of the total $9.7 billion or one-third of the total budget. From FY2016 to the proposed FY2018 budget, the overall budget declines $413 million or 14.25 percent. Given their share in the overall budget, essential services received the largest budget cuts in FY2018 (in thousands): education -176,000 (-10.5%), health -153,578 (-11.3%), justice -94,078 (-11.1%), UPR 202,719 (-23.2%), police -23,755 (-3.2%) and municipalities -175,000 (-44.3%). Pension were maintained level funded from the prior year, but when FY2016 is used as a baseline, pensions for commonwealth's retirees were cut -81,031 or -24.8 percent. The only line item that increased over this period was the budget office account used to centralize payments—that among others would include future debt service — with a $2.4 billion increase from FY2016 to FY2018, representing a corresponding increase from 3 percent to 26 percent of the overall budget.

The question of how much would be the so-called haircut,[6] which will determine actual debt service in subsequent years, is pending in federal court bankruptcy procedures.

FY2016 was the last year that the commonwealth paid debt services prior to the stay granted by PROMESA. Table 4 summarizes the commonwealth's Consolidated and General Fund budgets from FY2015 to FY 2018 (Recommended) including debt payments, federal funds and Act 154 contributions. PROMESA's stay saved the commonwealth a cumulative $8.3 billion in FY2017 and FY2018 when debt payments in FY2015 and FY2016 are use as a baseline. To put this figure in perspective, savings in debt payments on average amounted to 12 percent of the General Fund and 13 percent of the Consolidated Budget. For example, total revenues from sales tax used for debt service to pay COFINA bondholders alone would have exceeded $700 million in 2017. In the recommended FY2018 budget, federal funds account for $6 billion or 30 percent of the total $20.4 Consolidated Budget, and Act 154 accounts for $2.1 billion or 23 percent of the General Fund. Both federal revenue sources are critical to the Commonwealth, and both are dependent on future congressional and presidential action. The austerity described above would be severely harsher if the subsidization provided by federal funds or the tax treatment of CFC's changes in the future.

According to PROMESA, the Commonwealth's annual budgets must correspond to the Fiscal Plan approved by the Oversight Board. Though there have been multiple versions of the Fiscal Plan, as it is negotiated between the Oversight Board and the governor, there are two approved versions of the plans. The first was submitted in March of 2017, pre-Hurricane María, and the most recent in August of 2018 and incorporates disaster relief in ten-year projections. Table 5 summarizes the average annual budget allocation in the Fiscal Plan based on ten-year financial projections included in the plan, which include the projected federal funding for disaster relief. These projections are based on a plethora of assumptions, among which are the

Table 3: Puerto Rico General Fund Budget FY 2015 to FY 2018

(in thousands)

Agency	FY 2016	FY 2017	FY 2018 Rec.
Education	1,985,496	1,674,497	1,498,497
Health (a)	1,372,534	1,356,794	1,203,216
Justice (b)	883,680	848,853	754,775
UPR	869,696	872,432	669,713
Police	804,946	734,061	710,306
Pension (c)	407,219	326,188	326,188
Municipalities	365,700	394,730	219,730
Budget Office	304,397	1,234,595	2,443,116
Other	1,751,640	1,544,850	1,458,459
Public Debt	951,210	-	-
Total	9,696,518	8,987,000	9,284,000

Notes
(a) Includes: Administración de Seguros de Salud de Puerto Rico, Departamento de Salud, Administración de Servicios de Salud Mental y Contra la Adicción, Administración de Servicios Médicos de Puerto Rico, Cuerpo de Emergencias Médicas de Puerto Rico, Salud Correccional. (b) Includes: Departamento de Corrección y Rehabilitación, Tribunal General de Justicia, Departamento de Justicia. (c) Includes: Sistema de Retiro de Maestros, Sistema de Retiro de Empleados del Gobierno y La Judicatura (Sistema Central).
Source: Oficina de Gerencia y Presupuesto, Gobierno de Puerto Rico, PROMESA Requirement #1A, Recommended General Fund Budget by Concept and Source of Funds FY 2018 (rounded to thousands).

Gross National Product (GNP) growth rate, population and migration, and reform measures to improve revenue collections and reduce expenses, among many others.

Following International Monetary Fund-like structural reforms implemented in other countries or jurisdictions "without monetary policy options and high informal labor markets," the Fiscal Plan proposes labor, energy, ease of doing business and education reforms intended to have a positive impact on economic performance that according to projections will allow for an annual average of $1.5 billion or 9 percent increase in revenues. On the revenue side, in addition to a continuation of Federal Transfers for an average of $7.8 billion annually, the Fiscal Plan estimates a steady decline in projected Act 154 revenues from $2.1 billion in 2017 to an annual average of $1.6 billion. Given the ambiguity about future congressional appropriations for the Affordable Care Act (ACA), the Fiscal Plan preclude the Governor from including this funding past the expiration of the current grant after FY2019. This exclusion represents an annual average loss of $1.8 billion. In addition to revenue measures, the Fiscal Plan estimates that cost saving measures will add on average $2.9 billion annually. The combined net impact of revenue generation and cost savings measures is projected to an annual cash flow for debt services of $787 million a year. By any measure, projected debt service in the ten-year fiscal plan amounts to about a fifth of what debt services would have been in the absence of PROMESA. Not one creditor would be paid in full given these numbers. The question of how much would be the so-called

Table 4: Budget, Federal Funds and Debt Paymnets (Million)

	FY 2015	FY 2016	FY 2017	FY 2018 Rec.
Consolidated Budget	26,987	27,856	25,678	20,433
Federal Funds	6,182	6,709	6,643	6,056
%	0.23	0.24	0.26	0.30
Debt Payment	4,187	3,522	1,499	130
%	0.16	0.13	0.06	0.01
General Fund	9,479	9,697	8,987	9,284
Foreign (Act 154)	1,943	1,862	2,078	-
%	0.20	0.19	0.23	-
Debt Payment	1,136	1,072	24	-
%	0.12	0.11	0.00	-

Source: Oficina de Gerencia y Presupuesto, Gobierno de Puerto Rico, PROMESA Requirement #1C, #1D, Recommended General Fund Budget by Concept and Source of Funds FY 2018, Recommended Consolidated Budget by Concept and Source of Funds FY 2018, and Apendice Estadistico, Informe Economico del Gobernador, 2017, Table 27 - PUERTO RICO GOVERNMENT NET RECURRENT REVENUES: FISCAL YEARS.

haircut,[6] which will determine actual debt service in subsequent years, is pending in federal court bankruptcy procedures.

The Fiscal Plan projects that federal disaster-relief funding will total $83 billion over the next decade, with the bulk of this funding $75 billion coming from the federal government and an estimated $8 billion from private insurance. The portion of disaster relief funding considered in the Fiscal Plan projections amount to an average of $6.1 billion annually. By all counts, this injection of liquidity will play a significant role in the economic recovery of Puerto Rico over the next decade. The impact of the proposed reforms and cost saving measures and injection of disaster relief funding on the overall economic performance of Puerto Rico is illustrated by the projected GNP for the ten-year period (Graphic 3). The baseline for comparison is the GNP reported in the Fiscal Plan 2017 before the advent of Hurricane María and without the implementation of the proposed reforms. As suggested by post-disaster recovery data from many other countries (cited in the Fiscal Plan 2018), in 2018, the impact of Hurricane María resulted in an immediate GNP decline of 7.4 percent. The injection of recovery funding will result in an initial increase to 4 percent of GNP in 2019, gradually declining to 2 percent by 2022 and then hovering around negative one percent beginning in 2023 and for the rest of the period ending in 2026. In other

Table 5: Summary of Financials for 10-Year Projections (Average from 2017 to 2026)

Revenues Before Measures	17,081
Projected Act 154 Revenues	1,548
Loss of Affordable Care Act ("ACA")	-1,792
Federal Transfers	7,785
Revenue Measures	1,544
Revenues After Measures	18,471
Expenses Before Measures	-20,251
Expense Measures	2,854
Expenses After Measures	-17,682
Cash flows pre-Measures	-3,171
Net impact of measure	4,399
Cash Flow Available for Debt Service	787
Projected Public Disaster Relief Funding	7,225
Private Insurance	2,667
CDBG Cost Share	271
Adj. Public Disaster Relief Funding	6,065

Source: Commonwealth of Puerto Rico, Fiscal Plan to the Financial Oversight and Management Board for Puerto Rico, October 14, 2016 and March 13, 2017.

Graphic 3: Fiscal Plan 2017 and 2018 GNP Growth

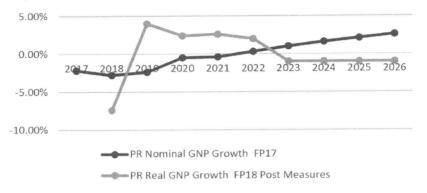

words, the Fiscal Plan alarming projections are that Puerto Rico—a decade after the enactment of PROMESA, the implementation of significant IMF-like structural reforms as suggested by the "Krueger Report," and the injection of disaster-relief funding—would continue in a protracted economic recession.

In sum, the Oversight Board's policies of balanced budgets and fiscal austerity, even in the context of projections of substantial disaster recovery funding, are insufficient and not likely mechanisms for overcoming the economic crisis. The projections of the fiscal plan suggest that additional economic stimulus policies are necessary to turn the Puerto Rico economy around and induce sustained economic recovery. The next section of the study examines the stimulus policies identified by the Congressional Task Force on Economic Growth in Puerto Rico and the Oversight Board.

PROMESA and Economic Development

PROMESA, in addition to providing for the restructuring of the Puerto Rican debt and the establishment of an Oversight Board, includes other provisions of great importance to long-term economic development that makes this legislation far reaching into Puerto Rico's future. The Congressional Task Force on Economic Growth in Puerto Rico (the "Task Force") was created as part of PROMESA to recommend policy options for sustainable long-term economic growth and job creation. Of special consideration are three industries: manufacturing, energy, and health. Each of these industries is vital to the economic stability and growth of the Puerto Rican economy, and the U.S. Congress and the President are instrumental in enacting policy.

In December 20, 2016, the Task Force released its final report on policy recommendations for supporting economic growth for Puerto Rico. Of these key policy recommendations, health care is by far the one with significant costs to the federal government. The catastrophic impact of Hurricane Maria on Puerto Rico and specifically in its health system, brought urgency to resolving Medicaid funding. In February of 2018, President Donald Trump signed a bill allocating $4.8 billion to fund Puerto Rico's

Medicaid program for two years. However, in the absence of Congressional action to close the structural disparity in funding, the Fiscal Plan approved by the Oversight Board calls for "savings" of $6.123 billion in ten years for health programs servicing the most vulnerable populations—children, seniors, and the poor. Budget cuts will affect basic coverage for "primary needs" such as prescription medications, dental services, private nursing, prosthetic devices, physical and occupational therapy, optometry, hospice services, and services for speaking, hearing, and language disorders.

However, as significant as the recommendations made by the Task Force are the policy proposals considered but for which there was no consensus and were not made. One of the key policy areas in which the Task Force failed to propose concrete policy recommendations is labor market reform. The Task Force recommended for Congress to consider the merits of giving Puerto Rico greater flexibility in unemployment compensation benefits to increase employment. Besides this timid proposal, the Task Force did not recommend the extension of the Earned Income Tax Credit (EITC) to Puerto Rico as recommended by President Obama (Cornwell 2016). Puerto Rico has a substantially lower labor force participation when compared to any other state. The EITC encourages labor force participation and increases labor supply by making work more attractive to low-wage workers. The EITC may also serve as a policy to mitigate the massive exodus of Puerto Ricans to Florida and other states.

The inclusion of Puerto Rico in the EITC has been a priority for the Democratic leadership in Congress. According to a paper authored by Arthur MacEwan and J. Tomas Hexner (2016), there is a "lack of fairness" in the way residents of Puerto Rico are excluded from eligibility for the EITC and CTC. For example, assume two families each consisting of two parents and two young children that have earned income of $28,000 in 2015 but one family is in the states and one in Puerto Rico. Further, assume that each family pays the same in Social Security taxes ($1,736) and in Medicare taxes ($406) and have no federal income tax liability. The family in the states receives an EITC of $4,622 and a CTC of $2,000 for a total income of $32,480 or a 26 percent greater income than the Puerto Rican family. MacEwan and Hexner (2016) estimate that the cost of eliminating this disparity by extending the EITC and CTC to Puerto Rico on equal bases as the states would be about $1 billion annually.

In July of 2018, at the conclusion of its second year of operations, the Oversight Board filed the Annual Report for Fiscal Year 2018 and made several recommendations to the Federal Government (Financial Oversight & Management Board 2018). The report concludes that:

[T]he disaster relief funding is by no means a long-term solution to Puerto Rico's long standing structural problems. [T]he Oversight Board continues to believe that the Commonwealth's recovery and fulfillment of PROMESA's objectives will be significantly aided by the Federal Government's support in the following key Executive and Legislative areas [among others]:

- Legislate a long-term Medicaid program solution to mitigate the drastic reduction in federal funding for healthcare in Puerto Rico that will happen next year.
- The new international tax and base erosion rules of the U.S. Tax Code should be framed in a manner that will help Puerto Rico, as a U.S. territory, retain the current CFC base and to favorably compete with foreign jurisdictions in attracting new investments, and to comply with the fiscal plan.
- Recommend that Congress explore ways to minimize the challenges and maximize the opportunities of extending an Earned Income Tax Credit (EITC) to residents of Puerto Rico.
- Extend the full federal Child Tax Credit (CTC) to residents of Puerto Rico to allow otherwise eligible families in Puerto Rico with one child or two children to claim the additional child tax credit.

Clearly the Oversight Board recognizes that budget projections indicate that after the injection of disaster relief funding the economy will revert to a continued recession They recognize the potential impact that extending the Opportunity Zones program could have on a stagnant economy. Yet, to date, Congress has failed to act on the recommendations made by its own Task Force and recently endorsed by the Oversight Board. All in all, the proposed package of economic stimulus legislation that emanates from the Task Force and the Oversight Board recommendations might be similar in scope to President Obama's package of $7 billion, of which $1.4 billion were for federal agencies and $5.6 billion for the state government, through the American Recovery and Reinvestment Act of 2009 (ARRA). ARRA funding was spent from 2009 to 2013, a similar stimulus package would have to be extended for a longer period of time and would have to include Medicaid parity as a separate line item. However, because most of the ARRA funds were intended to maintain police and other essential public services, the allocations of funds to stabilize the health system in Puerto Rico, support families and incentivize labor force participation should have a bigger multiplier effect and long-lasting impact on the island's economy.

Discussion and Conclusions
It is too early for a final verdict on the long-term impact of PROMESA on the Puerto Rico economy. For one, there are too many unfolding processes, from the restructuring of the debt to the revamping of the infrastructure damaged by the hurricane, to the impact of structural fiscal reforms. There are, however, some important implications from the data and analysis presented above. To judge the law's effectiveness is important to assess how far it addresses the commonwealth's three key problems: too much debt, a budget that exceeds revenues, and, most importantly, whether it can support a battered economy. For one, PROMESA allowed Puerto Rico to undertake a necessary restructuring of its public debt. The Oversight Board approved the filing of

close to $50 billion of the commonwealth's debt under Title III of PROMESA, which can significantly reduce or eliminate the debt and lower payments to creditors. What levels of the debt are restructured and how much money retirees get back from their pensions are issues that are now in the hands of New York Federal Judge Swain, who oversees Title III proceedings. She will also preside over dozens of lawsuits that have been filed contesting a myriad of issues related to the government's finances.

The Oversight Board's fiscal policy prescriptions, often described as draconian, are intended to balance the commonwealth's budget. With severe population exodus and concomitant declines in tax revenues, austerity is unavoidable. The math to reach this conclusion is as simple as it is difficult to restructure annual budgets. Since Governor García-Padilla declared that Puerto Rico's debt was unpayable in 2015 and the subsequent stay effective when PROMESA was enacted in 2016, besides a minimal payment of $328.7 million of interest on general-obligation debt, Puerto Rico has not made payments on the debt. Yet government revenues have continued to fall short of covering expenditures. Given that Puerto Rico lacks access to borrowing in capital markets, even in the context of no payments to bondholders budgets have to be cut, or new sources of revenues have to be found, such as higher taxes or the privatization of public assets.

The difficulty for the administration and the Oversight Board is in how to balance a budget while minimizing austerity to preserve adequate public services, protect the most vulnerable sectors of the population and continue to invest on economic development and job creation. The ten-year fiscal plan approved by the board included, among others, cuts to the University of Puerto Rico, health care cuts that could lead to thousands of Puerto Ricans losing their insurance, a 10 percent reduction of certain pension benefits, and even significant cuts to the legislative branch. Until the advent of Hurricane María, the fiscal plan also called for debt services of up to a billion dollars annually though these payments represent, on average, less than 20 cents on the dollar of what is currently owed to creditors. No one knows for sure what long-term economic effect austerity measures will have, how much of the debt service the government will eventually have to pay, and whether or when the economy will grow. What we do know, based on the government's own financial projections, is that austerity alone will not solve the problem. Puerto Rico cannot simply cut its way into solvency.

In the core principles for a revised Fiscal Plan to account for the adverse economic impact of Hurricane Maria submitted at the end of January 2018, the Oversight Board guidelines include "sufficient resources to ensure appropriate immediate emergency response and recovery effort in anticipation of federal funds, including provision of public safety, healthcare and education, in order to avoid increased outmigration"; [and a] capital expenditure plan [that] must provide the basis for a long-term economic recovery plan for Puerto Rico, focusing on increased and expedited support for rebuilding critical infrastructure such as energy, water, transportation, and housing" (Financial Oversight and Management Board 2017). As a group of distinguished economists and policy analysts asserted, "These are positive statements" (A Fiscal Plan for Puerto Rico Recovery n.d.).

Yet, achieving the goals of restoring fiscal stability and access to credit markets while preserving adequate public services and investing in economic development is untenable in the absence of substantive investment of federal resources and of congressional policies that incentivize private capital investment in Puerto Rico. The effects of the policies implemented by the Oversight Board on Puerto Rico's economic development are still an open question and critically dependent on further congressional action.

Hurricane María deepened an already unfolding humanitarian crisis.

Clearly, Hurricane María changed everything. By all counts, Hurricane María had a devastating effect on the economy though its real impact will take years to assess. Hurricane María deepened an already unfolding humanitarian crisis. Prior to the hurricane, the recession has forced over half a million Puerto Ricans to move from the island to the U.S., and with more emigrating every day it is expected that the depopulation of Puerto Rico will continue unabated. In addition, high unemployment and low labor force participation rates are enduring indicators of economic stagnation and consequently about half the population lives in poverty. About 18 percent of housing units are vacant. Puerto Rico's recovery from a debilitating economic recession since 2006 became more daunting post Hurricane María. Whether Congress and President Trump will be moved by the impact of Hurricane María on the island to support the proposed package of economic stimulus legislation recommended by the Task Force and the Oversight Board remains elusive. PROMESA was enacted based on the Republican majority premise that it will not become a "bailout" of Puerto Rico or the bondholders. The recommendations made by the Congressional Task Force on Economic Growth in Puerto Rico and the Oversight Board are necessary steps in a variety of ways the U.S. government can support Puerto Rico's economic recovery.

ACKNOWLEDGEMENTS

I appreciate the invaluable comments and suggestions from anonymous referees and other colleagues. The opinions and conclusions expressed here are my own and do not represent the official standing of Centro, Hunter College, CUNY or the opinions of others who have shared with me their comments and suggestions for this essay. In addition, I would like to thank Kathya Severino, Víctor Martínez and Rafael Pérez for their invaluable research assistance.

NOTES

[1] Title I, Sec. 101(a) Purpose. S. 2328 (114th): PROMESA.

[2] There are three market dominant credit rating agencies: Moody's Investors Service, Standard & Poor's, and Fitch Ratings. Collectively they control approximately 95 percent of the industry, with the two largest rating agencies—Moody's, S&P—controlling roughly 80 percent market share globally.

[3] The act states, "The provisions of this act shall prevail over any general or specific provisions of territory law, State law, or regulation that is inconsistent with this Act."

[4] A public enterprise is a quasi-public business organization wholly or partly owned by government controlled through a public authority and an appointed board of directors.

[5] Entities not included in the Fiscal Plan included: PREPA, PRASA, Children's Trust Fund and PRHFA.

[6] "In debt restructuring agreements, a haircut is a percentage reduction of the amount that will be repaid to creditors" (Who Needs a Haircut n.d.).

REFERENCES

A Fiscal Plan for Puerto Rico Recovery. n.d. <http://recovery4pr.org/>.

Another Fine Debt Crisis. 2015. *The Ecnomist* 30 June.

Associated Press. 2017. Puerto Rico Hit with 1st Lawsuit from Bondholders. *Fox News* 2 May. <http://www.foxnews.com/world/2017/05/02/puerto-rico-hit-with-1st-lawsuit-from-bondholders.html/>.

_____. 2018. Puerto Rico Warns of 11 Percent GDP Drop in New Fiscal Plan. *VOANews* 25 January. <https://www.voanews.com/a/puerto-rico-warns-of-11-percent-gdp-drop-in-new-fiscal-plan/4224543.html/>.

Ayala, César. J. and Rafael Bernabe. 2007. *Puerto Rico in the American Century: A History since 1898*. Chapel Hill, NC: University of North Carolina Press.

Backdoor Bailout' Boosts Puerto Rico's Revenues. 2014. *Reuters* 10 February. <http://www.reuters.com/article/usa-puertorico-tax-idUSL2N0LF1BE20140210/>.

Bail-Out By The Back Door: A Tax Loophole Helps Keep Puerto Rico Solvent. 2014. *The Economist* 30 January.

Basas, Daniel. 2017. Puerto Rico Oversight Board Asks Court to Enforce Furloughs. *USA Breaking News* 4 August. <https://www.usabreakingnews.net/2017/08/puerto-rico-oversight-board-orders-furloughs-governor-defiant/>.

Bernal, Rafael. 2017. Puerto Rico Governor Defies Oversight Board on Worker Furloughs. *The Hill* 4 August. <http://thehill.com/latino/345409-puerto-rico-governor-defies-oversight-board-on-worker-furloughs/>.

Beyer, Scott. 2015. Puerto Rico, at 11.5%, Has America's Highest Sales Tax. *Forbes* 17 August. <https://www.forbes.com/sites/scottbeyer/2015/08/17/puerto-rico-at-11-5-has-americas-highest-sales-tax/#22a18570308f>/.

Bradford, Hazel. 2017. Puerto Rico Governor Signs Pension Reform Law. *Pensions&Investments* 25 August. <http://www.pionline.com/article/20170825/ONLINE/170829881/puerto-rico-governor-signs-pension-reform-law/>.

Brannon, Ike. 2017. Puerto Rico's Faux Pension Reform. *The Weekly Standard* 24 May. <http://www.weeklystandard.com/puerto-ricos-faux-pension-reform/article/2008192/>.

Brown, Nick. 2015. Puerto Rico to Default on Some Debts, Will Pay GO Debt. *Fox Business* 30 December. <http://www.foxbusiness.com/markets/2015/12/30/puerto-rico-to-default-on-some-debts-will-pay-go-debt-18982121.html/>.

Cornwell, Susan. 2016. Obama Urges Doubling Tax Cedit for Low-Income Childless Workers. *Reuters* 9 February. <https://www.reuters.com/article/obama-budget-taxcredit-idUSL2N15O0QN/>.

Costa, Denis. 2017. Oversight Board Approves Fiscal Plan with 10% Pension Cut. *El Nuevo Día* (English edition) 13 March. <https://www.elnuevodia.com/english/english/nota/.>

Delgado, José. 2016. Democrats Under Pressure, Trade Unions That Are Key for Their Electoral Mobilization Ask Them to Account Over H.R. 5278. *El Nuevo Día* (English edition) 21 May. <http://www.elnuevodia.com/noticias/politica/nota/democratsunderpressure-2201385/>.

Dietz James L. 1982. Puerto Rico in the 1970s and 1980s: Crisis of the Development Model. *Journal of Economic Issues* 16(2), 497–506.

_____. 1987. *Economic History of Puerto Rico: Institutional Change and Capitalist Development*. Princeton, NJ: Princeton University Press.

Fact Sheet: Union Recommendations on Amendments to PROMESA (Endorsed by AFL-CIO, ACSME, UAW, SIU, and UFCW). 2016. <https://morningconsult.com/wp-content/uploads/2016/04/FINAL-PROMESA-Fact-Sheet.pdf/>.

Feliciano, Zadia M. 2018. IRS Section 936 and the Decline of Puerto Rico's Manufacturing. *CENTRO: Journal of the Center for Puerto Rican Studies* 30(3), 30–42.

Farone, Alexandra. 2017. Puerto Rico Governor Signs Controversial Labor Reform Bill. *Jurist* 27 January. <http://www.jurist.org/paperchase/2017/01/puerto-rico-governor-signs-controversial-labor-reform-bill.php/>.

Financial Oversight and Management Board for Puerto Rico. 2017. Minutes of the Eleventh Meeting of the Board. 5 December.

_____. 2018. Annual Report Fiscal Year 2018. 30 July.

Giel, Dawn. 2018. Puerto Rico Unveils Revised Fiscal Plan: No Debt Service Payments for the Next 5 Years. *CNBC* 25 January. <https://www.cnbc.com/2018/01/25/puerto-rico-unveils-revised-fiscal-plan-no-debt-service-payments-for-the-next-5-years.html/>.

González, Joanisabel. 2017. No Reverse on Furloughs. *El Nuevo Día* (English edition) 11 August. <https://www.elnuevodia.com/english/english/nota/noreverseonfur-loughs-2348141/>.

Ismailidou, Ellie. 2015. Puerto Rico Sees First-Ever Default: What's Next for Bond Investors. *Market Watch* 3 August. <http://www.marketwatch.com/story/what-puerto-ricos-missed-debt-payment-means-2015-07-16/>.

Krueger, Anne O., Ranjit Teja and Andrew Wolfe. 2015. Puerto Rico–A Way Forward. <http://www.gdb.pr.gov/documents/puertoricoawayforward.pdf/>.

MacEwan, Arthur and J. Tomas Hexner. 2016. Including Puerto Rico in the Earned Income Tax Credit and Full Child Tax Credit. GDS Working Paper 2016-9, 11 October. Center for Global Development and Sustainability, Brandeis University.

Márquez, Carlos and José L. Carmona. 2011. The Age of Consequences. *Caribbean Business* 28 July. <http://www.rafaelhernandezcolon.org/Comunicado/CB%20July%2028,%20 2011-%20The%20Age%20of%20Consequences.pdf/>.

Mora, Marie T., Alberto Dávila and Havidán Rodríguez. 2018. Migration, Geographic Destinations, and Socioeconomic Outcomes of Puerto Ricans during *La Crisis Boricua*: Implications for Island and Stateside Communities Post-Maria. *CENTRO: Journal of the Center for Puerto Rican* Studies 30(3), 208–29.

Mugabi, Frank Ikonero, Stacy M. Paz, Gerald Rokoff, Bruce J. Wein and Drew M. Young. 2018. Tax Cuts and Jobs Act Could Have Significant Impact onSstructuring of US and Foreign Investments. *DLA Piper* 4 January. <https://www.dlapiper.com/en/us/insights/publications/2018/01/tax-cuts-and-jobs-act/>.

Oversight Board and Puerto Rico Government Clash over Pensions. 2017. *Puerto Rico Report* 9 August. <https://www.puertoricoreport.com/oversight-board-puerto-rico-government-clash-pensions/#.Wl4vwqinGUk/>.

Preliminary Details and Analysis of the Tax Cuts and Jobs Act. 2017. *Tax Foundation* 18 December. < https://taxfoundation.org/final-tax-cuts-and-jobs-act-details-analysis/>.

Puerto Rico's Governor Says "Government is Bankrupt." 2009. *CNN* 3 March. <http://www.cnn.com/2009/WORLD/americas/03/03/puerto.rico.economy/index.html?_s=PM:WORLD/>.

Puerto Rico, Investors Look to Ex-IMF Officials for Help –WSJ. 2015. *Reuters* 13 April. <http://www.reuters.com/article/puertorico-imf-idUSL4N0XA1ZY20150413/>.

Schroeder, Peter and Sylvan Lane. 2016. House passes Puerto Rico rescue. *The Hill* 9 June. <http://thehill.com/policy/finance/282895-house-votes-to-rescue-puerto-rico/>.

Spalding, Rebecca. 2017. Puerto Rico Board Rejects Governor's Plan to End Debt Crisis. *Bloomberg* 9 March. <https://www.bloomberg.com/news/articles/2017-03-09/puerto-rico-board-rejects-governor-s-plan-for-ending-debt-crisis/>.

State Public Pension Investments Shift Over Past 30 Years. 2014. Report from The Pew Charitable Trusts and the Laura and John Arnold Foundation. <https://www.pewtrusts.org/~/media/assets/2014/06/state_public_pension_investments_shift_over_past_30_years.pdf/>.

Statistical Appendix of the Economic Report to the Governor Economic. 2016. Program for Economic and Social Planning of the Planning Board. <http://www.jp.gobierno.pr/>.

Summary of Judge Laura Taylor Swain's Orders on The FOMB's Motions to Dismiss the Governor's and Legislature's Complaints. 2018. Comité Oficial de Retirados (COR) 7 August. <https://www.porturetiro.com/noticias/summary-of-judge-laura-taylor-swains-orders-on-the-fombs-motions-to-dismiss-the-governors-and-legislatures-complaints/>.

U.S. Public Law 114-187. 2016. Puerto Rico Oversight, Management, and Economic Stability Act or PROMESA. 114th Congress. <https://www.congress.gov/bill/114th-congress/senate-bill/2328/>.

Valentín Ortiz, Luis J. 2016. Uncertainty Clouds One-Fourth of Puerto Rico's Revenues. *Caribbean Business* 14 July.

Walsh, Mary Williams. 2017. Puerto Rico Declares a Form of *Bankruptcy*. *The New York Times* 3 May.

Who Needs a Haircut. n.d. *StackExchange*. <https://english.stackexchange.com/questions/248172/who-needs-a-haircut/>.

VOLUME XXX • NUMBER III • FALL 2018

An Analysis of Puerto Rico's Debt Relief Needs to Restore Debt Sustainability

PABLO GLUZMANN, MARTIN GUZMAN AND JOSEPH E. STIGLITZ

ABSTRACT

This paper makes two contributions. First, we examine the macroeconomic implications of Puerto Rico's Fiscal Plan certified in March 2017 for fiscal years 2017–18 to 2026–27. Second, we perform a Debt Sustainability Analysis (DSA) that incorporates the expected macroeconomic dynamics implied by the Fiscal Plan in order to compute Puerto Rico's debt restructuring needs. We detect a number of flawed assumptions in the Fiscal Plan that lead to an underestimation of its contractionary effects on the island's economic activity. We conduct a sensitivity analysis of the expected macroeconomic dynamics implied by the plan that allows us to construct more realistic scenarios of Puerto Rico's debt restructuring needs. We show that the island's current debt position is unsustainable, and compute the necessary debt relief to restore sustainability under different sets of assumptions. The paper offers insights for designing a plan of action for resolving Puerto Rico's current debt crisis that will remain valid after the certification of a new fiscal plan. [Key words: Puerto Rico's debt, debt restructuring, Debt Sustainability Analysis, sensitivity analysis, macroeconomics, debt relief]

Pablo Gluzmann (gluzmann@yahoo.com) holds a Ph.D. in Economics and is a researcher at Consejo Nacional de Investigaciones Científicas y Técnicas (CONICET) and the Centro de Estudios Distributivos Laborales y Sociales (CEDLAS), professor at the Universidad Nacional de La Plata (Argentina), and Director of Labor Database For Latin America (LABLAC, CEDLAS and the World Bank). His research fields are income distribution and poverty, and macroeconomics.

1. INTRODUCTION

Puerto Rico's economy has been suffering a recession for more than a decade. The recession has led to a debt and economic crisis. The ultimate goal of this paper is to offer insights for designing a plan of action for resolving Puerto Rico's current debt crisis.

Our contribution is thus twofold. First, we examine the macroeconomic implications of Puerto Rico's Fiscal Plan that has been approved for fiscal years 2017-18 to 2026-27, as it is a crucial element for a computation of Puerto Rico's debt restructuring needs. Second, we perform a Debt Sustainability Analysis (DSA) that incorporates the expected macroeconomic dynamics implied by the Fiscal Plan in order to compute the island's restructuring needs.

We stress two important caveats. First, we note that the computations included in this paper were performed before the hurricanes Irma and Maria hit Puerto Rico. We claim that the methodological and empirical analysis offered in this paper will serve as the basis to update the computations when more precise information on the costs of the hurricanes becomes available.

Second, this paper does not study the causes that led to the debt crisis. The reader interested in an analysis of the factors that contributed to the unsustainable growth of Puerto Rico's debt is referred to Caraballo-Cueto and Lara (2017), and the references therein. Caraballo-Cueto and Lara (2017) offer a thorough analysis that connects the evolution of Puerto Rico's debt to deindustrialization. The study points to the fragility of an economic model focused on tax-incentivized industrialization as a major determinant of the unsustainable debt dynamics experienced by the island. The authors provide evidence that supports the hypothesis that a deindustrializa-

Martin Guzman (mg3463@columbia.edu) is Associate Professor at the Columbia Business School and at the Department of Economics, University of Buenos Aires. He is a member of the Institute for New Economic Thinking Research Group on "Macroeconomic Efficiency and Stability," co-chair of Columbia Initiative for Policy Dialogue's Taskforce on Debt Restructuring and Sovereign Bankruptcy, and a non-resident Senior Fellow at the Centre for International Governance Innovation. His research fields are macroeconomics, sovereign debt, and economic development.

Joseph Stiglitz (jes322@columbia.edu) is University Professor at Columbia University. In 2001, he was awarded the Nobel Prize in Economics for his analyses of markets with asymmetric information, and was a lead author of the 1995 Report of the Intergovernmental Panel on Climate Change, which shared the 2007 Nobel Peace Prize. In 2011, Time named him as one of the 100 most influential people in the world. His most recent books are *The Price of Inequality: How Today's Divided Society Endangers Our Future* (W.W. Norton and Penguin/Allen Lane, 2012); *Creating a Learning Society: A New Approach to Growth, Development, and Social Progress, with Bruce Greenwald* (Columbia University Press, 2014); *The Great Divide: Unequal Societies and What We Can Do About Them* (W.W. Norton and Penguin/Allen Lane, 2015); *Rewriting the Rules of the American Economy: An Agenda for Growth and Shared Prosperity* (W.W. Norton, 2015); and *The Euro: How a Common Currency Threatens the Future of Europe* (W.W. Norton and Penguin/Allen Lane, 2016).

tion process, triggered by a change in US tax and trade policies and the subsequent failure of the island's government and private sector to adapt, led to a secular decline of the economic activity that was followed by a reduction in government revenues and increasing levels of debt.[1]

Besides this introduction, this paper includes five other sections. Section 2 introduces the conceptual framework that serves as the basis of our analysis of the Fiscal Plan and the computation of the debt restructuring needs. The conceptual analysis notes that the design of a restructuring proposal must take into account that the relationship between debt restructuring and fiscal policies exhibits bi-directional causality. On one hand, absent macroeconomic policies that expand the aggregate demand, Puerto Rico will not recover; and if the economy does not recover, Puerto Rico will not be able to pay its creditors without imposing severe damages on its nearly 3.5 million residents. On the opposite direction of causality, a larger debt reduction would imply that the territory would have more resources for expansionary macroeconomic policies, making the recovery more feasible and full repayment of the restructured debt more likely.

Section 3 examines the Fiscal Plan certified in March 2017 for the period 2017–2026. It first discusses its assumptions. We claim that some of its critical assumptions are unsound and analyze their implications. We identify a number of core flaws in its design and perform a sensitivity analysis, with respect to the assumptions, for the fiscal multipliers and the effects of the structural reforms. This analysis suggests that the fall in real GNP over the next decade was likely to be significantly larger than what the plan had predicted.

Section 4 presents a computation of Puerto Rico's debt restructuring needs. We first demonstrate that the island's current debt position is unsustainable. Assuming the fiscal plan will be respected, absent a debt restructuring, the territory would be forced to sustain primary fiscal surpluses between 3.5 percent and 7.4 percent of GNP from 2027 onwards, forever. But pursuing such a fiscal surplus would lead to a contraction that would make the collection of the necessary tax revenues to achieve it simply untenable, rendering the fiscal surplus unfeasible. We compute the necessary debt reduction to restore debt sustainability for different combinations of assumptions. We report the following main conclusions:

(i)   When we maintain the assumptions of the Fiscal Plan, we find that the necessary reduction of Puerto Rico's debt to restore debt sustainability should include a full cancellation of the interest payments that are scheduled not to be repaid in the Fiscal Plan, plus a face value reduction that should lie roughly between 45 and 65 percent of the current debt stock of $51.9 billions included in the Fiscal Plan.

(ii) However, the relevant universe of the public sector's debt obligations may go beyond the debts included in the Fiscal Plan, as the sustainability of the public sector's debt may also depend on the sustainability of a large part of debt issued by other public entities that is not included in the Fiscal Plan.

When we compute the necessary relief assuming that the relevant stock of debt corresponds to the total debt of the public sector,[2] which increases the relevant stock to $72.2 billions, we obtain that the necessary reduction includes full cancellation of unpaid interest plus a face value reduction of between 60 and 73 percent of this alternative relevant stock of public debt.

(iii) Under a more comprehensive range of assumptions for fiscal multipliers that includes both the assumption of the Fiscal Plan and other more realistic scenarios, and dismissing the unjustifiably optimistic positive assumed effects of the structural reforms on GNP growth for the period 2017–2026, we conclude that if the fiscal plan is implemented, the territory would need full cancellation of interest payments not scheduled for payment in the Fiscal Plan plus a face value reduction that lies between roughly 50 and 80 percent to restore debt sustainability – and again, the necessary reduction is larger if we take $72.2 billions instead of the just $51.9 billions included in the Fiscal Plan as the relevant universe of debt obligations.

Our computations are conservative, as we are not addressing how migration flows will be affected by the deeper depression that the fiscal plan is projected to generate, and more importantly, we are maintaining the fiscal plan's controversial assumption that the territory will somehow manage to achieve a steady state annual nominal GNP growth rate of 2.6 percent without having implemented any expansionary aggregate demand policies. Thus, the range of the values of necessary debt relief that we obtain must be considered as a lower-bound.

The structure of seniority will imply that not all bondholders will get the same discount. Our analysis does not study how the debt write-off will be distributed among bondholders, but simply provides a perspective on the macroeconomic needs. The distribution of losses will be determined by legal considerations that go beyond the object of this study.

We argue that in order to deal with the uncertainty that will underlie the implementation of the fiscal plan and the debt restructuring, the restructuring process could be improved with the inclusion of GNP linked bonds that align debt payments with Puerto Rico's capacity to pay. By definition, these bonds improve the sustainability of the restructured debt and align the incentives of the debtor and the creditors such that the creditors would also benefit from a stronger recovery.

Finally, section 5 concludes with a summary of the policy implications of the analyses and findings of the paper for resolving Puerto Rico's social, economic, and debt crisis.

2. CONCEPTUAL FRAMEWORK
2.a. PUBLIC DEBT SUSTAINABILITY AND MACROECONOMIC DYNAMICS

A public debt sustainability analysis must be able to answer the two following questions:

Q1. Is public debt sustainable with high probability?

Q2. If it isn't, what are the restructuring needs in order to restore debt sustainability?

Answering Q1 and Q2 requires a definition of the concept of debt sustainability.

The economic definition of public debt sustainability refers to the capacity of the government to satisfy its intertemporal budget constraint (IBC) without resorting to a debt default. The IBC states that the present discounted value of primary fiscal surpluses has to be equal to the value of outstanding debt. Each trajectory of states is associated with an IBC. Formally, in an infinite time setup we can describe the IBC in one trajectory of states as:

$$d_t^* = \sum_{j=0}^{\infty} (1+r)^{-j} s_{t+j} \qquad \text{(IBC)}$$

. if

$$\lim_{j \to \infty} \frac{1}{(1+r)^j} d_{t+j} = 0 \qquad \text{(TC)}$$

where the condition (TC) is known as the government's transversality condition, $d_t^* = (1+r)d_{t-1,t}$ denotes debt to output ratio at the start of period t, s_t is the primary fiscal surplus to output ratio in period t, and $1 + r = \frac{1+R}{1+g}$, where R is the nominal interest rate and g is the growth rate of output (for simplicity we denote them as constant). In the context of Puerto Rico, we will use GNP as the measure of output.

More generally, the definition of debt sustainability may also refer to other economic or non-economic principles that are meant to ensure an efficient functioning of debt markets and the respect human rights. For instance, debt could be considered unsustainable if full payment would entail the need to cut on essential public services.[3] Therefore, the satisfaction of the government's solvency condition is a necessary but not a sufficient condition for debt sustainability, as the territory's development needs have to be taken into account. Relatedly, defining debt sustainability also requires a definition of the relevant universe of creditors. Defining the universe of creditors in a public debt restructuring is different than in a corporate debt restructuring, as the creditors of a country need not be only the formal creditors but also the informal ones—as pensioners and workers.

Public Debt and Macroeconomic Dynamics
The objects of each side of the IBC are not independent. The capacity to collect revenues depends on the level of economic activity. In turn, the level of economic activity depends on fiscal policies. But the space of feasible fiscal policies depends on the debt burden. Formally, the primary fiscal surpluses that enter the IBC must be consistent objects that respect the functional relationship between fiscal policies, economic activity, and fiscal revenues. The consideration of these endogenous feedback effects in a system in which fiscal outcomes, the level of economic activity, and the borrowing costs are endogenous variables is central in any analysis of debt sustainability, and missing it leads to flawed estimates of the implications of debt policies.

Puerto Rico's deep and long-lasting downturn has put the economy into a demand-constrained regime. Such a situation calls for the application of macroeconomic policies that expand the aggregate demand—a basic principle of macroeconomic theory. Implementing expansionary macroeconomic policies requires the capacity for financing them. But a country that is in a demand-constrained regime and faces a debt burden that is unsustainable lacks the capacity for expansionary policies. Instead, the unsustainable debt position becomes a drag for economic growth. The logic is simple: when the debt position is perceived as unsustainable with a high probability, the cost of refinancing debt increases; this in turn increases the burden of interest payments, and decreases the available resources net of interest payments for financing public policies. Attempting to force full repayment under those conditions creates a destabilizing dynamic. The induced fiscal austerity decreases aggregate demand, which in the demand-constrained regime leads to a deeper recession, which in turn leads to a debt position perceived as even more unsustainable, and so on. Indeed, the idea that fiscal austerity could somehow restore debt sustainability in an already depressed economy, in times in which the private sector is also contracting, without contemplating the possibility of destabilizing contractionary spirals, is ill conceived and not aligned with sound macroeconomic theory or evidence.[4] The uncertainty created by an unresolved debt problem also deters new investment in the economy, so that in addition to the negative impact on aggregate demand there is an adverse effect on aggregate supply.[5] [6]

Thus, in these circumstances—those prevailing today in Puerto Rico—the recovery of debt sustainability is a necessary condition for economic recovery: There is no possibility of implementing the policies needed for macroeconomic recovery when debt is unsustainable. To restore debt sustainability, debt must be restructured—a restructuring that goes beyond just "reprofiling," e.g. changing the maturity of the obligations. Even creditors as a group may benefit from a restructuring, because the expansionary effects that it allows increases the size of the pie that is distributed among the claimants.[7]

We have just described the ex-ante effects of unsustainable debt—costs that are borne well before a default actually occurs. In addition, there may be large costs which occur when the default actually occurs, and the anticipation of these costs themselves can have adverse effects in the present. The theoretical literature suggests various channels through which debt defaults are associated with output losses as the result of, for example, reputational damage and international trade exclusion costs (e.g., Eaton and Gersovitz 1981; Bulow and Rogoff 1989; Cole and Kehoe 1998; Aguiar and Gopinath 2006; Arellano 2008).[8] However, the empirical literature suggests that the major costs have been those associated with the impact of defaults on domestic bondholders (Sandleris, 2016).[9] [10]

Relationships between Fiscal Policies, Revenues, and GNP Growth: The Fiscal Multipliers

The effects of the fiscal policies that are included in a macroeconomic plan depend on the size of fiscal multipliers, i.e. the parameters that describe the impact of fiscal policies on the level of economic activity. Thus, any fiscal plan must aim at making realistic assessments on the values of the fiscal multipliers.

There are different types of multipliers. The "spending to output multiplier" refers to the effect of changes in public spending on output. The "tax rate to output multipliers" refer to the effects of changes of different tax rates on output; from the tax multipliers, we can infer the values of the "revenues to output multipliers," which indicate how a variation in fiscal revenues will affect output. Finally, the 'spending to revenues multipliers' indicates how a change in public spending will affect tax revenues through the effects that it will have on the endogenous tax bases.

There is a sizable empirical literature that estimates different types of fiscal multipliers for different regions or countries, in different stages of the cycle, and with different methodologies. Although to our knowledge there are no precise estimates for Puerto Rico, the literature offers valuable insights for assessing what assumptions are sensible at the moment of studying the consequences of a fiscal plan for the island. This section offers a brief review of the main findings from that literature. Some of the finds of the empirical literature are that (i) fiscal multipliers are state-dependent;[11] (ii) there are negative endogenous feedback effects from fiscal contractions;[12] and (iii) fiscal multipliers depend on the exchange rate regime: Consistent with the predictions from economic theory, the empirical literature finds that they are larger in economies operating under predetermined exchange rates than under flexible exchange rates.[13]

A simple corollary of the multipliers' state-dependence is that there is uncertainty about the values of multipliers in a particular economy at a particular time. Certainly, there is no precise knowledge about the correct distributions for the values of multipliers for Puerto Rico. Extrapolating values found for US regions or other economies may be of help, but an analysis for Puerto Rico must take into account that the territory is currently in a deep recession and faces the possibility of large out-migration, so that multipliers are likely to be larger than what is obtained for US regions in more "normal" recessions.

The uncertainty about the values of the multipliers has practical implications for an analysis of debt sustainability and for the study of the consequences of a fiscal plan. It makes sensitivity analysis with respect to the baseline assumptions an especially necessary part of the exercise. Our analysis will include a sensitivity analysis that refers to the ranges of estimates that we report in this section.

The stochastic nature of the DSA

Given that any analysis is made under uncertainty, the implication is that the assessment of debt sustainability must be stochastic (see IMF 2013; Celasun, Debrun and Ostry 2006; Consiglio and Zenios 2015, 2017; Guzman and Heymann 2015; Guzman and Lombardi 2017). There may be multiple states of nature, and each state of nature will have a different associated intertemporal budget constraint. This is why we assess debt sustainability from a stochastic perspective, requiring only that there the condition of debt sustainability holds *with a high probability*.

2.b. EMPIRICAL EVIDENCE ON DEBT REDUCTION AND MACROECONOMIC PERFORMANCE

The empirical evidence is consistent with our earlier analysis suggesting that debt relief has beneficial economic effects for debtor countries. Reinhart and Trebesch (2016) examine the economic performance of debtor countries during and after sovereign debt relief operations, for samples that cover the periods 1920–1939 for defaults on official (government to government) debt and 1978–2010 for emerging markets defaults with private creditors. They find that per capita GDP increases 11 percent for emerging markets and 20 percent for advanced economies during the five years following a restructuring that results in exiting from the state of default. They also find a strong increase in average ratings for emerging markets—a result predicted by economic theory, as the market perceptions of debt sustainability should improve if the debt restructuring is effective in resolving the debt crisis. Besides, debt levels decline strongly following the exit of crises. Within five years, total government debt/GDP falls by 27 percentage points across emerging market episodes and by 22 percentage points in the sample of defaults with official creditors. However, they find that not every type of restructuring is associated with improvements in economic performance and ratings: the effects are significant only in deals that involve face value reductions. Reprofiling deals, such as operations with maturity extensions and interest reductions, were not associated with improvements in economic performance.

Recent commentaries and research have made the mistake of looking at what has been the average in past restructurings as a guide for appropriate future debt policies (Edwards 2015a, 2015b). But what has been the norm in recent practice should instead be taken as representative of what is unacceptable. The amount of relief that distressed countries have obtained has generally been insufficient to resolve debt crises. Indeed, restructurings are coming in the form of "too little and too late" (cf. Guzman, Ocampo, and Stiglitz 2016). From 1970 to 2010, between 49.9 percent and 60 percent of sovereign debt restructurings with private creditors were followed by another restructuring or default within 3 to 7 years, respectively (Guzman and Lombardi 2017, based on data from Cruces and Trebesch 2013), the figures suggest that restructuring processes have too often been ineffective at providing enough relief to restore debt sustainability with high probability.

Among the successful cases, two stand out—at least in terms of their magnitude and the attention they have received in the literature. One of them is the case of West Germany following World War II. West Germany obtained significant debt relief through the London Debt Agreement (LDA). The case is studied by Galofré-Vilà et al. (2016), who conclude that West Germany's spectacular recovery would have not been possible without the LDA. The significant debt write-down released resources for fiscal policies that allowed the pursuing of the public policies that the recovery required. Absent such a relief, West Germany would have been forced to obtain sizable fiscal surpluses that would not only have undermined the recovery, but would also have fostered political instability, potentially renewed geopolitical conflict, and ultimately be economically self-defeating.

The other case was Argentina's debt restructuring following the default of 2001—the largest recorded sovereign default in history at the time. The country followed a strategy that resulted in significant debt relief (see Basualdo et al. (2015); Guzman (2016); Chodos (2016); and Cruces and Samples (2016) for details), which created space for fiscal policies that played a crucial role in the fast and large recovery that the country experienced following the default.[14] However, the country also got immersed in a complex legal dispute with holdout bondholders—bondholders who decide to not cooperate in restructuring negotiations even when a large majority accepts the proposal of the debtor—including the so-called vulture funds who bought debt at a low fraction of its face value when it was already in default, sued the country in US courts seeking full payment and won, blocking the finalization of the restructuring process and also the country's access to international credit markets for more than a decade. The case is also telling of the complexities of resolving debt crisis under severe gaps in the legal frameworks.

Among the recent unsuccessful cases, Greece stands out. The case is extensively analyzed by Varoufakis (2016). The management of Greece's ongoing debt crisis is an example of *too little* and *too late*. After a few years of recession and of an unsustainable debt position, the country restructured its debt in 2012. But the restructuring was not effective to restore debt sustainability. It came with conditions of fiscal austerity imposed by the Troika that undermined the possibility of escaping the recession. The draconian demands have continued since then. The Troika later imposed a program for reducing Greece's public debt to GDP ratio that included a target of primary surplus of 3.5 percent of GDP for 2015, and 4.5 percent of GDP from 2015 onwards, forever. Predictably, such a program has not restored Greece to prosperity. The country continues to struggle, and throughout this period, opportunities have vanished for many Greeks. The unemployment rate was 7 percent in 2008 and skyrocketed since then, growing higher than 25 percent; it was 23 percent in 2016. Youth unemployment statistics are even more alarming. The youth unemployment rate peaked at 60 percent in 2013, then declined to 47 percent at the time of this study after many migrated or stopped looking for jobs.

2.c. PROJECTIONS

The model we employ for projecting the debt repayment capacity respects the functional relationships assumed by the Fiscal Plan. The growth rate of real GNP, g_t^y, is defined as

$$g_t^y = g_t^b + g_t^d + g_t^s$$

where is the real GNP growth, g_t^b is the baseline real GNP growth rate g_t^d is the growth rate of real GNP that comes from fiscal policy measures, and g_t^s is the growth rate in real GNP that comes from structural reforms, in all cases between years $t - 1$ and t. The growth rate of real GNP that comes from fiscal policy measures is given by

$$g_t^d = \frac{\Delta RGNP_t^d}{RGNP_{t-1}}$$

where $RGNP_t$ is the real GNP in year t, and

$$\Delta RGNP_t^d = \alpha_{Y,G}\Delta G_t + \alpha_{Y,T}\Delta T_t^C + \alpha_{Y,T}\Delta T_t$$

where $\alpha_{Y,G}$ is the public spending to real GNP multiplier and $\alpha_{Y,T;t}$ is the fiscal revenues to real GNP multiplier.

The ΔT_t^C component denotes the necessary change in tax revenues to compensate the initial variation due to the change in public spending in year t:

$$\Delta T_t^C = -\alpha_{T,G;t}\Delta G_t$$

where $\alpha_{T,G;t}$ is the public spending to fiscal revenues multiplier that denotes the endogenous feedback effect that a contraction of public spending creates on fiscal revenues through the fall in economic activity.[15]

Informed by the literature (see section 2.A above), we project the real and nominal GNP for each possible combination of the following parameters: $\alpha_{Y,G} = \{1,1.34,1.5,2,2.5,3,3.5\}$, $\alpha_{Y,T} = \{0,0.5,1,1.34\}$, and $\varepsilon_{T,G} = \{0,0.1,0.2,0.3,0.4,0.5,0.6,0.7\}$ where $\varepsilon_{T,G}$ is the elasticity of fiscal revenues to public spending,

$$\varepsilon_{T,G} = -\alpha_{T,G;t}\frac{G_t}{T_t}$$

We are making a conservative assumption for the tax revenues to real GNP multiplier, under the premise that part of the increases in tax revenues will fall on agents with low marginal propensities to consume. Our projections would be more pessimistic if we chose the same range for $\alpha_{Y,T}$ as for $\alpha_{Y,G}$.[16]

The nominal GNP growth rate is denoted by g^y, where

$$g_t^Y = g_t^y + \pi_t + g_t^y\pi_t$$

and where π_t is the rate of inflation between years $t - 1$ and t.

The real GNP in period t is given by

$$RGNP_t = RGNP_{t-1}(1 + g_t^y)$$

and the nominal GNP in period t is given by

$$NGNP_t = NGP_{t-1}(1 + g_t^Y)$$

Our choice of parameters for the multipliers $\alpha_{Y,G}$, $\alpha_{Y,T}$ and the elasticity $\varepsilon_{T,G}$ results in 192 combinations of parameters that can be defined as "scenarios". We project real and nominal GNP for each of those 192 scenarios.

3. AN ANALYSIS OF THE FISCAL PLAN 2017-2026[17]

In this section, we examine the macroeconomic implications of Puerto Rico's Fiscal Plan that had been approved for fiscal years 2017–18 to 2026–27, as it is a crucial element for a computation of Puerto Rico's debt restructuring needs. The Fiscal Plan presented by the Government of Puerto Rico had been certified by the Oversight Board on March 13, 2017.

The plan includes a detailed path of policies, including spending and tax policies as well as structural reforms. It offers a projection of the effects of those policies on Puerto Rico's GNP for the ten-year period under a set of assumptions regarding

Table 1

Fiscal year ending June 30 ($ in millions)	2017	2018	2019
PR Nominal GNP Growth	(2.2%)	(2.8%)	(2.4%)
Revenue before Measure	$18,952	$17,511	$16,407
Nointerest Exp. before Measures	($17,872)	($18,981)	($19,233)
Cash flows pre-Measures	$1,000	($1,470)	($2,826)
Measures			
Revenue Measures	-	924	1,361
Expense Measures	-	951	2,012
Net impact of measures	-	1,875	3,393
Cash flows post-Measures, before Debt Service	$1,000	$404	$567

Fiscal year ending June 30 ($ in millions)	2020	2021	2022
PR Nominal GNP Growth	(0.5%)	(0.4%)	0.3%
Revenue before Measure	$18,434	$16,494	$16,590
Nointerest Exp. before Measures	($19,512)	($20,477)	($20,477)
Cash flows pre-Measures	($3,077)	($3,456)	($3,886)
Measures			
Revenue Measures	1,384	1,531	1,633
Expense Measures	2,415	2,983	3,156
Net impact of measures	3,799	4,515	4,789
Cash flows post-Measures, before Debt Service	$722	$1,059	$903

Source: Fiscal Plan 2017–2026.

the macroeconomic effects of fiscal policies, the effects of the structural reforms, the migration flows, the baseline growth rate of GNP (that describes the scenario that would prevail in absence of new policy measures), and the inflation rate.

On the demand side, the program is characterized by fiscal contraction over the entire decade but mainly concentrated in years 2018 and 2019. Regarding the structural reforms, the plan features four packages that are classified as (i) improve the ease of business activity, (ii) improving capital efficiency, (iii) energy reform, and (iv) promoting economic development. The concrete measures include (textually reproduced from the approved Fiscal Plan, p. 23):

- Institute public policy measures aimed to attract new businesses, create new employment opportunities, and foster private sector employment growth to increase labor demand.

Table 1 (continued)

Fiscal year ending June 30 ($ in millions)	2023	2024	2025
PR Nominal GNP Growth	1.0%	1.6%	2.1%
Revenue before Measure	$16,746	$16,953	$17,204
Nointerest Exp. before Measures	($20,884)	($21,310)	($21,973)
Cash flows pre-Measures	($4,139)	($4,357)	($4,769)
Measures			
Revenue Measures	1,740	1,752	1,766
Expense Measures	3,255	3,357	3,724
Net impact of measures	4,995	5,108	5,491
Cash flows post-Measures, before Debt Service	$857	$751	$722

Fiscal year ending June 30 ($ in millions)	2026	'17 - '26 total	
PR Nominal GNP Growth	(0.5%)	(0.4%)	
Revenue before Measure	$18,434	$16,494	
Nointerest Exp. before Measures	($19,512)	($20,477)	
Cash flows pre-Measures	($3,077)	($3,456)	
Measures			
Revenue Measures	1,384	1,531	
Expense Measures	2,415	2,983	
Net impact of measures	3,799	4,515	
Cash flows post-Measures, before Debt Service	$722	$1,059	

Source: Fiscal Plan 2017–2026.

- Change welfare and labor incentives to encourage greater sector participation, thus increasing labor supply.
- Centralize, streamline, and modernize and expedite permitting processes; increase business friendly environmental and economic growth.
- Lower marginal tax rates and broaden the tax base; simplify and optimize the existing tax code to achieve gains in efficiency, ease of doing business and reducing tax evasion.
- Reduce unnecessary regulatory burdens to reduce the drag of government on the private sector.
- Augmenting competitiveness by investing in critical infrastructure and quality of public services in roads, ports, telecommunications, water and waste, knowledge services, and other strategically important sectors.[18]

Table 2

Year	2017	2018	2019	2020	2021	2022	2023	2024	2025	2026
PR Annual Inflation Rate %	-0.2	1.2	1.0	1.0	1.1	1.3	1.5	1.5	1.6	1.6

Source: Fiscal Plan 2017–2026.

Table 3

Year	2017	2018	2019	2020	2021	2022	2023	2024	2025	2026
Baseline Real GNP Growth (%)	-2.4	-1.31	-1.39	-1.44	-1.47	-1.49	-1.50	-1.51	-1.52	-1.53

Source: Fiscal Plan 2017–2026.

Table 4

Year	2017	2018	2019	2020	2021	2022	2023	2024	2025	2026
Impact of structural reforms on real GNP growth (%)	0	0	0	0	0	0.5	1	1.5	2	2.5

Source: Fiscal Plan 2017–2026.

- Leverage key public assets through long-term concessions to optimize quality of public infrastructure, services to public and sustainable operations and maintenance.
- Implement management system to boost development of critical projects through expedited processes.
- Leverage and facilitate expedited private sector investments in modern, cost-efficient, and environmentally compliant energy infrastructure; reform PREPA operations and services to clients; and allow for greater competition in energy generation.
- Promote productivity growth, attract FDI & incentivize investments in technology through collaboration with the private sector.
- Externalize the overseeing of marketing efforts and continuity under a single brand and as a unified front representing all of Puerto Rico's tourism components.

Table 1, reproduced from the Fiscal Plan (p.10), summarizes the fiscal measures and the projections for the growth rate of nominal GNP.

The plan assumes a constant annual population growth rate of -0.2 percent for the entire period and an evolution of the inflation rate as described in Table 2.

As publicly reported, the plan assumes that the multiplier associated with fiscal contractions will be 1.34, which means that every dollar of contraction in the primary surplus will be associated with a fall in GNP of 1.34 dollars. The Fiscal Plan assumes baseline real GNP growth rates for the decade as described in Table 3 (i.e. these are the growth rates that would have occurred, in the absence of the Plan's changes in policy).[19]

The plan also assumes that the effects of the structural reforms will kick in by 2022 and will make a contribution to real GNP growth as described in Table 4.

Critiques

Our analysis of the fiscal plan detects a number of core flaws in its design:

(I)   The plan is based on assumptions that are not sensible: thus it fails to appropriately recognize the magnitude of the destabilizing dynamics that it would create.

(II) The plan falls short on presenting a debt restructuring and sustainability analysis, and as we have already explained, such an analysis is essential for making reasonable growth forecasts. Instead, it simply specifies what is the amount that must be repaid to creditors during the next decade, without being explicit about the longer-term obligations that the island will face and their sustainability.

We discuss each of these in turn. Specifically:

1. The values of fiscal multipliers used for the GNP projections are overoptimistic.

The value for the multiplier associated with the fiscal contraction of 1.34 is close to the lower-bound of the estimates corresponding to times of recession, as described in the review of the literature in section 3. That value corresponds to estimates for US regions in recessions,[20] but Puerto Rico is suffering a depression that is deeper than a "normal" recession. Multipliers are likely to be larger for deep recessions. This is especially so in the case of Puerto Rico, given the likely effect of a deep recession on migration.[21] And even if the assumption is considered sensible, a robust plan should consider the consequences of deviations from it. It is not only the point estimate what matters, but also the distribution.

2. The endogenous feedback effects that the fall in economic activity would have on fiscal revenues are not taken into account.

While the assumption on the fiscal multiplier cannot be classified as a wrong assumption—but simply as an overoptimistic one—ignoring the effects that the fall in economic activity would have on tax revenues is a plain mistake, one that leads to an underestimation of the contractionary impact of the proposed fiscal policies. Implicitly, the projections assume that the elasticity of public spending on tax revenues is zero—as tax revenues fall as the economy contracts, to meet the fiscal targets, public expenditures have to fall. But this induced contraction of expenditures then has a further contractionary effect. The Board's analysis seems to have ignored these feedback effects.[22]

3. The plan assumes that the territory will begin to experience a recovery starting in 2022 entirely because of structural reforms that mostly affect the supply side. This assumption gooes against sound macroeconomic theory, because Puerto Rico's economy is a deman-constrained regime.

In a supply-constrained regime, structural reforms that remove obstacles to supply formation will likely have expansionary effects. But Puerto Rico's economy is in a demand-constrained regime. Thus, the assumption that supply-side reforms will be the driver of economic recovery is not well-founded. On the contrary, any spending-reducing reform as cuts in pensions will more likely deepen the recession in the short-term.

In summary, the entire reasoning of the fiscal plan for how Puerto Rico will recover relies on an assumption that is not aligned with sound economic theory. Puerto Rico will not manage to recover if it does not implement policies that push aggregate demand while the economy is in a demand-constrained regime. And the Plan provides no argument for how in the foreseeable future Puerto Rico will shift away from a demand constrained economy.

4. The assumption on migration flows assume that migration pressures will not intensity with the projected contraction in economic activity.

Puerto Rico's population has declined from approximately 3.8 million in 2000 to a little more than 3.4 million in 2016. Between 2010 and 2016, the annual rate of population contraction exceeded 1 percent, and reached 1.8 percent in 2016. A deeper recession—as anticipated by the Board's plan—will further decrease opportunities in the island, fueling more migration to the mainland. And yet the plan assumes that the migration flows will taper off, with the population declining by only 0.2 percent per year over the 2017–2026 period. This is an unrealistic assumption.[23]

An intensification of migration outflows as a result of the contractionary effects of the Plan would accelerate the fall in fiscal revenues. Then, to achieve the revenue targets stated in the Fiscal Plan, the adjustments would need to be larger—but that would trigger further contractions in economic activity and would increase the per capita burden for those remaining in the island, leading to a destabilizing dynamic that the Fiscal Plan fails to recognize.

Figure 1

Assuming the Fiscal Plan's assumption on structural reforms hold

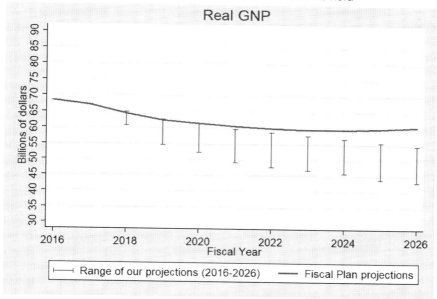

Assuming structural reforms have no effect on GNP

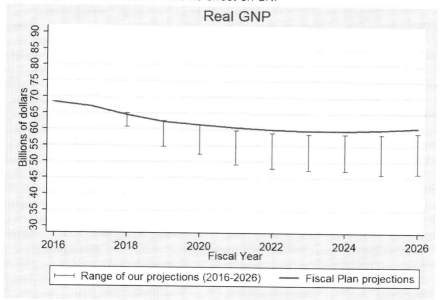

5. The plan does not present a proposal for debt restructuring.
The plan simply states what is the amount that must be repaid to creditors during the next decade, but it falls short on the specifics of a restructuring plan as, for instance, on the amount of relief that the territory should obtain to restore debt sustainability. This is a mistake, because the possibilities that the territory will face in terms of fiscal policies are contingent on the restructuring it achieves; and those fiscal policies in turn will affect output, employment, migration, and tax revenues.

There is a sixth issue that deserves attention. The annual growth rates of nominal and real GNP are assumed to reach 2.6 percent and 1 percent respectively in 2026. It is not specified whether these assumptions correspond to a steady state.[24] Assumptions about future growth obviously affect the sustainability of the debt after 2026; market perceptions about debt sustainability obviously affect the interest rates the territory will have to pay; and this in turn affects (for reasons already explained) the territory's macroeconomics.

Finally, the exercise of projecting the effects of public policies must take into account that there is uncertainty about the values that the relevant parameters and the magnitude of the shocks that the island will experience. The sensitivity analysis, where changes in the assumptions are analyzed, must be part of the projection analysis. We next engage into such an exercise.

Projections: Sensitivity analysis
In order to address the limitations of the Fiscal Plan's forecasts, we conduct a sensitivity analysis of the expected implied macroeconomic dynamics. This allows us to construct more realistic scenarios of Puerto Rico's debt restructuring needs. We project the trajectories under alternative assumptions for fiscal multipliers described in Section 2.A above, maintaining the same assumptions of the Fiscal Plan for the trajectory of baseline real GNP growth and the annual inflation rates until 2026. We maintain those assumptions because our initial goal is to assess how the GNP projections react to changes in the values of the fiscal multipliers. We assume that the component of the fiscal primary balance that corresponds to the line "Measures" in Table 1 is the "unanticipated" component of the fiscal policy, to which the multipliers apply—the Fiscal Plan assumes the same.

Our choice of parameters for the multipliers , , and the elasticity results in 192 combinations of parameters that can be defined as "scenarios." We project real and nominal GNP for each of those 192 scenarios. Figure 1 shows the ranges of our projections, as well as and the Fiscal Plan's projections, for the real GDP, for two scenarios: in panel A, the Fiscal Plan's assumptions on the effects of structural reforms on GNP are maintained, while in panel B the comparison is made under the assumption that the Fiscal Plan's structural reforms have no effect on GNP.

Our projections strongly suggest that the Fiscal Plan's projections are overoptimistic. They lie on the most optimistic bound within the range of assumptions on the values of multipliers that are aligned with the empirical evidence. The magnitude of

Figure 2

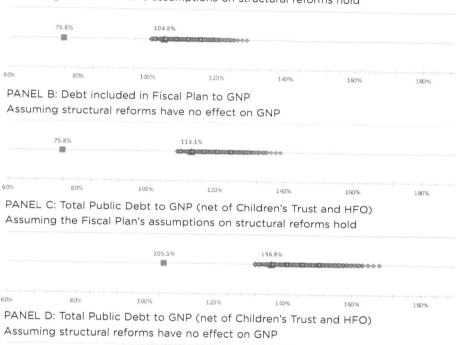

PANEL A: Debt included in Fiscal Plan to GNP
Assuming the Fiscal Plan's assumptions on structural reforms hold

PANEL B: Debt included in Fiscal Plan to GNP
Assuming structural reforms have no effect on GNP

PANEL C: Total Public Debt to GNP (net of Children's Trust and HFO)
Assuming the Fiscal Plan's assumptions on structural reforms hold

PANEL D: Total Public Debt to GNP (net of Children's Trust and HFO)
Assuming structural reforms have no effect on GNP

the differences between our range of projections and the projections of the Fiscal Plan is noticeably larger if we dismiss the positive effects that the structural reforms are assumed to have on GNP by the Plan.

And even under those optimistic assumptions, the plan falls into an "austerity trap": the magnitude of the targets for primary surpluses leads to a decrease in GNP over a decade that is larger than the reduction in the stock of debt, thus leading to an increase in the debt to GNP ratio by 2026. If there was no reduction in the debt principal, and if missed payments either of interest or principal were capitalized at zero interest rate, the total public debt to GNP ratio would rise from 1.09 in 2016 to 1.41 in 2026 in the scenario projected by the Fiscal Plan. (It is this "austerity trap" which has led to the dire outcomes in Greece, where, after its austerity program and after successive debt restructurings, the debt GDP ratio is higher than it was in the beginning of the crisis.)

And as figure 2 shows, the magnitude of the austerity trap will likely be larger, as the projected debt to GNP ratio for 2026 is even larger in the large majority of the postulated scenarios.

True, the lower-bound of our projections corresponds to projections that may be too pessimistic. Prospects should be certainly better if there is a restructuring that restores sustainability, as the baseline growth rate of GNP would probably be larger if the debt position of the territory is perceived as sustainable by market participants. But our projections call the attention on the deeply negative consequences that the implementation of the Fiscal Plan could have for Puerto Rico's economy. And our projections still ignore the larger effects that the fall of economic activity could have on migration outflows. [25]

4. A COMPUTATION OF PUERTO RICO'S DEBT RELIEF NEEDS

In this section, we perform a Debt Sustainability Analysis (DSA) that incorporates the expected macroeconomic dynamics implied by the Fiscal Plan in order to compute Puerto Rico's restructuring needs. The analysis includes a computation of the amount of debt relief that is required in order to restore Puerto Rico's public debt sustainability. More specifically, we compute the reduction in the value of Puerto Rico's public debt that would make full repayment of the restructured debt feasible, being consistent with the Fiscal Plan assumptions that the country will achieve a real GNP growth rate of 1 percent in 2026, and that will settle on that rate as a steady state.

Our DSA takes the premise that the Fiscal Plan will be respected. We assume that any discrepancy between the Fiscal Plan's GNP projections and realizations will be addressed in a way that respects the schedule of debt payments—or equivalently, the schedule of cash after measures available for debt service—established in the Fiscal Plan. Therefore, each projection will lead to the same face value of debt in 2026, because by construction we force the economy to do whatever it takes to reach the targets of fiscal revenues included in the Fiscal Plan. But each scenario will be associated with different GNP trajectories, as shown in figures 1 to 4. Thus, for each of the 192 scenarios that are defined by the assumed range of fiscal multipliers, we obtain a different value of the debt to GNP ratio for 2026, , as depicted in figure 2.

For each of those 192 projected debt to GDP ratios, we need to respond the following questions:

    a.) What path of primary fiscal surpluses would the economy require after 2027 to satisfy the government's IBC?

    b.) Is that path economically feasible?

    c.) If it is not, what is the size of the debt write-down that would make the satisfaction of the government's IBC feasible with high probability?

Answering these questions requires taking a stance on the relationship between fiscal policies and GNP growth. We use exactly the same functional form that is used for the projections of the Fiscal Plan, but as explained previously, we run the projections under a set of assumptions that include those of the Fiscal Plan as well as others, informed by the empirical literature.

To perform the computations required to answer questions (a) to (c), we make the following additional assumptions:

Assumption i. We take the value of the fiscal surplus to GNP ratio of 2026 as the new structural fiscal balance for year 2027—the first year for which there is no information from the Fiscal Plan. This is an optimistic assumption—one that assumes that the reforms and policies included in the plan will be as effective as assumed and will remain in place after 2026. If anything, this assumption leads to an underestimation of Puerto Rico's debt relief needs—consistently with our strategy of making assumptions in each step of the analysis that imply that our computations of the debt relief needs must be interpreted as lower bounds.

Assumption ii. With the same goal of making our computations a representation of lower-bounds, we assume that the interest payments that are missed during the period 2017-2026 are capitalized after being rolled-over to 2027 at zero interest rate.

Assumption iii. We assume that by 2027 the economy will have already settled on a trend of real GNP growth rate of 1 percent, as predicted by the fiscal plan. We also assume that the inflation rate will settle on a trend of 1.6 percent per year after 2026—which is the inflation rate the Fiscal Plan assumes for 2026. As discussed above, these are controversial assumptions. If the country does not implement policies that push aggregate demand, the real and nominal growth targets will likely not be met. Again, the goal is to err on the underestimation side of relief needs rather than on the overestimation side.

Assumption iv. Finally, we assume that the nominal interest rate stabilizes at 6 percent after the restructuring, which corresponds to a scenario of a risk free nominal interest rate of 3 percent, recovery of sustainability with probability 95 percent, and recovery rate of 46 percent in case of default. The online appendix presents the sensitivity analysis regarding this assumption.[26]

The debt stabilizing primary fiscal surplus to gnp ratio

We search for the value of the debt stabilizing primary fiscal surplus to GNP ratio in a steady state situation. We denote this variable in scenario i as s^i, and it is defined as

$$s^i = d^i \frac{(R - g^B)}{1 + g^B}$$

where g^B is the steady state nominal GNP growth, and, as defined before, d^i is the debt to GNP ratio in scenario i, and R is the nominal interest rate that corresponds to the situation where debt has been stabilized. The debt stabilizing primary fiscal surplus denotes the value of the primary fiscal surplus as a ratio of GNP that must be achieved to satisfy the government's intertemporal budget constraint. But that value may or may not be feasible, i.e. it may or may not be achievable once we take into account the endogenous feedback effects between fiscal policies and economic performance.

Let s^i_{2026} be the structural primary fiscal balance by the end of 2026 in scenario i, i.e. the new primary fiscal balance in absence of measures by the time the Fiscal Plan ends. From 2027 onwards, we do not take a stance on what component of the primary

Table 5: Debt-stabilizing primary fiscal surplus, R=0.06, g =0.026

Scenarios	Measure of debt	Fiscal Plan assumptions on sructural reform	Mean	Minimum	Maximum
192	Total public debt net of Children's Trust and HFO	No	5.8%	4.9%	7.4%
192	Debt included in Fiscal Plan	No	4.3%	3.7%	5.2%
192	Total public debt net of Children's Trust and HFO	Yes	5.3%	4.6%	6.7%
192	Debt included in Fiscal Plan	Yes	3.9%	3.5%	4.7%

balance (revenues or spending) will have to be adjusted in order to achieve the target of primary surplus defined for each scenario. Therefore, we assume the same multipliers for tax revenues and public spending for each combination i: $\alpha_{G,Y}^{i} = \alpha_{T,Y}^{i} = \beta^{i}$. We redefine the function that determines the effects of fiscal contractions on real GNP growth as

$$\alpha_{G,Y}^{i} = \alpha_{T,Y}^{i} = \beta^{i} \quad (1)$$

which, as stated, is the same function used for the Fiscal Plan projections.[27]

Computing s^{i} requires a series of iterations until the economy stabilizes on a path of constant nominal GNP growth and stable debt-to-GNP ratio.

The iteration process works as follows:

Step 1: Under the *Assumption ii*, we compute d^{i} for each i for 2026.

Step 2: For each d_{2026}^{i}, we compute s^{i}. If $s^{i} \neq s_{2026}$, the economy will not be in a steady state situation, and then we need to compute g_{2027}^{nY}, where g_{2027}^{nY} is the nominal growth rate of GNP in scenario . This will result in a new d_{2027}^{iY} that will differ from d_{2026}^{iY}.

Step 3: For the new value of d_{2027}^{iY}, we compute again the new s^{i}. If $s^{i} \neq s_{2027}$, then $g_{2027}^{nY} \neq g_{2027}^{B}$, and we need to compute d_{2028}^{i}.

Step 4 to N: This iteration will continue until $s_{t}^{i} = s_{t-1}^{i}$, with $g_{t-1}^{nY} = g_{t}^{nY} = g^{B}$. At that moment (step N), we get a constant s^{i} that satisfies the government's IBC.[28]

Results: The debt stabilizing primary fiscal surpluses to GNP and the evolution of debt to GNP ratios

In the absence of restructuring, the debt included in the Fiscal Plan to GNP ratio would have to stabilize at values from 1.04 (when $\alpha_{G,Y}$ = 1.34, $\alpha_{G,T}$ = 0, $\alpha_{T,Y}$ = 0) to 1.45 (when $\alpha_{G,Y}$ = 3.5, $\alpha_{G,T}$ = 0.7, $\alpha_{T,Y}$ = -1.34), and the total public debt (net of Children's Trust and HFO) to GNP ratio would have to stabilize at values from 1.38 to 2.04. The lower bound of 1.04 corresponds to s = 0.035, and the upper bound corresponds to s = 0.074. Under the Fiscal Plan assumptions, those ratios take values of 1.08 and 1.43 respectively, and in 2026 they take values of 1.04 and 1.36 respectively.

Therefore, in absence of any relief, Puerto Rico should achieve primary fiscal surpluses between 3.5% and 7.4% of GNP after the end of the Fiscal Plan, forever. Under the Fiscal Plan's assumptions, the primary surpluses after 2028 would have to be 3.5% or 4.7% of GNP, forever, depending on whether the relevant debt stock is the one included in the Fiscal Plan or the total public debt net of Children's Trust and HFO. Table 5 summarizes these findings.

On the feasible primary fiscal balance paths

The functional form (1) used for the Fiscal Plan projections relates the growth rate of GNP to the change in the primary surplus, but it does not relate it to the level of the primary surplus. Thus, according to their model, even if the government is forced to sustain primary surpluses of 7 percent of GNP forever, that would not affect the (growth) performance of the economy in the long term. The only period in which economic activity would be affected would be the one in which the large contraction to achieve the target of 7 percent occurs.

But such premise is, of course, not valid over the entire range of primary surplus levels. The need to maintain massive primary surpluses for a long time would have significant effects on the possibilities of the government to make investments in infrastructure, health, or human capital, or to implement other development policies. A draconian plan as requiring constant primary surpluses between 3.5 to 7.4 percent of GNP would entail drastic permanent cuts to spending in these areas, and that would have long term effects. The targets would likely be inconsistent with the baseline assumption of convergence to a real GNP growth rate of 1 percent. (Moreover, such draconian measures would further encourage migration, making the growth targets even more unrealistic.)

The IMF DSA framework and its fan charts approach provide a helpful basis for complementing our analysis. IMF (2011) recognizes that sustained large surpluses are not common, and incorporates this constraint in its debt sustainability analyses; it reports that out of a sample of 87 countries, only 16 countries (less than 20 percent) sustained primary surpluses exceeding 5 percent of GDP for five years or longer. Some of these episodes of sustained large surpluses were related to specific conditions that are not easily applicable to most countries. Out of the 16 countries that recorded episodes of sustained surpluses, five had this performance in connection to exogenous factors—large increases in revenues related to natural resources

(Botswana, Chile, Egypt, and Uzbekistan) or transfers arising from customs union membership (Lesotho). Episodes of sustained large surpluses in the absence of facilitating exogenous factors have been limited to 11 countries (13 percent of the sample). And a few of these countries ran large primary surpluses in the absence of a large debt burden (Denmark, New Zealand, Turkey). The ones that sustained surpluses exceeding 5 percent of GDP for five years or longer at times where debt levels were above 60 percent of GDP were Belgium, Canada, Dominica, Israel, Jamaica, Panama, Seychelles, and Singapore. And no country targeted those values forever.

Besides, there is no evidence that supports the premise that targeting those high primary fiscal surpluses has been associated with recoveries in situations of distress. Indeed, four of those eight economies faced situations that are significantly different from that of the debt distress Puerto Rico is facing (Belgium, Canada, Israel, and Singapore were in situations where austerity could ensure the sustainability of the public sector without triggering a self-defeating macroeconomic process. For instance, Canada had the good fortune of having a flexible exchange rate regime and having its major trading partner, the US, experience a boom.). While Dominica combined a debt restructuring in 2004 with an average primary fiscal surplus of 3.9 percent of GDP for the period 2004–2008, it had only an average fiscal surplus of 1.19 during the decade that followed the restructuring; Jamaica has been keeping sizable primary fiscal surpluses since its last debt restructuring in 1990, on average of 7.48 of GDP, and the economy has suffered the consequences: the unemployment rate has kept at two digits for almost the entire period, and the government's debt to GDP ratio is at about the same levels now as in 1990, above 120 per cent; Panama combined two debt restructuring episodes in 1994 and 1996 with an average primary fiscal surplus of 1.08 percent of GDP in the decade that followed the latter restructuring; and Seychelles combined a debt restructuring in 2010 with an average primary fiscal surplus of 5.98 percent of GDP during the period 2010-2015—in a context of significant increases in the prices of its exports.

Most important, the primary surplus is an endogenous outcome; if a country recovers due to the implementation of an appropriate mix of policies that include a debt restructuring, obtaining primary surpluses becomes a more likely outcome.

In summary, while there is no evidence that suggests that a country in a situation of debt distress, in a demand-constrained regime, can do well by avoiding a restructuring through the achievement of very large primary fiscal surpluses, there is evidence that long periods of large primary fiscal surpluses are very rare, and that a restructuring has been almost always ultimately unavoidable under those circumstances.

We conclude that if Puerto Rico's government needs to collect primary surpluses in the order of 3.5 percent to 7.4 percent of GNP after 2027 forever, this means that Puerto Rico's debt is almost surely unsustainable, and that it needs to be restructured to a level where the required path of primary fiscal surpluses becomes feasible.

Figure 3: Necessary face value reduction under the Fiscal Plan assumption on the effects of structural reforms on GNP growth – Relevant debt: Debt included in Fiscal Plan

Panel A: As % of total relevant debt

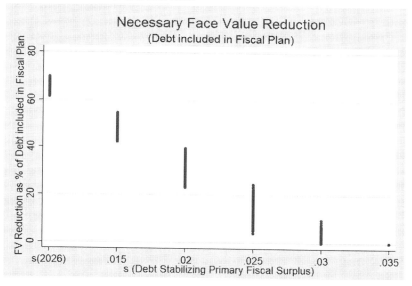

Panel B: In billions of $

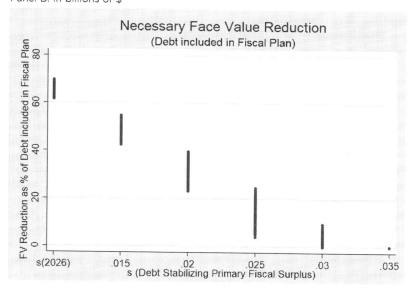

Table 6: Necessary face value reduction under the Fiscal Plan assumption on the effects of structural reforms on GNP growth, as percent of total relevant debt — Relevant debt: Debt included in Fiscal Plan

Debt stabilizing primary surplus to GNP since 2027	No. of scenarios	Min Face Value Reduction (% of total current public debt)	Max Face Value Reduction (% of total current public debt)	Face value reduction under Fiscal Plan multiplier assumptions
s2026	192	61.6	69.8	63.0
0.015	192	42.4	54.7	44.4
0.02	192	23.2	39.7	25.9
0.025	192	4.0	24.6	7.4
0.03	192	0.0	9.5	0.0
0.035	192	0.0	0.0	0.0

Figure 4: Necessary face value reduction under the Fiscal Plan assumption on the effects of structural reforms on GNP growth – Relevant debt: Total Public Debt Net of Children's Trust and HFO

Panel A: As % of total relevant debt

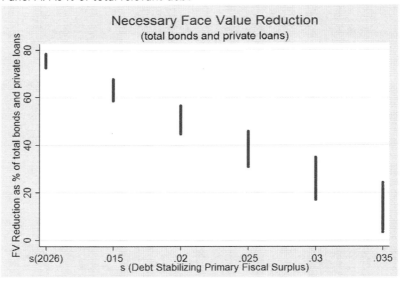

Figure 4 (continued)

Panel B: In billions of $

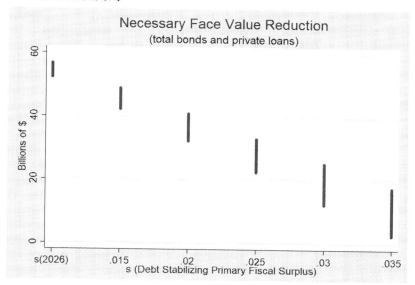

Table 7: Necessary face value reduction under the Fiscal Plan assumption on the effects of structural reforms on GNP growth, as % of total relevant debt – Relevant debt: Total Public Debt Net of Children's Trust and HFO

Debt stabilizing primary surplus to GNP since 2027	No. of scenarios	Min Face Value Reduction (% of total current public debt)	Max Face Value Reduction (% of total current public debt)	Face value reduction under Fiscal Plan multiplier assumptions
s2026	192	72.4	78.3	73.4
0.015	192	58.6	67.5	60.1
0.02	192	44.8	56.6	46.8
0.025	192	31.1	45.8	33.5
0.03	192	17.3	35.0	20.2
0.035	192	3.5	24.1	6.9

Figure 5: Necessary face value reduction under the assumption that structural reforms have no effects on GNP growth – Relevant debt: Debt included in Fiscal Plan

Panel A: As % of total relevant debt

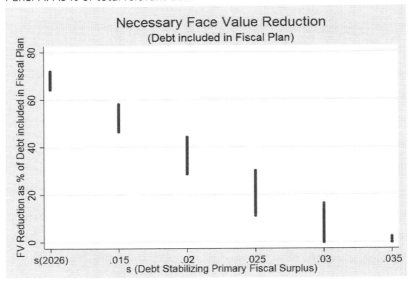

Panel B: In billions of $

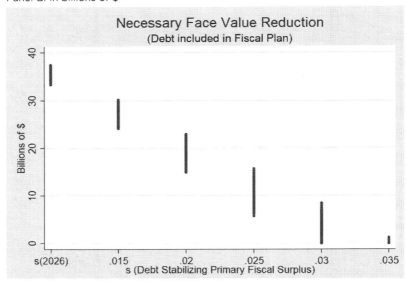

Table 8: Necessary face value reduction under the assumption that structural reforms have no effects on GNP growth, as % of total relevant debt – Relevant debt: Debt included in Fiscal Plan

Debt stabilizing primary surplus to GNP since 2027	No. of scenarios	Min Face Value Reduction (% of total current public debt)	Max Face Value Reduction (% of total current public debt)	Face value reduction under Fiscal Plan multiplier assumptions
s2026	192	64.4	72.0	65.7
0.015	192	46.6	58.1	48.5
0.02	192	28.8	44.1	31.3
0.025	192	11.0	30.1	14.1
0.03	192	0.0	16.1	0.0
0.035	192	0.0	2.2	0.0

Figure 6: Necessary face value reduction under the assumption that structural reforms have no effects on GNP growth, as percent of total relevant debt – Relevant debt: Total Public Debt Net of Children's Trust and HFO

Panel A: As % of total relevant debt

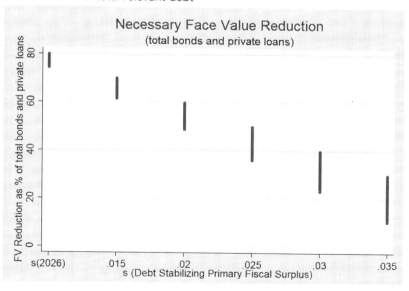

Figure 6 (continued)

Panel B: In billions of $

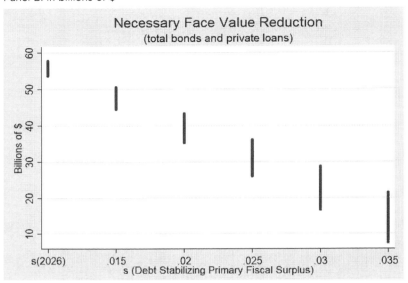

Table 9: Necessary face value reduction under the assumption that structural reforms have no effects on GNP growth, as percent of total relevant debt—Relevant debt: Total Public Debt Net of Children's Trust and HFO

Debt stabilizing primary surplus to GNP since 2027	No. of scenarios	Min Face Value Reduction (% of total current public debt)	Max Face Value Reduction (% of total current public debt)	Face value reduction under Fiscal Plan multiplier assumptions
s2026	192	74.4	79.9	75.3
0.015	192	61.6	69.9	63.0
0.02	192	48.9	59.8	50.7
0.025	192	36.1	49.8	38.3
0.03	192	23.3	39.8	26.0
0.035	192	10.5	29.7	13.6

Figure 7: Sustainable debt under the Fiscal Plan assumption on the effects of structural reforms on GNP growth, in billions of $

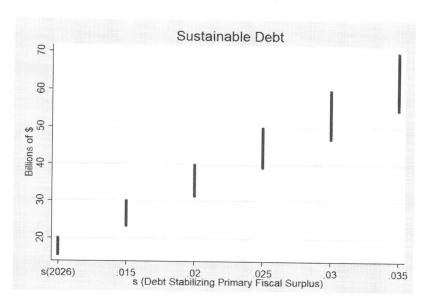

Table 10: Sustainable debt under the Fiscal Plan assumption on the effects of structural reforms on GNP growth, in billions of $

Debt stabilizing primary surplus to GNP since 2027	No. of scenarios	Sustainable Debt (Billions of USD)		
		Minimun	Maximun	Under government multiplier assumptions
s2026	192	15.7	19.9	19.2
0.015	192	23.5	29.9	28.8
0.02	192	31.3	39.9	38.5
0.025	192	39.2	49.8	48.1
0.03	192	47.0	59.8	57.7
0.035	192	54.8	69.8	67.3

Figure 8: Sustainable debt under the assumption that structural reforms have no effects on GNP growth, In billions of $

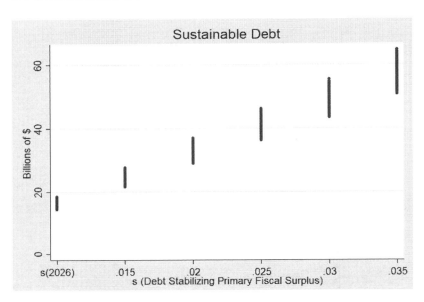

Table 11: Sustainable debt under the assumption that structural reforms have no effects on GNP growth, In billions of $

Debt stabilizing primary surplus to GNP since 2027	No. of scenarios	Sustainable Debt (Billions of USD)		
		Minimun	Maximun	Under government multiplier assumptions
s2026	192	14.5	18.5	17.8
0.015	192	21.8	27.7	26.7
0.02	192	29.0	37.0	35.7
0.025	192	36.3	46.2	44.6
0.03	192	43.5	55.4	53.5
0.035	192	50.8	64.7	62.4

Table 12: Fiscal Plan projections of primary fiscal surpluses to GNP ratio, 2017-2026

Year	2017	2018	2019	2020	2021	2022	2023	2024	2025	2026
5	0.0161	0.0107	0.0089	0.0114	0.017	0.0145	0.0137	0.0118	0.0112	0.0122

Source: Fiscal Plan 2017–2026.

Computing the necessary debt relief to restore debt sustainability

The debt position that can be deemed as sustainable with high probability depends on the path of fiscal policies that are considered feasible.

To compute the necessary relief to restore sustainability, we first compute the stabilizing debt to GNP ratio for values of from the value that corresponds to each of our projections for 2026, s_{2026} (the range of these values goes from 0.012 to 0.016) to a maximum of 0.035. Next, we calculate the necessary relief for restoring sustainability as the difference between the debt to GNP ratio in scenario i in 2026 and the stabilizing debt to GNP ratio for $s = \{s_{2026}, 0.015, 0.02, 0.025, 0.03, 0.035\}$.

We perform these computations for two groups of scenarios:
(i) First, we assume that the Fiscal Plan's assumptions on the effects of the structural reforms on GNP hold.
(ii) Second, we assume that the structural reforms stated in the Fiscal Plan have no effects on GNP growth during the period 2017-2026.

The results are summarized in figures 3 to 8 and in tables 6 to 11. The results show the necessary face value reduction in the different scenarios under analysis for restoring debt sustainability, assuming the debt service scheduled in the Fiscal Plan will be respected, and not taking into account the devastating effects of the hurricanes Maria and Irma as well as the effects of the Federal aid as a response to those natural disasters.

To reach a conclusion on the necessary relief needs for Puerto Rico, we need to take a stance on the set of feasible values of s. Even under the most optimistic projections the economy is projected to have a lower GNP in 2026 than in 2016, and as was described above, the projected debt to GNP ratio absent a restructuring is projected to be larger. The Fiscal Plan projects the evolution of primary fiscal surplus to GNP ratios that is described in Table 12. Requiring a larger after 2027 than the values of s_{2026} would not be a sensible stance; the economy is projected to be in worse in shape 2027 than at the moment we perform this analysis, hence being even more ambitious in terms of the fiscal targets would not lead to better outcomes than the ones projected for the next decade. Instead, being overly ambitious with the primary fiscal surplus targets would most likely lead to another lost decade after 2027.

For a stable primary fiscal surplus after 2027 that takes values between s_{2026} and 1.5 percent of GNP, the necessary debt reduction includes the full cancellation of interest payments not scheduled for repayment in the Fiscal Plan plus a face value reduction that under the Fiscal Plan assumptions should be between 44.4 percent and 63 percent if the relevant debt stock is $51.9 billions (table 6, column "Face value reduction under Fiscal Plan multiplier assumptions"), and between 60.1 percent and 73.4 percent if the relevant debt stock is $72.2 billions (table 7, column "Face value reduction under Fiscal Plan multiplier assumptions"). Under a broader range of assumptions that include different values for the fiscal multipliers and under the assumption of no effects of structural reforms on GNP growth, the debt reduction should include the full cancellation of interest payments not included in the Fiscal Plan plus a face value reduction of between 46.6 and 72 percent if the relevant debt stock is the one included in the Fiscal Plan of $51.9 billions (Table 8, column "Min Face Value Reduction" for $s = 0.015$ and column "Max Face Value Reduction" for $s = s_{2026}$, respectively), or between 61.6 and 79.9 percent if the relevant debt stock is the figure of $72.2 billions that we achieve once we take into account other debts not included in the Fiscal Plan (Table 9, column "Min Face Value Reduction" for and column "Max Face Value Reduction" for $s = s_{2026}$, respectively). Clearly, Puerto Rico needs substantial relief. But the interpretation of these results must take into account important caveats, to which we next turn our attention.

Interpretation of our results

Our computations show that in order to restore debt sustainability with high probability the restructuring should deliver a substantial reduction of Puerto Rico's debt. The figures we presented are "macroeconomic" figures that do not establish how the debt write-off should be distributed across the different bond series. And these are conservative estimates due to a number of reasons.

First, throughout we have kept all the computations the Fiscal Plan's assumption that annual real GNP growth will reach 1 percent in 2027, and we assume that this will correspond to a new steady state. But if the Fiscal Plan 2017–2026 is respected, for the reasons discussed in this study, getting to that state will be an unlikely outcome. If no expansionary aggregate demand policies are implemented to escape out of the current depression, the necessary relief to restore sustainability will have to be even larger. Puerto Rico has no debt service capacity today, and if it does not recover, it will not improve its payment capacity in the future either.

Second, as we described above, in every step of our analysis we made conservative assumptions as to err on the "too little" side of debt relief.

A final caveat is that we do not study how the write-off will be distributed, and this is an issue that will have macroeconomic effects. The expansionary effects of the restructuring will be increasing in the fraction of the write-off that falls on external bondholders, rather than on domestic bondholders, as the marginal propensity to spend in Puerto Rico's economy is lower for external than for domestic bondholders. The evidence supports this basic theoretical insight, as it shows that the macroeconomic costs of a default are increasing in the proportion of debt held by domestic residents (see Alessandro 2011;

Guembel and Sussman 2014) and are highly related to the transmission through the balance sheets of domestic banks (cf. Gennaioli, Martin, and Rossi 2014).[29]

GNP linked bonds

A non-contingent debt relief is always exposed to the risk that ex-post the relief ends being "too little"—harming the recovery—or "too much"—implying that creditors could have got more without undermining sustainability. To deal with the uncertainty that is present at the time of the restructuring, the debt restructuring could include GNP growth linked bonds, which relate the debt payments to the evolution of the territory's GNP. These instruments would improve sustainability, as the payments would be related to the payment capacity of the debtor; and they would also align the interests of creditors and the debtor, as both would benefit from a larger recovery. The economic rationale has been largely developed in the literature.[30]

Despite their virtues, the implementation of this type of contingent debt has not been straightforward. In practice, securities with a return linked to economic growth have been issued only in the context of a few debt restructurings, including those in Bulgaria (1994), Argentina (2005),[31] Greece (2012), and Ukraine (2015). To date, no advanced economy has issued growth-indexed bonds in normal times. But the support in policy spheres has been increasing (Blanchard, Mauro, and Acalin, 2016).

5. CONCLUSIONS

The most urgent policy that Puerto Rico needs is a debt restructuring that provides substantial debt relief. This paper made two main contributions that intend to shed light on the island's debt restructuring needs. First, we examined the consequences of the Fiscal Plan for the period 2017–2026 and identified a number of problems with its assumptions. Second, our analysis informs what are the actual restructuring needs of the country.

ACKNOWLEDGEMENTS

We wish to thank Gustavo J. Bobonis, Deepak Lamba-Nieves, Sergio M. Marxuach, Daniel Santamaria Ots, Brad Setser, Zaakir Tameez, and Jennifer Wolff for valuable discussions; Espacios Abiertos and its director Cecille Blondet-Passalacqua for the encouragement and support to our work on Puerto Rico's debt crisis; and four anonymous reviewers and participants of a seminar at the University of Puerto Rico Law School for useful comments. Usual caveats apply. Martin Guzman and Joseph Stiglitz are grateful to the Institute for New Economic Thinking for supporting their research agenda on debt crises resolution.

NOTES

[1] For a non-technical account of the evolution of events that preceded the debt crisis, see Guzman (2018).

[2] Net of Children's Trust's and HFA's debts, the reason for excluding the debts of those two entities being that their payment is not the responsibility of residents of Puerto Rico.

[3] The literature on the principles that should be respected in a restructuring process significantly grown over the last few years. For instance, see Blankenburg and Kozul-Wright (2016), Bohoslavsky and Goldmann (2016), Goldmann (2016), Guzman and Stiglitz (2016a, 2016b), Kolb (2006), Raffer (2016), and Li (2015).

[4] See, for example, Jayadev and Konczal (2010, 2015), Auerbach and Gorodnichenko (2012a, 2012b, 2012c, 2012d); Eggertsson and Krugman (2012); Herndon, Ash, and Polish (2014), Jorda and Taylor (2013); see also the commentaries by Krugman (2010, 2013, 2015) and Stiglitz (2010a).

[5] See Krugman (1988a). The destabilizing dynamics at play in the context of a financial crisis has been thoroughly analyzed in the macroeconomics literature by seminal authors as Fisher (1933), Keynes (1936), Minsky (1977, 1992), Kindleberger (1978), Leijonhufvud (1981), Stiglitz and Heymann (2014), Koo (2003), and Eggertsson and Krugman (2014), among many others.

[6] In Puerto Rico, the sub-utilization of factors can rapidly turn into migration, a phenomenon that would not be captured by measures of intensity of use of the available factors of production.

[7] This claim has been demonstrated by Krugman (1988b), who demonstrates that the expected present discounted value of payments for creditors takes the shape of a Laffer curve as a function of the value of the debtor's total liabilities. The reason is that the probability of default, and thus the interest rate, is an increasing function of the debt burden. Sachs (1989) also emphasizes the potential welfare benefits of forgiving debt in a situation of debt overhang, in a model where both creditors and debtors can gain from a partial debt write-down, since an excessive debt stock and the prospect of large future debt repayments act as a tax on domestic investment and depress the present value of claims held by investors. Under those conditions, debt relief should be followed by a period of higher growth.

[8] The theoretical literature suggests, however, that the costs arising from the exclusion from financial markets may be less than is often feared, because capital markets are forward looking. Indeed, by reducing existing debt obligations, a default may make lending to the country more attractive. See Stiglitz (2010b).

[9] Debt restructuring renegotiations under insufficient legal frameworks for dealing with col-

lective action problems also result in inefficient delays that reduce output (Benjamin and Wright 2009; Pitchford and Wright 2012).

[10] The literature also suggests that defaults have dire political consequences for incumbent governments and finance ministers (Borensztein and Panizza 2009).

[11] Auerbach and Gorodnichenko (2012b, 2012c), using regime-switching models, estimate the effects of fiscal policies over the business cycle and find that fiscal policy is considerably more effective in recessions than expansions. They provide estimates for multipliers for disaggregate spending variables for US regions. Military spending has the largest multiplier: estimates range from 3.69, with standard error of 0.83 (Auerbach and Gorodnichenko, 2012c) to 1.67, with standard error of 0.72 (Auerbach and Gorodnichenko, 2012b). The estimates for non-defense spending multipliers range from 1.34, with standard error of 0.31, to 1.09, with the same standard error. These values demonstrate the effect of $1 of additional spending on output; for example, according to Auerbach and Gorodnichenko (2012c) an additional dollar of public spending in the non-defense sector increases output by $1.34. In the expansion, the defense spending multiplier changes sign: it ranges from -1.03, with standard error of 0.25 (Auerbach and Gorodnichenko, 2012c), to -0.43, with standard error of 0.24 (Auerbach and Gorodnichenko, 2012b). And the non-defense spending multiplier keeps the positive sign but the magnitudes are smaller: it ranges from 1.17, with standard error of 0.15 (Auerbach and Gorodnichenko, 2012c), to 1.03, with the same standard error (Auerbach and Gorodnichenko, 2012b). Auerbach and Gorodnichenko (2012a) also estimate fiscal multipliers for OECD economies. The effects in recessions are stronger for this group of economies: Their point estimate is that an increase of government purchases of $1 results in about $3.50 of added GDP when the economy is weak, with a 90 percent confidence interval running from 0.6 to 6.3. On the other hand, in times of a strong economy, added government purchases reduce GDP, according to the point estimate. The confidence interval for that estimate includes moderate positive values. In all those estimates, the effects of fiscal policies are not necessarily concentrated in one year, but can be accumulated over time. The IMF has also recognized the importance of considering the non-linear nature of multipliers (Blanchard and Leigh, 2013). This recognition received special attention as the calls for a reconsideration of the methodology for assessing debt sustainability and the assumptions on multipliers had intensified after the dramatic consequences that the underestimation of the impact of fiscal austerity had for Greece, and also for other European economies in distress (see Guzman and Heymann, 2015). Another estimate is provided by Nakamura and Steinsson (2014), who using historical data on military procurement to estimate the effects of government spending, obtain a so-called "open economy relative multiplier" of approximately 1.5—the "open economy relative multiplier" estimates the effects on output that an increase in government spending in one region of the union relative to another, and differs from the "closed economy aggregate multiplier" that is estimated using aggregate US data. More recently, Chodorow-Reich (2017), based on an analysis of the American Recovery Reinvestment Act and of a survey of empirical studies, suggests that his "preferred" point estimate of the cross-sectional fiscal spending to output multiplier lies around 1.8.

[12] Auerbach and Gorodnichenko (2012b, 2012c) also offer evidence on the impulse-responses regarding the effects of an increase in public spending on tax revenues. For non-defense

spending, the tax revenues response to an increase in $1 ranges from $0 to $1. See the Figure A.3 in the appendix of Auerbach and Gorodnichenko (2012c) and the Figure A.3 in the appendix of Auerbach and Gorodnichenko (2012b).

[13] See Ilzetki, Mendoza, and Végh (2012).

[14] In a context of favorable international conditions and under the implementation of a policy of competitive and effectively multiple real exchange rates, GDP grew more than 8 percent on average from 2003 until the eruption of the global financial crisis in 2008 (see also Damill, Frenkel, and Rapetti (2015) for a more comprehensive description of the post-default dynamics, and Guzman, Ocampo, and Stiglitz (2018) for a description of the rationale of those policies and their importance in the Argentine post-default recovery). These conditions are markedly different than the ones Puerto Rico will face after its debt restructuring.

[15] The latter multiplier includes the time sub-index , because we assume constant values for the elasticities of fiscal revenues to public spending, hence the multiplier will vary over time with the variations in the fiscal revenues to public spending ratio.

[16] Not all the measures on the fiscal revenues side will lead to a reduction of Puerto Ricans' spending. For instance, while the Fiscal Plan plans to replace Act 154 by taxes that would achieve the current revenues over the next decade, if Act 154 was replaced with a tax that is paid by multinationals there would be no associated depressing effect on Puerto Rico's economy. Our conservative range of assumptions for the multiplier of tax revenues on output accounts for the possibility of a less depressing effect of revenues measures relative to public spending measures. It must be noted, however, that there is uncertainty about Act 154 being replaced by a scheme that has no cost on Puerto Ricans. This will depend on Federal policies that are beyond Puerto Rico's reach, which adds a layer of uncertainty to the projections of the effects of the Fiscal Plan. This uncertainty is indeed a matter of major concern. Makoff and Setser explain that "how Puerto Rico will do so [Act 154 will eventually be replaced by a set of taxes that maintain current levels of revenue over the next 10 years] is a great mystery: nobody has explained how Puerto Rico will continue to collect the same amount of revenue from the tax-allergic multinational corporations if federal forbearance on credibility lapses" (2017, 23).

[17] For a non-technical summary of the findings presented in this section, see Guzman and Stiglitz (2017).

[18] Public investments do not only affect supply formation but also have demand multiplier effects.

[19] These assumptions were made by the Fiscal Board and accepted by Puerto Rico's government.

[20] The definition of a recession comes from a calibration that is consistent with the duration of recessions according to the NBER business cycle dates since 1946.

[21] While migration is likely to reduce the need for certain categories of government expenditures, these effects are likely to be overwhelmed by the effects on the territory's income and tax revenues.

[22] If it did take those endogenous feedback effects into account, this would mean that the multiplier associated with the contraction in spending assumed by the plan is not 1.34 but lower.

[23] Makoff and Setser provide a detailed analysis of Puerto Rico's migration dynamics in its recent history and argue that the Fiscal Plan's assumptions on migration over the next decade are off. In their words: "Something is off here. How does the economy drop by 12 percent over

10 years and the population by only two percent? How does the rate of net migration improve from its current run rate of -2 percent a year to only -0.2 percent a year at the same time that the island is being hit by a significant cut in jobs and services? Absent a miraculous shift in household sentiment, Puerto Rico's population will certainly fall by more than the plan projects" (2017, 16). They also observe that the Puerto Rico Institute of Statistics reported that the new Census Bureau outmigration projection for the next 10 years is 1.4 percent annually.

[24] An additional concern, not analyzed in this study but in Makoff and Setser (2017), is that the baseline trend of Puerto Rico's economy may be worse than projected by the Fiscal Plan. They point out that while the Fiscal Plan takes a continued fall of the economy on its historic trend (about 1.5 percent a year since 2005) as the baseline scenario, this is a controversial assumption, "because the territory's historic downward trajectory likely would have been much worse if it were not for the billions of dollars injected into the economy through emergency federal transfers (Obamacare, the American Recovery Act stimulus and the backdoor transfer provided by the federal tax treatment of Act 154), the commonwealth's aggressive debt financings (primarily general obligation, "GO," and sales tax backed, "COFINA," bonds), and the depletion of Puerto Rico's public pension plan assets to pay benefits (Makoff and Setser 2017, 16).

[25] The fiscal plan does not specify whether the output growth baseline assumptions already incorporate the effects of a planned debt restructuring. If they do, the projections would be including the effects of a debt restructuring through the baseline assumptions instead of doing it through the macroeconomic multipliers that would be associated with the need for lower primary fiscal surpluses. If the baseline assumptions already incorporate the effects of an eventual restructuring, incorporating those effects in the macroeconomic multipliers would lead to an overestimation of the beneficial effects of a restructuring—they would be counted twice. It is possible though to replicate the analysis under alternative (less optimistic) baseline assumptions to deal with this possibility. All the codes for the projections are publicly available at <http://espaciosabiertos.org/analisis-de-alivio-de-deuda-para-sostenibilidad-del-pais/>.

[26] <http://espaciosabiertos.org/wp-content/uploads/2018/01/Online-Appendix-DSA-2018.01.pdf

[27] For each public spending to real GNP multiplier, once we take into account the endogenous feedback effects from public spending contractions on tax revenues, we can find a lower associated value of .

[28] In essence, this procedure computes the fixed point that satisfies both equation (1) and the intertemporal budget constraint associated with each scenario.

[29] There are important binding constraints for designing a selective default strategy that requires targeting the bondholdings of foreigners, as these bonds are actively traded in secondary markets (see Broner, Martin, and Ventura 2010; Broner and Ventura 2011). However, the transfer from domestic bondholders to the territory that the restructuring would entail will still be expansionary in the short run if the government uses the funds for policies that have a larger macroeconomic expansionary effect. And the larger space for public policies can also have positive long-term consequences.

[30] See Borensztein and Mauro (2004) for a review, and Barr, Bush, and Pienkowski (2014) for a more recent contribution, as well as Robert Shiller's related proposal to create "macro mar-

kets" for GDP-linked securities (Shiller 1993, 2003).

[31] Argentina implemented a variant of known as GDP warrants. But the results of the experiment were ambiguous. On the one hand, the warrants paid off extremely well, benefitting the creditors who kept them in their portfolios. But on the other hand, they were not well received by markets at the time of issuance. This may have had to do with their complex design, that made pricing difficult: the trigger for the payment was a threshold growth rate of GDP, but the formula for the amount of payments depended on the difference between the actual level of GDP and a threshold level (see Cruces and Samples (2016), Guzman (2016), and Benford, Best, and Joy (2016) for details).

REFERENCES

Aguiar, Mark and Gita Gopinath. 2006. Defaultable Debt, Interest Rates and the Current Account. *Journal of International Economics* 69, 64–83.

Alessandro, Mauro. 2011. Three Essays on Sovereign Debt and Financial Markets. Ph.D. dissertation, MIT.

Arellano, Cristina. 2008. Default Risk and Income Fluctuations in Emerging Economies. *American Economic Review* 98(3), 690–712.

Auerbach, Alan and Yuriy Gorodnichenko. 2012a. Fiscal Multipliers in Recession and Expansion. In *Fiscal Policy after the Financial Crisis*, eds. Alberto Alesina and Francesco Giavazzi. Chicago: University of Chicago Press.

_____. 2012b. Measuring the Output Responses to Fiscal Policy. *American Economic Journal – Economic Policy* 4, 1–27.

_____. 2012c. Measuring the Output Responses to Fiscal Policy. NBER Working Paper No. 16311.

_____. 2012d. Output Spillovers from Fiscal Policy. NBER Working Paper No. 18578.

Barr, David, Oliver Bush and Alex Pienkowski. 2014. GDP-Linked Bonds and Sovereign Default. In *Life After Debt*, eds. Joseph Stiglitz and Daniel Heymann. 246–75. London: Palgrave Macmillan.

Basualdo, Eduardo, Pablo Manzanelli, Mariano Barrera, Andrés Wainer,and Leandro Bona. 2015. Deuda externa, fuga de capitales y restricción externa. Desde la última dictadura militar hasta la actualidad. CEFIDAR, Documento de Trabajo No. 68, Abril.

Benford, James, Thomas Best and Mark Joy. 2016. Sovereign GDP-Linked Bonds. Bank of England, Financial Stability Paper No. 39, September.

Benjamin, David and Mark L. J. Wright. 2009. Recovery Before Redemption: A Theory of Delays in Sovereign Debt Renegotiations. SSRN <https://papers.ssrn.com/sol3/papers.cfm?abstract_id=1392539/>.

Blanchard, Olivier and Daniel Leigh. 2013. Growth Forecast Errors and Fiscal Multipliers. IMF Working Paper, Research Department, WP/13/1.

Blanchard, Olivier, Paolo Mauro and Julien Acalin. 2016. The Case for Growth-Indexed Bonds in Advanced Economies Today. Peterson Institute for International Economics Policy Brief 16-2.

Blankenburg, Stephanie and Richard Kozul-Wright. 2016. Sovereign Debt Restructurings in the Contemporary Global Economy: The UNCTAD Approach. *Yale Journal of International Law* 41(2), 1–7.

Bohoslavsky, Juan Pablo. 2016. Economic Inequality, Debt Crises and Human Rights. *Yale Journal of International Law* 41(2), 177–99.

Borensztein, Eduardo and Paolo Mauro. 2004. The Case for GDP-Indexed Bonds. *Economic Policy* 19(38), 166–216.

Borensztein, Eduardo and Ugo Panizza. 2009. The Costs of Sovereign Default. *IMF Staff Papers* 56(4), 683–741.

Broner, Fernando, Alberto Martin and Jaume Ventura. 2010. Sovereign Risk and Secondary Markets. *The American Economic* Review 100(4), 1523–55.

Broner, Fernando and Jaume Ventura. 2011. Globalization and Risk Sharing. *The Review of Economic Studies* 78(1), 49–82.

Bulow, Jeremy and Kenneth Rogoff. 1989. A Constant Recontracting Model of Sovereign Debt. *Journal of Political Economy* 97, 155–78.

Celasun, Oya, Xavier Debrun and Jonathan Ostry. 2006. Primary Surplus Behavior and Risks to Fiscal Sustainability in Emerging Market Countries: A "Fan-Chart" Approach. International Monetary Fund Working Paper 06/67.

Chodorow-Reich, Gabriel. 2017. Geographic Cross-Sectional Fiscal Spending Multiplier: What Have We Learned? NBER Working Paper No. 23577, July.

Chodos, Sergio. 2016. From the Pari Passu Discussion to the "Illegality" of Making Payments: The Case of Argentina. In *Too Little, Too Late: The Quest to Resolve Sovereign Debt Crises.* 77–83. New York: Columbia University Press.

Cole, Harold L. and Patrick Kehoe. 1998. Models of Sovereign Debt: Partial versus General Reputations. *International Economic Review* 39, 55–70.

Consiglio, Andrea and Stavros A. Zenios. 2015. Risk Management Optimization for Sovereign Debt Restructuring. *Journal of Globalization and Development* 6, 181–213.

_____. 2017. Stochastic Debt Sustainability Analysis for Sovereigns and the Scope for Optimization Modeling. *Optimization and Engineering* 8(2), 537–58.

Cruces, Juan José and Christoph Trebesch. 2013. Sovereign Defaults: The Price of Haircuts. *American Economic Journal: Macroeconomics* 5, 85–117.

Cruces, Juan Jose and Tim Samples. 2016. Settling Sovereign Debt's Trial of the Century. *Emory International Law Review* 31, 5–47.

Damill, Mario, Roberto Frenkel and Martín Rapetti. 2015. Macroeconomic Policy in Argentina During 2002–2013. *Comparative Economic Studies* 57(3), 369–400.

Eaton, Jonathan and Mark Gersovitz. 1981. Debt with Potential Repudiation: Theoretical and Empirical Analysis. *Review of Economic Studies* 48, 289–309.

Edwards, Sebastian. 2015a. Sovereign Default, Debt Restructuring, and Recovery Rates: Was the Argentinean 'Haircut' Excessive? *Open Economies Review* 26, 839–67.

_____. 2015b. Argentina's Haircut as an Outlier. *VoxEU* 4 March.

Fisher, Irving. 1933. The Debt-deflation Theory of Great Depressions. *Econometrica: Journal of the Econometric Society* 1(4), 337–57.

Galofré-Vilà, Gregori, Martin McKee, Christopher M. Meissner and David Stuckler. 2016. The Economic Consequences of the 1953 London Debt Agreement. National Bureau of Economic Research Working Paper No. 22557.

Gennaioli, Nicola, Alberto Martin and Stefano Rossi. 2014. Sovereign Default, Domestic Banks, and Financial Institutions. *The Journal of Finance* 69(2), 819–66.

Goldmann, Matthias. 2016. Putting your Faith in Good Faith: A Principled Strategy for Smoother Sovereign Debt Workouts. *Yale Journal of International Law* 41(2), 117–40.

Guembel, Alexander and Oren Sussman. 2009. Sovereign Debt Without Default Penalties. *The Review of Economic Studies* 76(4), 1297–320.

Guzman, Martin. 2016a. Reestructuración de Deuda Soberana en una Arquitectura Financiera-Legal con Huecos. *Revista Jurídica, Universidad de Puerto Rico* 85(3), 611–27.

_____. 2016b. An Analysis of Argentina's 2001 Default Resolution. Centre for International Governance Innovation Paper No. 110.

_____. 2018. Down for the Count? *Milken Institute Review* 27 April. <http://www.milkenreview.org/articles/down-for-the-count/>.

Guzman, Martin and Daniel Heymann. 2015. The IMF Debt Sustainability Analysis: Issues and Problems. *Journal of Globalization and Development* 6(2), 387–404.

Guzman, Martin and Domenico Lombardi. 2017. Assessing the Appropriate Size of Relief in Sovereign Debt Restructuring. Columbia Business School Research Paper No. 18-9.

Guzman, Martin, Jose Antonio Ocampo and Joseph E. Stiglitz, eds. 2016. *Too Little, Too Late: The Quest to Resolve Sovereign Debt Crises*. New York: Columbia University Press.

Guzman, Martin, Jose Antonio Ocampo and Joseph E. Stiglitz. 2018. Real Exchange Rate Policies for Economic Development. *World Development* 110, 51–62.

Guzman, Martin and Joseph E. Stiglitz. 2016a. Creating a Framework for Sovereign Debt Restructuring that Works. In *Too Little, Too Late: The Quest to Resolve Sovereign Debt Crises*, eds. Martin Guzman, Jose Antonio Ocampo and Joseph E. Stiglitz. Chapter 1. New York: Columbia University Press.

_____. 2016b. A Soft Law Mechanism for Sovereign Debt Restructuring Based on the UN Principles. *International Policy Analysis* October.

_____. 2017. PROMESA's Dangerous Premises. *Project Syndicate* 18 September.

Hagan, Sean, Maurice Obstfeld and Poul Thomsen. 2017. Dealing with Sovereign Debt—The IMF Perspective. <https://blogs.imf.org/2017/02/23/dealing-with-sovereign-debt-the-imf-perspective/>.

Herndon, Thomas, Michael Ash and Robert Pollin. 2014. Does High Public Debt Consistently Stifle Economic Growth? A Critique of Reinhart and Rogoff.

Cambridge Journal of Economics 38(2), 257–79.

Ilzetzki, Ethan, Enrique G. Mendoza and Carlos A. Végh. 2013. How Big (Small?) are Fiscal Multipliers? *Journal of Monetary Economics* 60(2), 239–54.

IMF. 2011. Modernizing the Framework for Fiscal Policy and Public Debt Sustainability Analysis. Prepared by the Fiscal Affairs Department and the Strategy, Policy, and Review Department. Approved by Carlo Cottarelli and Reza Moghadam.

_____. 2013. Staff Guidance Note for Public Debt Sustainability Analysis in Market-Access Countries. Approved by Siddharth Tiwari.

Jayadev, Arjun and Mike Konczal. 2010. The Boom not the Slump: The Right Time for Austerity. University of Massachusetts Boston, ScholarWorks at UMass Boston, Economics Faculty Publication Series.

_____. 2015. Searching for Expansionary Austerity. University of Massachusetts Boston Working Paper.

Jordà, Òscar, and Alan M. Taylor. 2013. The Time for Austerity: Estimating the Average Treatment Effect of Fiscal Policy. Working Paper No. 19414. National Bureau of Economic Research.

Keynes, J. M. 1936. *The General Theory of Employment, Interest and Money.* London: Macmillan and Co., Limited.

Kindleberger, Charles. 1978. *Manias, Panics, and Crashes: A History of Financial Crises.* New York: Palgrave Macmillan.

Kolb, Robert. 2006. Principles as Sources of International Law (with Special Reference to Good Faith). *Netherlands International Law Review* 53(1), 1–36.

Krugman, Paul. 1988a. Market-Based Debt-Reduction Schemes. NBER Working Paper No. 2587.

_____. 1988b. Financing vs. Forgiving a Debt Overhang. *Journal of Development Economics* 29(3), 253–68.

_____. 2010. Myths of Austerity. *The New York Times* 1 July.

_____. 2013. How the Case for Austerity has Crumbled. *The New York Review of Books* 6 June.

_____. 2015. The Expansionary Austerity Zombie, The Conscience of a Liberal. *The New York Times* 20 November.

Koo, R. 2003. *Balance Sheet Recession: Japan's Struggle with Uncharted Economics and Its Global Implications.* New York: John Wiley & Sons.

Leijonhufvud, Axel. 1981. *Information and Coordination: Essays in Macroeconomic Theory.* New York: Oxford University Press.

Li, Yuefen. 2015. The Long March Towards an International Legal Framework for Sovereign Debt Restructuring. *Journal of Globalization and Development* 6(2), 329–41.

Makoff, Gregory and Brad Setser. 2017. Puerto Rico Update: PROMESA, Population Trends, Risks to the Fiscal and Economic Plan — and Now Maria. CIGI Paper No. 146.

Minsky, Hyman P. 1977. The Financial Instability Hypothesis: An Interpretation of
      Keynes and an Alternative to "Standard" Theory. *Challenge* 20(1), 20–7.
_____. 1992. The Financial Instability Hypothesis. Levy Economics Institute
      Working Paper No. 74.
Nakamura, Emi and Jon Steinsson. 2014. Fiscal Stimulus in a Monetary Union:
      Evidence from US Regions. *The American Economic Review* 104(3), 753–92.
Pitchford, Rohan and Mark L. J. Wright. 2012. Holdouts in Sovereign Debt
      Restructuring: A Theory of Negotiation in a Weak Contractual
      Environment. *Review of Economic Studies* 79, 812–37.
Raffer, Kunibert. 2016. Debts, Human Rights, and the Rule of Law: Advocating a
      Fair and Efficient Sovereign Insolvency Model. In *Too Little, Too Late: The
      Quest of Resolving Sovereign Debt Crises*, eds. Martin Guzman, José Antonio
      Ocampo and Joseph Stiglitz. 253–68. New York: Columbia University Press.
Reinhart, Carmen M. and Christoph Trebesch. 2016. Sovereign Debt Relief and Its
      Aftermath. *Journal of the European Economic Association* 14, 215–51.
Sachs, Jeffrey. 1989. The Debt Overhang of Developing Countries. In *Debt
      Stabilization and Development*, eds. Guillermo A. Calvo, Ronald Findlay,
      Pentti Kouri and Jorge Braga de Macedo. New York: Basil Blackwell.
Sandleris, Guido. 2016. The Costs of Sovereign Default: Theory and Empirical
      Evidence. *Economia* 16(2), 1–27.
Shiller, Robert J. 1993. *Macro Markets: Creating Institutions for Managing Society's
      Largest Economic Risks*. Oxford: Clarendon Press.
_____. 2003. *The New Financial Order: Risk in the 21st Century*. Princeton, NJ:
      Princeton University Press.
Stiglitz, Joseph E. 2010a. The Dangers of Deficit Reduction. *The Economists' Voice*
      7(1), 1–3.
_____. 2010b. Sovereign Debt: Notes on Theoretical Frameworks and Policy
      Analyses. In *Overcoming Developing Country Debt Crises*, eds. B. Herman,
      J.A. Ocampo, and S. Spiegel. 35–69. New York: Oxford University Press.
Stiglitz, Joseph, and Daniel Heymann, eds. 2014. *Life After Debt: The Origins and
      Resolutions of Debt Crisis*. New York: Springer.
Varoufakis, Yanis. 2016. Greek Debt Denial. In *Too Little, Too Late: The Quest of
      Resolving Sovereign Debt Crises*, eds. Martin Guzman, José Antonio Ocampo
      and Joseph Stiglitz 84–108. New York: Columbia University Press.

Energy Policies in Puerto Rico and their Impact on the Likelihood of a Resilient and Sustainable Electric Power Infrastructure

EFRAÍN O'NEILL-CARRILLO AND MIGUEL A. RIVERA-QUIÑONES

ABSTRACT

Hurricane María uncovered the vulnerabilities and frailties of Puerto Rico's electric infrastructure--in particular, the anachronism of the present fossil-based, centralized generation in a Caribbean island with an excellent, distributed solar resource. However, transitioning to a different, more resilient and sustainable infrastructure requires much more than just bringing technological gadgets to communities or implementing microgrids. Without an understanding of Puerto Rico's social contexts and its energy policy history, any transformation initiative is at risk of failure, or as has happened in the past, will mostly benefit the many outsiders anxious to make business while leaving Puerto Ricans with technological nightmares or unintended consequences. This paper strives to remind policymakers (local and federal) of recent local policies and discuss how their outcomes exemplify the challenges that need to be addressed for a transition to a more distributed, sustainable and resilient electric infrastructure while truly fostering local socio-economic development. [Keywords: Electric energy, PREPA, sustainability, energy policy, electric infrastructure, distributed energy]

Efraín O'Neill (efrain.oneill@upr.edu) is Professor of Electrical Engineering at the University of Puerto Rico-Mayagüez. He is a Registered Professional Engineer and Senior Member of IEEE. He has been an ABET evaluator since 2006. Dr. O'Neill led the first distributed generation (DG) studies in Puerto Rico in 2002 and the first local microgrid studies. He is author of renewable energy and energy policy studies that have significantly influenced the local electric energy sector.

Introduction

After hurricane María hit Puerto Rico, all essential services, water, communications and electric energy collapsed. Many roads were destroyed, damaged, flooded, or obstructed due to landslides. News from some areas in Puerto Rico, especially the center of the island, were impossible to get due to an almost complete collapse of the communication infrastructure of the island. Furthermore, federal relief after the disaster arrived later and more slowly to Puerto Rico when compared to other affected areas in the continental U.S. This is due to the islanded condition and the distance from the closest continental U.S. port, as well as specific policy and institutional reasons. Had this been an earthquake, the death toll would have been enormous because the state government did not have the tools for a quick and efficient response. Hurricane María showed how vulnerable and alone Puerto Ricans are.

Why was the aftermath of María different than other post-hurricane recoveries? The winds and rain were unprecedented for modern Puerto Rican society; thus, the damage was unprecedented as well. The strongest hurricane in the last 80 years to go over Puerto Rican land (Georges) was a Category 3 hurricane. At the time (1998), Puerto Rico's economy was not as weakened as it had been previous to María; infrastructure-related agencies were still financially stable and were able to respond immediately; additionally, communications did not collapse completely after Georges.

The Federal government must ensure that the emergency relief and reconstruction funds are used effectively, not only for the immediate crisis, but to begin addressing the many aspects of emergency response that need fixing in the territory. This kind of approach will help reduce the amount of relief funds required during and after future emergencies, especially for the electric infrastructure. However, transitioning to a different, more resilient and sustainable infrastructure requires much more than just bringing technological gadgets to communities or implementing microgrids.

The first part of the paper provides relevant background on Puerto Rico and on its electric power infrastructure. Without an understanding of Puerto Rico's social contexts any transformation initiative risks failure, or as has happened in the past, will mostly benefit the many outsiders anxious to make business while leaving Puerto Ricans with technological nightmares or unintended consequences. Geri and McNabb's *Energy Policy in the U.S.: Politics, Challenges, and Prospects for Change* is used as framework to explain some of the outcomes of recent energy policies. Fur-

Miguel A. Rivera-Quiñones (miguel.rivera24@upr.edu) is Assistant Professor of Political Science at the University of Puerto Rico-Rio Piedras. He holds a PhD in International Relations from the University of Sussex, specializing in global political economy. He worked at the Institute of Development Studies (IDS) in the United Kingdom, where he was part of DFID-funded research project on livelihoods vulnerability in Bangladesh and lectured at the M.A. program on Governance and Development. He has 12 years of experience in projects related to policy processes, public financing, debt crisis and development in Argentina, Puerto Rico, Haiti, Pakistan, Bangladesh, Zambia and South America.

thermore, how PREPA's transformation efforts fell short is discussed. Finally, despite the deep financial problems and the aftermath of María, the potential for true transformative actions is looked at, emphasizing local distributed energy resources.

This paper is a reminder, especially for policymakers (local and federal), of recent local energy policies and discuss how their outcomes exemplify the challenges that need to be addressed for a transition to a more sustainable and resilient electric infrastructure while truly fostering local socio-economic development. In this article it is argued that the introduction of new technologies and Federal funding for infrastrucutre are not enough for a transition toward a sustainable and resilient electric infrastructure. For a transition in this direction, PREPA's governing structures should be decentralized and participatory, infrastructure investments should aim at a sustainable energy model and reforms should be framed with participation of all local political parties. The reform initiatives undertaken between 2007 and 2014 are used as case studies to show how recent experiences can inform proposed reforms. Process tracing was used as the method for analyzing the official documents and secondary sources used for documenting this study. The importance of using process tracing in this research is that it allows us to build a comprehensive and accurate account of the policy process used as a case study (Ludwig 2015, 5).

Brief History of Puerto Rico's Electric Power Infrastructure
A key factor of Puerto Rico's "economic miracle" in the mid-20th century was the electrification of the territory. This occurred with support from the Federal government through the "Puerto Rico Emergency Relief Administration" (PRERA), established in 1933 to give special attention to Puerto Rico's dire conditions during the Great Depression. In 1935 PRERA was substituted by the Puerto Rico Reconstruction Administration (PRRA), which used a two-pronged approach: dealing with unemployment and establishing an economic reconstruction program, including the rural electrification program, that allowed the construction of hydroelectric plants and distribution lines (Látimer 1993). Puerto Rican engineer Antonio Lucchetti was in charge of the local and federal efforts related to the hydroelectric program. In 1941 the Puerto Rico Water Resources Authority (AFF, its acronym in Spanish) was created through Act 83 to plan, design, construct, operate and maintain Puerto Rico's electric infrastructure. It has been the sole provider of electricity in Puerto Rico since 1941. It used the Tennessee Valley Authority (TVA) as a model to create a public power company (owned by the state government). Before that, private companies dominated the electric sector focusing on areas where their business could prosper, while not serving rural and remote areas. As part of the plans to take many Puerto Ricans out of the dire conditions they lived in during the 1930s, Antonio Lucchetti proposed to integrate all electric power systems in Puerto Rico. It was a socio-economic development strategy in which economies of scale would make electricity cheaper, industrial activity could be promoted and electricity would be affordable for more people. The private companies did not accept this easily, and complicated

court battles ensued. In the end, war time circumstances enabled the last acquisition of private power companies and the AFF was on its way to complete its mission: the electrification of Puerto Rico (Látimer 1993). Without the AFF's leadership, Puerto Rico's electrification would not have been as fast and as inexpensive as it was. It is important to emphasize that Lucchetti placed much attention in responsibly managing municipal bond issuances to build and support AFF's key infrastructure projects.

Before María hit, Puerto Rico's electric power infrastructure had an installed generating capacity of more than 5,000 MW, transmission lines of 230 kV and 115 kV, a sub-transmission system of 38 kV and thousands of distribution lines of diverse voltages (13.2 kV, 8.32 kV, 7.2 kV, 4.16 kV). A key technical weakness was that most of the central generating capacity is in the south, while the area with the largest power demand (and economic activity) is in the north. Thus, the transmission lines going from south to north were vital for Puerto Rico's economy and daily life[4] (Ortega 2017). The isolated nature of the electric system means that Puerto Rico does not have external support in case of major power disruptions.

PREPA's planning and operating vision was based on hierarchical control, centralized generation and top-down planning, with a condescending attitude toward non-PREPA persons, who just "could not understand the complexity of the electric grid."

The AFF successfully accomplished its founding mission in the 1970s. By then, many people began pointing out the need to make reforms to the AFF. This reform movement was fueled by the OPEC embargo of 1973, and indeed, many good initiatives took place, including the creation of a state energy office in 1977 to lead energy policy development and implementation in Puerto Rico. Unfortunately, once the '70s and early '80s oil crises went away, many of those reforms were abandoned or limited (O'Neill 2012). Even though its name changed in 1979 to the Puerto Rico Electric Power Authority (PREPA), the corporation's mission essentially remained the same as the one given in 1941.

Efforts to reform PREPA were unsuccessful through the '80s,' 90s and the first decade of the 2000s. Some groups insisted on reforming PREPA, and many ideas were presented to do just that. However, PREPA's management would repeatedly oppose any proposed changes arguing that it was against their given mission of providing electricity at the least cost possible. PREPA's management lobbied periodically in the Legislature to stop attempts to amend PREPA's law and its mission, claiming possible breaches of the Trust Agreement with bondholders. In many of these cases, PREPA would be supported by the Government Development Bank (BGF, its acronym in Spanish). PREPA's planning and operating vision was based on hierarchical control, centralized generation and top-down planning, with a condescending attitude toward non-PREPA persons, who just "could not understand the complexity of the electric grid." In a way, PREPA's management, through the last forty years, acted in the same way that the private companies did when they opposed the integration of the disconnected, private electrical systems in Puerto Rico: clinging to a way of running electrical systems that was losing touch with what Puerto Rico needed from its electric infrastructure.

Meanwhile, the social, environmental and economic costs of existing energy sources and practices continued to grow, and Puerto Ricans got used to patterns of inefficient and irresponsible energy use. Through the last quarter of the 20th century the territory remained 99 percent dependent on oil, the most expensive and polluting fossil fuel. This resulted in uncertainty in electricity prices (the cost of fuel was a pass-through charge to customers in the electric bill). The oil dependence was reduced in the early 2000s, when two independent power producers began operations in Puerto Rico. EcoEléctrica & AES use natural gas and coal, respectively, to generate electric power that they sell directly to PREPA under the federal mandate of the Public Utilities Regulatory Act (PURPA). However, Puerto Rico still depends on fossil fuels, not available locally. Furthermore, the environmental costs of coal and oil are still not properly accounted at the local or federal levels.

There were many factors that led to PREPA's financial debacle, such as the exodus of 1,000 industrial clients, excessive electric energy use patterns and the lack of public engagement. However, there were two main causes of PREPA's crisis: the multiple and constant interventions from party politics and politicians; and a narrow planning vision. Every political party that governed Puerto Rico used PREPA and other public institutions for its own purposes (Pantojas-Garcia 2016; Glanz and Robles 2018). As a public power company, it is acceptable for a Governor to provide policy direction to decisions related to electric infrastructure. In PREPA's case, however, policy directions were distorted, and sometimes supplanted by political directions, thus crushing the benefits of having an autonomous, public power company leading and managing the local electric infrastructure. For example, PREPA did not change its basic rates for 27 years (1989 to 2016), mainly due to political intervention even though by the late 1990s and early 2000s (after the departure of about 1,000 industrial clients); it was evident the basic rate structure was not enough to maintain PREPA operations. Basic rates were used to cover operating costs not including the cost of fuel. Thus, although customers would see high electricity costs, on average more than 70 percent of PREPA's income, would go to pay for fuel (billed to customers directly through an adjustment clause in the electric bill). PREPA kept issuing municipal bonds to artificially keep the same rate structures. It is important to note that PREPA might have identified and corrected inefficiencies (technical and organizational) to improve its finances and reduce its reliance on the municipal bond market.[5]

A narrow planning vision of top PREPA management degraded the public power model that Lucchetti established and that had served Puerto Rico well for many decades. The conservative, centralized planning vision became deeply engrained in management, regardless of who was Executive Director and who was in the Governing Board. The 2012 election of two consumer representatives to the Governing

Board brought some public access to PREPA, as well as a different, user-centered perspective (Cotto 2012; Irizarry 2013). Nevertheless, this was just a temporary shift. For example, the Integrated Resource Plan (IRP) presented by PREPA in 2015, insisted on the dominance of the centralized model, belittled the importance of conservation and efficiency, and refused to embrace Puerto Rico's local renewable resources. The IRP was a sad contrast to the fighting spirit of Lucchetti and his struggle to provide the island with an instrument for socio-economic development (i.e., the AFF). For Lucchetti, Puerto Rico's needs were first, not PREPA, which existed to serve the people. On the other hand, in the last forty years it seemed that PREPA's needs were first, not Puerto Rico's. It is important to point out that Puerto Rico needs PREPA's managers and planning professionals--people who know the electrical infrastructure and its limits well. The needed electric transformations require their support, knowledge and expertise in support of a new vision.

Sustainable energy policies and actions should come from a shared vision of Puerto Rico's future, and how energy strategies (electric energy as a subset) should be transformed to support that shared vision of our future. Understanding the local energy policy history is essential in crafting a shared energy vision, and in any plans to build a resilient and sustainable electric power infrastructure.

Synopsis of Energy Policies in Puerto Rico

A look back is necessary in order to learn from past mistakes and to understand the local context before committing to any energy future. This is especially true in Puerto Rico, given that technological solutions have been proposed and even built in the past without truly considering the local social contexts, resulting in unintended, negative consequences. The book by Geri and McNabb *Energy Policy in the U.S.: Politics, Challenges, and Prospects for Change* provides a suitable policy theory framework to understand some of the energy policies in Puerto Rico. Their definition of public policy describes it as a plan that guides a government or its agencies in actions dealing with issues of public concern, that shapes and is shaped by laws (Geri and McNabb 2011). But public policy is also shaped by public opinion: unless the public supports a policy, it will not succeed.

A comprehensive and coordinated energy policy is vital for a nation, not just isolated energy laws. However, a comprehensive energy policy does not happen often. Four main stakeholder energy perspectives exist based on very different values and goals: supply, demand, national security and environment. Energy policies are usually framed by some stakeholders more than others: The struggle at federal and state levels, and in public opinion, is often framing the problem (whose frame will "win" and why?). Major energy stakeholders, with political and/or economic influence, lobby to ensure that legislation unfavorable to their interests does not get passed or that favorable legislation passes (Geri and McNabb 2011). Thus, producing a comprehensive energy policy is very difficult. Another energy policy challenge is the short memory of policymakers. Policies do not change until elected politicians perceive a change in public opinion or new conditions force changes (Geri and McNabb 2011). Policy- makers often overlook the reasons behind existing policies when changing them, and whether existing policies are addressing an actual need or not.

In Puerto Rico there have not been consistent and enduring energy strategies and policies. The few instances that clear energy policies emerged were brief (e.g., the efforts of the late 1970s), but diverse sectors could not rally in support of a comprehensive energy policy that could withstand leadership changes in the local government. Changes in energy policy directions have been an obstacle to implement truly sustainable energy strategies and alternatives. This in turn has impeded approaching Puerto Rico's energy challenges from a holistic perspective. One notable exception was the net metering law, Act 114-2007 "Ley para establecer un programa de medición neta," which ordered PREPA to establish a net metering program for residential, commercial and industrial clients. The law was backed by a broad range of citizen and industry organizations as well as academia. A study from the Electric Power Research Institute (EPRI), commissioned by PREPA, found that there were no major obstacles for interconnection of distributed generation (key technical aspect to establish net metering). Act 248-2008 "Enmiendas al Código de Rentas Internas de Puerto Rico y a la Ley de Contribución Municipal sobre la Propiedad" provided customers with economic incentives to install renewable energy systems in their premises, which was later substituted by incentives from Act 83-2010 "Ley de Incentivos de Energía Verde de Puerto Rico." By 2017 more than 100 MW had been installed in net-metered systems at all levels, mostly photovoltaic (PV) systems in residential, commercial and industrial rooftops. Even though there have been problems with third-party ownership contracts and with permit delays from PREPA, as of December 2017 the net metering policies had been the most successful in moving the citizenry towards renewable energy (O'Neill 2016a).

Unfortunately, other recent energy policies and supporting laws have had limited success or unintended, negative consequences. For example, a wheeling mandate included in Act 73-2008 "Ley de Incentivos Económicos para el Desarrollo de Puerto Rico" ordered PREPA to establish a program through which a private generator could sell its energy to a private client via Puerto Rico's grid. As of December 2017, there was not even one wheeling transaction. This effort was perceived as a benefit for industrial clients without paying attention to the rate and service impact on other customers. The legislative process did not account for the legal, technical and social complexities of the Puerto Rican electric infrastructure. Furthermore, there was no regulatory framework to properly manage this type of operation that would ensure a safe and fair wheeling program (O'Neill 2016a). There was no technical study of the feasibility of wheeling in Puerto Rico. Nowadays, with the shift in focus to more distributed energy options due to Hurricane María, wheeling might not make much sense, considering it is still a centralized option that depends on vulnerable transmission lines to operate.

On the other hand, there have been good ideas turned into local energy policies that failed during the implementation stage. Act 82-2010 "Ley de Política Pública de Diversificación Energética por Medio de la Energía Renovable Sostenible y Alterna en Puerto Rico" set renewable energy goals for the first time in Puerto Rico through a renewable portfolio standard (RPS): 12 percent renewable energy by 2015, 15 percent for 2020 and 20 percent by 2035. The law ordered the creation of a market for renewable energy credits (REC), through which the amount of renewable energy sold at retail would be accounted for purposes of compliance with the RPS. Unfortunately, PREPA's Governing Board signed more than 60 contracts (power purchase agreements, PPAs) to buy more than 2,200MW from proposed large-scale renewable energy systems, at prices higher than previous PPAs PREPA had signed, and assigning value to the RECs even though the REC market had not been established yet. It is very important to remind policymakers that PREPA had signed, by 2009, PPAs for the purchase of wind energy at $0.09 per kWh (without RECs) as part of a plan to integrate 350 MW of large-scale wind energy systems (Cordero 2009). Thus, it makes no economic sense that the PPAs signed later by PREPA up to 2012 were for $0.125 per kWh plus 2.5 cents per kWh for wind energy (a total of $0.15 per kWh for wind) and for $0.15 per kWh plus 3.5 cents per kWh for solar energy (a total of $0.185 per kWh for solar). Furthermore, there was no technical way to integrate 2,200 MW of renewable energy in a system whose peak power demand was around 3,000 MW at the time (without causing severe stability and service problems in the power grid). Had PREPA stuck with its original plan to regionally integrate wind energy, after a competitive bidding process, in the best places (environmentally, socially and technically), at the lowest possible prices, Puerto Rico would have had today much more than the 2 percent we have of renewable energy participation. Further details of the erratic, local energy policies can be found in O'Neill (2016ab).

In summary, there have been examples of good policies (e.g., net metering and the RPS) that have suffered from obstacles or implementation errors, mainly from PREPA.

Stakeholder Engagement As Part of the energy Policy Process

The short memory of policymakers in Puerto Rico, and their susceptibility to be influenced by stakeholders with economic and political power, warrants a different approach to establish policies in support of sustainable and resilient energy strategies and technologies. An approach grounded in people's concerns and lived experience is suggested in Geri and McNabb 2011. Policy communities can be created to discuss energy visions and the policies of support that are needed. Minimum common ground can be identified through dialogue among sectors having different perspectives, and used to build the shared energy vision mentioned earlier. "Forums that encourage the formation and maintenance of cross-cutting relationships at the local level must be nurtured," while experts can become "skilled facilitators of citizens, to help them engage in policy discourse" (Geri and McNabb 2011). A local example of such forums is the Energy Roundtable, created in 2008 as a reaction to the public debate in Puerto Rico about wheeling. This was a multi-sector group composed of representatives from academia, community organizations, industry, the state energy office, PREPA's management and PREPA's largest labor union that was able to craft a shared vision for the future of the electric system in Puerto Rico (O'Neill 2016c).[6]

Puerto Rico's energy policy was defined as a continuous process of planning, inquiry, execution, evaluation and improvement regarding all energy issues.

Using the visions proposed by various citizen groups, including the Energy Round-table and Town Hall meetings held in three municipalities in Puerto Rico during March 2013 (Gobernador anuncia... 2013), a new paradigm in energy policy was established, first through the governor's executive order 2013-39 "Orden Ejecutiva del Gobernador para la creación del Consejo de Autonomía Energética para Puerto Rico" (MicroJuris 2013), and later through Act 57-2014 "Ley de Transformación y Alivio Energético de Puerto Rico." Puerto Rico's energy policy was defined as a continuous process of planning, inquiry, execution, evaluation and improvement regarding all energy issues. This approach intended to expand the scope of energy policy beyond laws and regulations, for example, with a new focus on citizen participation. This was a more holistic, integrated approach to energy policy never before formalized in Puerto Rico. The process is illustrated in Figure 1, where specific activities are listed, as well as the expected time frames to complete or begin (months through one year). The objective of Figure 1 is to show the breadth of policy actions that were pursued to transform the energy regime. Executive order 2013-39 also established an Energy Autonomy Advisory Board to lead the initiatives needed to execute the new energy policy. The Board was composed of three citizen-experts in energy-related matters and one representative from each of the following: Energy Affairs Administration (state energy office), PREPA, Planning Board, Governor's office, Transportation & Public Works Department and the Natural & Environmental Resources Department.

Other Policy Initiatives between 2013 and 2014

The new energy policy approach was supported by the National Governors Association (NGA) under a DOE grant. Puerto Rico competed with proposals from state governments in the U.S. and was selected for participation along with three other jurisdictions: Arizona, Minnesota and Mississippi (States to Focus on Economic Development... 2013). NGA's "Policy Academy on Targeting Clean Energy for Economic Development" began in 2013 and ended in 2014. Puerto Rico's participation focused on promoting the local energy industry through local resources (renewables, conservation and efficiency), on supporting PREPA reform actions and on studying local biofuel opportunities. NGA coordinated workshops, seminars and consulting contacts with energy experts that allowed the Puerto Rico team to develop a framework to link energy to economic development objectives and sustainability goals. Results were presented on July 16, 2014, during an NGA Energy Summit held in Caguas that included a panel with participation from Hawaii's regulator and DOE. Unfortunately, the event was not covered by the local media and the Governor's office did not release the final report of the NGA project (as of December 2017, the NGA project report had not been published). Nevertheless, the recommendations from that initiative were used by the state energy office in its policy development efforts, and many of the ideas obtained from that Policy Academy were used to inform the process that resulted in the approval of Act 57-2014 (discussed in the next section).

Another relevant policy initiative was the creation of an Electric Reliability Advisory Board through Executive Order 2013-40 "Orden Ejecutiva del Gobernador para la creación del Consejo de Confiabilidad Eléctrica." The Board was composed of two citizen-experts in electric power systems and one representative from each of the following: the Energy Affairs Administration (state energy office), the Planning Board and the Governor's office. The Reliability Board was tasked with estimating how much renewable energy could be safely interconnected to Puerto Rico's electric power grid. Sixty-four power purchase agreements (PPAs) were signed by PREPA between 2009 and 2012, plus 600 MW on master agreements, for a total of over 2,200 MW of large-scale renewable energy (mostly solar, some wind). No scientific study was performed to ensure that the electric grid was able to handle such large quantities of renewable energy. The reliability of Puerto Rico's electric system would have been affected since the daily peak electric demand was around 3,000 MW at the time. During October 2013, the Board stated in its report to the Governor that no more than 800 MW of renewable energy could be safely integrated to the electric grid at that time. The Board recommended to allocate a reasonable amount within those 800 MW to rooftop PV systems (Laureano 2013). The Board also mediated between PREPA and large-scale renewable energy project developers over proposed minimum technical requirements (MTR). The work by the Board informed some of the operational aspects included in Act 57-2014.

A New Mission for PREPA

A key goal in PREPA's transformation was changing its mission from "electrifying Puerto Rico" to "supporting sustainable energy in Puerto Rico" (from Executive Order 39). Besides the work described in the previous section, citizen input from formal reports, written depositions and results from Town Hall Meetings in Caguas, Adjuntas and Mayaguez were also used to create the most comprehensive reform in PREPA's history. It is important to mention that more citizen engagement meetings were planned, but pressure from influential stakeholders in the media forced the engagement process to be cut short. On October 23, 2013, the main components of PREPA's transformation were presented by the Governor in a public forum (García Padilla presenta plan de reorganización en la AEE 2013). On January 2014, bills to amend PREPA's Law (Senate Bill 881 and House Bill 1620), to create a new regulator and to modify the state energy office (Senate Bill 882 and House Bill 1618) were finally submitted to the Legislature, containing the product of a year of work, input from hundreds of stakeholders as well as input from reports from diverse groups.

Figure 1: Puerto Rico's energy policy on executive order #39.

- Formalize an energy plan with a clear vision of energy sustainability
- Coordinate inter-agency collaborations in energy matters
- Propose ways to harmonize existing laws, propose comprehensive reforms to PREPA
- Define a Citizen Forum that would allow a constant and early energy dialogue with citizens in a way that enables them to understand energy initiatives during early stages to make suggestions or present alternatives.

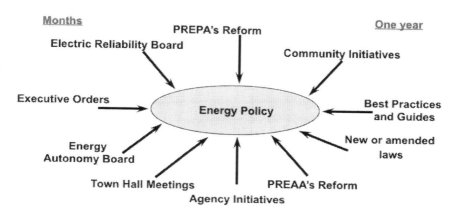

After a difficult negotiating process, including merging various energy bills that had been presented in the Legislature; Act 57-2014 (Ley de Transformación y Alivio Energético de Puerto Rico) emerged in May 2014. Although not perfect, it had the main elements to begin a transition to a sustainable electric infrastructure. For the first time in 73 years, a comprehensive reform of PREPA's law gave it a new mission: to provide reliable electric energy, contributing to the general welfare and to a sustainable future for the People of Puerto Rico, maximizing the benefits and minimizing the social, environmental and economic impacts. PREPA was ordered to focus on customer service and citizen participation. Act 57-2014 aligned PREPA's law and mission to sustainable development and emission reduction goals through explicit mandates to promote renewable and sustainable energy. PREPA was ordered to begin changing Puerto Rico's infrastructure so as to maximize renewable energy usage in a safe and reliable way. The law also mandated PREPA to reduce red tape for residential and commercial rooftop PV systems below 25 kW.

The law also created a regulator for the electric power sector (Energy Commission of Puerto Rico, CEPR in Spanish), and also a utility consumer advocate (OIPC in Spanish). The state energy office was given a new mission, a new name (OEPPE in Spanish) and became an independent identity for the first time in its history. An important task given to OEPPE was to determine the maximum level of renewable energy that the local electric infrastructure could safely integrate, at a reasonable cost, and the most appropriate technologies and places for such integration.

Stakeholder Engagement in Act 57-2014
One of the main differences between Act 57-2014 and previous energy policy initiatives was the focus on citizen participation. The reasoning behind this emphasis was the need to identify minimum common ground over which a shared vision could be created. As mentioned earlier, citizen forums are needed to reach that shared vision. Citizen participation outlets are aligned with the main values of "public power companies" such as PREPA, which was already structured in seven operational and commercial regions (Arecibo, Bayamón, Caguas, Carolina, Mayagüez, Ponce, San Juan).[7] Act 57-2014 allowed PREPA to establish agreements with NGOs, Academia or other citizen organizations in each of its seven regions. The main objective of the public empowerment initiatives was to engage citizens as much as possible, and as early as possible in key decisions, major projects and proposals that might impact communities.

The main objective of the public empowerment initiatives was to engage citizens as much as possible, and as early as possible in key decisions, major projects and proposals that might impact communities.

The task to ensure citizen participation in rate revisions fell unto the regulator (CEPR), and the utility consumer advocate (OIPC). The OIPC had ample powers to execute its mandate, including the ability to go to court in defense of consumers, even against the CEPR if necessary. Citizen participation in integrated resource planning processes was the responsibility of the state energy office (OEPPE). Figure 2 illustrates the general structure of the electric power sector in Puerto Rico as a result of Act 57-2014.

Since each PREPA region has its particularities, it was expected that citizen participation would vary from region to region. Thus, the citizen participation clauses in Act 57-2014 were designed to provide flexibility to motivate participation from NGOs and other citizen groups that had long criticized PREPA's service and lack of transparency. The main objective was to empower the public through regional participation and support from the OIPC and the OEPPE as facilitators of citizen participation. Nevertheless, the potential for broad, citizen participation never materialized. Citizen groups did not take advantage of the participation opportunities, PREPA's crisis took over most of the attention, leaving little time to demand support for the citizen participation outlets. The absence of effective citizen participation is still a problem. For example, the FOMB consistently holds public hearing in New York city, limiting Puerto Ricans' participation and access in their proceedings.

Up to this point, key policy actions and related pitfalls from 2007 to 2014 have been presented and discussed. However, the reasons behind those policy actions are left as open questions. One possible explanation or motivation for these changes is that PREPA's problems could not be hidden anymore; and thus, the voices claiming for reform grew and sometimes joined forces. For example, the net metering law was passed with bipartisan support, and the wheeling clause passed because of strong support from the industrial sector. Since the 2008 election, both main parties had included in their government programs reforms to PREPA, including establishing a regulator. Act 82 and 83 of 2010 passed as part as reforms sought by Governor Fortuño, backed by industrial support and foreign investors who saw Puerto Rico as an opportunity for large-scale renewable projects (Cordero 2009). When Governor García Padilla took office, he ran with a program "Luz al final del camino," which presented comprehensive reforms for PREPA. The combination of those promises and strong public opinion against PREPA were some of the reasons for the reforms between 2013 and 2014. Regardless of the efforts between 2007 and 2014, a true transformation of the electric infrastructure of Puerto Rico has not really been executed yet.

Transformation Potential Despite the Financial Debacle

The energy policy actions in Puerto Rico from January 2013 to May 2014 strove to avoid the pitfalls of previous energy policies. Special attention was given to stakeholder engagement in the development of policy initiatives, as recommended by Geri and McNabb's *Energy Policy in the U.S.: Politics, Challenges, and Prospects for Change*. Act 57-2014 provided important opportunities to innovate in the electric power sector, to move forward with renewable energy, to implement a novel regulatory framework through the collaboration of CEPR, OIPC and OEPPE, and, for the first time, to integrate citizens in electric energy decisions. The effort failed in many areas.

As Act 57-2014 was being signed, PREPA's financial problems had taken center stage and dominated the focus of transformation efforts and media coverage. Most if not all other efforts were secondary matters. The CEPR, OEPPE and OIPC were never able to coordinate their work to maximize the scarce resources available for their tasks. It took too long to name the Commissioners to the CEPR; for example, the Commission's first significant order was in December 2014 (seven months after Act 57 was signed). The OIPC Director was named in 2015. Furthermore, the citizen participation opportunities provided for the first time in Act 57-2014 did not turn into real citizen engagement efforts. Positive outcomes from Act 57-2014 include the amount of information from PREPA made public for the first time through the CEPR-led proceedings (e.g., rate revision case, integrated resource planning evaluation). Also, the consultants hired by the CEPR yielded important work that provided good guidance for the first regulatory decisions. The problems related to Act 57-2014 could have been addressed, had there been the will to correct the shortcomings in the implementation of the law. A key principle that was initially followed in the policy efforts of 2013 and 2014, but was abandoned in the formulation and adoption stages, was a negotiation with other political forces in Puerto Rico. As stated in Geri and McNabb (2011) regarding the U.S., but with direct ap-

Figure 2: Main relationships in the electricity sector from Act 57-2014

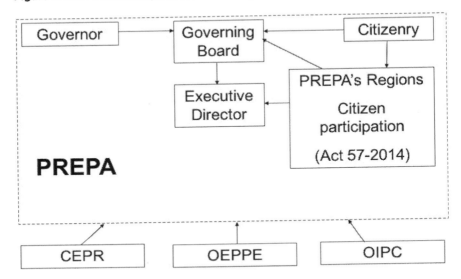

plication to Puerto Rico: "Without a commitment to define a sustainable future and strong bipartisan leadership, a sustainable energy policy cannot emerge." Because of the lack of bipartisan support for Act 57-2014, in January 2018 the new Governor announced plans to make major changes to the incipient regulatory framework and sell PREPA's generation assets (the privatization was also part of the mandate given by the U.S. Congress to the FOMB).

Regardless of the continued tradition of governing through party politics, a process that has plagued policy decisions since the 1960s, Puerto Rico still has the potential to innovate in many areas related to electric energy. In other words, regardless of the challenge presented by political interventions, there are many actions that can be implemented to deal with the electric energy challenges. The Achievable Renewable Energy Targets (ARET) study from the University of Puerto Rico-Mayagüez Campus (UPRM) showed that the solar resource is excellent (Irizarry 2009). Figure 3 shows one of the main contributions from that study, a solar irradiation map for Puerto Rico. Some estimates of the local "rooftop resource" show the potential for PV systems: residential rooftop area, 180,814,184 m2; commercial rooftop area, 7,300,000 m2; industrial rooftop area,2,702,545 m2.

The ARET studied also showed that the wind resource is acceptable, but its potential is not as good as the solar resource. The ARET study also discussed the potential of micro-hydro and biomass, although both of these have additional environmental and social hurdles to overcome. The waves in the North of the main island are excellent, however, the technology to extract energy from the waves is not as well developed as the PV option. Even though all resources must be explored to determine the best options, there is no doubt that the best resource, with commercially available technology, is the solar resource. Thus, a best technology practice would be to pursue aggressive deployment of rooftop photovoltaic systems (Irizarry 2009). That would also provide the best energy opportunity to spur local socio-economic development.

Puerto Rico also has great potential for socio-economic development and energy transformations through conservation and efficiency strategies and technologies. A best practice would be to support as broadly as possible, access to efficient equipment for all types of customers (industrial, commercial and residential). It is vital to begin considering conservation and efficiency as a local energy resource.

Puerto Rico needs to build the appropriate physical and social infrastructures that favor the use of local energy resources (the existing infrastructure does not). Another UPRM study concluded that Puerto Rico had already achieved grid parity in terms of costs for residential rooftop PV systems around 2010 (O'Neill 2013). Thus, we must envision and work on transitioning from the existing centralized, hierarchical, fossil-dependent electric infrastructure to a more distributed, sustainable infrastructure that favors the use of local energy resources and reduces the dependency on fossil fuels. Hawaii has a goal of 100 percent use of local energy resources by 2045, despite currently having a weaker electric infrastructure than Puerto Rico.

Figure 3: Estimated average insolation in Puerto Rico, kWh/m2 per year (Irizarry 2009)

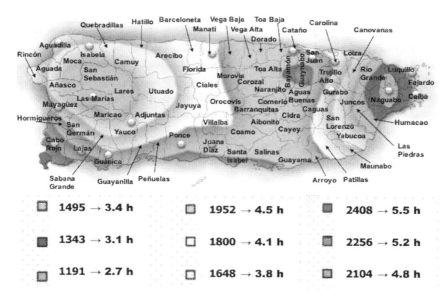

In the 1930s the local electric infrastructure was planned, designed and constructed to support the socio-economic development plans needed to overcome the critical situation of the time. In 2018, a shared vision of socio-economic development must be reached to address the existing critical period and to align accordingly the transformation of the electric infrastructure. The reforms to the local electric infrastructure require truly sustainable energy policies and actions (O'Neill 2014). Legally, that task falls under the state energy office (OEPPE), with support from the Energy Commission (with regards to electric energy). However, energy policy is not and should not be limited to laws or actions from government entities.

Distributed Energy to Transform the Electric Infrastructure

The crisis created by María calls for a new perspective regarding Puerto Rico's electric infrastructure. The reconstruction of Puerto Rico will require transparent oversight and management to ensure appropriate use of recovery funds. Whenever possible, the help or resources should not only be focused to address an immediate need, but should also be directed to supporting the longer-term recovery efforts. That is the case for the recovery of our infrastructure. Most of the infrastructure will be replaced, making this the moment to begin an electric energy revolution. Given Puerto Rico's particular context, traditional, centralized electric systems cannot continue to be the dominant model to follow. A more distributed approach should guide the reconstruction, which could not only result in a faster recovery in some areas, but would also support the much-needed transformation of Puerto Rico's electric infrastructure. Thus, a best technology practice is to give priority to the design and implementation of an infrastructure that enables the maximum possible use of distributed energy resources.

On September 15t, 2017, the *Energy Advisor* (Latin America Advisor) published an opinion article that included a brief description of benefits of distributed energy in the Caribbean context (How Resilient Is the Caribbean Basin's Energy Sector? 2017). The author stated that renewable-based microgrids would increase the resiliency of the power infrastructure in islanded/isolated locations. The dominant power model (centralized and fossil-burning) could be replaced by distributed, non-centralized, local energy resources (conservation, efficiency and renewable energy). Centralized power would be minimized and focused on supporting the usage of local resources. Within each microgrid a constant energy source would provide base load or continued operation at night. During emergencies, when centralized power would likely not be available (e.g., downed power lines), microgrids could still provide basic electricity needs and help re-establish normal operation of the power infrastructure. Despite the potential of microgrids, governments and vulnerable communities should not rush to "silver bullets" or "one size fits all" promises. Technological solutions abound during critical times, as do projects that yield economic benefit but do not fully address a social need, and do not increase local capacities or increase the resiliency of the local infrastructure. Good ideas or intentions may go wrong when the technology proposed is incompatible with the context or the social goal being pursued.

For example, renewable energy and microgrids seem a logical choice for Caribbean islands (e.g., Puerto Rico) or Pacific islands (e.g., Hawaii). Nevertheless, establishing effective and consistent energy policies is challenging, even more difficult than the technological and economic challenges. Renewable-based microgrids entail turning passive users to engaged energy actors. This new energy vision requires capacity building actions, as well as new responsibilities for the government, the workforce and the citizenry. Social agreements should guide and sustain policy directions that support the economic and technological changes needed for microgrids (How Resilient Is the Caribbean Basin's Energy Sector? 2017). It is vital to ponder the social nature of electric power systems, which makes them a powerful tool for either justice or injustice (social and environmental).

Good ideas or intentions may go wrong when the technology proposed is incompatible with the context or the social goal being pursued.

Although many regular citizens cannot access energy storage due to cost, the present crisis should encourage a move toward distributed storage systems that might serve communities in common areas ("community centers"). Thus, we must envision and work to implement solar communities, with the physical and social arrangements needed. Furthermore, to increase regional emergency preparedness around the territory, "emergency response hubs" must be established in each of the 78 municipalities. In municipalities with populations greater than 10,000 persons, multiple hubs may be needed. Additionally, more than one hub might also be needed in municipalities with irregular or challenging geography (e.g., towns in the mountainous central region). These emergency response hubs should have minimal infrastructure to allow each town emergency team to work in the immediate response during and after disasters. For example, microgrids should be established to provide electricity as part of a hub. With a distributed energy approach, the electric infrastructure would be more resilient and better prepared to face the impacts of natural disasters. A key technology practice is to begin studying, designing and implementing pilot projects that use microgrids in emergency hubs, at least one in each of the seven regions of PREPA.

The transformation of Puerto Rico's electric infrastructure requires answering the following questions: How long will a transition toward renewables take? What is the right mix of resources? What is the right mix of approaches (centralized vs distributed, regional vs island, regional vs community)? What is the right mix of funding sources (private, federal, cooperative, foundations, etc.)? One key challenge is the mistrust among some of the key stakeholders who are needed to answer these questions, especially between those with economic/political power and access, and those representing communities or environmental and social justice issues (How soon can Puerto Rico restore its electric grid? 2017).

A future envisioned by many (as proven through stakeholder engagement initiatives from 2013 to 2014) is the widespread use of rooftop solar systems (O'Neill 2013; O'Neill, Irizarry, Ortiz and Pérez 2016). But Puerto Rico cannot go from almost zero renewables to 100 percent renewables straight away. Hawaii, with more effective energy policies than Puerto Rico, and much more renewable energy participation, set its 100 percent goal for 2045. But a more diverse energy mix could be achieved within a few years in Puerto Rico, where renewables are the main player and big power plants have a supporting role. That requires Puerto Rico to move beyond political bickering and focus on rebuilding a more sustainable and resilient power system (O'Neill 2017). Supporting this is the fact that the cost of residential rooftop PV in Puerto Rico, net-metered, is 11 cents/kWh (O'Neill, Figueroa and Irizarry 2013). The electrical load is nearby; thus, there are no losses in the power lines. If 2 to 3 cents are added for grid services, the cost is still at 13-14 cents/kWh. The utility scale PV contracts signed by PREPA established a cost of 15 cents/kWh, plus up to 3.5 cents/KWh as RECs, for a total of 18.5 cents/kWh. In these cases, there are power line losses since those projects are connected at the transmission level. Those contracts were challenged in court by the Congress-appointed oversight board (from the PROMESA law). Although the FOMB withdrew their case, they are still pursuing reduced rates from those contract holders, a process that might end up in court once more or take months to clear (at least with the original contract-holders). Anyone trying to push those types of projects could be shut down by the people who had original contracts.

On the other hand, the distributed option is open at the residential, commercial or industrial level. Although there are short-term limits on how much and how fast distributed resources can be deployed, the distributed option is the best bet for Puerto Rico's energy future. The effects of hurricane María is further evidence that we cannot continue to completely depend on the centralized model, which should be minimized as much as possible. A system with distributed resources, despite being costlier than large-scale renewables (in a per Watt basis), provides the opportunity for better oversight of energy issues and creates a sense of ownership among users. Although Puerto Rico has enough insolation to meet our electricity demands, we still do not have a cheap, reliable and environmentally friendly way to store all that solar energy for use at night. At 11 cents per kWh, residential rooftop PV systems are much cheaper than the 20 cents a kWh on average paid to PREPA in 2017 and 2018. However, citizens still need to come up with the money to purchase the PV systems; and the infrastructure needs to be changed to support 100 percent renewables in Puerto Rico. One way to address this challenge is to provide financing options to make PV systems accessible to more citizens.

Distributed generation, especially rooftop PV systems, presents an opportunity for local socio-economic development. Most of the companies designing, installing and maintaining rooftop PV systems are local, small and medium companies. Thus, the economic activity generated is greater, since those local companies pay taxes in Puerto Rico, employ local people and generate other indirect economic activity. Furthermore, rooftop PV systems enable people to become active energy actors. The word "prosumer" has surfaced to refer to those consumers that are also energy producers. As many prosumers emerge in Puerto Rico, the possibility of creating solar community's increases. These solar communities are a means to achieve energy democracy and local empowerment (O'Neill 2016c; Jordán and O'Neill 2016; O'Neill et al. 2017).

A balanced view of the problem should be pursued. The centralized vision has advantages, and still has value. Acknowledging other perspectives does not weaken the distributed energy vision, but rather strengthens it by allowing a civilized conversation with those with differing points of view. Puerto Rico needs civilized conversations among stakeholders, given that PR had very few of those in the last thirty years (or maybe in its whole history). A key technology practice is to evaluate which centralized energy options would make sense to support and enable an increased use of local energy resources, closer to the points of use.

The Road Ahead

Some argue that PREPA's crisis is evidence that the public power model does not work. That is not true. If well-run, the public power model is effective and can still be useful in Puerto Rico. When comparing public power companies and investor-owned utilities in the U.S., one observes that average rates for residential and commercial clients are less in public power companies (although industrial rates are slightly better in private companies according to the American Public Power Association).

The distortions to the public power model from PREPA managers cannot continue, especially given the history of political interventions in PREPA. Act 57-2014 came too late; the legislative changes to PREPA's Board to make it "less political" failed (e.g., Act 4-2016 "Ley para la Revitalización de la Autoridad de Energía Eléctrica de Puerto Rico"). The new regulator (Puerto Rico Energy Commission) is still in its infancy, underfunded and vulnerable to political intervention, as shown by attempts in early 2017 to merge it with other regulatory entities. And this is not just because of the present-day local government. The previous administration from the other majority party did the same in early 2013 by signing into law changes to the composition of PREPA's board. Local politicians cannot resist the temptation to meddle in everything.

Simply privatizing generation, i.e., constructing new, privately run power plants, is not what the local electric infrastructure needs.

The PROMESA law suggests privatizing the power generation in Puerto Rico as a way to improve the local electric system. However, the aftermath of María warrants a deeper look into potential futures for Puerto Rico's electric infrastructure. Simply privatizing generation, i.e., constructing new, privately run power plants, is not what the local electric infrastructure needs. The problems with restoring power after María *were not* due to lack of generating plants, but the destruction of many of the transmission towers and lines that supply bulk power to load centers, and the destruction of most of the distribution lines that supply power to individual users. Depending 100 percent on the centralized model, and its vulnerabilities is the main cause for the delays in restoring power in Puerto Rico.

Since millions of dollars in federal money will be going to reconstructing the local electric infrastructure, those funds must be effectively used in ensuring that the new electric infrastructure is more resilient and robust to face future natural hazards. In the long-term, taking this approach now will save tax-payers money later. Of course, power had to be restored as soon as possible, but a new vision must guide the future of the electric infrastructure, and no short-term actions should be made that hinder the chances of transforming the local grid.

The recent attempts of reforming PREPA can provide useful lessons for the reconstruction of the electric system in Puerto Rico. For instance, any new policy should be framed in a multi-sector agreement among political parties, economic forces, environmental advocates and community leaders among others, with a minimum common ground over which energy vision should be pursued and how. Puerto Rican politicians and major political parties have proved incapable of reaching a consensus on socio-economic development strategies, including the proper handling of the local power infrastructure (e.g., maintenance, financial oversight and transformation of the electric grid). Recent energy policy processes shows that as soon as the opposing parties assume power, previous policies or the guiding principles of previous reforms are abandoned, To avoid this, a minimum policy agreement should be reached among stakeholders. Another important lesson that can be learned from recent attempts of reforming PREPA is the need for creating spaces for citizen participation in energy policy. Stakeholders engagement meetings must have a central role in providing better policy oversight, creating ownership among users and providing transparency to the implementation process.

Since the federal government is investing millions of dollars in the grid's reconstruction after María, it becomes necessary to establish mechanisms to ensure the problems that plagued PREPA do not resurface. Addressing the issues at hand (e.g., PREPA's debt; privatization; resiliency, renewables, conservation, efficiency; centralized vs distributed) require a non-political, objective entity, sensible and willing to adapt the diverse perspectives from local stakeholders. In this way, federal funds spent on the recovery really address the needs of the millions of Puerto Ricans through a resilient and adaptive electric system. Unfortunately, such an entity does not now exist in Puerto Rico.

An entity or mechanism should be put in place, similar to the PRERA and the PRRA, to sort out the electric energy options. Through a broad stakeholder engagement effort, it would guide the appropriate actions toward a sustainable and resilient future for the local electric infrastructure. Such an entity cannot be the FOMB, with its emphasis on repaying the debt, nor should it come about from PREPA or the local government. Although PREPA has been a public power company, it has also acted similarly to the rural electric coops, electrifying rural and isolated parts of Puerto Rico. Thus, the evaluation of the local electric future is not just a private vs public debate, it deserves a wider view, and probably leads to a new hybrid model that truly addresses the needs of the millions of residents in Puerto Rico. The convener or organizer of this effort must have federal support to avoid the problems that result when local political or economic forces capture the process (problems that many energy policies have had). However, the leadership of this effort must reside within Puerto Ricans, to ensure that the initiatives are not perceived as impositions from the outside and that there is local ownership of the process.

Researchers from the University of Puerto Rico (UPR) system could be part of an appointed, overseeing entity for the electric transformation of Puerto Rico. The UPR has expertise on most areas related to the operation of the electric infrastructure. For example, the Instituto Nacional de Energía y Sostenibilidad Isleña (INESI) is a system-wide platform that connects energy and sustainability researchers on all 11 UPR campuses. INESI also convenes an Energy Stakeholders Forum, which was based on and still follows the work and principles from the Energy Roundtable mentioned earlier. Other examples of successful UPR projects relevant to the creation of a sustainable and resilient electric infrastructure include energy collaborations with communities (O'Neill 2006, 2007, 2017) and with industry (López 2017), and projects studying new structure for distribution systems (Jordán 2016; Rodríguez 2016). Another sector that could make a significant contribution to the overseeing entity is the credit unions. "Cooperatives" (as credit unions are known in Puerto Rico) follow institutional values that are aligned to the socially based creation of an electric infrastructure in support of local socio-economic development.

Under any of the possible futures, and regardless of the final policy directions given by either Congress, the FOMB and/or the local government, the incipient state regulator CEPR, or whatever entity substitutes it, needs to be supported and strengthened. It is vital to have a strong, objective, transparent regulatory framework to give regulatory certainty, to reduce investment risk and to support whatever electricity future Puerto Rico decides to have. The conditions need to be created so that the regulator is able to grow as an objective, independent, non-political entity.

Next Steps toward a True Transformation

Any action taken to build a resilient, local electric infrastructure must include Puerto Ricans in the main roles (as the role Puerto Rican engineer Antonio Lucchetti had with the PRERA and PRRA). A top-down or imposed approach will not effectively address the contextual particularities existing in the territory, which must be closely considered for the success of any policy or strategy pursued in Puerto Rico. Recent local energy policies and their outcomes exemplify the challenges that need to be addressed for a transition to a more sustainable and resilient electric infrastructure. The introduction of new technologies or the inflow of Federal funds alone will not be enough for achieving the necessary electric transformations.

Another aspect to be considered is that, in the medium term, it is important to give Puerto Rico the necessary tools to create local socio-economic development. Puerto Rico cannot continue being held hostage in a prison that does not allow the territory to enjoy the tools available to states nor the trade and financial benefits at the international level. Since the U.S. Congress and the U.S. Supreme Court have left Puerto Rico without concrete options to recover from the present crisis, Federal intervention is necessary. Thus, it is of paramount importance to link the reconstruction of the electric system to a broader socio-economic development plan. The creation of a more sustainable and resilient electric energy system can become a key driver for local socio-economic development.

Since the U.S. Congress and the U.S. Supreme Court have left Puerto Rico without concrete options to recover from the present crisis, Federal intervention is necessary.

The decisions made in 2018 and the approach taken in the coming years for the reconstruction of our electric infrastructure will either facilitate or hinder Puerto Rico's chances for a sustainable and resilient energy future. With the appropriate vision and policies, a distributed energy approach combined with aggressive demand response programs could yield a resilient and sustainable electric infrastructure in Puerto Rico. The local nature of these distributed resources, combined with the work of well-organized communities can also yield local, sustainable socio-economic development that would remain in place once the federal support is eliminated or phases out. If the federal support, e.g., monetary and human resources, is not enough, then it would require Puerto Ricans to work even harder to realize this future of increased resiliency and sustainability through local energy resources.

The main policy recommendations for the electric transformation of Puerto Rico are:

- Puerto Rico's electric transformation should part of a broader socio-economic development strategy.
- Social considerations must become an essential part of the decision-making process, as important or even more, than technological issues or technology's best practices.
- Stakeholders and citizen engagement meetings should be a central component of the electric transformation.
- The creation of an independent, non-political, overseeing entity for the electric transformation of Puerto Rico with an objective and transparent regulatory framework. The entity would have a broad, multi-sector participation of local energy stakeholders.
- Researchers from the UPR system should be included as part of any entity overseeing the electric transformation of Puerto Rico.
- Capacity building actions among citizens are needed in order to promote a transition from passive users to engaged energy actors.

- Regardless of the chosen policy direction, the policy reforms should include the participation and support of all local political parties, to ensure continuity regardless of future changes in the ruling party.
- The electric system should be as decentralized as possible, in order to facilitate a more efficient post-disaster recovery.
- For a distributed energy policy, the planning of the electric infrastructure must give priority to change the design paradigm from centralized generation to distributed energy resources, especially locally available resources such as solar energy. Appropriate funding must be allocated to support this policy direction.

NOTES

[1] "Que existe el peligro de que por no poner a uso productivo una buena parte de los fondos que importamos, crezca más rápidamente nuestra deuda exterior de lo que crece nuestra capacidad para sufragar su servicio; lo que puede acercarnos a una difícil situación en nuestra balanza de pagos internacionales" (Baquero 1963).

[2] The Jones Act of 1920 requires the use of U.S. Merchant Marine and U.S. built ships. Since Puerto Rico is a U.S. territory, this restriction applies, increasing shipping costs between the continental U.S. and the territory.

[3] Graph by the Center for Puerto Rican Studies <http://centropr.hunter.cuny/>, data from the American Community Surveys.

[4] Although Puerto Rico is about 35 miles wide, the transmission lines that run from south to north go through a difficult and steep central mountain range. Thus, many failures in those transmission lines are difficult to repair. The damages to that infrastructure from María included the destruction of the transmission towers; thus, there was no way to deliver the power generated in the southern plants to supply the largest local demand in the North until new transmission towers and lines were built in such difficult terrain.

[5] These municipal bonds were issued by a public entity, and had triple tax exemption (local, state and federal).

[6] For the Energy Rountable's strategic plan see <http://iteas.uprm.edu/docs/Mesa_Dialogo_Documento_Plan_Estrategico.pdf/>.

[7] For PREPA's regions, see <http://www.aeepr.com/medicionneta/DOCS/Mapa%20Regiones.pdf/>.

REFERENCES

Baquero, Jenaro. 1963. La importación de fondos externos y la capacidad absorbente de nuestra economía. *Revista de Ciencias Sociales* 7(1–2), 79–92.

Burnett, Christina Duffy and Burke Marshall, eds. 2001. *Foreign in a Domestic Sense: Puerto Rico, American Expansion and the Constitution*. Durham, NC: Duke University Press.

Cordero, Miguel. 2009. Puerto Rico Electric Power Authority Project Development. Presentation at the Puerto Rico Projects Conference. October, San Juan, PR.

Cotto, Cándida. 2012. Juan Rosario y Agustín Irizarry: Informe al Pueblo de sus representantes en la AEE. *Claridad* 7 August.

García Padilla presenta plan de reorganización en la AEE. 2013. *El Nuevo Día* 23 October.

Geri, Lawrence A. and David E. McNabb. 2011. *Energy Policy in the U.S.: Politics, Challenges, and Prospects for Change.* Boca Ratón, FL: CRC Press.

Glanz, James and Frances Robles. 2018. How Storms, Missteps and an Ailing Grid Left Puerto Rico in the Dark. *New York Times* 6 May.

Gobernador anuncia conversatorios sobre temas energéticos. 2013. *El Nuevo Día* 17 March.

Microjuris. 2013. Gobernador firma órdenes ejecutivas que impulsarán la energía renovable. *Al Día* 14 May.

Greenberg, Scott and Gavin Skins. 2015. Tax Policy Helped Create Puerto Rico's Fiscal Crisis. *Tax Foundation* 30 June. Accessed 17 December 2017. <https://taxfoundation.org/tax-policy-helped-create-puerto-rico-s-fiscal-crisis/>.

How Resilient Is the Caribbean Basin's Energy Sector? 2017 *Energy Advisor* 15 September 1, 3, 6. <https://www.researchgate.net/publication/319721956_ENERGY_ADVISOR_How_Resilient_Is_the_Caribbean_Basin's_Energy_Sector/>.

How Soon Can Puerto Rico Restore Its Electric Grid? 2017. *Energy Advisor* 10 November 1, 3, 6. <http://docplayer.net/95612801-Qthree-quarters-of-puerto-rico-residents-are-still-without.html/>.

Irizarry, Agustín. 2013. El Dr. Agustín Irizarry Rinde Cuentas Sobre Su Labor En La Junta Gobierno De La AEE. Interview by Eliza Llenza. *YouTube Channel.* 15 August. Accessed 3 August 2018. <https://www.youtube.com/watch?v=nSxYaxnzcXs/>.

Irizarry Rivera, Agustín, J. Colucci-Ríos and Efraín O'Neill-Carrillo. 2009. Achievable Renewable Energy Targets for Puerto Rico's Renewable Energy Portfolio Standar. San Juan: Puerto Rico State Energy Office.

Johnson, Brendan. 1971. Puerto Rico: After 'Operation Bootstrap.' *New York Times* 8 April.

Jordán, Isaac L., Efraín O'Neill-Carrillo and Naysy López. 2016. Towards a Zero Net Energy Community Microgrid. 2016 IEEE Conference on Technologies for Sustainability. 9–11 October. Phoenix, AZ.

Kruger Anne, Ranjit Teja and Andrew Wolfe. 2015. Puerto Rico: A Way Forward. Government Development Bank, Puerto Rico. Accessed 9 August 2018. <http://www.gdb.pr.gov/documents/PuertoRicoAWayForward.pdf/>.

Látimer Eugenio. 1993. *Historia de la Autoridad de Energía Eléctrica.* San Juan: Autoridad de Energía Eléctrica.

Ludvig Norman. 2015. Interpretive Process Tracing and Causal Explanation. *Qualitative and Multi-method Research* 13(2), 4–9.

Laureano, Eva. 2013. Se contrató más energía renovable que la que se puede absorber en sistema AEE. *Noticel* 11 October.

López, Naysy, Agustín A. Irizarry-Rivera, Efraín O'Neill-Carrillo, Tom Key and Alexander W. Schneider. 2017. Industry-University Collaboration in Workforce Development: Results from a Short Course on IEEE Standard 762. 2017 IEE Frontiers in Education Conference. 18–21 October, Indianapolis, IN.

States to Focus on Economic Development through Clean Energy. 2013. *National Governors Association News* 30 October. Accessed 6 August 2018. <https://classic.nga.org/cms/home/news-room/news-releases/2013--news-releases/col2-content/states-to-focus-on-economic-deve.html/>.

O'Neill, Efraín. 2012. Una nueva AEE: energía eléctrica para la sociedad puertorriqueña del siglo XXI. Accessed 7 December. <http://iteas.uprm.edu/docs/Nueva_AEE_2012.pdf/>.

_____. 2016a. Evaluación de resultados de las leyes principales sobre Energía Eléctrica Renovable (2007 y 2008) *Dimensión* 30(1), 27–32. <http://www.ciapr.org/images/stories/Dimension/dimA30v1_web.pdf/>.

_____. 2016b. Evaluación de resultados de las leyes principales sobre Energía Eléctrica Renovable (2010 y 2014). *Dimensión* 30(2), 13–7. <http://www.ciapr.net/images/stories/Dimension/dimA30v2.pdf/>.

_____. 2016c. Transformaciones del sector eléctrico y el rol regulatorio. *Dimensión* 30(3), 7–12. <http://www.ciapr.org/images/stories/Dimension/05dimA30v3.pdf/>.

_____. 2017. After the Hurricane: Building Better Power Systems. Spark with Nora Young. *CBC Radio*, 3 November. <http://www.cbc.ca/radio/spark/370-hurricanes-and-power-grids-cellphone-privacy-and-more-1.4384889/after-the-hurricane-building-better-power-systems-1.4380208/>.

O'Neill, Efraín and Agustín Irizarry. 2006. Socially-Relevant Capstone Design Projects in Power Engineering. 2006 IEEE/PES Power Systems Conference and Exposition. 29 October–1 November, Atlanta, GA.

O'Neill, Efraín, Luisa Seijo, E. Dan Hirleman, Francisco Maldonado, Edgar Marti and Alejandra Rivera. 2007. Mentoring Interdisciplinary Service Learning Projects. Frontiers in Education Conference. October, Milwaukee, WI.

O'Neill, Efraín, A. Figueroa, Agustín Irizarry. 2013. Improved Permitting and Interconnection Processes for Rooftop PV Systems in Puerto Rico, University of Puerto Rico-Mayagüez, DOE SunShot.

O'Neill, Efraín, Agustín A. Irizarry-Rivera, Cecilio Ortiz, Marla Pérez-Lugo. 2016. The Role of Engineers as Policy Entrepreneurs toward Energy Transformations. Proceedings of the ASEE 123rd Annual Conference. June, New Orleans, LA.

O'Neill-Carrillo, Efraín, R. Santiago, Z. Méndez, H. Vega, J. Mussa and J. Rentas. 2017. Capstone Design Projects as Foundation for a Solar Community. Proceedings of the 47th ASEE/IEEE Frontiers in Education Conference, October, Indianapolis, IN.

Ortega, Melisa. 2017. Para mañana la interconexión de las líneas del norte y el sur. *El Nuevo Día* 22 October.

Pantojas-Garcia, Emilio. 2016. Is Puerto Rico Greece in the Caribbean? Crisis, Colonialism, and Globalization. *The Fletcher Forum of World Affairs* 40(1), 57–71.

Rohter, Larry. 1993. Puerto Rico Fighting to Keep Its Tax Breaks for Businesses. *New York Times* 10 May.

Rodríguez-Martínez, Manuel, Efraín O'Neill-Carrillo, María Pérez, Fabio Andrade, Wilson Rivera, Agustín Irizarry-Rivera, Rafael Rodriguez, Cecilio Ortiz and Eduardo Lugo. 2016. A Case for Open Access Smart Grids (OASIS). 2016 IEEE Conference on Technologies for Sustainability. 9-11 October, Phoenix, AZ.

Cabotage as an External Non-tariff Measure on the Competitiveness on SIDS's Agribusinesses: The Case of Puerto Rico

WILLIAM SUÁREZ II

ABSTRACT

This paper explores the multidimensional effects of an external non-tariff measure (NTM) on maritime transportation between the United States (US) and Puerto Rico (PR) trades. In particular, this research addresses the vulnerability level of PR's agrifood sector in relation to sustainability as a Small Island Developing State (SIDS) highly influenced by a larger economy. Due to the high potential of climate changes in the Caribbean, this study reviewed the effects of a maritime cabotage policy on a SIDS agribusinesses' logistic. Could a NTM affect the supply chain capabilities and the food security of a SIDS? What challenges and opportunities does the US Cabotage policy present for PR's agricultural sector's competitiveness? Based on mixing empirical analysis in an exploratory convergent design, the research categorizes the cabotage policy in relation to the effects on PR's agrifood supply chain, its port infrastructure, and its native agribusinesses' competitiveness. Results show the maritime cabotage itself is a constraint. However, the interactions with others NTMs, indirectly related to the cabotage but inherent to the political status and business relationship between PR and the US, add other limits. In addition, it revealed that internal factors have an impact on the efficiency and competitiveness of PR's agro-industrial sector. [Keywords: Food security; Small Island Developing State; Agrifood Supply Chain; Non-Tariff Measure; Agribusinesses Logistic; Maritime Cabotage; Supply Chain Capabilities; Vulnerability]

The author (w.suarezi.bcid@gmail.com) is Researcher at Bradford Centre for the International Development in the University of Bradford, UK. His research interests are focused on small economies' agrifood supply chain competitiveness, agrifood systems and food policy. He is adjunct Assistant Professor in Hostos College at City University of New York. He is former Executive Director of the Colegio de Agrónomos de Puerto Rico (2001–08).

1. Introduction

Puerto Rico has many strengths that include its political stability, literacy rates, dollarized economy, access to US markets, and absence of direct U.S. taxes (Collins et al. 2006). Ironically, Puerto Rico's particular political relationship with the U.S. is questioned due to its highly unequal society (IEPR 2018), higher than average price of goods (Marazzi-Santiago 2018), and an economic recession and staggering debt (Caraballo-Cueto and Lara 2018). To exacerbate the situation, recently, two consecutive hurricanes broke down Puerto Rico's national supply chain (Holpuch 2017).[1] These disasters helped reveal how some of the US Federal Government regulations could be affecting Puerto Rico's agrifood production and sustainable development.

It is not possible to understand the humanitarian crisis that ensued on September 2017 without considering the long-standing political and economic phenomena that preceded it. An exploration of Puerto Rico's Maritime Merchant Law, and its agricultural sector before Hurricane Maria are needed to situate multidimensional findings of this research. The findings could be meaningful to policymakers, other SIDS, and U.S. off-shore jurisdictions.

This paper does not assume a stance against the relationship between Puerto Rico and the US. This research approaches the phenomenon of the US Cabotage Act as a commercial relationship using an operational perspective focused on sustainable development and food insecurity.

1.1. The Jones Act 1920 as a non-tariff measure (NTM)

Since 1917, the relationship between Puerto Rico and the US has been linked with a "Jones Act" (Venator-Santiago 2017). Between 1917 and the mid-1930s the name "Jones Act" was popularly applied to various[2] US federal laws. Although different in intent (e.g., citizenship, cabotage), the term causes some confusion to this day (Rivera 2007; Dietz 1989). This paper is focused on the operational effects of the Wesley "Jones Act" or the Merchant Maritime Act. The Act was strategically designed as a reformulation[3] of the US maritime trade policies but legislated in 1920 as a framework for the US Cabotage structure between the US and its territories. With World War I as a context, the initiative was also supported by the US security/military apparatus to re-ordain and register all the US flagged carriers (Pantojas-García 1990). These trade restrictions, based on the Dutch and British imperial rules, have been building up through decades of administrative structures to benefit the US maritime industry (Santos 1997), whilst diluting its cost in terms of the total welfare among its mammoth economy and its more than 300 million consumers (USITC 1991). US cabotage policies are a complex combination of regulations to protect trade among its coasts, which in the long run has shrunk its national registered fleet (USGAO 1998). Currently in Puerto Rico, unlike other non-incorporated US territories,[4] this Act limits trades only to ships constructed and repaired in the US, operated by US citizens, and registered under the US flag (Torruellas 2017).

In some cases, policies designed for developed markets are not necessarily suitable for the less developed ones and/or small economy realities (Stiglitz 2010). That is the case because some policy instruments (such as NTM) could affect competitiveness creating hidden costs to trade and/or business behaviors, that by their particularity, may imply indirect effects on the agents (participants) (May 2015; Beghin 2013). Literature on this subject is scarce and limited when it comes to proposing methods to analyze multidimensional effects of a NTM on SIDS.

The US maritime cabotage could fit the above description. Unfortunately, the regulation has primarily been studied based on its welfare cost[5] (AMP 2018; Alameda and Valentín 2014; Cruz et al. 2014; Martínez 2014; Estudios Técnicos 2013; Lewis 2013; USGAO 2013). Another area which has received some attention is the market-political relations (Clar 2013; Collazo 2012; Frankel 2002; Santos 1997). Very little is said about agribusinesses or the regulation's interaction with the business environment in which chain actors operate.

Depending on location, transport costs on import values vary between 8 percent and 13 percent (Márquez-Ramos et al. 2007). Every time one maritime line buys another, two carriers merge or a group forms an alliance; the ports, terminals, and/or clients are affected in one way or another. In the next years, more consolidations are expected (Hopman and Nienhuis 2009). These maritime service patterns will have greater effects on the most dependent smaller markets, their connectivity, quality of services, local business environment, and well-being (Alameda and Valentín 2015; Chen et al. 2013). Since the agricultural sector nowadays accounts for less than 1 percent of PR's GDP and its capacity to export food is practically non-existent, promoting efficiencies in the agricultural sector has not been a priority. As a result, the literature is silent regarding Puerto Rico's agribusiness supply chain competitiveness.

On the positive side, Puerto Rico's agriculture has some characteristics of a competitive market.

1.2. Puerto Rico's agribusinesses sector in context

Puerto Rico's agricultural sector has lacked attention since the mid-1970s (Comas 2009). The disregard for local agriculture is evident when its economic contribution is considered. According to the Puerto Rico Planning Board (PRPB) (2015), PR's agriculture contributes 0.85 percent of the GDP or between $700 and 900 million per year, of which 55 percent is from animal production. In comparison to similar small economies—such as Singapore (0.09 percent), Hong Kong (0.1 percent), Bahrain (0.3 percent) and Ireland (1.6 percent)—the percentage of Puerto Rico's agricultural contribution seems to be relatively high. Overall, however, considering other factors from the World Economic Forum (2013), such as restrictions to trade, inequality levels (GINIc) and the cost of agricultural policies to access food, PR shows a lower performance.

Geographically speaking, Puerto Rico is no different from other SIDS in the region. Like them, PR is totally dependent on maritime transportation and shows a large imbalance in agricultural goods trade (FAO 2006). According to Setrini (2012), Puerto Rico's producers are squeezed between the low cost of industrial producers in the US and low-wage producers in the Caribbean and Latin American countries. On the positive side, Puerto Rico's agriculture has some characteristics of a competitive market. First, its market openness is as high as the rivalry between international and domestic (US Interstate Commerce Act) products and native producers (WEF 2013). Second, the local infrastructure permits native distributors to make 'just-in-time' purchases, thus giving fresh products more days on the shelf (Setrini 2012). Third, the number of producers[6] and buyers is relatively large. For instance, in 2012 the Puerto Rican food consumption expenditures were estimated to be $8.93 billion, making up 14.64 percent of the total consumption expenditures ($2,400 per capita/ year) in food (González and Gregory 2014).

Regarding imports, according to the PRPB (2015) using data of 2012, the value of the food and agricultural goods imported to Puerto Rico represents around 4 percent of all of Puerto Rico's importations. Interestingly, approximately 95 percent of the agriculture (livestock and food) goods imported to Puerto Rico is produced by 15 countries, but the vast majority (84 percent) comes from the North American Free Trade Agreement (NAFTA, currently named USMCA), namely the United States, Mexico, and Canada. The highest percentage (79 percent), nonetheless, comes as domestic trade from the US estimated to be worth $3 billion (USD).

Puerto Rico's agribusiness sector is highly susceptible to external shocks. These outside variables include other restricting factors from their trade with the US, such as sanitary and phytosanitary (SPS) measures. In addition, Puerto Rico's agribusiness is highly exposed to natural conditions (e.g., hurricanes, overflows) and a low level of added value in native production. These factors, according to González and Gregory (2014), have been detrimental to Puerto Rico's production over the last twenty years, particularly for crops—vegetables and root produce.

1.2.1. Grains and animal produce sectors

The strongest agricultural sector in Puerto Rico, and the most dependent on grain imports, is animal production. It is well known within the agricultural community that animal feed constitutes between 50 percent and 70 percent of production costs in this sector. In Puerto Rico, 100 percent of grains for feedstuff are imported making its strongest agricultural sector entirely dependent on maritime transportation. In the last decade, the number of grain-importing companies in Puerto Rico has dwindled (Departamento de Agricultura 2012). It seems that their disappearance has been affected by factors such as bankruptcy or consolidations, the grains' volatile costs, and the impact of trading costs.

The grain-importing sector is broken down into animal feed manufacturing and flour milling and baking. Puerto Rico's animal feed industry, as a production system, consists of four basic activities: grain buyers' resale, grain transformation, product trading with wholesalers and retailers, and secondary product sales to consumers.

In general, these are the first basic echelons in the animal production agrifood chain. Before the animal feed product is consumed, various processes are undertaken in the chain. They include grain producers at the farm level, grain elevators and sellers, transporters, surveyors and receivers, inspectors, regulators and other secondary activities associated with them (Morgan 2000). Grains are transported and delivered in dry bulk vessels separated by hatch. For each of these processes, some buyers are searching for a combination of low prices and high quality. Price is the most traditional decisional factor used in this business. Commonly, animal producers are not well informed about the technical–nutritional requirements of their animals, but they are highly aware of the costs for their own business. Consequently, farmers searching for lower prices for animal feed may ignore the importance of quality to the detriment of their animals' yield. Similarly, feed mill agribusinesses are focused on low-cost materials rather than improving efficiency through innovation and technology (Chavarría et al. 2002).

1.2.2. Fresh produce sector

World Bank (2015) data show that like some of the smallest Caribbean nations but unlike Jamaica, the Dominican Republic and Cuba, Puerto Rico's import of its food needs are high. Popularly it is estimated at above 80 percent. Around 70 percent of this amount is imported from the US markets and almost 92 percent specifically from the Jacksonville Florida Port (Comas 2009). The literature is much less informative about which products are considered in these percentages and whether Puerto Rico's production is enough to cover its market needs. Puerto Rico's market dependence on imported food may entail several dangers, beginning with the fact that in a national emergency the population would not be able to feed itself. Second, food imports depend on volatile export markets susceptible to periodic market access disruptions and external regulations. Unlike grain, produce imports are transported in refrigerated or controlled climate storage units. Third, climate change, with more frequent and severe events (e.g., hurricanes, floods) can seriously affect food supply available on the global market.

1.3. Theoretical stance

The scholarly silences mentioned earlier coupled with the political, regulatory and geographical particularities of PR call for an eclectic theoretical stance from which to explore Cabotage as a non-tariff measure (NTM) and its effects on the agrifood system. Consequently, the worldview guiding this research incorporates tenets from the field of development, engineering (i.e., agricultural, mechanical and industrial), management and logistics.

As mentioned, NTMs may affect trade and/or its supply chain (Beghin 2013). A threat to food security may arise through higher prices—making food unaffordable for many—or through food scarcity at any price—as a result of political, economic and mechanical issues (Hubbard and Hubbard 2013, 142). Consequently, the sustainable development aims (UNSDSN 2014) on the basis of food security became an important topic to evaluate SIDS' economic vulnerability. This research relies on Briguglio's (2003) factors of integrated supply chain and the level of dependence on strategic imports as basis to interpret national economic vulnerability. This research also considers Porter's (1985) proposal on "strategy and structure" importance in developing firms' competitive advantages but also the "forces" that might affect them. Exploring regulations with effects on the national vulnerability and firms' competitiveness, in this context, may support the local economic objectives but, more importantly, the nation's food security.

Competitiveness variables associated with market, infrastructure and government play an important role too via their different interactions with external and internal indicators. Their weight is important in competitive analyses at the firm, cluster, regional or national level (Porter 1985). At the firm level and arguing that tangible and intangible forms of resources have the potential to sustain or affect competitiveness, Barney (1991) developed the VRIO[7] framework to evaluate controlled/private assets. In the context of this study, a private asset can be a grain mill, which bases its activity in a common product around the world, which is considered rare to the people of Puerto Rico because it is not produced there. However, it is argued that sectoral, systemic and non-economic factors could also be highly influential on the competitiveness and therefore basic for the agrifood supply chain analysis (Rojas et al. 2000).

Latruffe's (2010) suggestions about the importance of the relationship among markets and/or between importers and suppliers, as competitiveness factors, were also considered. In addition, Brandon-Jones and colleagues (2014) highlight the firms' supply chain visibility[8]—particularly during the importation process—and the way in which it was considered. In this research, because the NTM under study is related to the maritime sector, the author looks upon the ideas of De Martino and Morvillo (2008) to identify systemic key factors of port competitiveness that exert an impact on the supply chain network.

To explore the multidimensional effects of the US Cabotage Act as an NTM, this research considered cabotage as an external regulation on Puerto Rico as a SIDS. In sum, the policies, protocols and decisions related to the Maritime Merchant Act, imposed on Puerto Rico, are controlled by the US Federal Government instrumentalities an applied as a "one size fits all" trade framework.

This study aims to demonstrate how the external policy measures affect the development and productivity between agents and domains,[9] namely the SIDS's native agribusinesses' importers' as agents and their supply chain system, infrastructure, and behavior as domains. The discussion centers on the operational dimension of the Act on Puerto Rico's agrifood logistics and its complexities. Puerto Rico's vulnerability and its food security are also presented as the basis on which to study the Cabotage phenomenon.

2. Methodology

This research incorporated a heterodox economic framework in a convergent mixed method design, where the researcher uses concurrent timing to implement the qualitative and quantitative strands and prioritizes both data equally (Creswell and Plano

2011).[10] This research was performed as an ongoing process starting in December 2014 and finishing in July 2016. Secondary quantitative data (i.e., reports between 2005 and 2015) of Puerto Rico from the External Trade Statistics and the US Department of Agriculture were analyzed to identify the price, origins, and restrictions of grains, respectively. Consumption analysis, national production, and farmland availability for the livestock sector were also assessed as basis of the analysis. The prices of grain in the domestic market (from 2010 to 2015) were investigated, from the end of the chain to the origin, using international market data as reference point. Additionally, the level of openness to trade in grains and the level of consumption and remoteness of those goods were considered. The quantitative analysis to evaluate the costs on the feedstuff formulations and its cost analyses are based on proportions of one macro ingredient[11] for dairy cattle, poultry, and hogs.

In regards to qualitative analysis, semi-structured interviews constituted the instrument for the primary data collection for the period between December 2015 and February 2015. A snowball sampling technique was used. Overall, import representatives were selected on the basis of the agribusinesses under analysis and the practical feasibility of accessing the companies. The semi-structured question instrument was designed using the variables of Porter's Diamond. Porter's framework helped identify factors related to the internal agribusiness competitiveness through the dimension of an external NTM. The instrument targeted the effect of the Cabotage Act (external NTM) on the agribusiness supply chain, the operational activities, the integration into the chain, business importing logistics, and secondary activities related to operational processes. Independent variables associated with maritime transportation, such as the role of government and non-governmental organizations, port mooring costs, handling fees, insurance and inspections were studied. Using NVivo, the data were coded for three dimensions: external, internal, and cultural factors. These dimensions were anchored in vulnerability to trade, the managers' perception of business competitiveness, the level of supply chain complexities, and the strategies implemented to deal with maritime transportation costs.

The primary data collection (i.e., interviews) was done in Spanish and conducted in Puerto Rico. The goal was to learn more about interviewees' perceptions, logistics, and strategies for dealing with the cabotage challenges in their business's supply chain. Categorical coding was applied to sort the findings into formulated concepts and areas of decisions (internal or external to the firm). Once the thematic networks had been created, the data were integrated and interpreted.

The sample was representative of the vast majority of the companies recognized in PR as native importing agribusinesses for the period between 2000 and 2015. The group consisted of seven fresh-produce importer companies in a market estimated at $230 million per year; three of them accounted for more than 75 percent of the produce sales. The second group was associated with the importing of grain, raw material, and other goods used in the animal feed sector with gross sales of about $200 million per annum. In this group of nine importing firms, all existing operational firms of animal feedstuff were interviewed, as well as representatives from two firms no longer in the market. The sector of fertilizers, in which the overall sales may reach over $40 million per annum, was not analyzed in this research. However, some of the participants were related to that agribusiness.

3. Discussion and empirical analysis

This section summarizes the data analysis and findings regarding the agrifood trade relationship between US and Puerto Rico and directly and/or indirectly related with the Cabotage phenomenon. Informative topics gathered through the fieldwork and some multidimensional effects of Cabotage are segmented in the following six subsections. Each one describes the scenario pre 2017 hurricanes considering hard-infrastructure, cross regulations, soft-infrastructure, agribusinesses firms (i.e., grain, fruit and vegetables), and emerging issues.

3.1. PR's port infrastructure

Puerto Rico has eleven official ports[12] registered under the Puerto Rico Ports Authority (PRPA) (USDoC 2015). Most of the maritime facilities are in the port of San Juan (North). Although the Ponce (South) and Mayagüez (West) ports fall under PRPA's jurisdiction, the ports were administratively delegated to public-private partnerships and municipalized, respectively.

For more than a decade, PRPA, which is governed by a board of directors headed by an executive director, has acted more like a real-estate corporation than a port-planning manager. By law (No. 125 of May 1942, as amended), the PRPA was created to own and manage all the sea and air facilities for cargo and passenger cruises in the Puerto Rican archipelago (OMB 2011).[13] Various agencies of the US Federal Government are related to PRPA, such as the US Environmental Protection Agency, the US Army Corp of Engineers and particularly the US Coast Guard. As a result, the PRPA's planning programs and some decisions are in a direct relationship with these agencies. According to some of the participants, some grants and technical assistance are provided annually by these and other US Federal Government agencies. PRPA investments are commonly focused on the airport infrastructure rather than the maritime port. However, PRPA is facing serious financial problems.

The interviewees agreed that private companies and not the PRPA provide most shipping industry services, including tugs, pilotage, fuel delivery, water supply, provisions, customs, water supply, and vessel maintenance. Since the Navieras de Puerto Rico was sold in 1995 due to questionable considerable losses (estimated at $350 million), the Government of Puerto Rico does not have a cargo fleet (Frankel 2002). Various interviewees support the idea that the whole operational transportation system is privatized but outdated and inefficient, with effects on Puerto Rico's market particularly on the native businesses.

San Juan's port is the only port in the north of the main island that is naturally protected from the strength of the Atlantic Sea. While San Juan is Puerto Rico's main port with 26 piers or dockyards, Ponce's (in the south) has the deepest draught (15 m in 3 dockyards and a road) and is the most recently redesigned. The cargo port of San Juan has a relatively tight entrance, and exiting might require a harbor pilot. According to the interviewed PRPA officials, the port offers a total of 4.6 hectares (ha) of space for loading/unloading cargo. All facilities are rented to private companies. In this port area the relationship is mixed. For instance, one of the three agribusiness grain importers has its own dockyard. Regarding the docking places of the other two grain firms, although the PRPA is the landlord, these are lent to them by long-term contracts. It is estimated that PR may have more than 30 private cargo dockyards, none of which pay fees to the PRPA and the majority of which are linked to an industrial business, but data to validate this claim were not available.

It is estimated that PR may have more than 30 private cargo dockyards, none of which pay fees to the PRPA and the majority of which are linked to an industrial business, but data to validate this claim were not available.

Due to the limitations in public investment funds, the PRPA's investment plan is currently based on a kind of public-private partnership promoting the terminals' modernization by its current operators. The interviewees report that the PRPA is using some formulas and fixing rent fees in the long term that are contingent to the investment. However, the draughts represent a limitation.

On the west coast, Guánica and Mayagüez specifically, some raw materials for agribusinesses and pharmaceuticals are received (USDoC 2015). However, in both municipalities the cargo dockyards used for agribusiness importers are private, which means they are totally administered by their owners. Fieldwork revealed that Guánica's bay is operationally limited by its natural draught (9 m at the entrance and 6.5 m at the dockyards). In the past, two agribusiness importers (i.e, Pro-Granos and Ochoa Fertilizer) had operations there. In Mayagüez, since StarKist tuna shut down its factory, the regional port has had a comparatively insignificant operation. Currently, its activity is basically nil. Although this region is historically less affected by destructive hurricanes (Mujica-Baker n.d), its lack of critical-mass (population) affects its business potential.

The US authority on ports is spread throughout all three levels of government—federal, state and local—but its Constitution grants the federal government exclusive jurisdiction over domestic waterways (Sherman 2002). Since Puerto Rico's bays are federalized, many activities are subject to control by the US Federal Government and a plethora of overlapping regulations. For example, investments must be authorized by the US Army Corps of Engineers and various other federal agencies. Before hurricane Maria, Puerto Rico's main lane in the port of San Juan was limited to 12.2 m (40') in depth.[14] Authorization of maintenance extraction procedures in the bay is relatively easy to undertake, but according to some of the interviewees authorization could take almost a year and for major dredging extractions is very unlikely—if not impossible—to obtain. Additionally, the cost of extraction procedures would imply a huge expense for Puerto Rico. The cost of renovating every pier and dockyard in the port should also be included because many of them were designed in the 1940s under different conditions and requirements. Lower draught limits sea trade mostly to modern and efficient vessels. To offer a comparison, the South America's main ports show—an overall draught average—1.3 m (4.2') deeper than Puerto Rico's main port. Wilmsmeier and Sánchez (2015) report that between 2012 and 2014 the average draught on the east coast (ECSA) of that region is 13.3 m (43.6') and the maximum draught 14.5 m (47.6').

Another weakness of Puerto Rico's port system is its infrastructure, which is basically owned by domestic (US) firms; thus, foreign direct investment in the maritime infrastructure is practically non-existent (Estudios Tecnicos 2013). According to some of the interviewees, the lack of services to repair vessels is another disadvantage. So far, the majority of the tugboats, barges, ferries, ships, and other commercial and public vessels are repaired abroad. The Dominican Republic and a few small islands in the Caribbean or the south of the US are the most common places, but for Jones Act vessels, their repairs are limited to US territories. Apparently, for decades, PR's market has had no interest in providing this kind of service. Burns (2015) sustains that generally vessel maintenance programs are a lucrative business in high trade markets because they have ramifications for logistics and reduce the number calling for services.

Finally, the lack of stability in the PRPA's direction is an internal (Puerto Rico) issue that was presented as one of the causes for the loss of regional competitiveness. Between 2008 and 2017, the PRPA had seven executive directors. Certainly, the high turnover of managers may affect negatively long-term planning actions. However, in summary, Puerto Rico's ports seem affected by overlapping jurisdictional regulations, the lack of a system of proactive improvements, and clear direction focused on logistic performance, facilities' optimization, and a culture of efficiency.

3.2. Maritime firms, containerization, and cross regulations

Various maritime companies hold their main service in the area, but literature on this particular seems limited. Since 2013, whilst the claims[15] for cabotage liberalization in Puerto Rico have become more popular, some of these firms announced aggressive investment plans and terminal modernization programs. Interviewed PRPA officials informed that the biggest coastal areas in San Juan are rented to Crowley and Sea Star Lines. It is understood that, overall, around 16 maritime (domestic and foreign) service providers[16] operate in Puerto Rico. However, the vast majority of the infrastructure and terminal operations are carried out by these two main domestic firms.

The US maritime firm Crowley has been one of the biggest in the US for more than a century. It has served the domestic market of Puerto Rico (approximately 38 percent)[17] for over five decades and has over 200 employees. In the US, it is a huge maritime firm providing services from the most basic logistics to naval design and building. Its operation in Puerto Rico (in 31 ha) is based on roll-on/roll-off (RO-RO) vessels, but in 2014 it reported the acquisition of new ships for 2017. Two brand-new Liquefied Natural Gas (LNG) ships with capacity for 900 containers will be part of its fleet to serve Puerto Rico's market. Additionally, Crowley will invest approximately $45 million in a new maritime cargo terminal (in San Juan), as part of a long-term contract lent agreement with the PRPA (Sin Comillas 2015). In 2015, they conducted a full renovation and draught of the dockyard and acquired three new cranes for containers, power stations for refrigerated containers, new generation containers and ISO tanks, and equipment to manage containers on the ground. In addition, a new logistics yard design for easy trucking access started in 2016. They reported that the whole investment is over $400 million (Han 2017).

According to the interviewees, TOTE Maritime operates the second domestic firm: Sea Star Lines. Its Puerto Rico operations, based in Jacksonville, Florida, started in the 1970s and represent approximately between 25 percent and 32 percent of all Puerto Rico's domestic traffic (as of 2014). Whilst Sea Star has previously concentrated on domestic cargoes, they recently acquired the firm Tropical Shipping exclusively dedicated to international trade (TOTE Service 2014). In addition, between late 2016 and mid-2017, two new LNG high-tech ships were added to its fleet. So far, Sea Star Lines is the only paperless terminal operator company in Puerto Rico. Many of its procedures to track, trace, and pick up containers are digitalized or performed by a scanning system. As part of its transformation, in 2017, Sea Star announced an investment between $10 and $25 million in its terminal to become more modern with a full containers tracking system (CTS), chassis, drivers, buyers, and other security devices (Sin Comillas 2016).

While it should be highlighted that the purchasing pronouncement made by Crowley and TOTE—each buying two new LNG ships made in the US— a business decision, it is also highly influenced by the US Merchant Maritime Act and its overlapping regulations. The literature sustains that international shipbuilders are well experimented and also significantly cheaper than their US competitors (Donga 2015; UNCTAD 2013; Hopman and Nienhuis 2009).

The third-biggest area of (30 ha) was administered by Horizon, but during this research, the firm decided to close operations and the PRPA was selecting a new operator. According to the research participants, Horizon was a mixed company attending to approximately 35 percent of the international and 30 percent of the domestic carriers to/from Puerto Rico with particular interest on reefers.

Another domestic company that operates in Puerto Rico is Trailer Bridge, based in Jacksonville, but in comparison with the companies mentioned earlier, it has limited space, managing around 15 percent of all Puerto Rico's domestic trade. It is more focused on lift-on/lift-off (LO–LO) and RO–RO vessels but also manages highly diversified containers. Although not a contractor of the PRPA, it is in partnership with the maritime firm International Shipping, which is a native company dedicated to international trade and stevedoring with a PRPA long-term contract. It is an example of a partnership between two relatively small maritime service providers, one based in Jacksonville and the other based in San Juan, offering global access to Puerto Rico. Luis Ayala-Colón SCs, focused on international cargoes, is the fifth maritime firm. It is an experimented local-native operator, which although limited in resources provides stevedoring services to international carriers, as well as some domestic ones.

To contrast Puerto Rico's domestic maritime firms, the two US off-shore states, Alaska and Hawaii, have only two main operators each: TOTE (Sea Star in Puerto Rico) and Matson, and Matson and Pasha, respectively. These are highly specialized container management companies. Nevertheless, the new configuration in these markets reduced competition and strengthened the players. For instance, Matson bought Horizon's Alaska service and competes with TOTE. In Hawaii, the firm Pasha, which operates RO–RO tonnage in this market, acquired Horizon's Hawaii operation to compete with Matson.[18] However, unlike the mentioned US off-shore states, Puerto Rico's population, market, and container traffic are higher.

Although all of these companies are recruiters of local talent, only Horizon and Ayala-Colón boards are in the majority local investors. The maritime firm Island Stevedoring is a small, local company dedicated to carrying construction materials, such as wood and pipes, paper, less than a container's load (LCL) and cars. Many international lines of transport, such as Maersk, Norton Lilly International, Oceanic General Agency, Henríquez & Assoc and Pérez & Cia use Puerto Rico's ports (*Noticel* 2015); however, they have service agreements with the maritime service providers mentioned above. Therefore, international companies have no similar infrastructure or investment in Puerto Rico's ports. Among other reasons, the majority of imports to Puerto Rico are domestic, and the costs of initiation in this business are very high. As a result, partnerships with the operators mentioned above seem to be an acceptable business model for them.

All the mentioned maritime firms in Puerto Rico are well equipped to manage containers efficiently. It is important to clarify that containers' sizes are measured by density thus using equivalent units. For international trades, the sizes were standardized in 20' (TEU) and 40' (FEU), while in domestics the sizes are determined by each country (Burns 2015). For instance, in the US, container sizes are 45', 48', and 53' long. This offers more options to trade but as the volume becomes higher (in equivalent units), its relative gross cargo weight (gcw) becomes lower because its dimensions are not yet designed to handle the same rigors as sea (international) containers. Perishable produce such as vegetables and fruits are transported regularly using refrigerated or climatized containers named reefers. Containers over 45' equivalent units are relatively rare for reefers, but this situation may change in the future. Nevertheless, interviewed produce importers reported challenges to maritime firms since Horizon's closing, including: the availability of vessels suited to transport high number of reefers at once, adequate space equipped for reefers once in the yard, and high density for storage. Regarding the first challenge, reefer ships differ from general container carriers in their power generation and electrical distribution

Figure 1: Port efficiency in Latin America and the Caribbean; Extracted from: Morales-Sarriera et al (2013).

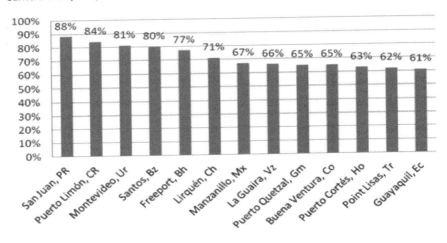

equipment (Burns 2015). Although limited, reefers can be carried in general design vessels, but this is a challenge because in addition to the lack of space and good balance for containers' stackability, they are generally limited in power connections. The reported issues of adequate space and storage might be related to lack of investments and issues of flows and terminal designs. Grain traded in domestic journeys is commonly transported in dry-bulk vessels or barge carriers due to its capability to travel inland (across rivers). The fieldwork shows that in Puerto Rico these cargoes are directly managed by the importing grain company rather than some of the "port service providers" or "terminal operators"

Using data between 1999 and 2009, the Inter American Development Bank ranked the technical efficiency of containers at the port of San Juan as first among other 62 ports in Mexico, the Caribbean, and Central and South America (Morales-Sarriera et al. 2013) (Fig. 1). Between 2008 and 2016, the port of San Juan was ranked (63, 71, 72, 79, 80, 92, 94 to 94, respectively) in the list of top 100 world ports in container traffic (AAPA 2017). In 2017, based on container traffic, Lloyds Maritime Intelligence launched its top 100 ports rank (Nightingale 2017). On that list, the lowest traffic was 1.4 million TEU. Puerto Rico's numbers are even lower, thus not included. At the domestic level, the US Department of Commerce (2015) classified San Juan as 13th of the 38 US ports in total volume (MT) transported. In the value of goods imported from the US, the port of San Juan is classified 17th of 38 ($11.7 billion in 2012) and 19th of 38 in the value of goods exported to the US ($4.4 billion in 2012) (USDoC, 2015). The majority of goods (food and grains) imported to Puerto Rico are carried through San Juan. Clearly, while these rankings show that at least 1.2 million TEU are annually managed by the maritime firms in Puerto Rico, a reduction in container traffic is evident. However, not much has been said about logistics, efficiency, infrastructure, dry-bulk activities, and/or performance variables of Puerto Rico's port.

According to Szakonyi (2014), the southbound rates of transport from Jacksonville to San Juan are between $2,600 and $3,400 per twenty-foot equivalent unit (TEU), with dry-box prices on the lower side and reefers priced higher. Although not specifically clear, these TEU rates imply a higher cost to trade forty-foot equivalent unit (FEU) containers. Furthermore, he affirms that northbound rates on the same route are between $500 and $700 per TEU. He suggests that the export cost per dry container from PR to Jacksonville is basically non-existent because the vessel's operational costs and drayage to Florida might be equivalent to the number of full containers loaded (FCL). Maritime transportation providers should develop logistics to guarantee the full return of containers and worst-case scenario with no less than 25 percent FCL; otherwise, operational costs would become more expensive or unsustainable (Burns 2015).

Currently, the costs on Puerto Rico northbound domestic routes are lower than that percentage[19] (Szakonyi 2014). Although recognizing that Puerto Rico's market is far more crowded than that of Alaska and Hawaii, there has been a reduction (around 12 percent) in the total of containers at domestic imports to Puerto Rico, which could be associated with Puerto Rico's economic depression (Fig. 2). However, a pattern of reduction in the number of containers from Puerto Rico to the US was previewed by Frankel (2002) almost two decades ago.

At the International Convention of Safe Containers in 1972 a resolution for the safety traffic of containers was adopted. It promoted among members some human life safety measures during container management, such as maximum gross weight or ratings, handling, stacking, and whether under a single bill of lading or under separate bills of lading (IMO 2014). In the US, since 1997 containers have faced some management restrictions by the Intermodal Safe Container Act (Public Lax 102-548, Oct. 1992). This act regulates the loaded container from its place of origin to its place of destination in multimodal transportation. The gross cargo weight (gcw) is also regulated according to the container size. Currently, at the international level, this kind of regulation is common in developed and in some less developed countries. However, this research revealed that the gcw limits in the US are lower (40' max gcw 20 MT) than in Mexico (40' max gcw 21 MT), Canada (40' max gcw 21.8 MT), or the UK (40' max gcw 26 MT) and Japan (40' max gcw 30 MT). Furthermore, the gcw is even less strict for shipping containers from less developed countries such as the Dominican Republic (40'max gcw 31 MT). This limit on gcw could have an impact in PR's container traffic but also on space optimization, efficiency, and cost analysis.

Unlike domestic ships, foreign vessels and/or containers require authorization from US agencies, such as the Coast Guard, Custom Border Patrol, the Department of Agriculture (APHIS & PPQ), and in some cases the Health Department. The Government of Puerto Rico has very limited or no jurisdiction over this matter. As a result, the intervention of a registered "custom broker" is required. Around 22 brokers are recognized

Figure 2: Percentage of change in the US container trade with PR (2008–2013); Extracted from: Szakonyi (2014).

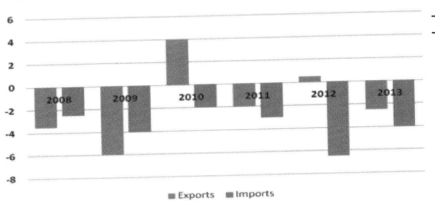

and authorized by the US federal agencies to provide services in Puerto Rico (Anaya-Oviedo 2012). On the contrary, the protocols in Puerto Rico for domestic (US) cargoes are relatively fast or unnecessary because they are considered to have been inspected or to be from a safe place. The interviewees reported that once these containers have been unloaded, the importers may receive the cargo in as little as two hours. However, for international cargoes these processes may take between 24 and 48 labor hours after the docking. The Puerto Rico ratio of container volume per year (domestic: international) could be estimated as a ration of 70:30; hence, it is a predominantly domestic market. To contrast this average time with other SIDSs' processes, Puerto Rico's protocols seem to take longer than those of the Mauritius Islands, which according to official data average between 30 and 60 minutes (World Bank 2015). For perishables, freshness is related to quality, and thus longer container times mean the product's shelf life is affected and the time for consumers' use is lessened. Therefore, consumers pay for a short-life product.

Data about the domestic maritime transportation rates are limited, and for this research it was generated through interviews (Table 1). It should be mentioned that the majority of the participating firms were reluctant to share their official annual contracts showing the fixed prices rate for containers. Nevertheless, the differences in price are noticeable among importing companies (Co), more specifically in trades from Jacksonville. Higher freight rates have an impact on all aspects of the economy, all the way down to the consumers themselves.

3.3. Digitization, environment, route optimization & cost of energy

Digitization in this field stands for a highly technological system to identify, track, and trace containers during the stevedoring process. It includes assigning chassis, tracking and measuring the whole process until the container is exported from its or-

Table 1: Price per FEU refrigerated containers and distance (n.m.) from the port of origin to the port of San Juan, PR.

Origin	Distance (n.m.)	Days	Co 9	Co 10	Co 11	Other
				Value in USD		
Jacksonville, US	1333	4	5,350	4,500	4,000	6,300***
California, US‡	*	9	N/P	9,000	10,500	-
Miami, US	1057	3.5	N/P	N/P	N/P	6,688
Philadelphia, US	*	8				-
Sto. Domingo, DR	300	0.7	2,200	2,300	2,250	1,057-1,240**
Pto. Limón, CR	1342	2.5	2,800-3,300	N/P	2,500	-
Nicaragua†	1500	3.5-5.5	2,400-3,300	N/P	2,500	-
Colombia†	-	-	3,450	-	-	-

Note: 12th of December - 10th of February. ‡Inland to Jacksonville. †Port was not mentioned
** 45 foot NOT refrigerated container from Haina Port. The rate varies by volume; the first is 7 containers vs. 1 container, respectively.
*** The price for 45-foot containers is $300 higher.

igin to its arrival. In Puerto Rico, such technology system is in early stage, not widely used, or inexistent.[20] Although the process is quite dynamic digitalization of Puerto Rico is limited in comparison with other SIDSs markets, such as Singapore and Hong Kong. Unlike airports, it seems that seaports have the disadvantage of a relatively low traffic of people and thus fewer funds to improve areas, logistics, and efficiency in processes. Seaports lack priority unless a union declares a lockout and/or during a climatic phenomenon or a humanitarian crisis.

Environmentally, sea ports' locations are highly vulnerable to climate effects such as rising sea levels, intensive hurricanes, among others. These events can cause heavy flooding at ports and operation disruptions. For example, in 2000 Hurricane George caused serious damage and destruction to practically all the basic port facilities and terminals, blocking the main entrance of the port of San Juan, devastating Puerto Rico's economy for months. Fortunately, during hurricanes Irma and Maria the damages to infrastructure on Puerto Rico's main ports were not as serious as they were in the 2000. However, many of the commercial port terminals in Puerto Rico are outdated. This is particularly obvious in the private terminals of the grain-importing firms. For instance, the majority of dockyards and commercial terminals in the ports of San Juan and Mayagüez are very close to the sea level. Therefore, ordinary operations would be affected if the level rises by more than a meter. Since most port activities in Puerto Rico are privatized, the PRPA is not directly responsible for implementing environmental initiatives associated with clean air programs and emission controls imposed by some other local and federal agencies. Hence, little effort has been made to adapt Puerto Rico's cargo ports and their infrastructure to the impacts of climate change.

Transporting dry-bulk materials requires different supply chain management from transporting containers. An increase in annual rainfall or precipitation rates may affect its logistics. For example, grains delivered in dry bulk vessels are unloaded under an open sky; thus, an increase in the frequency of heavy rain periods would bring delays in the process and demurrage fees.[21] With regards to fresh produce containers, their refrigeration needs, such as electrical devices, entail risks of storm-water effects.

On the other hand, Ponce's port is spacious and ready for containers and investments.

During this research, I was informed that the Government of Puerto Rico does not have an executive plan or maritime analyst to promote the optimization of commercial sea routes as is happening for airlines and cruise lines. Through a cross-analysis of commercial sea routes, more possibilities to trade with other Latin American countries could be identified, helping in planning and profitability. On the subject of space optimization, the ports of San Juan and Mayagüez are substantially limited in growth and storage areas. Areas for storing containers are practically non-existent in Mayagüez. San Juan is a highly populated port city where urban growth takes priority and has a great influence on the limited space available. This space issue will represent more challenges to adapt the facilities to the local contexts, and it will probably affect the insurance cost rates. On the other hand, Ponce's port is spacious and ready for containers and investments. Although it was designed for a trans-shipment operation, it has been underdeveloped since its inauguration, arguably, due to its lack of critical-mass.

Companies hold additional inventories to respond to delivery delays and product unreliability. This practice may increase costs for inventory, storage space, energy, and so forth. In the case of produce importers, due to its perishability, the inventory levels are low, but its climatized storages demand high energy consumption. In regards to the grain importers, an efficient goods unloading and its transformation requires highly energy dependent colossal machinery. As a result, on these two sectors the price of energy is an important internal variable for competitiveness (Fig. 3). However, Puerto Rico's energy system is poorly maintained and highly dependent on petroleum. Thus it is substantially influenced by the oil price, which is an external variable with impact on the cost of all its derivatives (transportation, fertilizers, pesticides, etc.).

Figure 3: Cost of energy (kW/h) in US jurisdictions (2012); Extracted from: US Energy Information Administration (2015)

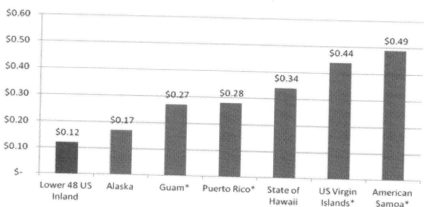

3.4. Grain importers

Puerto Rico's animal feed mill sector currently consists of eight firms, but three of them were recently consolidated. Altogether, they represent around $250 million in sales per year. Their domestic and foreign imports could be estimated to be approximately $130 million and $35 million, respectively, per year.[22] None of Puerto Rico's grain firms have a logistics division or internal personnel dedicated to or specialized in optimizing the freight cost. In all of them, the grain-importing process is led and authorized by the manager or CEO. Two firms are not factually grain importers but raw material importers for animal feed production. In this research, these two importers are considered to be 'complementary companies.' One of them imports liquids; and the other, vitamins and minerals. Both are vital echelons in the elaboration process of the feedstuff. Certainly, these two firms are not directly affected by the volatile international cost of grain, but they are importers affected by the cost of maritime transport.

Grain imports in Puerto Rico are carried in barges and charter ships, all of them directly contracted by the grain importers. All firms have external (outside Puerto Rico) agreements with grain exporters and/or business advisory services based in the US. Sea transportation is supplied by external providers because none has vessels as part of its inventory. One has a long-term agreement with a domestic maritime firm providing a barge used twice or more per month.

Grain is considered to be a storable commodity that is produced every year. Its prices are forecasted and set on future prices affected by many variables; thus, its purchase and delivery may represent challenges. For instance, in addition to the cost of grain, the barge sets its rates for this journey, which may change weekly. The rates could vary by the grain's city of origin, the carrier's number of stops, fuel, volume, weather conditions, storage costs, local conditions, supply and demand, and other factors. These factors are named the '*basis*,' because they are the difference between the current local cash price and the future price of the contract with the closest delivery month (Hofstrand 2009).

Puerto Rico's tropical weather affects grain storage. Regularly, it is limited to a period of three to four months once received. Nevertheless, the firms are technically working below their storage capacity level. Except for one firm, the lack of a dockyard infrastructure and draught may limit PR's grain importers' firms to vessels no more than 7 meters in depth. In this case, docking dry bulk cargo ships with 25,000 tons or more (7.50 m) will be problematic in grain importers facilities. This is not a problem for the river barges frequently used by the grain producers in the US, but commonly limited in capacity (between 12,000 and 18,000 tons).

Due to the limits of Puerto Rico's animal feed market, grain importers share vessels and commodities to reduce their cost of transportation or to take advantage of bigger volumes in the commodity for a better price. Although negotiations and accords between the local grain importers seem not to be complex, the logistics and shipping coordination require precision and operational agreements.

The grain-importing firms have a direct relationship with equipment, ships and their crew, and many other processes related to their goods. In this research, none of the interviewees identified negative experiences with the crew of a foreign maritime provider. On the contrary, the majority of the participants highlighted their professionalism, particularly that of the ship leaders. Regarding ship maintenance, various participants said the foreign ships that generally arrive in PR show a level of maintenance and sophistication that is higher than that of the domestic fleet. The conditions of the domestic fleet were seriously criticized by many of the interviewees.

My experience with foreign crews is that they are very skilled, they are people with ... Just as an example, in the last foreign ship arrival that I had the captain was a veteran, an ex-commander of a Russian nuclear submarine. What of both vessels would require the most highly trained personnel? We were talking frankly for a while.

The cost of the domestic product versus the foreign one should not include other expenses associated with shipping. Although it could be logical to think the value of the commodity would not take the transportation cost into consideration, two of the participants categorically affirmed that, on the contrary, this is the case for foreign imports. They posited that the price per MT reported by the foreign exporters includes all transportation services until delivery, and that is not the case for domestic suppliers. Following their experience, they estimated that overall, although varying monthly, the domestic transportation cost is between $8 and $30 per MT higher than the foreign cost. In the low-cost scenario, their decision to import is based more on quality than on price. However, the quantitative data to support their argument were not provided.

Table 2: Over-cost of transportation ($8.00) per maize (MT) for Puerto Rico's farmers by sector

A. Dairy Farms

Year	% Domestic origin/yr	Cost per unit/yr	Fixed No. units 2012	Total cost for the sector	Farms 100-199 units	200-299 units	300-350 units
2010	72%	$15.12	90,000	$1,360,800.00	$2,260.44	$3,764.88	$4,914.00
2011	57%	$11.97	90,000	$1,077,300.00	$1,789.52	$2,980.53	$3,890.25
2012	48%	$10.08	90,000	$907,200.00	$1,506.96	$2,509.92	$3,276.00
2013	36%	$7.56	90,000	$680,400.00	$1,130.22	$1,882.44	$2,457.00
2014	75%	$15.75	90,000	$1,417,500.00	$2,354.68	$3,921.75	$5,118,75

B. Poultry Farms

Year	% Domestic origin/yr	Units per farm/C	Cost per farm/yr	Total cost for the sector
2010	72%	30,000	$2,801.87	$196,141.14
2011	57%	30,000	$2,218,15	$155,270.49
2012	48%	30,000	$1,867.92	$130,754.09
2013	36%	30,000	$1,400.94	$98,065.57
2014	75%	30,000	$3,648.27	$255,379.09

C. Hog Farms

Year	% Domestic origin/yr	Cost per unit/yr	Fixed No. units 2012	Total cost for the sector	Farms 100-199 units	200-299 units	300-399 units	400-499 units
2010	72%	$0.77	55,000	$42,588.00	$255.53	$425.88	$596.23	$766.58
2011	57%	$0.61	55,000	$33,715.50	$202.29	$337.16	$472.02	$606.88
2012	48%	$0.52	55,000	$28,392.00	$170.35	$283.92	$397.49	$511.06
2013	36%	$0.39	55,000	$21,294.00	$127.76	$212.04	$298.12	$383.29
2014	75%	$0.81	55,000	$44,362.50	$266.18	$443.63	$621.08	$798.53

The suggested over-cost was considered to estimate the effects on the cost by unit of production. Variables such as the average volume of feedstuff consumed by the three main animal production sectors of PR (dairy cow [9 Kg/day per unit]; poultry farms [8.5 MT/day per flock]; swine farms [1.2Kg/day per unit]), the proportion of maize (65-70 percent) in a basic formulation in PR, and the percentage of domestic imports of maize per year were considered (Table 2).

These analyses only considered the over-cost of maize as a heavy grain. Soy meal, corn gluten, fishmeal, and wheat-meal are also common ingredients used in feedstuff formulations in Puerto Rico, and many of them are imported. However, the data available on these other ingredients are mixed with data on other products, not accurately classified or, in the case of corn gluten, the percentages in the formulations are relatively smaller. In addition, some of the ingredients or wheat by-products used in formulations are produced in Puerto Rico, and the data are not available.[23]

For contrasting services, other factors were presented and described to the participants to particularize the differences between domestic and foreign maritime services. These factors were punctuality, intercommunication, product management, and cultural issues (Table 3).

3.5. Fruit and vegetables importers
The majority of the fresh-produce importers in Puerto Rico are native-family agribusinesses. Although few in number, they supply almost 75 percent of the imported produce to feed the total market. The remaining 25 percent is from transnational companies that focus on processed products rather than fresh goods.

For fruits, the cycle begins on the (US) west coast, then moves to the south coast until winter when Peru and eventually Chile become the suppliers until late spring, when they return to California.

Puerto Rico's data on the value of imports, particularly for agriculture and food produce from the US, show a pattern of increase in foods and some reduction in the agriculture group. However, Puerto Rico's dependency on other markets to sustain its more basic needs for food is certainly more dramatic when the transportation service is totally privatized, and the market is relatively limited in its ability to adopt counterbalance measures. In addition, the purchasing strategies, in this importing sector of Puerto Rico, follow the US season of production, which means that when the US market lacks some produce, its importers look abroad.[24] As a result, except for some roots or tanniers (so far not produced in the US), the fresh-produce importers have their itinerary of purchasing starting and ending with US production. For instance, for green leaves, their main suppliers are the West Coast of the US, then in mid-autumn Mexico, then in the spring the southeast coast of Canada, and then Cali-

Table 3: Puerto Rico's agribusiness importers' perception of Latin American exports

QUALITY

	Firm	Packaging	Product	Handling
PRODUCE	10	HQ	HQ	HQ
	9	HQ	Good	Good
	11	Medium	Good	Medium
	13	Medium	Low	Good
GRAIN	1	N/A	Medium	-
	2	N/A	HQ	Good
	3	N/A	HQ	Good
	5	N/A	Medium	-
	8	N/A	-	Good

INSECURITY

	Firm	On Trade (Distrust)	Technical	SPS Regulations	Political Stability
PRODUCE	10	Low	Medium	High	Low
	9	Low	Medium	VH	Low
	11	Low	Medium	High	Low
	13	Medium	VH	VH	Low
GRAIN	1	VH	-	VH	-
	2	Low	Medium	VH	Low
	3	VH	VH	VH	Medium
	5	VH	VH	VH	VH
	8	VH	High	Low	VH

INTERCOMMUNICATION

	Firm	Language Issues	Phone/Fax	Online
PRODUCE	10	Low	Low	VH
	9	Low	High	Medium
	11	Low	Medium	High
	13	Low	Medium	Medium
GRAIN	1	High	High	Low
	2	VH	VH	Medium
	3	VH	High	High
	5	High	VH	-
	8	High	High	High

fornia until the next cycle. For fruits, the cycle begins on the (US) West Coast, then moves to the South Coast until winter when Peru and eventually Chile become the suppliers until late spring, when they return to California. These systematic forms of trading follow the US market because, from the perspective of volume, they can buy at lower prices in comparison with Puerto Rico. As a result, the US purchasers and consolidation firms, in partnership with Puerto Rico's importers, may supply foreign products in accordance with the restrictions of applicable SPS measures at relatively competitive prices for their standards. Inevitably, the domestic (US) maritime service providers have to be contracted to carry these supplies to Puerto Rico.

Due to the fact that perfect substitution is not always possible in this business, the Cabotage Act is a given constraint on this market. We have to deal with it, hence reducing the time and many of our efficiencies.

Liberalization could bring some changes to competition and the cost of trade might be lower. It is likely that the cost of importing raw materials would be lower, as well as the rates for transporting manufactured food. The latter scenario may need more analysis, particularly from the perspective of the current limited national food production. Currently, native food manufacturing in Puerto Rico is practically non-existent, and around 65 percent of products are imported from the US. The remaining percentage is imported from countries to which the US Cabotage Act does not apply. Therefore, a reduction in the cost of domestic transportation should also reduce the cost of domestic imports made under a similar sanitary and phytosanitary (SPS) framework to PR.

The negative effects of this would be on the local producers. They would have to reduce their prices to compete with the domestic imports in unfair conditions and lack of volume. In that sense, a relaxation in the Cabotage Act on the manufactured goods would be beneficial for the importers and supermarkets, but it might be a hard punch for the native agriculture rather than a benefit. However, if it is about price competition, currently the native producers are highly affected by the produce from the Dominican Republic that has a similar productive season and lower cost to produce than PR.

Puerto Rico's importers are not restricted to importing products only from the US market; thus, the market could be considered as an open market. However, for importing food and agricultural products, other NTMs have to be taken into account. Consequently, the application of all the US regulations to food, labeling, canning, and so forth on Puerto Rico's market reduces the number of places to trade. Furthermore, whilst for the domestic imports the inspection protocols at the port are practically non-existent, at the foreign imports they are complex. The delay in trucking a container will depend on the ship's arrival time and the number of containers queuing. It is not unusual for foreign arrivals between 15:00 and 17:00 to schedule an inspection time 24 hours later.

For instance, once the containers have been discharged from the ship and the process of container recognition begins, consisting of inspection, fumigation and other red-tape procedures, they are normally completed in 12 to 72 labor hours.[25]

In my professional experience dealing with the elements of quality, produce management and packaging, I have not noticed big differences between foreign and domestic produce. However, the SPS inspections and port complexities on imports from abroad are the major obstacle to looking more to Central and South American suppliers.

To contrast the maritime services, the participants were invited to identify the differences between domestic and foreign companies. These factors were coded in three groups: quality,[26] insecurity, and intercommunication (Table 3). Regarding delays or inaccuracies in the delivery schedules or ETA, the participants affirmed that it would depend on the maritime firms. Some lines are much more punctual than others, but interviewees categorized the foreign maritime firms as the group with the most frequent occurrence of unpunctuality. Since Horizon's closure, the domestic transport is showing more problems due to the lack of space.

Concerning the intercommunication issues, which are those associated with identifying problems in shipping or tracking containers, all participants said domestic firms are more diligent or at least it is easier to obtain information from their website or by email. Apparently, domestic firms are perceived more "client oriented"[27] about informing issues on board that may cause delays or other problems that would be managed in advance, if the importer was informed. One of the participants said that a reason to hire a third party contractor was precisely to reduce logistical uncertainties due to the lack of communication of the foreign maritime firm contracted by its produce supplier in Latin America.

One dimension that is not directly associated with the Cabotage Act but may influence the cost of trade is the years of business partnerships between importers and suppliers. Purchasing teams are focused on the same companies that traditionally were trading with without seeking competitors. This is not a negative point when it is part of a dynamic market analysis but it might be when purchasing decisions are taken without an ample analysis of providers. The interviewed firms are based on 'high reliability' of their suppliers; thus, searching for new providers is undertaken sporadically. Although the rates for transporting inland are higher than the sea freight rates,[28] a business partnership extending over years has a higher probability of trade than searching for options abroad and in better conditions.

You are making me reflect hard about it. I have to admit that with some frequency we begin the searching process to eventually supply a client, but at the end of the day my purchasing team selects the same provider that traditionally supplies us. We are always doing the same. Although it is 'better the devil you know', we are in a comfort zone. Lack of doing different things and trying to search for options at least to identify other possible providers.

All of the participant firms in this category expressed their disagreement with the application of the US Cabotage Act to PR's market. Their most common argument was based on the over-cost added to imports. A few of them argued the lack of competition of maritime transporters in PR is the most problematic issue, but a bigger problem is the lack of vessels properly prepared for reefers. According to them, both scenarios are having serious effects on their businesses, increasing the cost for the consumers.

The maritime market needs more service providers because currently the fresh-produce importers are choosing between a single, faster, limited-space company (Sea Star) and a firm with space in a slow vessel (Crowley). Both scenarios limit our businesses. I am of the belief that having more ways for transporting imports or having faster ships to trade, the local businesses would be much better and our consumers too.

Here is an example of how cabotage may restrict the supply chain logistics on this economic sector. One of the most frequent suppliers of potatoes in Puerto Rico has its origins in the port of Halifax in Canada, which also carries other supplies to some of the British Caribbean Islands. Consequently, to optimize the shipping and reduce inefficiencies and time, one possible option could be to stop in New York to collect some products for Puerto Rico. However, this is not allowed by the US Cabotage; as a result, the importer should schedule a US-flagged vessel to obtain these products or transport them by inland trucking to the Jacksonville Port, which has more frequent trips to San Juan.

The cabotage limitation for the use of foreign vessels affects my logistic optimization and as a result the price to do business and my produce on the shelf.

3.6. Other emerging topics
A basic flow chart about the Cabotage's layers was developed (Fig. 4) to show layer of elements affected (directly or indirectly) by the Act during the agrifood importing activities. Certainly, many other elements might be considered.

The following example of costs was used by one participant. He said a 40 percent reduction in the current cost of domestic transportation would reduce the basic cost of farming.

A 100 pound (45.4 kg) bag of fertilizer in the US is around $3.50, but in PR due to the freight cost it is between $0.10 and $0.14 per 50 pounds (22.7 kg) over the original cost. As a result, the importer is paying around $0.22 extra just for bringing the produce from the US. It means that the basic price of 100 pounds (45.4 kg) of this fertilizer will start at $3.72. However, the importer should add its expenses and profit, almost 9% of the cost ($0.37); therefore, the consumer will be paying easily $4.10. Certainly, this is not a big deal for a casual consumer, but the $0.60 means money for a regular farmer.[29]

Many additional variables over the price of the commodity affect produces cost, such as the cost of its management, refrigerated containers, transportation (inland and ocean), logistics and regulatory frameworks. Additionally, the elements of relatively low volume, little competition in the market (lack of production), and low availability of domestic maritime transporters cause the price of the affected goods, such as fruits and vegetables, to rise disproportionately.

It is like a tax to preserve inefficiency but in a category of products that, according to the International Health Organization, should be more consumed by the people.

Another dimension was presented by the expectancy of new higher capacity ships that will be incorporated into Puerto Rico's market in a year. Undeniably, new and efficient vessels to transport reefers are highly necessary. The pace of the international maritime providers in the last decade was moving in a similar direction to become more efficient (Burns 2015). However, sustainability patterns in Puerto Rico's businesses are not well known; thus, business decision-making tends to consider limited scenarios of almost five years without much analysis of the underlying elements. Therefore, if Puerto Rico's economic situation is taken into account— a reduction in population and exportation; the cost of energy; and the reduction in the annual family expenses at the supermarket level[30]—how will the (four) new ships exclusively for Puerto Rico's route be cost-effective for the current domestic[31] maritime providers?

4. Conclusion

Puerto Rico's development is immersed in a historical structure of dependency in which government intervention, production inefficiencies, and a large economy (the US but previously Spain) had control over Puerto Rico's growth. To guarantee this, customs control, cabotage, and other regulatory frameworks in favor of the US corporations were established. The "US Jewel of the Caribbean" seems to be an inefficient, uncompetitive, and expensive place to produce, highly controlled by US multinationals and experiencing a high level of brain drain (out-migrants to the US). Its soon-to-be-decade-old depressed economy and approximately 12 percent sustained unemployment in a restricted trade framework, limits the possibilities for participating actively in the global economy and trading with more flexible markets. Some lessons from Puerto Rico's experience could be meaningful to other territories, and this research offers a different approach through mixed method to evaluate the effect of a NTM to trade on SIDS agrifood supply chain.

1. A restriction on the main transportation on a SIDS market (without any inland connection among suppliers) affects the importers' capacity.
2. Cabotage requirements and its cross regulations have direct and indirect effects early on Puerto Rico's agribusiness supply chain activities.
3. The US Maritime Merchant Act limits the range of suppliers affecting the supply

Figure 4: Diagram of some interrelated elements

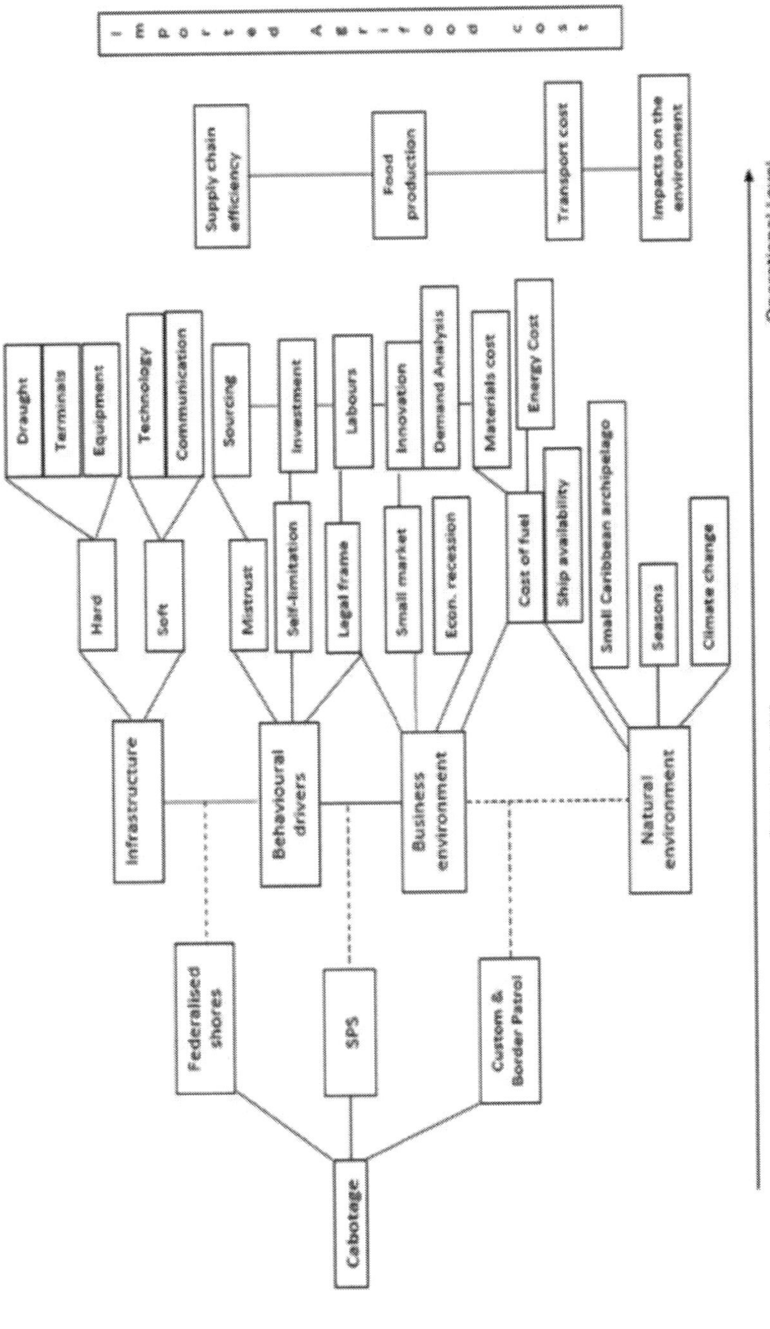

chain of PR's agribusinesses based on imports from the US.

4. Puerto Rico's agribusiness importers, despite having options to import from abroad, are limited because they have to comply with other factors affecting their decisional process to purchase. For instance, the US sanitary and phyto-sanitary restrictions, the US weight limits on containers, the lack of volume in their market, lack of cash flow, obsolete infrastructure on their terminals, and the lack of consolidation services from abroad.

5. The data on the costs associated with freight are under the control of the maritime transportation firms, thus private. Its rates or patterns are neither published nor centralized or collected by the Government of Puerto Rico. This lack of access to data only allows the shippers to allocate specific routes among themselves at predetermined rates. Those with higher volumes get the better rates and priority.

6. The vulnerability of Puerto Rico's market was highlighted by the closure of Horizon in December 2015. After hurricane Maria (September 2017), maritime domestic firms in Puerto Rico did not have enough (cost-benefit) capacity to deal with extraordinary situations to ensure a continuous flow of cargo to Puerto Rico. In addition, the lack of sustainable operations on the ports of Mayagüez and Ponce, constraint even more the supply chain. Currently, a few fleet ships are suitable for fresh food containers and/or reefers, but some importers said although the scenario is improving. Hundreds of containers are still left-behind in Florida due to lack of space on cargo vessels. Maria's emergency demonstrated maritime firms' limitations of space. However, during the period of this research, it was anticipated because the number of ships available for reefers was only one.

7. Areas of opportunity at the internal level regarding supply chain competitiveness of the sectors under exploration were identified.

Bearing in mind this research was founded on most of the sustainable development goals, the analysis of cabotage shows multidimensional effects on food availability and accessibility trigger vulnerability. The cost of energy in Puerto Rico, influenced by its obsolete and highly dependent fossil fuel system, is also affected by the US Cabotage when equipment and some fuel are transported from there.. In addition, port maintenance activities (e.g., dredging, electric submarine cable), exploratory activities as seen and renewable projects such as ocean wind farms are affected by the Act. The energy cost and the extra cost of transportation (on fuel, containers, grains, etc.) are considered by the participants as the most important factor with effects on Puerto Rico's agrifood supply chain. Unfortunately, sea transportation restrictions and their complex structures and layers of service costs developed through the years make it difficult to estimate the real cost of this NTM on the agribusiness sector. However, the most frequent journeys to Puerto Rico are made by domestic vessels. The importers expressed their preferences for the US market and in the case of animal feedstuff, Puerto Rico's farmers are absorbing that overcost.

The sum of all these factors—internal and external—affect Puerto Rico's agrifood sector. Liberalizing cabotage without any investments or internal changes could reduce the price of many goods related to farming in the short term, but in the long term would have a negative effect on Puerto Rico's native agribusiness importers. Probably, they will be affected by the foreign price structure of goods with potential effects reducing the number of native agribusinesses and eroding Puerto Rico's food sovereignty potential. On the other hand, preserving the law as it is would maintain the same business structures and its vulnerabilities without a sustainable solution for Puerto Rico and its competitiveness. Strategic investments in commercial ports' lanes and terminals' infrastructure, automating and digitizing processes, promoting rivalry among maritime firms, strengthening the local industry firms' supporters, and manufacturers' product diversification would be the key to a healthier competitiveness environment. Other dimensions such as fiscal (inventory taxes), geographical (incentives for densification of two of the main port-cities), firms (operational inefficiencies), and anthropological issues related to the local producers' behavior are indirect dimensions that might bring vulnerabilities to PR's food supply chain.

ACKNOWLEDGEMENTS

The author recognizes the collaboration of Drs. Ana Rodríguez and Zaira Arvelo for their comments on editing and Drs. David J. Potts and Hossein Jalilian—from the Bradford Centre of International Development, University of Bradford in the United Kingdom—for their advice, guidance, and help during this research.

NOTES

[1] For this purpose, agrifood is considered as a business of producing food linked to agriculture production, which in a system is developed according to the local resources, cultural, and social productive characteristics. The food supply chain, on the other hand, considers the variables on an effective system between "farms and forks." It includes production, infrastructure, delivery, technological changes, environmental issues, sustainable management, and governance structures.

[2] During that period the US Congress approved, at least, three different laws named Jones Act. The Jones-Shafroth Act that regulates PR's citizenship; the one about Land Grant Colleges (UPR-RUM) Bankhead-Jones Act, 1935; and the one related to Cabotage, which is the one written by Wesley Jones, as the Maritime Merchant Act of 1920 (46 USC Title, Chapter 24; many sections on related topics).

[3] Since 1789, the U.S. Law requires US workers, crew, and flagged ships for domestic maritime transportation. A few maritime laws were approved between 1810 and 1887. Eventually, due to its lack of competitiveness for shore-side support functions many US shipping firms disappears into consolidations. US shipping faced significant cost disadvantages from the turn of the 20th century (Sagers 2006).

[4] American Samoa, Mariana Island, and the Virgin Islands.

[5] Cabotage welfare costs on PR's economy, although without agreement from the academic community, have been estimated between $0 million and $400 million per year.

[6] Overall around 11,000 farmers and native agribusiness for the time of the fieldwork

[7] VRIO (Valuable; Rare; costly to Initiate; Organized to capture value). These four segments are conformed by variables (infrastructure, location, reputation, economic performance, environment threat, social complexity, operational, innovation, and capabilities) to evaluate firms' competitive advantage cycle.

[8] Visibility in the supply chain refers to risk reduction, proactively tracking products, and identifying potential disruptions.

[9] Gorton and associates (2013) outlined a framework to evaluate the relationship of elements and determinants of competitiveness in agriculture supply chain.

[10] Due to the limitations of well-defined theoretical frameworks for the analysis of NTMs, this exploratory research follows a pragmatic stance.

[11] In a basic formulation for animal feed mill, the most common macro-ingredients are maize, soy, wheat, and fishmeal. The quantitative analysis was analyzed using a gravity model (formula).

[12] San Juan, Guayanilla, Humacao, Jobos, Ponce, Mayagüez, Fajardo, Guánica, Aguadilla, Arecibo and Yabucoa (USCoC 2015). So far, the last two are limited to oil imports. Ponce & Mayaguez are delegated port thus not administered by PRPA.

[13] Puerto Rico's archipelago includes the ports of Vieques and Culebra.

[14] Some atmospheric phenomenona such as hurricanes may provoke high movements of sediments reducing port depths.

[15] Between 2011 and 2013 some organizations, the 2012 political campaign, and eventually a few Puerto Rican Congressmen, the Governor of Puerto Rico, and the US Resident Commissioner of Puero Rico, publicly converged on the needs of a solution in benefit of Puerto Rico's competitiveness. By the Recovery Act of 2009 many projects of infrastructure in the US were developed. Eventually, the sea-port activities were included.

[16] Private firms dedicated to any activity related to the shipping process of importing and exporting, such as terminal operators, maritime lines, docking or vessel repairs or mechanics, stevedoring, port logistics distribution, docking support, and so on. Anaya-Oviedo (2012) explores this in more detail.

[17] Percentages were mentioned during the interviews. No quantitative data to sustain it were provided or analyzed. However, similar approximations are presented by Szakonyi (2014) and Comas (2009).

[18] See e.g. Szakonyi (2014) for a succinct analysis.

[19] The effects of containers reduction towers northbound could be associated with the deindustrialization process described by Caraballo-Cueto and Lara (2018).

[20] Anaya-Oviedo (2012) reports that 36 percent of the custom-brokers in Puerto Rico consider the use of the technology in this process to be below the regular level (4/7); 80 percent of the maritime service providers consider that inland access to terminals and port facilities in San Juan is poorly maintained and/or underdeveloped, and 40 percent of them believe that sea roads of the San Juan Port are underdeveloped. Similarly, 50 percent of them have the same opinion about the lack of cranes and equipment in terminals.

[21] Demurrage fees could vary among firms but in some cases could be such as $2,000 per hour and other $10,000 per day or fraction.

[22] Available data on Puerto Rico's external trade as an animal feed data segment show lower values because they consider as cereals some particular grains that are frequently used in animal feed mills; hence, they are not classified in their section.

[23] This is the case of wheat mesh and the premixed micronutrients' formulation. The formula used is basically 70 percent of maize. Unit is a cow in production for dairy farm. In poultry farms, the analysis considered four flocks per year but five in 2014. In hog farms, the production cycle (C) is between 125 to 200 days under ordinary conditions.

[24] Particularly to the Latin American markets but it is fundamentally lead by seasonality.

[25] The working hours of the port inspectors of the USDA and the PRDA differ by season and are fewer than those of the private service providers.

[26] The code related to Quality included: punctuality, packaging, product, and handling. The code of Insecurity included distrust on issues related to sanitary and phytosanitary policies to trade, political stability, and technical or management issues at port level or with carriers. The code of intercommunication focused on cultural issues (such as language, meanings, and metric systems), and most frequent methods of communication.

[27] Participants perceived that the domestic maritime firms are more informative and diligent than the foreign one.

[28] An anecdotal example was the case of purchasing green leaves from California and transporting them to Jacksonville. The inland rate is over $6,000, and the sea rate from Jacksonville to San Juan is around $4,000. Consequently, a container of 900 cartons of lettuce is almost $10 per box over the produce price as a result of the cost of transport.

[29] Although fertilization is a relatively common routine practice and its volume depends on soil conditions and crop requirements, in tropical soils the use of 2,800 kg per acre is considered to be a very basic measure. Using that on the example, the extra cost of transport only will represent $616 (USD) per acre over the cost of the product.

[30] MIDA (2014) estimates a reduction of 14 percent less than in 2013.

[31] The price of Crowley and Sea Star new LNG ships (two each) for Puerto Rico was estimated to be over $150 million per ship.

REFERENCES

Alameda, J. and J. Valentín. 2014. El impacto de la Jones Act en Puerto Rico. Discusión, Análisis y Medición. Accessed 10 August 2014. <http://docplayer.es/14543370-Impacto-economico-del-jones-act-en-la-economia-de-puerto-rico-discusion-analisis-y-medicion.html/>.

American Association of Port Authorities (AAPA). 2017. World Port Rankings 2008–2016. Accessed 10 July, 2018. <www.aapa-ports.org/>.

American Maritime Partnership. 2018. Impact of Jones Act on Puerto Rico. Commissioned to Reeve & Associates and Estudios Técnicos, Inc. Accessed 18 July 2018, <https://www.americanmaritimepartnership.com/puerto-rico-economy/>.

Anaya-Oviedo, C. Y. 2012. Factores que obstaculizan el proceso de importaciones hacia Puerto Rico desde el punto de vista de corredores de aduana y navieros. MBA thesis, University of Puerto Rico, Mayagüez.

Barney, J. 1991. Firm Resources and Sustained Competitive Advantage. *Journal of Management* 17(1), 99–120.

Beghin, J. C. 2013. *Non-Tariff Measures with Market Imperfections*. Bingley, UK: Emerald Group Publishing Limited.

Brandon-Jones, E., B. Squired, C. W. Autry and K. J. Petersen. 2014. A Contingent Resource-based Perspective of Supply Chain Resilience and Robustness. *Journal of Supply Chain Management* 50(3), 55–73.

Briguglio, L. 2003. The vulnerability index and small island developing states: A review of conceptual and methodological issues. AIMS Regional Preparatory Meeting, Review of the Barbados Program of Action, 1–5 September, Cape Verde.

Burns, M. G. 2015. *Port Management and Operations*. Boca Ratón, FL: Taylor and Francis Group, CRC Press.

Caraballo-Cueto, J. and J. Lara. 2018. Deindustrialization and Unsustainable Debt in Middle-Income Countries: The Case of Puerto Rico. *Journal of Globalization and Development* 8(2), doi:10.1515/jgd-2017-0009.

Chavarría, H., P. Rojas and S. Sepúlveda. 2002. *Competitividad: Cadenas agroalimentarias y territories rurales. Elementos conceptuales*. San José, Costa Rica: IICA Publicaciones.

Chen, T., P.T-W. Lee and Notteboom, T. 2013. Shipping Line Dominance and Freight Rate Practices on Trade Routes: The Case of the Far East-South Africa Trade. *International Journal of Shipping and Transport Logistics* 5 (2), 155–73.

Clar, J. 2013. Rethinking the Puerto Rican Commonwealth Model through a Lens of Internationalization. *Fletcher Forum of World Affairs* 33(3), 151–62.

Collazo, H. 2012. Informe sobre la Ley de Cabotaje. Comision de derecho y relaciones internacionales. Colegio de Abogados de Puerto Rico, Julio.

Collins, S., B.P. Bosworth and M. Soto-Class. 2006. *The Economy of Puerto Rico. Restoring Growth*. Washington, DC: Brooking Institution Press.

Comas, M. 2009. Vulnerabilidad de las cadenas de suministros, el cambio climático y el desarrollo de estrategias de adaptación: El caso de las cadenas de suministros de alimento de Puerto Rico. Ph.D. dissertation, University of Puerto Rico.

Creswell, J. W. and V.K. Plano-Clark. 2011. *Designing and Conducting Mixed Methods Research*. 2nd ed. California: SAGE publications Ltd.

Cruz, N. E., M. Ortiz, V.A. Dones and E. Ortiz. 2014. The Maritime Laws of the United States of America and Their Impact in Puerto Rico's Current Economy. *Inter Metro Business Journal Spring* 10(1), 18–26.

De Martino, M. and A. Morvillo. 2008. Activities, Resources and Inter-organizational Relationships: Key Factors in Port Competitiveness. *Maritime Policy and Management* 35(6), 571–89.

Departamento de Agricultura. 2012 Resumen del consumo agrícola de Puerto Rico en el año 2010-11. División de Estadísticas, Departamento de Agricultura, Estado Libre Asociado de Puerto Rico.

Dietz, J. L. 1989. *Historia económica de Puerto Rico*. Spanish ed. San Juan: Ediciones Huracán, Inc.

Donga. 2015. Korea regains no. 1 spot in shipbuilding orders in Q1. *Dong- A ILBo News Room* 6th April. Accessed 7th May 2015. <http://english.donga.com/srv/service.php3?bicode=020000&biid=2015040687128/>.

Estudios Técnicos, Inc. 2013. The Maritime Industry in Puerto Rico. Private study commissioned by the Maritime Alliance, San Juan.

FAO. 2006. *Statistical Yearbook Country Profile 2005–2006*. New York: United Nations.

Frankel, E. G. 2002. Study of Economic Impact of Cabotage and Alternative Strategies to Cabotage in U.S. Trade. Study commissioned for the Development Bank of the Commonwealth of Puerto Rico. Brookline, MA.

González, G. M. and A. Gregory. 2014. Economic Development Plan for Agriculture Sector. In Economic Development Plan for Puerto Rico 2015. Puerto Rico Planning Board (PRPB), Governor Office, Commonwealth of Puerto Rico, October, Chapter 2.

Gorton, M., C. Hubbard, and I. Fertö. 2013. International comparison of product supply chains in the agri-food sector: Determinants of their competitiveness and performance on EU and international markets. *COMPETE*, 3, Germany: Institute of Agricultural Development in Transition Economies.

Han, E. 2017. Crowley's new STS cranes arrive in San Juan. *Maritime Link* 23rd of March. Accessed 10 January 2018. <www.marinelink.com/news/crowleys-cranes-arrive423487/>.

Hofstrand, D. 2009. Corn and Soybean Price Basis. *Ag Decision Maker-University Extension,* File A2-40, December. Iowa: Iowa State University Press.

Holpuch, A. 2017. Puerto Rico supply failure stops food and water reaching desperate residents. *The Guardian* 29 February. Accessed 1 October 2017. <https://www.theguardian.com/world/2017/sep/29/puerto-rico-crisis-supply-food-water/>.

Hopman, H. and U. Nienhuis. 2009. The Future of Ships and Shipbuilding – A Look into the Crystal Ball. In *Future Challenges for the Port and Shipping Sector,* eds. H. Meersman, E. Van de Voorde and T. Vanelslander. 27–52. London: MPG Books Ltd.

Hubbard, L. J. and C. Hubbard. 2013. Food Security in the United Kingdom: External Supply Risks. *Food Policy* 43, 142–7.

International Maritime Organization (IMO). 2014. *International Convention for Safe Containers, 1972.* 2014 edition. London: IMO Publishing.

Instituto de Estadísticas de Puerto Rico (IEPR). 2018. Informe sobre desarrollo humano. Puerto Rico 2016. San Juan: Instituto de Estadísticas. Accessed 18 May 2018. <https://estadisticas.pr/en/publicaciones/informe-sobre-desarrollo-humano-de-puerto-rico-2016/>.

Junta de Planificación de Puerto Rico (PRPB). 2015. Índice de indicadores económicos años 2005–2015. Accessed 11 February 2016. <www.jp.pr.gov/>.

Latruffe, L. 2010. Competitiveness, Productivity and Efficiency in the Agricultural and Agrifood Sectors. *OECD Food, Agriculture and Fisheries Papers,* No. 30. OECD Publishing. Accessed 23 April 2014. <http://dx.doi.org/10.1787/5km91nkdt6d6-en/>.

Lewis, J. 2013. Veiled Waters: Examining the Jones Act's Consumer Welfare Effect. *Issues in Political Economy* 22, 77-113.

Marazzi-Santiago, M. 2018. Puerto Rico and the Jones Act. *Hispanic Economic Outlook* Spring, 9–13.

Márquez-Ramos, L., I. Martínez-Zarzoso, E. Pérez-García and G. Wilmsmeier. 2007. Determinantes de los costes de transporte marítimos. El caso de las exportaciones españolas. *Información comercial Española* 834, 79–94.

Martínez, F. 2014. The impact of the Jones Act (1920) on the economy of Puerto Rico: Potential assistance tools for policy makers. Guaynabo: Fundación Carvajal, Inc.

May, D. 2015. Behavioural Drivers of Business Competitiveness in Agriculture. *Agricultural Economics Review* 16 (2), 73–94.

MIDA. 2014. Deposition RS 237 – April 2013, by Mr Manuel Reyes Alfonso, Executive Vice-President. Presented on 28th January, Commission of Civil Rights, Citizens Participation and Social Economy, Senate of Puerto Rico, San Juan.

Morales-Sarriera, J., T. Serebrisky, G. Araya, C. Briceño-Garmendia, and J. Schwartz. 2013 Benchmarking Container Port Technical Efficiency in Latin America and the Caribbean. Working Paper Series, No. IDB-WP 473. Washington: Inter-America Development Bank.

Morgan, D. 2000. *Merchants of Grain.* Nebraska: An Authors Guild Backinprint.com Edition; iUniverse, Inc.

Nightingale, L. 2017. Lloyds List One Hundred Ports. *Lloyds Maritime Intelligence.*

Noticel. 2015. ¿Cuántos barcos continúan en ruta a PR tras hundimiento de 'El Faro'? *Noticel.com* 6 October. Accessed 6 October 2015. <www.noticel.com/noticia/181754/cuantos-barcos-continuan-en-ruta-a-pr-tras-hundimiento-de-el-faro.html/>.

Pantojas-García, E. 1990. *Development Strategies and Ideology. Puerto Rico's Export-Led Industrialization Experience*. London: Lynne Rienner Publishers, Inc.

Porter, M. E. 1985. *Competitive Advantage: Creating and Sustaining Superior Performance*. First Free Press Export Edition, 2004. New York: Free Press.

Oficina de Gerencia y Presupuesto de Puerto Rico (OMB). 2011. Puerto Rico Ports Authority Act. No. 125 of May 7, 1942, as amended. Compiled till June, by the Office of Management and Budget Library.

Rivera, A. I. 2007. *Puerto Rico ante los retos del siglo XXI. Cambio económico, cultural y político en los inicios del nuevo siglo*. San Juan: Ediciones Nueva Aurora.

Rojas, P., S. Romero, and S. Sepúlveda. 2000. Algunos ejemplos para medir competitividad. Serie de Cuadernos Técnicos, No. 14. Competitividad de la agricultura: Cadenas agroalimentarias y el impacto del factor localización espacial. CODES – Instituto Interamericano de Cooperación para la Agricultura (IICCA). San José, Costa Rica: IICA Publicaciones.

Sagers, C. 2006. The Demise of Ocean Shipping Regulations: A Study in the Evolution of Competition Policy and the Predictive Power of Microeconomics. *Vanderbilt Journal of Transnational Law* 39, 779–818.

Santos-Santos, H. I. 1997. Cabotage Laws: A Colonial Anachronism. *Revista del Derecho Puertorriqueño* 36, 1–20.

Setrini, G. 2012. Cultivating New Developments Paths: Food and Agriculture Entrepreneurship in Puerto Rico. Puerto Rico Economy Project Working Paper, MIT Political Science Department.

Sherman, R.B. 2002. Seaport Governance in the United States and Canada. American Association of Port Authorities. Accessed 20 February 2017. <http://library.arcticportal.org/1601/>.

Sin Comillas. 2015. Crowley invierte $48.5 millones en construcción de muelle. *Periódico Digital Sin Comillas.com* 12 May. Accessed 12 May 2015. <http://sincomillas.com/crowley-invierte-48-5-millones-en-construccion-de-muelle/>.

_____, 2016. TOTE Maritime e INTERSHIP crean la principal operación de terminales en Puerto Rico. *Periódico Digital Sin Comillas.com* 3 August. Accessed 4 August 2016. <http://sincomillas.com/tote-maritime-e-intership-crean-la-principal-operacion-de-terminales-en-puerto-rico/>.

Stiglitz, J. 2010. *Freefall. Free Markets and the Sinking of the Global Economy*. United Kingdom: Penguin Books, Ltd.

Szakonyi, M. 2014. How will Horizon's Exit Affect the Puerto Rico Trade? *Journal of Commerce.com* 14 November. Accessed 10 December 2014. <http://www.joc.com/maritime-news/>.

Torruellas, J.R. 2017. To Be or Not To Be: Puerto Ricans and Their Illusory US Citizenship. *CENTRO: Journal of the Center for Puerto Rican Studies* 29(1), 108–35.

TOTE Service. 2014. Saltchuk announces acquisition of Tropical Shipping. *TOTE Press Releases* 8 April. Accessed 23 May 2015. <http://toteservices.com/2014/04/08/saltchuk-announces-acquisition-of-tropical-shipping/>.

UNCTAD. 2013. *Review of Maritime Transportation, 2013.* Trade Logistics Branch of the Division on Technology and Logistics. New York: United Nations Publications.

UNSDSN. 2014. Issue Brief: Goals, Targets and Indicators for Sustainable Agriculture. Sustainable Agriculture and Food Systems, February. New York: United Nations.

US Department of Commerce (USDoC Census Bureau). 2015. General Data. Various Years 2010–2014. Official website, US Department of Commerce. Accessed 30 July 2015. <https://www.census.gov/quickfacts/table/IPE120214/72/>.

US Energy Information Administration. 2015. State Electricity Profiles. Various Years. Accessed 8 November 2015. <http://www.eia.gov/electricity/state/archive/2012/>.

US General Accountability Office (USGAO). 2013. Puerto Rico: Characteristics of the Island's Maritime Trade and Potential Effects of Modifying the Jones Act. No. 13-260, March.

———. 1998. Maritime Issues: Assessment of the International Trade Commission 1995. *Economic impact of the Jones Act RCED 9896R,* March.

USDA-NASS. 2015. US Census of Agriculture, 2008–2014. US Department of Agriculture, National Agricultural Statistics Service. Accessed 30th of June, 2015. <http://www.nass.usda.gov/>.

Venator-Santiago, C.R. 2017. A Note on the Puerto Rican Denaturalization Exceptions of 1948. *CENTRO: Journal of the Center for Puerto Rican Studies* 29(1), 224–37.

Wilmsmeier, G., and R. Sanchez. 2015. Capacidad de contenedores en las rutas principales de América del Sur: los desafíos para el sistema portuario. *CEPAL, Boletín Marítimo y Logístico* No. 58, September.

World Bank. 2015 Data of Logistics and Performance. Accessed 18 February 2016. <http://data.worldbank.org/>.

World Economic Forum (WEF). 2013. Global Competitiveness Report 2013–14. Full data edition. Geneva. Accessed 20 August 2014. <www.weforum.org/gcr/>.

Migration, Geographic Destinations, and Socioeconomic Outcomes of Puerto Ricans during *La Crisis Boricua*: Implications for Island and Stateside Communities Post-Maria

MARIE T. MORA, ALBERTO DÁVILA AND HAVIDÁN RODRÍGUEZ

ABSTRACT

Hurricane Maria struck Puerto Rico at a time the island was encountering what had already been described as a humanitarian crisis brought upon by more than a decade of a severe economic crisis. In this manuscript, we provide an overview of the conditions that led to and resulted from *La Crisis Boricua*, including the record level of net outmigration that occurred even before Hurricane Maria. We also analyze the overrepresentation of non-Puerto-Rican migrants (based on self-identification) in the recent island-mainland migration flow. Moreover, we discuss interstate differences in the socioeconomic characteristics, including the rates of impoverishment, among recently arrived Puerto Ricans from the island in the largest receiving areas. This information can be used to inform policymakers, social workers, and social scientists about potential challenges incoming migrants may encounter as they settle into their mainland communities. Finally, we highlight some of the challenges and opportunities Puerto Rico and Puerto Ricans will continue to face while rebuilding. [Key words: Demographic shift; Island-Mainland Migration; Economic crisis; Hurricane Maria; Poverty; Puerto Ricans]

Marie T. Mora (Marie.Mora@utrgv.edu) is Professor of Economics at the University of Texas, Rio Grande Valley. Her research focuses on the socioeconomic outcomes of Hispanic populations. In addition to numerous journal articles and book chapters, her publications include *Population, Migration, and Socioeconomic Outcomes among Island and Mainland Puerto Ricans: La Crisis Boricua* (Lexington, 2017) with Alberto Dávila and Havidán Rodríguez, the award-winning *Hispanic Entrepreneurs in the 2000s: An Economic Profile and Policy Implications* (Stanford University Press, 2013) with Alberto Dávila, and three edited volumes.

With wind speeds of 155 miles per hour, just two miles shy of a Category 5 hurricane and equivalent to an EF-3 tornado, Hurricane Maria ripped through Puerto Rico on September 20, 2017, leaving behind a trail of catastrophic destruction, suffering, and death. In the immediate aftermath, Maria left the island's then-3.3 million American citizens without electricity (over a million of whom would remain without it for more than four months), running water, telecommunications, and transportation systems. Other critical necessities, such as food supplies, drinking water, and medicine were in short supply. Nearly a year later, the official death toll was raised after considerable public pressure from 64 to 2,975 fatalities,[1] which represented 0.09 percent of Puerto Rico's entire population.

During the initial aftermath of Hurricane Maria, the media reported on Puerto Rico's critical social and economic issues confronting the island's population, as well as an anticipated massive outmigration, but less publicized was that the island had already been described as encountering a humanitarian crisis resulting from a severe economic crisis surging for more than a decade. There is no question that Hurricane Maria exacerbated the effects of this crisis—which we refer to as *La Crisis Boricua*[2] (Mora, Dávila and Rodríguez (henceforth, MDR), 2017a)—and intensified the net outmigration from the island, already at a record high. However, with a bankrupt government, a shrinking and rapidly aging population, an already deteriorated infrastructure, and a weak business sector and labor market, Maria has prolonged the uncertain and challenging near- and long-term future of the Commonwealth.

In this manuscript, we first provide an overview of the conditions that led to and resulted from La Crisis Boricua. One of these outcomes has been the record level of net outmigration, which, as we report below, was over 597,000 people between 2006 and 2017. The vast majority of this group moved to the mainland, including into Florida (an "old new" destination) and other non-traditional areas. We also show that a non-trivial number of these island-to-mainland migrants did not identify themselves as Puerto Rican. We then discuss interstate differences in the socioeconomic

Alberto Dávila (adavila@semo.edu) is Dean and Professor of Economics at Southeast Missouri State University. His research focuses on Hispanic labor market outcomes, immigration, and the U.S.-Mexico border. In addition to numerous journal articles and book chapters, his publications include *Population, Migration, and Socioeconomic Outcomes among Island and Mainland Puerto Ricans: La Crisis Boricua* (Lexington, 2017) with Marie T. Mora and Havidán Rodríguez; and the award-winning *Hispanic Entrepreneurs in the 2000s: An Economic Profile and Policy Implications* (Stanford University Press, 2013) with Marie T. Mora; and two edited volumes.

Havidán Rodríguez (Havidan@albany.edu) is President and Professor at the University at Albany, State University of New York. His research focuses on the social science of disasters as well as socioeconomic outcomes of Hispanic populations. In addition to numerous journal articles and book chapters, his publications include *Population, Migration, and Socioeconomic Outcomes among Island and Mainland Puerto Ricans: La Crisis Boricua* (Lexington, 2017) with Marie T. Mora and Alberto Dávila, and three edited volumes.

characteristics among recently arrived Puerto Ricans from the island. As part of this discussion, we provide a detailed analysis of their poverty rates to illustrate that Puerto Ricans moving to the mainland are not homogeneous with respect to their socioeconomic outcomes. While at the time of writing this manuscript, the data were not available to fully analyze these differences post-Maria, all estimates of the major destination areas point to the same areas where pre-Maria migrants were moving, particularly Florida (e.g., Hinojosa, Román and Meléndez 2018; see also MDR 2019). It follows that the socioeconomic and demographic characteristics of pre-Maria migrants can be used to inform policymakers, social workers, and social scientists about potential issues post-Maria migrants may encounter as they settle into their mainland communities. Finally, we highlight some of the challenges and opportunities we anticipate Puerto Rico will encounter as the island continues to recover from Maria.

Background on La Crisis Boricua

Hurricane Maria struck at a time when the Commonwealth and its 3.3 million residents had been encountering more than a decade of an unrelenting economic crisis. La Crisis Boricua technically started in 2006—the year we refer to as "the perfect storm" (MDR 2017a)—although it had been brewing for years if not decades beforehand. One major factor that precipitated La Crisis Boricua was the complete expiration of Section 936 of the Internal Revenue Service Code on December 31, 2005; Section 936 had provided U.S. corporations in Puerto Rico tax breaks on goods produced in Puerto Rico. Its repeal resulted in a scaling back and, in some cases, relocation of businesses, and a corresponding loss of jobs in both labor-intensive and capital-intensive industries.[3] These losses essentially led to a domino effect of lost tax revenue, a loss in public sector jobs as the government worked to restructure its budget, and a loss of bank deposits and capital, thus leading to additional employment losses. Moving forward, if the recently approved 12.5-percent tax on income from intellectual property in Puerto Rico is implemented (e.g., Coto 2017; Mazzei 2017),[4] a continued scaling back of manufacturing firms (especially in medical manufacturing) and additional job losses on the island are expected, independent of Hurricane Maria.

Many of these conditions overlap and have fed into the severity of La Crisis Boricua and the massive population exodus from the island both pre- and post-Maria.

Since 2006, the island has only had one year of positive economic growth (in 2012), prompting scholars to refer to this period as "Puerto Rico's Depression" and "lost decade" (e.g., Caraballo Cueto and Lara 2016). Even under its optimistic scenario, the economic projections made by the Puerto Rico Planning Board (Junta de Planificación) in 2016 indicated that the economic contraction would continue through at least fiscal year 2017. Estudios Técnicos, Inc. (a Puerto Rican economics consulting firm) projected in late 2016 that the contraction would continue until 2020, and it would not be until 2034 that Puerto Rico's economy would be restored to its 2006 level. Following the decimating impacts of Maria on the island's industry and the expected imposition of the intellectual-property tax noted above, the timeline of these projections appears unattainable.

Some of the major challenges the island faces relate to the net outmigration and ensuing significant demographic shift, its unprecedented debt and "oversight" leg-islation, and, consequently, the lack of resources and financial autonomy to rebuild. Other critical factors include a perennially weak labor market and a dilapidated in-frastructure, including for healthcare. Many of these conditions overlap and have fed into the severity of La Crisis Boricua and the massive population exodus from the island both pre- and post-Maria.

Migration and Demographic Shift. Even before Hurricane Maria, as we report else-where (MDR 2017a), La Crisis Boricua led to the largest number of net outmigrants from the island, and the second largest on a scale relative to the population size (the largest be-ing during the Great Migration of the 1950s). Coupled with low fertility rates and a high life expectancy, the recent net outmigration has left Puerto Rico with a dwindling and rapidly aging population. The island's population declined on net by nearly half a million people, from 3.8 million in 2006 to 3.3 million in 2017.[5] At the same time, the average age of the island's population increased by 4.5 years (from 36.2 years to 40.7 years) and the percentage of the population ages 65 and older rose by six percentage points (from 12.9 percent to 18.9 percent) between 2006 and 2016.[6] To compare, the U.S. mainland popula-tion also grew older during this time, but it did so more slowly, with the average age rising by 1.8 years (from 36.7 years to 38.5 years), and the percentage ages 65 and older rising by 2.8 percentage points (from 12.4 percent to 15.2 percent of the population). This de-mographic shift has important ramifications for the future of the island's economy, labor force, and its deteriorating and overstretched healthcare sector.

Puerto Rico's Debt and PROMESA. Hurricane Maria hit Puerto Rico at a time when the government did not have viable fiscal policy options nor the legislated au-thority to rebuild. With the island's loss in credit ratings on municipal bonds in 2014, the government's unprecedented and expanding public debt (described in 2015 by the then-governor as a "death spiral") at $74 billion plus another $49 billion in unfunded pension obligations, and a series of defaults on debt payments starting in July 2015, even without subsequent federal legislation, the island's government would have been unable to use traditional fiscal policy tools to rebuild the economy and reverse the tide of net outmigration. As we have previously discussed (MDR 2017a, 2017b), attempts to restructure its budget starting in 2006 led to a significant loss in public-sector jobs; a corresponding reduction in public services; and the imposition of a relatively high sales tax (*Impuesto a las Ventas y Uso* – IVU), first implemented at 7.0 percent in 2006 but raised in 2015 to 11.5 percent, a level higher than any state sales tax.

Unable to file for federal protection under Chapter 9 of the U.S. Bankruptcy Code due to Puerto Rico's status as a U.S. territory, the federal government's response to provide "assistance" was the Puerto Rico Oversight, Management, and Economic

Stability Act (PROMESA), signed into law by President Obama in June 2016. The PROMESA Oversight Board was essentially granted unilateral power over Puerto Rico's finances and the island's economic future. As we note in other work (MDR 2017a), criticisms of the Board include that it does not address Puerto Rico's chronic socioeconomic issues such as its weak labor market or widespread poverty; its lack of accountability to the Puerto Rican people; the lack of experience in economic reform of the Board members (e.g., Furth 2016); and the interpretation by many that the charge and scope of the Board signal Puerto Rico's *de facto* colonial status as opposed to a self-governing territory.[7] As such, the Puerto Rican government's hands remain tied with respect to budgetary decisions to assist the island in rebuilding after Hurricane Maria without approval from the Oversight Board.

Weak Labor Market. For years, the labor market in Puerto Rico has been characterized by high unemployment rates, low labor force participation rates (LFPRs, which are some of the lowest in the world), and low employment population ratios (e.g., MDR 2017a, 2017b). Between 2006 and 2016, among civilians ages 16 and older, the unemployment rate and LFPR were, respectively, 17.4 percent and 46.1 percent on the island, compared to 7.9 percent and 64.1 percent on the mainland. In our previous work (MDR 2017a), we further reported that the unemployment rate would have been considerably higher on the island if the LFPR had not declined during La Crisis Boricua. As noted earlier, Puerto Rico lost a significant number of jobs in the manufacturing industry with the expiration of Section 936, as well as in the public sector, as the government attempted to address its fiscal crisis. The significant loss in jobs has been one of the factors that led to the massive net exodus from the island in recent years. Indeed, work-related issues—moving because of a job or to find a job on the mainland—were the primary reasons *two-thirds* of migrants aged 25-64 left Puerto Rico in the midst of La Crisis Boricua (MDR 2017a).

In light of the island's weak labor market conditions, moreover, it is not surprising that poverty rates have remained high for years. To illustrate, we estimate that the average poverty rate in Puerto Rico was 45.2 percent between 2006 and 2016, which more than thrice exceeded the mainland's average poverty rate of 14.7 percent during this time and more than twice exceeded the highest state poverty rate (22.1 percent, in Mississippi). Still, as we discuss later in this manuscript, the poverty rates among recent Puerto Rican migrants in mainland traditional settlement areas tend to be considerably higher than on the island (see also MDR 2017a).

Deteriorating Healthcare Infrastructure. The decrease in public-sector employment and under-funded healthcare systems exacerbated the deteriorating socioeconomic conditions in Puerto Rico during La Crisis Boricua. We discuss elsewhere (MDR 2017a) that in 2016, 92 percent of the island's *municipios* were categorized by the U.S. Health Resources and Services Administration as Medically Underserved Areas (Levis 2016), and the population's healthcare system was expected to continue to deteriorate even before Maria due to declining income and state funding along with "the graying of Puerto Rico's doctors" (*New York Times* 2017). The outmigration of physicians has compounded the overstretched nature of the healthcare industry and the aging of the doctors (e.g., Allen 2016). For insight into the scale, we estimate that the number of physicians and surgeons in Puerto Rico declined more sharply (by 26.4 percent, from 8,870 to 6,527) than the population (12.2 percent), while their average age increased (from 48.0 to 52.0 years) between 2006 and 2016. As the disproportionate outmigration of younger people has likely continued post-Maria, the increasingly elderly population remaining in Puerto Rico will continue to strain the outstretched healthcare system.

Outmigration and the Puerto Rican Diaspora: 2006–2017 (Pre-Maria)

As these changes indicate, Puerto Rico was already in crisis mode before Hurricane Maria. For more details behind the massive population exodus, as shown in Table 1, the island's total population declined on net by more than 468,000 residents (from

Table 1: Estimates of Net Migration from Puerto Rico: 2006–2017

Characteristic	Estimates
Population of Puerto Rico, July 1, 2006	3,805,214
Population of Puerto Rico, July 1, 2017	3,337,177
Total change in population between 2006 & 2017	-468,037
Natural increase (live births – deaths) between July 1, 2006 & July 1, 2017	129,164
Estimated net migration from Puerto Rico between July 1, 2006 & July 1, 2017	-597,201
Net migration as percentage of 2006 population	-15.7%
Estimated net migration from Puerto Rico between July 1, 2006 & July 1, 2016	-528,923
Estimated net migration from Puerto Rico to the U.S. mainland	-503,092
Estimated net migration from Puerto Rico to other countries or other U.S. territories	-25,831

Source: Authors' estimates using data from the U.S. Census Bureau for population size and natural increase (http://www.census.gov/popest/estimates.html), most recently from December 2017; and the 2006-2016 ACS/PRCS data from the IPUMS.
Notes: The population estimates pertain to July 1, 2006 – July 1, 2017. As such, the effects of Hurricane Maria are not included.

Figure 1: Percent of Recent Migrants on the Mainland and Island Residents Who Self-Identify as Puerto Rican: 2006-2017

Panel A:
Percent of Recent Island-to-Mainland Migrants Who Self-Identify as Puerto Rican

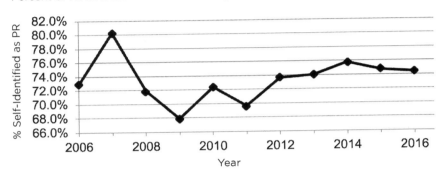

Panel B:
Percent of Recent Island ResidentsWho Self-Identify as Puerto Rican

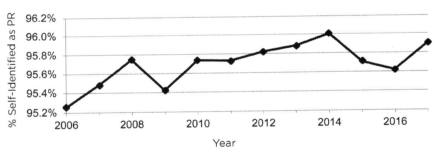

Source: Authors' estimates using 2006-2016 ACS and PRCS data in the IPUMS; and the U.S. Census Bureau (2018a) for 2017.
Notes: Ethnic self-identification is based on the Hispanic ethnicity question. Appropriate sampling weights are employed. The 2017 data for Panel A were not publicly available when this manuscript was written. The 2017 data for Puerto Rico were only collected through mid-September by the U.S. Census Bureau.

3.8 million to 3.3 million) between July 1, 2006, and July 1, 2017. Natural increase was positive over the 12-year period, with over 129,000 more live births than deaths on the island.[8] As such, more than 597,000 people migrated from the island on net to the U.S. mainland and other countries between 2006 and 2017—the largest number of net out-migrants in the island's recorded history. On a relative scale, this represented a 15.7 percent loss of the island's 2006 population, the year La Crisis Boricua began, resulting in the largest relative population loss since the Great Migration of the 1950s. At that time, net-outmigration represented more than one-fifth (21.3 percent) of the island's population (MDR 2017a). Meléndez and Hinojosa (2017) projected shortly after Maria, the island would lose another 477,335 residents to the mainland by 2019. This means that within two years of Maria, the island may lose close to the same number of residents due to net outmigration as during the previous 12 years, thus compounding the demographic shift and significant population decline.

It should be noted, however, that while the vast majority of these migrants move to the U.S. mainland, there are net outflows to other countries as well (MDR 2017a). As seen in the bottom part of Table 1, over 503,000 people moved from the island to the continental U.S. between July 1, 2006 and July 1, 2016, while nearly 26,000 moved to other countries. Future studies should explore the international dimension of the Puerto Rican diaspora.

Moreover, not all of the migrants identify themselves as Puerto Rican in the Hispanic ethnicity question in the ACS and PRCS, suggesting the island's population loss of Puerto Ricans, while massive, is not quite as large as the total number of net outmigrants suggests. As seen in Panel A of Figure 1, since peaking in 2007, on an annual basis self-identified Puerto Ricans represented between two-thirds (67.8 percent in 2009) and three-quarters (75.8 percent in 2014) of migrants from the island to the mainland. However, with only one exception between 2009 and 2014, there was an increased presence of self-identified Puerto Ricans in the annual migrant outflow. Since 2009, these changes generally mirrored the changes in the percentage of island residents who identified themselves as Puerto Rican (see Figure 1, Panel B). The percentage of island residents who reported Puerto Rican ethnicity subtly increased annually from 95.4 percent in 2009 to a high of 96.0 percent in 2014; while it fell in 2015 and 2016, this share increased again to 95.9 percent before Maria's landfall in 2017.

Comparing the two panels of Figure 1 reveals several interesting findings. First, the number of Puerto Ricans who left the island since 2006 – while large – is by definition, smaller than the total number of people who migrated. Second, migrants who did not identify themselves as Puerto Rican were significantly overrepresented in the net migration flow. For example, in 2016, one-fourth (25.5 percent) of the migrants to the continental U.S. did not self-identify as Puerto Rican, which was nearly six times greater than the 4.4-percent representation of non-self-identified Puerto Ricans among island residents that year, suggesting those remaining behind had stronger ethnic ties to the island. Third, Figure 1 illustrates how changes in the self-identified Puerto Rican representation among the migrant outflow parallel subtle changes in the self-identified ethnic representation of island residents.

Figure 2: Island-Mainland Migration of Puerto Ricans by Year: 2006-2017

Panel A:
Island-Mainland Migration

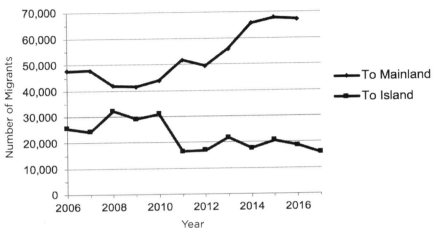

Panel B:
PR Population in Specific Areas

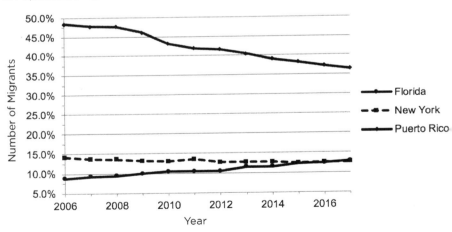

Source: Authors' estimates using 2006-2016 ACS and PRCS data in the IPUMS, and the U.S. Census Bureau (2018) for 2017.

Notes: These estimates only include those who self-identified as Puerto Rican in the Hispanic ethnicity question. Panel B indicates the percentage out of the total Puerto Rican population living in the three areas shown. Appropriate sampling weights are employed. The 2017 data for Puerto Rican migrants from the island in Panel A were not publicly available when this manuscript was written. The 2017 data for Puerto Rico were only collected through mid-September by the U.S. Census Bureau.

Still, the disproportionate number of non-Puerto-Rican migrants should not be interpreted as a sign that the Puerto Rican diaspora is modest. The numbers of self-identified Puerto Ricans moving stateside are historic and dwarf the numbers of those moving to the island, particularly after 2010. For visual clarity, Panel A in Figure 2 presents the numbers of self-identified Puerto Ricans moving to the island on an annual basis between 2006 and 2017, and from the island between 2006 and 2016 (2017 data were not yet publicly available). Coinciding with the recovery in the mainland labor market after the Great Recession, with few exceptions, the number of Puerto Ricans leaving the island escalated after 2010, although this tendency started slowing after 2014. The number of those moving from the mainland to the island fell sharply between 2010 and 2011, and then fell again in 2017 before Hurricane Maria.

Panel B in Figure 2 provides additional insight into the Puerto Rican diaspora by showing how the geographic distribution of the self-identified Puerto Rican population was shifting away from the island before Maria, a point we extensively discuss in our book (MDR 2017a). Between 2006 and 2017, the percentage of the Puerto Rican population who lived on the island sharply declined on an annual basis. While in 2006 nearly half of all Puerto Ricans resided in Puerto Rico, by 2017 (based on data collected through mid-September), this figure was just over one-third (36.4 percent). This figure further shows that the share of the Puerto Rican population residing in New York slightly fell during this time, from one out of seven (14.1 percent) to one out of eight (12.7 percent) Puerto Ricans.

At the same time, this figure illustrates how the representation (and number) of Puerto Ricans living in Florida (considered to be an "old new" destination area)[9] has steadily increased since 2006. Florida received a full third of all migrants from the island since the start of La Crisis Boricua and was a net receiver of interstate migrants (MDR 2017a), which resulted in its prominence as a major Puerto Rican settlement area. By 2017, one out of every eight Puerto Ricans (12.8 percent) resided in Florida (an increase from one out of 12 (8.8 percent) in 2006), such that Florida surpassed New York as the state with the largest number of Puerto Rican residents (an estimated 1.13 million versus 1.11 million). With the intensified outmigration following Hurricane Maria, all estimates indicate that the Puerto Rican population in both Florida and New York increased, especially in Florida (Hinojosa, Román, and Meléndez 2018; MDR 2019).

As discussed below, these migration patterns have implications for both island and mainland communities. To better visualize these geographic shifts in the settlement patterns of Puerto Ricans, Figure 3 displays the numbers of Puerto Ricans who moved between the island and the seven largest receiving states between 2006 and 2016: Florida (which received 33.4 percent of all incoming migrants from Puerto Rico), Pennsylvania (which received 9.4 percent), New York (8.4 percent), Texas (7.1 percent), Massachusetts (6.5 percent), New Jersey (5.1 percent), and Connecticut (4.3 percent). This figure also shows migration into and out of Puerto Rico.

Figure 3: Island-Mainland Migration of Puerto Ricans by Largest Receiving Areas: 2006-2016

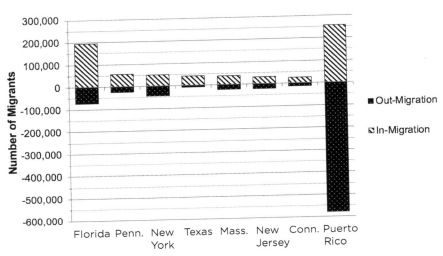

Source: Authors' estimates using 2006-2016 ACS and PRCS data in the IPUMS.
Notes: These estimates only include those who self-identified as Puerto Rican based on the Hispanic ethnicity question. Appropriate sampling weights are employed. These flows account for migration between Puerto Rico and the mainland; they do not include interstate nor international migration. Because these are aggregated over the timeframe, people who moved back and forth between the island and mainland are counted more than once.

At least three striking features can be observed. First, Puerto Rico represented the largest receiving area of island-mainland Puerto Rican migrants between 2006 and 2016; more migrants moved from the states to the island than from the island into any single state during La Crisis Boricua (see MDR (2017a) for more details). Second, more than twice as many Puerto Ricans left the island than those who arrived. As such, on a net basis, Florida represented the largest receiving area of Puerto Rican migrants, a position the state has maintained post-Maria (e.g., Hinojosa, Román, and Meléndez et al. 2018; MDR 2019). Third, while Texas ranked fourth (behind Florida, Pennsylvania, and New York) among the states with respect to incoming migrants from the island, it ranked second (after Florida) when considering *net* migration between the island and mainland from 2006 to 2016. Because post-Maria migration estimates point to destination patterns similar to those among pre-Maria migrants, despite its newness as a destination area, Texas is likely one of the key states impacted by the post-Maria migration.

Geographic Differences and Implications of the Characteristics of Incoming Migrants

What are the implications for the major receiving areas on the mainland? As we discuss in other work (MDR 2017a), the average characteristics of Puerto Ricans migrating stateside before Hurricane Maria as well as the reasons they were moving varied considerably depending on their stateside destination. To illustrate, Table 2 shows selected average socioeconomic and demographic characteristics of recent Puerto Rican migrants between the ages of 25 and 64 in the seven largest receiving states between 2006 and 2016.[10] For comparison, we also provide these characteristics for Puerto Ricans on the island.

Of the states shown, recent migrants in Texas fared the best between 2006 and 2016 with respect to residing above the poverty line; 13.9 percent of the new Puerto Rican adults in Texas were impoverished, which was less than half of the next lowest poverty rate (32.0 percent, in Florida), and a third of the poverty rate among island residents (41.0 percent). The recent migrants who fared the worst in this regard (even more so than Puerto Ricans who did not leave the island) tended to be those who settled in traditional receiving areas. Nearly six out of ten new migrants of prime working age in Pennsylvania, New York, Massachusetts, and Connecticut lived below the poverty line between 2006 and 2016, compared to four in ten of adults in Puerto Rico.

Between 2006 and 2016, less than one-third (30 percent) of those in Massachusetts and Connecticut were employed, compared to half in Florida and New Jersey, and nearly three-quarters (72.7 percent) in Texas.

It is not surprising that these differences conform to differences in other characteristics observed in Table 2. For example, in most cases recent migrants in the traditional settlement states had relatively low employment rates and schooling levels. Between 2006 and 2016, less than one-third (30 percent) of those in Massachusetts and Connecticut were employed, compared to half in Florida and New Jersey, and nearly three-quarters (72.7 percent) in Texas. Moreover, recent migrants in Massachusetts and Connecticut had less than 11 years of schooling on average and approximately 60 percent did not speak English well. Those in other traditional areas also had less than a high school diploma on average, which was below the average schooling (12.5 years) among Puerto Ricans in the same age range who lived on the island.[11] In contrast, recent Puerto Rican migrants in Texas and to a lesser extent in Florida had relatively high levels of education (14.4 years and 13.1 years, respectively) and English fluency rates.

Therefore, coupling the differences in the average characteristics of pre-Maria migrants with the similarities in the pre- and post-Maria migration destination areas, the integration process of Puerto Ricans moving into Florida and Texas post-Maria will likely differ from those moving into New York and other traditional

Table 2: Selected Average Characteristics of Recent Puerto Rican Island-to-Mainland Migrant Adults by Receiving Area, and of Puerto Ricans in Puerto Rico: 2006–2016

Characteristic	Florida	Penn.	New York	Texas	Mass.
Poverty rate	31.99%	59.08%	58.28%	13.91%	58.41%
Employed	51.60%	44.55%	38.33%	72.71%	30.31%
Education	13.090	11.871	11.848	14.408	10.778
Age	39.940	37.161	41.737	36.187	42.726
Limited English fluency	36.07%	46.21%	40.48%	18.05%	59.94%
N (unweighted)	693	137	183	186	156
N (weighted)	105,276	24,646	21,251	24,576	18,434

Characteristic	New Jersey	Conn.	Other States	Puerto Rico
Poverty rate	37.96%	57.35%	37.63%	40.1%
Employed	49.35%	29.52%	57.10%	51.1%
Education	11.873	10.190	12.791	12.491
Age	40.437	42.540	38.383	44.057
Limited English fluency	38.32%	59.03%	34.17%	63.39%
N (unweighted)	119	83	558	168,743
N (weighted)	15,572	11,815	71,795	19,655,323

Source: Authors' estimates using 2006-2016 ACS and PRCS data in the IPUMS.
Notes: These estimates only include adults between the ages of 25 and 64 who self-identified as Puerto Rican in the Hispanic ethnicity question. Appropriate sampling weights are employed. Recent migrants include those who migrated to the mainland within the past 12 months. The poverty rates exclude those living in group quarters. The unweighted N is the sample size and the weighted N is the estimated size of the population the sample reflects over the entire time frame, such that people are counted more than once in Puerto Rico.

Puerto Rican settlements. For example, as with pre-Maria migrants (MDR 2017a), those going to Texas might encounter greater issues related to work that matches their skills or finding housing close to their jobs (in light of their relatively high employment and education levels), whereas those moving into traditional areas might be more likely to encounter challenges in terms of transitioning into the labor force, returning to school, or becoming fluent in English (given their relatively low employment rates, schooling levels, and English-language proficiency).

   A More Detailed Analysis of Poverty Rates. Differences in employment/population ratios, educational attainment, English fluency, and other characteristics among Puerto Ricans partly explain geographic variations in the incidence of poverty across states and between the mainland and island. At the same time, we know from our previous work that observable characteristics do not fully explain these differences (e.g., MDR 2017a), raising questions about their integration and near- and long-term socioeconomic outcomes in their new communities. For more insight, we next present the role that such characteristics play in the interstate differences in poverty rates among the newly settled Puerto Rican migrants on the mainland, with a specific breakdown for the role of education (in light of the stark contrast in average schooling levels across the receiving areas) versus other characteristics. For this analysis, we use U.S.-born non-Hispanic whites as the comparison group, as their poverty rates reflect basic structural and economic conditions on the mainland.

   In particular, following the Oaxaca-type decomposition method (Oaxaca, 1973), we estimate the following probit regression models for non-Hispanic whites between the ages of 25 and 64 to obtain their structure of the incidence of poverty, first related to education and then accounting for additional characteristics:

   (1) *Resides in Poverty = f(Education),* and
   (2) *Resides in Poverty = f(Education, Other Human Capital, Employment, Demographic, Time),*

where the dependent variable *Resides in Poverty* equals one for individuals residing below the poverty line and equals zero otherwise. In Equation (2), the vector *Other Human Capital* includes characteristics typically associated with the likelihood of being impoverished in the literature, including age (as a proxy for experience), age2 (to account for nonlinear effects of age on socioeconomic outcomes), and limited English-language fluency. *Employment* is a binary variable equal to one for individuals who were employed (and equals zero otherwise),[12] while the vector *Demographic* includes the demographic characteristics of gender, family structure (marital status (including married and spouse present; married and spouse absent; single, never married; and divorced, widowed, and separated) plus the number of children at home), and residence outside of a metropolitan area. Finally, *Time* includes a set of binary variables indicating the year of the survey to account for changes in structural conditions that changed over the duration of the timeframe analyzed.[13]

   We then apply these probit regression estimates to residents in each state to impute their likelihood of being impoverished, given their education levels and other

Figure 4: Total and Decomposed Poverty Rates of Recent Puerto Rican Migrants versus U.S.-Born Non-Hispanic Whites by Major Receiving Area on the Mainland: 2006-2016

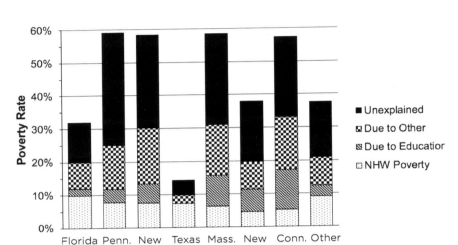

Source: Authors' estimates using 2006-2016 ACS and PRCS data in the IPUMS.
Notes: These estimates only include adults between the ages of 25 and 64 who were not residing in group quarters. Puerto Ricans only include those who self-identified as such in the Hispanic ethnicity question. Appropriate sampling weights are employed. The total height of the combined rectangles equals the total poverty rate of recent Puerto Rican migrants from the island in the area. Adding together the "Unexplained," "Due to Other," and "Due to Education" poverty-rate gaps equals the total gap in poverty rates between recent Puerto Rican migrants and U.S.-born non-Hispanic whites (NHWs) on the mainland in each area. The "Due to Education" gap in Texas is not visible because it is essentially zero (-0.3 percentage points). Details can be obtained from the authors. The unweighted (weighted) sample sizes of recent Puerto Rican migrants were 675 (representing 103,702 people) in Florida; 123 (23,692) in Pennsylvania; 173 (20,394) in New York; 165 (22,807) in Texas; 151 (18,058) in Massachusetts; 116 (15,262) in New Jersey; and 83 (11,815) in Connecticut.

socioeconomic and demographic characteristics. Based on Equation (1), the difference between these predicted outcomes for recent Puerto Rican migrants and U.S.-born non-Hispanic whites yields the Puerto Rican/non-Hispanic-white poverty-rate differential explained by differences in their educational attainment. Comparing the results from Equations (1) and (2), we can estimate how much the differences in other characteristics between Puerto Ricans and non-Hispanic whites further contribute to their respective poverty rates. The remainder of the differential reflects the portion that these observable characteristics do not explain. For ease of interpretation, we present the results from this decomposition analysis in Figure 4 for recent Puerto Rican migrants in the largest receiving states (also see Note 13).

Consistent with our previous work covering a shorter time frame (MDR 2017a), the poverty rates of recent Puerto Rican migrants in all areas between 2006 and 2016 were considerably higher than those of U.S.-born non-Hispanic whites, with the largest differences occurring in Pennsylvania (59.1 percent versus 7.7 percent, or 54.1 percentage points), Massachusetts and Connecticut (over 52 percentage points), and New York (50.8 percentage points); the smallest ones occurred in Florida (22.1 percentage points) and particularly in Texas (6.6 percentage points). Differences in education and other observable characteristics between recent Puerto Rican migrants and non-Hispanic whites explain considerable portions of these poverty-rate differentials (shown by the segments of "Due to Education" and "Due to Other"); nevertheless, Texas aside, the unexplained gaps remain in the double digits.

Taking the case of Florida, for example, Figure 4 shows that recent Puerto Ricans migrants had an average poverty rate of 32.0 percent between 2006 and 2016, which tripled the 9.9-percent poverty rate among U.S.-born non-Hispanic white adults. Of the 22.1-percentage-point disparity between the two groups, differences in education accounted for a modest 2.0 percentage points, while other observable characteristics accounted for an additional 7.9 percentage points. This leaves an unexplained poverty-rate gap of 12.2 percentage points (the solid shaded portion).

The relative unexplained poverty rate was highest among recent Puerto Rican migrants in Pennsylvania (34.2 percentage points), as gaps in their average education levels and other traits combined only accounted for about a third of the total differential of 51.4 percentage points (4.0 percentage points from schooling, and 13.2 percentage points from other characteristics). The unexplained poverty-rate differentials were also considerable in New York and Massachusetts (around 28 percentage points) as well as Connecticut (over 24 percentage points). In contrast, recent Puerto Ricans in Texas fared the best (4.4 percentage points) in terms of unexplained poverty-rate differentials with U.S.-born non-Hispanic whites, but even in that state, education gaps did not play a role (since their schooling levels were relatively high), while other observable characteristics only explained a third (2.2 percentage points) of the total impoverishment gap. The magnitude of the unexplained poverty-rate differential is admittedly small in Texas compared to such differentials in other states, but it remains non-trivial. This result may stem from the relatively large incidence of "overeducation" we previously identified for Puerto Ricans in Texas (MDR 2017a), in which their earnings were below those of non-Hispanic whites with similar skills.

In all, these differences indicate that Puerto Ricans moving into the traditional receiving areas encounter integration and socioeconomic challenges different from those in new destinations. Past socioeconomic disparities, including those historically transmitted through the labor market and other forms of institutional discrimination (e.g., Veléz 2015; Burgos and Rivera 2012; Vélez and Burgos 2010; Enchautegui 1992; Rodríguez 1992; Rodriguez 1989), may continue to be perpetuated among post-Maria migrants in these communities. Indeed, recently Diversitydatakids.org (2016) reported that based on a series of neighborhood-level indicators related to education, health/environment, and social and economic opportunities, Puerto Ricans living in the northeast, especially in traditional settlement areas (including in New York, Pennsylvania, and Massachusetts) have had the lowest access to such opportunities. Their opportunities were greater in Florida and particularly in Texas.

Therefore, social workers, community activists, and policymakers (including at the local level) should keep in mind the potentially different needs (such as employment assistance and school enrollment) to best facilitate the successful short-term integration and long-term socioeconomic outcomes of post-Maria migrants and their families. In the newer destination areas such as Texas, in which Puerto Rican migrants appear to be faring relatively well, but not as well as expected given their relatively high skill levels. It follows that assistance for new migrants might yield greater returns in such areas if efforts focus on disseminating information on employment opportunities best aligned to workers' skills or housing near their work.

Discussion and Concluding Remarks

With its 3.2 million American citizens in 2018, Puerto Rico has a larger population than 21 states as well as Washington, DC. Yet unlike states, Puerto Ricans on the island do not have voting representation in the U.S. Senate and House of Representatives, nor can they cast a vote in Presidential elections. Post-Maria, the Puerto Rican diaspora (already at a record level due to La Crisis Boricua) has intensified, and will likely have long-term effects on both the island and mainland well beyond the traditional Puerto Rican communities. These effects include continued demographic shift, an increased presence in areas beyond traditional Puerto Rican stateside communities, and a potential greater impact in local, state, and national elections.

Moreover, in light of the geographic differences in the socioeconomic and demographic characteristics of recent migrants from Puerto Rico, a "one size fits all" approach to assist these migrants with settling into their new stateside communities would presumably be less efficient than tailoring such assistance to meet their needs. Given the relative socioeconomic success of Puerto Ricans moving to Florida and especially to Texas *vis-à-vis* traditional destination areas, the migrants in these areas may be better served through assistance in finding employment matched to their skills or housing near their jobs. In contrast, given their high poverty rates as well as low average schooling levels, low rates of English proficiency, and low employment rates in traditional settlement areas, efforts might be better spent in assisting recent migrants with finding work, affordable housing, or opportunities to return to school.

In terms of impediments to alleviate the conditions on the island, without Hurricane Maria the island was already working through the implications of its $123 billion in debt ($74 billion in public debt and $49 billion in unfunded pension obligations). Beyond lacking financial capital, Puerto Rico currently lacks the authority and autonomy to rebuild the island's economy and infrastructure due to PROMESA. As we have noted elsewhere (e.g., MDR 2017a), with PROMESA and the Oversight Board's charge (which is not accountable to Puerto Rico); the island's net population loss (although not all of the out-migrants self-identify as Puerto Rican); a possible restructuring of the island's income taxes and minimum wages; the potential 12.5-percent intellectual property tax on mainland-owned companies in Puerto Rico; the slow rebuilding of the island's infrastructure; the overstretched healthcare sector; and the island's high sales tax,[14] Hurricane Maria compounded the challenges Puerto Rico was encountering after more than a decade of La Crisis Boricua.

The island's demographic shift has been notable, particularly in terms of the shrinking and rapidly aging population due to massive outmigration and low fertility rates on island, which we expect has only been exacerbated by the aftermath of Maria. Beyond the continued population exodus, consequences in prolonging the humanitarian crisis include additional suffering, disease/illness (both physical and mental), and fatalities affecting millions of American citizens in Puerto Rico, especially when considering the island's medically underserved status. The longer the crisis takes to address, the longer will be the vicious cycle of net outmigration, demographic shift, and economic decline.

There are some potential glimmers of hope, however. One is that the rebuilding and aid should serve as an economic stimulus and conceivably slow the tide of net outmigration. In fact, in October 2018, FocusEconomics predicted positive economic growth on the island in fiscal year 2019, which would be its first positive growth since 2012. Another is that rebuilding the island's infrastructure provides opportunities to incorporate greater efficiencies and strategically target industries aligned with the island's competitive advantages, including its location and educated population. Moreover, Hurricane Maria has increased awareness about Puerto Rico's status and relationship with the mainland, which could result in support and action from Congress to help address Puerto Rico's chronic socioeconomic issues, such as its perennially weak labor market and high rates of impoverishment. This possibility is more likely now than in the past in light of the 5.6 million (and rising) Puerto Ricans on the mainland who have Congressional representation and a vote in Presidential elections.

ACKNOWLEDGEMENTS

We thank Edwin Meléndez, Héctor Cordero Guzmán, María Enchautegui, José Caraballo Cueto, Mario Marazzi-Santiago, Xavier Totti, the *CENTRO Journal* reviewers of this manuscript, and various participants at the 2017 Puerto Rican Studies Association Summit on Puerto Rico/Puerto Ricans; the April 2018 "Meet the Authors" at the Center for Puerto Rican Studies, Hunter College; and the American Society of Hispanic Economists' panel discussions at the 2018 Allied Social Science Association annual meetings and the 2018 Western Economic Association annual meetings. All errors in fact or interpretation are our own.

NOTES

[1] The estimated 2,975 fatalities was based on a Puerto Rican government-commissioned report by George Washington University's Milken Institute School of Public Health (2018). However, other widely circulated estimates placed the death toll considerably higher (e.g., Kishore et at. 2018).

[2] Our use of this term is not meant to suggest that the crisis was "made in Puerto Rico." As we discuss in our book (MDR 2017a), Puerto Rico's complicated relationship with the U.S., including U.S. policies that directly affect the island but are outside of the island's control, set the stage for the crisis years, if not decades, before 2006.

[3] We estimated a loss of 37,400 (28.5 percent) of manufacturing jobs between 2006 and 2014 (MDR 2017b). While we cannot tie all of these job losses to the expiration of Section 936, a considerable number would have been directly related. It should also be noted that these losses were in both labor-intensive and capital-intensive manufacturing jobs, although based on our estimates (MDR 2017b), less educated workers were seemingly disproportionately displaced.

[4] The federal tax overhaul approved by Congress in December 2017 includes a 12.5-percent tax on intellectual property held in "foreign jurisdictions." Despite its territorial status, Puerto Rico is considered to be "foreign" for tax purposes.

[5] Previous estimates of Puerto Rico's 2006 population placed it at 3.9 million; however, the U.S. Census Bureau downwardly revised this figure to 3.8 million in its intercensal estimates.

[6] Unless otherwise noted, our estimates are based on the annual American Community Surveys (ACS) and the Puerto Rico Community Surveys (PRCS) in the Integrated Public Use Microdata Series (IPUMS), provided by Ruggles and associates (2018). Since 2006, these datasets have included an approximate one-percent sample of all residents in the 50 states, Washington, DC, and Puerto Rico on an annual basis. The 2017 IPUMS data were not available when this manuscript was written.

[7] For example, in response to PROMESA, Nobel Laureate Joseph Stiglitz and Martin Guzman (2017) described Puerto Rico as "*de facto* an American colony" and the April 2017 *Harvard Law Review* (2017) stated that "PROMESA is much closer to legislation envisioned within a colonial relationship than a federal one; the Puerto Rican people certainly seem to see it as such...."

[8] It is worth noting that the magnitude of the natural increase declined on an annual basis over the 12 years, such that between 2016 and 2017, it turned negative, with 1,065 fewer live births than deaths (28,267 versus 29,332), thus expediting the net population loss that year (U.S. Census Bureau 2017b).

[9] As we note in other work (e.g., MDR 2017a), Florida started emerging as a major destination

area for Puerto Ricans in the 1970s, when migration patterns shifted due to the de-industrialization and relatively high cost-of-living in the traditional settlement areas (e.g., Delerme 2013; Silver 2010).

[10] For a more detailed discussion of how recent Puerto Rican migrants compared to other Puerto Ricans on the mainland with respect to their geographic differences in socioeconomic and demographic characteristics, including birthplace, see MDR (e.g., 2017a).

[11] The relatively low education levels among recent Puerto Rican migrants in traditional settlement areas vis-à-vis Puerto Ricans on the island fits with our previous work showing that highly educated migrants were not disproportionately represented in the net migration flow (e.g., MDR 2017a, 2017b). Further suggestive evidence can be found in the island's rising real Gross Domestic Product per capita and real Gross National Product per capita between 2010 and 2016 (Jansen 2018), which is consistent with the case that more productive workers were less likely to migrate on average. The issue of how the skill distribution of island-mainland migrants has affected real output produced by workers remaining on the island goes outside of the scope of this manuscript, but it serves as a worthy topic for future exploration.

[12] We are aware that employment itself is a socioeconomic outcome (as is labor force participation). While this issue goes beyond the scope of our study, future scholars should more fully explore the overlapping factors between employment and the incidence of poverty among Puerto Rican migrants living stateside, taking into account whether they left the island for work-related purposes or other reasons.

[13] The empirical results from estimating the probit regression models (which can be obtained from the authors) conform to those reported in the literature. For example, education, age, English-language fluency, being employed, being male, living with a spouse, the absence of children, and residing in metropolitan areas each significantly related to a lower likelihood of residing below the poverty line, ceteris paribus. The coefficients on each of the regressors are statistically significant at the one-percent level except for age; however, the joint effect of age and age2 is statistically significant at the one-percent level. The total sample size of U.S.-born non-Hispanic whites used in this analysis was 11,622,219. The sample sizes of recent Puerto Rican migrants in each state are reported in the footnote to Figure 4.

[14] The relatively high cost of living on the island has also been attributed to the 1920 Jones Act (also known as the Merchant Marine Act), as transported goods between the island and mainland must be shipped via U.S.-owned, U.S.-built, and U.S.-crewed carriers.

REFERENCES

Allen, Greg. 2016. SOS: Puerto Rico is Losing Doctors, Leaving Patients Stranded. *National Public Radio* 12 March. Accessed 15 May 2017. <http://www.npr.org/sections/health-shots/2016/03/12/469974138/sos-puerto-rico-is-losing-doctors-leaving-patients-stranded/>.

Caraballo Cueto, José and Juan Lara. 2016. From Deindustrialization to Unsustainable Debt: The Case of Puerto Rico. Unpublished paper, University of Puerto Rico at Cayey, October 2016. Accessed 6 April 2017. <https://www.researchgate.net/project/From-deindustrialization-to-unsustainable-debt-The-Case-of-Puerto-Rico/>.

Cohn, D'Vera, Eileen Patten and Mark Hugo López. 2014. Puerto Rican Population Declines on Island, Grows on U.S. Mainland. Washington, DC: Pew Research Center Hispanic Trends, 14 August.

Coto, Danica. 2013. Doctors Flee Puerto Rico for U.S. Mainland. *Associated Press* 17 April. Accessed 27 May 2017. <https://www.yahoo.com/news/doctors-flee-puerto-rico-us-mainland-165338626.html/>.

_____. 2017. Puerto Rico Fears Economic Downturn from New Tax Overhaul. *Associated Press* 20 December. Accessed 15 February 2018. <https://hosted.ap.org/article/9 36cd122496c4b2b86e75e171f119a95/puerto-rico-fears-economic-downturn-tax-reform-bill/>.

Delerme, Simone. 2013. The Latinization of Orlando: Race, Class, and the Politics of Place. Ph.D. dissertation. Rutgers University.

Diversitydatakids.org. 2016. Hispanic National Origin and Neighborhoods of Opportunity. The Heller School for Social Policy and Management, Brandeis University, 17 October. Accessed 19 October 2017. <http://www.diversitydatakids.org/data/library/59/ hispanic-national-origin-and-neighborhoods-of-opportunity/>.

Enchautegui, María E. 1992. Geographical Differentials in the Socioeconomic Status of Puerto Ricans: Human Capital Variations and Labor Market Characteristics. *International Migration Review* 26(4), 1267–90.

FocusEconomics. 2018. Puerto Rico Economic Outlook. 9 October. Accessed 10 October 2018. <https://www.focus-economics.com/countries/puerto-rico/>.

Harvard Law Review. 2017. Developments in the Law – U.S. Territories. *Harvard Law Review* 130, 1617–727.

Hinojosa, Jennifer, Nashia Román and Edwin Meléndez. 2018. New Estimates: 135,000+ Post-Maria Puerto Ricans Relocated to Stateside. Centro Brief RB2017-03, March. <https://centropr.hunter.cuny.edu/sites/default/files/data_sheets/PostMaria-New-Estimates-3-15-18.pdf/>.

Kishore, Nishant, et al. 2018. Mortality in Puerto Rico after Hurricane Maria. *New England Journal of Medicine* 379, 162–70.

Levis, Maria. 2016. Your Money Or Your Life: Federal Policies And Health Disparities In Puerto Rico. *Health Affairs Blog* 13 June. Accessed 26 May 2017. <http://healthaffairs.org/blog/2016/06/13/your-money-or-your-life-federal-policies-and-health-disparities-in-puerto-rico/>.

Mazzei, Patricia. 2017. Months after the Storm, Puerto Rico Stares Down another Blow: The Tax Bill. *New York Times* 16 December.

Meléndez, Edwin, and Jennifer Hinojosa. 2017. Estimates of Post-Hurricane Maria Exodus from Puerto Rico. Centro Research Brief RB 2017-01, October. <https://centropr. hunter.cuny.edu/sites/default/files/RB2017-01-POST-MARIA%20EXODUS_ V3.pdf/>.

Milken Institute School of Public Health. 2018. *Ascertainment of the Estimated Excess Mortality from Hurricane Maria in Puerto Rico.* Washington, DC: George Washington University.

Mora, Marie T., Alberto Dávila and Havidán Rodríguez. 2017a. *Population, Migration, and Socioeconomic Outcomes among Island and Mainland Puerto Ricans: La Crisis Boricua.* Lanham, MD: Lexington Books.

———. 2017b. Education, Migration, and Earnings of Puerto Ricans on the Island and U.S. Mainland: Impact, Outcomes, and Consequences of an Economic Crisis. *Migration Studies* 5(2), 168–89.

———. 2019. Puerto Rican Migration and Mainland Settlement Patterns Before and After Hurricane Maria. *The Minority Report* 1(Winter), 4–7

Oaxaca, Ronald. 1973. Male-Female Wage Differentials in Urban Labor Markets. *International Economic Review* 14, 693–709.

Rodriguez, Clara E. 1989. *Puerto Ricans: Born in the USA.* Boston: Unwin Hyman.

Rodríguez, Havidán. 1992. Household Composition, Employment Patterns, and Income Inequality: Puerto Ricans in New York and Other Areas of the U.S. Mainland. *Hispanic Journal of Behavioral Sciences* 14(1), 52–75.

Ruggles, Steven, Katie Genadek, Ronald Goeken, Josiah Grover, and Matthew Sobek. 2018. Integrated Public Use Microdata Series: Version 6.0 [dataset]. Minneapolis: University of Minnesota, <www.ipums.umn/>.

Silver, Patricia. 2010. 'Culture Is More than Bingo and Salsa': Making *Puertorriqueñidad* in Central Florida. *CENTRO: Journal of the Center for Puerto Rican Studies* 22(1), 57–83.

U.S. Census Bureau. 2017a (and related years). Annual Estimates of the Resident Population for the United States, Regions, States, and Puerto Rico: April 1, 2010 to July 1, 2017. Washington, DC: U.S. Census Bureau, Population Division, December.

———. 2017b (and related years). Estimates of the Components of Resident Population Change for the United States, Regions, States, and Puerto Rico: July 1, 2016 to July 1, 2017. Washington, DC: U.S. Census Bureau, Population Division, December.

———. 2018. American FactFinder (2017 ACS 1-Year Estimates). Accessed 26 September 2018. <https://factfinder.census.gov/faces/nav/jsf/pages/searchresults.xhtml?refresh=t#none/>.

Vélez, William. 2015. The Status of Puerto Ricans in New Destination: Towards a New Framework. Unpublished manuscript, University of Wisconsin, Milwaukee.

Vélez, William and Giovani Burgos. 2010. The Impact of Housing Segregation and Structural Factors on the Socioeconomic Performance of Puerto Ricans in the United States. *CENTRO: Journal of the Center for Puerto Rican Studies* 22(1), 174–98.

Two Sides of the Coin of Puerto Rican Migration: Depopulation in Puerto Rico and the Redefinition of the Diaspora

JENNIFER HINOJOSA

ABSTRACT

Puerto Rican migration caught nationwide attention after Hurricane Maria impacted the island. It was a culmination of more than a decade of economic stagnation that led to Puerto Rico's declining population while stateside Puerto Ricans experienced a population growth. This study examines the impact of post-Hurricane Maria on the Puerto Rican exodus and Puerto Rican diaspora in the U.S. mainland. The purpose of this paper is to measure post-Hurricane Maria exodus and how settlement patterns have reinforced dispersion in the diaspora. The findings from this study shed light on the migration estimations using the School Enrollment Migration Index (SEMI) relative to other migration data sources and dispersed settlement patterns of Puerto Rican migrants data from the Federal Emergency Management Agency (FEMA) and Department of Education(s). More importantly, I argue that existing data sources on Puerto Rican migration are not sufficient to estimate Puerto Rican migration, especially during a time when migration estimates were immediately needed to determine where the migrants relocated to within the U.S. mainland post-Hurricane Maria and the dispersion of Puerto Rican settlement has been magnified as a result of post-Hurricane Maria migrants. [Keywords: Puerto Rico, Migration, Puerto Rican Diaspora, Hurricane Maria, Settlement Patterns, Student Enrollment Migration Index (SEMI)]

The author (jhinojos@hunter.cuny.edu) is a research associate and data center coordinator at the Center for Puerto Rican Studies at CUNY Hunter College. She holds a Master's of Science in Geographical Sciences from University of Maryland, College Park and MA in Geography from SUNY Binghamton University. She interned at the Brookings Institution's Metropolitan Policy Program in Washington D.C. Her research interests include GIS, socioeconomic disparities, migration, and demography.

INTRODUCTION

In the last decade, we have witnessed the resurgence of the Puerto Rican population in the United States through the lens of scholarship, politics, and within U.S. local communities. Recent Puerto Rican migration, driven by two major historical events in Puerto Rico—the 2006 onset of the economic crisis and Hurricane Maria in 2017—give a contemporary view of the fast-paced socioeconomic and demographic effects it has had on both Puerto Rico and receiving states in the U.S. mainland. The increasing geographic dispersion among stateside Puerto Ricans has intensified by the incoming Puerto Rican newcomers during both migration waves, especially after Hurricane Maria in September 2017. Puerto Rican migration today continues to be driven by Puerto Rico's lack of employment opportunities; however, as shown in recent events like Hurricanes Irma and Maria in September 2017, migration has been driven by environmental forces as well.

In this article, I introduce an alternative indicator to measure migration known as "Student Enrollment Migration Index" or SEMI. SEMI is a migration index that can be used in the short-term to estimate out-migration from Puerto Rico to the U.S. mainland while other traditional migration sources such as the Department of Transportation (net movement of passengers), Puerto Rico's Department of Health (Vital Health statistics), and U.S. Census Bureau (American Community Survey and Puerto Rican Community Survey) are otherwise unavailable for months. Hurricane Maria redefined Puerto Rican migration in the 21st century and data collection approaches. Thus, SEMI can be used in the interim and can meet the demands from policymakers and other stakeholders with readily usable and reliable data. I argue that SEMI can be used as an alternative measure to estimate Puerto Rican migration without waiting for estimates for months at a time. Secondly, I argue that the magnitude of the recent migration surpassed previous migration waves in a short period of time and how it has not stopped relative to other Puerto Rican migration periods. Lastly, I argue how post-Hurricane Maria reinforced dispersed settlement patterns beyond states of traditional settlement in the diaspora. My analysis is guided by the following questions: 1. How does post-Hurricane Maria exodus compare with that of previous migration waves? 2. How does SEMI compare to other traditional migration data sources? and 3. Where did post-Hurricane Maria migrants relocate? The organization of this paper is as follows: (1) a brief overview of Puerto Rican migration literature between 1940s and present day; (2) the alternative data and methodology to assess post-Hurricane Maria Puerto Rican migration; and (3) discuss settlement patterns of present-day migration from Puerto Rico to stateside and the implications for Puerto Rico.

PUERTO RICAN MIGRATION LITERATURE

The dominant explanation for Puerto Rican migration is that it is driven by the economic ties between the U.S. mainland and Puerto Rico. This perspective explains the structural forces behind Puerto Rico and the U.S. mainland's economies for prior migration waves, and it continues to explain the Puerto Rican population movement under the 2006 economic crisis migration wave. On the other hand, the recent 2017 post-Hurricane Maria migration wave, coupled with the effects of the 2006 economic crisis period, produced a new wave of migrants in terms of cohort's magnitude and dispersed settlement patterns. Research on Puerto Rican migration from the island to the U.S. mainland is well documented by various demographers, sociologists, and other social scientists, and it can be traced back as far as the 20th century (Godoy et al. 2003).

Economic Migration

Puerto Rico's economy has become more integrated into the U.S. economy over the years. In addition, economic and social policies promoted migration between the U.S. and Puerto Rico (Centro de Estudios Puertorriqueños 1979; Maldonado 1979; Enchautegui 1993; Whalen 2001; Meléndez 2015). The cyclical economic upturns and downturns between the U.S. mainland and Puerto Rico that impacted the migratory flows has been well documented (Macisco 1968; Centro de Estudios Puertorriqueños 1979; Enchautegui and Freeman 2005). In other words, when Puerto Rico's economic conditions worsens, it produces a wave of out-migration of Puerto Rican migrants and when the U.S. mainland's economy worsens, up to the last decade, there was a return migration from the stateside U.S. to Puerto Rico (Whalen 2005).

Puerto Rico's population continues to be a source of labor for the U.S. labor market; thus, selective characteristics of the Puerto Rican migrants and their settlement patterns also changed overtime (Meléndez 1994; Meléndez and Visser 2011). For example, during the Great Migration period (1940s–1950s), a surplus of unemployed low-skilled laborers was a main problem and migration to the U.S. mainland's agriculture and factory jobs was a way to alleviate Puerto Rico's unemployment. This cohort's settlement patterns were mostly described as concentrated communities throughout the Northeast and Midwest urban areas, and parts of the western coastal states, such as Hawaii and California (Macisco 1968; Maldonado 1979; López 2005; Delgado 2005).

Past social and economic policies such as Operation Bootstrap, the Migration Division's contract labor programs, and the recruitment of men and women in the military and factories during post-World War II era, are examples of policies that has led many Puerto Ricans to migrate to and from the island and the U.S. Furthermore, extending U.S. citizenship to Puerto Ricans through the 1917 Jones Act facilitated migration without legal barriers. Existing Puerto Rican communities throughout the mainland—especially in traditional states of settlement such as states in the Northeast region, parts of the Midwest, and West (specifically Hawaii and California)—was initiated by contract labor programs in the stateside agricultural and other industries that provided job opportunities that other groups declined (Maldonado 1979; Whalen and Hernandez 2001; Enchautegui 1993). Maldonado (1979) argued the origins of communities beyond New York City as a result of agriculture and industrial labor migration from Puerto Rico to areas like Buffalo, New York (upstate), Pennsylvania, Ohio, Indiana, Wisconsin, and California. Puerto Rican migration today continues to be economically driven due to a weak economy island with lack of job opportunities and economic mobility (Meléndez and Visser 2011; Birson and Meléndez 2014).

Post War II (late 1940s to 1960s)

Economically, Puerto Rico underwent rapid structural changes during the Great Migration period. Puerto Rican migration increased after the Second World War as a result of high unemployment rates heavily influenced by the decline of the sugar industry. For example, in the early phase, the island's transitioned from rural to an industry-based economy and displaced many farm workers, especially in the island's rural *municipios*. Studies documented how such labor force migrated to the island's large metropolitan areas and/or the U.S. mainland to meet the demands for both skilled and semi-skilled laborers (Centro de Estudios Puertorriqueños 1979; Whalen and Vázquez-Hernández 2005; Godoy et al. 2003). According to various studies, the first wave of migrants contained both unskilled and semi-skilled workers (Centro de Estudios Puertorriqueños 1979; Maldonado 1979; Perloff 1975; Mills et al. 1950; Fitzpatrick 1968). The economic ties between the U.S. and Puerto Rico reinforced migration to the extent of creating policies and relocation hubs for incoming Puerto Rican migrants (Whalen and Vázquez-Hernández 2005). Labor recruitments and chain migration also contributed to the rapid increase of the Puerto Rican population in the United States. Puerto Ricans were the first significant group to migrate into the U.S. mainland by air travel. It also important to note, previous small waves of Puerto Rican migration established communities within New York City and during the first major wave, these enclaves functioned as a destination point for many incoming Puerto Ricans. Furthermore, the enclaves provided a sense of community and social network for new Puerto Rican migrants. Lastly, chain migration also maintained a steady flow of Puerto Rican migrants to New York City because of family and friends already living.

In 1947, the Migration Division of the Department of Labor of Puerto Rico played a pivotal role in Puerto Rican settlement patterns throughout New York State as well as other areas of highly concentrated Puerto Rican communities. It was established by the U.S. and Puerto Rican governments to provide Puerto Ricans with job opportunities, vocational skills, and to prepare them to compete in the U.S. labor market (21 Puerto Rican Women Here as Domestics 1948a). Its first U.S. mainland office opened in New York City in 1947. The Migration Division fostered Puerto Ricans to find jobs in the service, factory-related industries, and agricultural industry (upstate New York). The Migration Division also functioned as way mobilize and distribute incoming Puerto Ricans throughout the U.S. mainland.

Migration flows during the Great Migration period was at its highest after World War II, between 1946 and 1964, due to labor force demand in the U.S. mainland (Whalen 2005). However, measuring migration during this period produced an array of estimates due to inconsistency and unreliable data sources (Godoy et al. 2003; Fitzpatrick 1968). Sandis (1970) work referenced the inadequacies of using the 1960 decennial data from the U.S. Census Bureau to characterize Puerto Rican migrants during the Great Migration.

Migration flowed toward the Northeast, mainly to New York City. In terms of settlement patterns, Puerto Ricans were concentrated in the Northeast and Midwest region's central city areas. However, once deindustrialization took place in United States, many Puerto Ricans have either permanently returned back to Puerto Rico or made repeated migration(s) to and from Puerto Rico and the U.S. mainland.

Circular Migration (1970s–2000s)

Repeated migration to and from Puerto Rico and the U.S. mainland, known as circular migration of the Puerto Rican population, took place between the 1970s and 2000s. Various scholars define circular migration differently, in terms of length-of-stay both on the island and the U.S. mainland, number of trips between the states, and characteristics of the migrants (Godoy et al. 2003; Duany 2002). The circular migration period was a time when Puerto Ricans were viewed as a very mobile community because of the back-and-forth movement for economic opportunities, such as seeking jobs, in either Puerto Rico or the U.S. mainland (Duany 2002; Enchautegui 1993). In other words, migration was driven by economic forces. Puerto Ricans who left the island during the 1970s and 2000s were migrating in search of better economic opportunities. On the other hand, some scholars found that return migrants composed of Puerto Rican individuals and/or households migrated to the U.S. mainland during the Great Migration and were economically displaced due to the replacement of service-related jobs by industrial jobs in the central cities (Enchautegui 1993). For example, for Puerto Rican communities in New York City, the 1970s and 1980s were the most difficult decades, which resulted an economically distraught labor market. Puerto Ricans were among the poorest. "Among Hispanics, between 1970 and 1985 Puerto Ricans experienced a sharp deterioration in economic well-being while Mexicans experienced the modest, and Cubans substantial, improvement in economic status" (Tienda 1989). Employment demands were no longer needed in both unskilled and uneducated workers, especially in New York City's industrial sectors, as well as other urban areas (Barnes 2002).

The unprecedented growth of the stateside Puerto Rican population fueled by both natural increase and migration from Puerto Rico and migration to Florida was a recurring theme across studies examining Puerto Rican migration between 2006 and 2016.

Economic Crisis Migration (2006 through 2016)

Since 2006, the island has experienced the largest GDP decline in history. The economic crisis negatively affected both private and public sectors and population, ultimately leading many individuals and families to leave the island for the U.S. mainland in increasingly large numbers. On the other hand, the United States faced its own economic downturn attributed to the housing market crash in 2008.

In the context of Puerto Rican migration during the economic crisis period, scholars have pointed out two types of migration patterns: (1) migration from Puerto Rico and (2) interstate migration among mainland Puerto Ricans, mainly to the sunbelt states (Concepción Torres 2008; Meléndez and Visser 2011; Meléndez and Birson 2014; García-Ellín 2014; Franqui-Rivera 2014; Silver 2017; Silver and Vélez 2017; Mora et al. 2018). The unprecedented growth of the stateside Puerto Rican population fueled by both natural increase and migration from Puerto Rico and migration to Florida was a recurring theme across studies examining Puerto Rican migration between 2006 and 2016.

García-Ellín (2014) discussed the internal migration of stateside Puerto Rican out of states of traditional settlement like in the Northeast and Midwest to states of new areas of settlement such as the U.S. South between 2001 and 2011. The author used aggregated data from Integrated Public Use Microdata Series (IPUMS) from the U.S. Census Bureau's American Community Survey (ACS), one-year samples. He found that state-to-state migration among Puerto Ricans contributed to the growth of the Puerto Rican population in the South, especially in Florida (García-Ellín 2014). Franqui-Rivera (2014) described military bases and service in the armed forces contributed to the Puerto Rican population growth in states of new settlements beyond traditional states. Both island-born and stateside born Puerto Ricans in the armed forces contributed to the diaspora of the Puerto Rican communities throughout the U.S. mainland, especially in the southern states as a result of becoming familiar with the area after completing initial training the U.S. mainland (Franqui-Rivera 2014; Silver 2010).

Silver and Vélez (2017) found that Puerto Rican settlement to central Florida occurred prior to the "economic crisis period" and were composed of Puerto Ricans from the Great Migration period, mainly from the Northeast and Midwest. Puerto Rico's economic crisis was also a major factor for Puerto Ricans from Puerto Rico to relocate to central Florida with the help of family and friends through social network ties.

Puerto Rican migration among mainland Puerto Ricans and from the island created the newly expanded diaspora communities, throughout the U.S. south and occurred during the economic crisis, in other words, migration from Puerto Rico and interstate migration from Puerto Ricans from other mainland states. Furthermore, Silver (2014) discussed the rising Puerto Rican population in the U.S. South, especially in states like: Georgia, Mississippi, North Carolina, South Carolina, and Tennessee (Silver 2014). Furthermore, the characteristics of both island-born and stateside born Puerto Ricans moving to the U.S. South differs by showing higher educational attainment and higher-paying occupational opportunities (Silver 2014).

Post-Maria Migration (2017–present)

On September 20, 2017, category 4 Hurricane Maria entered through Yabucoa, in the southeastern region of the island with wind speeds of up to 155 mph, and diagonally reached to the northwest region, Arecibo, with wind speeds of 115 mph. Damages related to flooding, structural, and electrical destroyed numerous homes, schools, businesses, and hospitals throughout the island. More importantly, Hurricane Irma, a category 5 hurricane, also passed north of Puerto Rico, two weeks prior Hurricane Maria leaving many without power and causing flash flooding (Johnson et al. 2017). Both storms, especially Hurricane Maria, induced one of the largest out-migration from Puerto Rico to the U.S. mainland in a short period of time. The magnitude of the post-Hurricane Maria migration has never been seen in Puerto Rico's history.

Environmental migration, coupled with the effects of the economic crisis and slow recovery/humanitarian aid, were push factors for relocation to the U.S. mainland. Puerto Rican migration during this period was heavily documented by news media outlets and mainly revolved around migration estimate (the number of Puerto Ricans who fled Puerto Rico) and the states that received the most migrants, as a result of the storm. Unlike prior Puerto Rican migration waves, assessing Puerto Rican migration during Hurricane Maria period differed due to lack data availability at a short period of time. Immediately following Hurricane Maria devastation in Puerto Rico, migration data was needed among public officials and government agencies to prepare housing, educational, economic, and medical needs for incoming evacuees to their states. However, local government and public agencies were not prepared for the magnitude of the incoming evacuees to their home state(s) and failed to take notice of an already existing and continuous Puerto Rican migration happening prior to the September 2017 hurricanes (both Maria and Irma). As a result, data related to incoming post-Hurricane Maria migrants were essential to understand and grasp the incoming new residents to their communities. As a result, alternative techniques and non-traditional migration sources were used to measure the magnitude of post-Hurricane Maria migration. Such alternative methods included tracking smartphone data usage and using non-traditional migration sources like student enrollment data reported by Department of Education that received displaced students from Puerto Rico.

A New York-based tech company developed a technology collecting a mobile phone data of the number of individuals who moved from Puerto Rico to the U.S. mainland and vice versa, between October 2017 and February 2018. Teralytics estimated about 407,465 Puerto Ricans relocated from Puerto Rico to the United States in a span of five months. However, during the same time period, the company analyzed a return migration of 359,813 individuals. Based on these numbers, the estimated net migration would be 47,652, probably an undercount when compared to other available data. To begin with, the data refer to owners of mobile phones who activated their accounts when traveling stateside. By implication the estimate excludes individuals that do not own a mobile phone or activated their account because of roaming costs or other considerations. Findings from this study concluded Florida followed by New York, Texas and Pennsylvania were among the top four states for Puerto Ricans relocating immediately following Hurricane Maria. According to the tech company, mobile data may become a new way to track human migration, especially after a natural disaster strikes an area, like Puerto Rico. A major concern in collecting such information is privacy among the mobile device users. As some view this as an invasion of their privacy especially data related to location.

We are calling this new alternative methodology the School Enrollment Migration Index (SEMI)....

Puerto Rico's Financial Oversight and Management Board (FOMB) played a role in providing post-Hurricane Maria estimates. FOMB's January 2018 New Fiscal Plan adopted Lyman Stone's population projection of a 7.7 percent population decline in 2018 (Government of Puerto Rico 2018). However, various revisions were made and the recent October 2018 'New Fiscal Plan' reported a population decline of 5.1 percent, with an estimated total population of about 3.16 million inhabitants in the island in 2018. Recent U.S. Census population data estimates Puerto Rico's population to be 3.19 million in 2018, between July 1, 2017, and July 1, 2018 (U.S. Census Bureau 2018a).

Lastly, CUNY Hunter College's Center for Puerto Rican Studies (Centro) released four reports related to migration estimate and settlement pattern trends among the displaced Puerto Rican migrants. The first two reports estimated Puerto Rican migration post-Hurricane Maria utilizing previous migration patterns based on data from the U.S. Census Bureau's American Community Survey/Puerto Rican Community Survey and student enrollment data of school districts in the United States that received displaced students from Puerto Rico by the selected state's Department of Education (Meléndez and Hinojosa 2017; Hinojosa, Román and Meléndez 2017; Hinojosa, Meléndez and Román 2018; Hinojosa and Meléndez 2018). The most recent Centro report (2018), released one year after Hurricane Maria, presented a new alternative methodology to estimate Puerto Rican migration using a combination of school enrollment data from Puerto Rico's Department of Education and the U.S. Census Bureau's American Community Survey (ACS) data. We are calling this new alternative methodology the School Enrollment Migration Index (SEMI) (Hinojosa and Meléndez 2018). This is further explained in the data and methods section.

METHOD AND DATA

Data Sources

Reliable data sources to estimate Puerto Rican migration is a topic that continues to be debated and unavoidable among scholars today. Similar to other studies estimating population movement to and from Puerto Rico, I use micro-level data from the 2006 and 2017 Puerto Rican Community Survey and American Community survey (one-year estimates) conducted by the U.S. Census Bureau. Both datasets allow the

Figure 1. Post-Hurricane Maria Data Sources and Availability, January 2017 to September 2018

PBE																				
								NMP												
								SEMI												
								2018 Population Estimates (U.S. Census Bureau)												
2017 ACS (1-year estimates)																				
JAN	FEB	MAR	APR	MAY	JUN	JUL	AUG	SEP	OCT	NOV	DEC	JAN	FEB	MAR	APR	MAY	JUN	JUL	AUG	SEP
2017	2017	2017	2017	2017	2017	2017	2017	2017	2017	2017	2017	2018	2018	2018	2018	2018	2018	2018	2018	2018

extrapolation of Puerto Rican migrants who currently live on the mainland and those who migrated from Puerto Rico one year ago from the non-moving Puerto Rican population (Godoy et al. 2003; García-Ellín 2014; Birson and Meléndez 2014; Meléndez and Visser 2011; Birson 2014; Franqui-Rivera 2014). In addition to using the U.S. Census Bureau's American Community Survey, I also rely on student enrollment data from Puerto Rico's Department of Education and data from Federal Emergency Management Agency's (FEMA) change of address database.

Prior estimates of the magnitude of the population movement between Puerto Rico and the United States post-Hurricane Maria have been based on the net movement of passenger, mobile telephone data (Echenique and Melgar 2018), or projections based on recent migration trends from Puerto Rico to the U.S. Immediately following the storm, alternative data sources were not available to measure the magnitude of the net migration. Generally, social scientists—such as demographers, sociologists and economists—have relied on a few methods and data sources to estimate Puerto Rican migration. These are:[1]

1. Demographic balancing equation (PBE),[2] using data from the Puerto Rico Department of Health and the U.S. Census Bureau Population Estimates.
2. Net Movement of Passengers (NMP), using data from the U.S. Bureau of Transportation Statistics.
3. Place of residence the prior year using data from the American Community Survey (ACS) of the U.S. Bureau of the Census.

However, these methods are not conducive to estimate Puerto Rican migration in the short term, especially in the aftermath of catastrophic events such as Hurricane Maria. As shown in Figure 1, the estimates produced by these more common measures tend to converge over long periods of times, even though the NMP tends to show more volatility (*i.e.*, wider variation) than the estimates derived from the ACS or the PBE. The main issue with the three available data sources and methods to estimate migratory flows from the island to stateside are their ready availability. The PBE, for instance, relies on population, mortality, and birth data that are typically reported annually for the prior year fiscal year (ending on June 30). Therefore, there is a lag in time capturing current conditions.

Similarly, the ACS data is based on a random survey of the population and the data is published about a year after the end of the year it is collected. The NMP data is an indirect method to estimate migration and typically would lag about six months after it is collected. Because the duration of travel for a significant portion of passengers tends to be short and traveling is by nature frequently seasonal, NMP is more volatile than other available data and is generally interpreted primarily as an early indicator of migration flows. For example, the latest NMP data available is as of June 2018, therefore, this indicator does not fully capture the total net migration estimate for the entire calendar year 2018 (see Figure 1). These time-lag issues are compounded by the fact that Hurricane Maria struck in Puerto Rico September 20, 2017, and migration data collected by the ACS for the last quarter of 2017 will be combined with the data for the previous eight months of that year, diluting the impact of the storm on migration over the entire twelve-month period, leading to lower estimates. Using data collected from these sources would therefore reduce the actual magnitude of the post-hurricane exodus.

Since Hurricane Maria made landfall in September 2017, data collection and estimate quality for the most recently released 2017 ACS, conducted both in the U.S. and Puerto Rico,[3] do not precisely reflect post-Hurricane Maria actual impact (U.S. Census Bureau 2018b). First, the 2017 ACS population estimates in the United States, which measure household interstate mobility, include households surveyed from January 2017 to December of 2017 (see Figure 1). This survey would include a representative sample of the population arriving from Puerto Rico collected after September 2017 when Hurricane Maria struck Puerto Rico and induced a massive emigration from the island. Yet, according to the U.S. Census Bureau survey protocols, evacuees from Puerto Rico would only be counted as emigrants in the 2017 survey if they had arrived in the U.S. prior to the hurricane's landfall or planned to stay in the U.S. for two or more months. Therefore, population and migration figures reported for 2017 by the U.S. Census Bureau are likely to underestimate actual changes in residence between Puerto Rico and the U.S. in 2017, and by implication total population and migration estimates. The 2017 American Community Survey (one-year estimate) was released on September 2018 and reported Puerto Rico's population as 3,337,177. However, this population count depicts 8.5 months of 2017,[4] due to data collection suspension after the storm (see Figure 1).[5] The latest population estimate, released in December 2018, by the U.S. Census Bureau's Population Estimate, reported a population estimate of 3,195,153 between July 1, 2017, and July 1, 2018. Furthermore, the U.S. Census Bureau states Puerto Rico's population declined by 129,848 people and mostly attributes that decrease to out-migration. On the other hand, migration estimates based on the PBE for the fiscal year that ends on June 30 of 2017 and this excludes the impact of Hurricane Maria from their 2017 estimates.

School Enrollment Migration Index (SEMI)

To measure post-Hurricane Maria migration estimates, I use data from 2017–2018 and 2018–2019 student enrollment count from Puerto Rico's Department of Education and data from the U.S. Census Bureau's 2013–2016 American Community Survey and Puerto Rican Community Survey (one-year estimates). According to

Hinojosa and Meléndez (2018), to estimate the number of migrants from Puerto Rico to the United States Post-Hurricane Maria, they developed an alternative method using student population losses reported by Puerto Rico's Department of Education as a source of data.[6] This new method produces a suitable migration estimate shortly after school enrollment is completed by the Department of Education at the beginning of every semester, thus producing a timely leading indicator of migration flows. The School Enrollment Migration Index (SEMI) is defined as:

SEMI= $\Delta SE_{0,1} \times (A/C)$,

where $\Delta SE_{0,1}$ refers to the change in student enrollment between period 0 and 1, and (A/C) is the ratio of the total adult migrant population (19 years and over) and non-school-age children (4 years or less) relative to school-age children (5 to 18 years old).

To establish the "A/C" ratio, the authors calculate the averages for Puerto Rican school-age children and total adult migrants using data from the yearly surveys of the American Community Survey from the U.S. Bureau of the Census between 2013 and 2016 (Hinojosa and Meléndez 2018). This ratio is then used to estimate the total migration that corresponds to the number of children assumed to have relocated stateside. In other words, the data on public school enrollment change from Puerto Rico's Department of Education is extrapolated to estimate the total post-Hurricane Maria exodus from Puerto Rico on a semester basis, at the beginning of the academic year in August, and at the beginning of the calendar year in January. The current estimate of 159,415 and up to 176,603 emigrants (upper bound) from the island was derived by using Puerto Rico's Department of Education's student matriculation loss in public schools between 2017 and 2018 (the academic year when Hurricane Maria made landfall in Puerto Rico) and the present academic year, 2018–2019. Between both academic years, there was a reported public-school student population loss of nearly 40,000 students, from 346,096 students from 2017–2018 to 306,652 students.

Geographical Information Systems (ArcGIS)
Geographical Information Systems are a combination of software modules that provide a toolbox for conducting spatial analysis. To illustrate Puerto Rican relocation post-Hurricane Maria, this paper utilizes one of the functions provided by ArcMap 10.2.2. Data are classified by natural breaks and are portrayed as shaded colors to indicate the spatial distributions of post-Hurricane Maria migrants at various scales within stateside. Requested data from the Federal Emergency Management Agency's (FEMA) change of address database from February 2018 (5 months post-Hurricane Maria) and August 2018 (11 months post-Hurricane Maria) was used to map the settlement patterns of displaced migrants from Puerto Rico who changed their mailing address from Puerto Rico to stateside U.S. (at the county level). Again, due to unavailable data from the U.S. Census Bureau's American Community Survey,

FEMA's change of address dataset is among the first data sources to illustrate relocation patterns. Two sets of maps are illustrated at the county level to analyze post-Hurricane Maria settlement patterns. It is important to note that FEMA data is not a representative sample of the post-Hurricane Maria migration; it only counts households who officially changed their mailing address at the state of relocation from Puerto Rico.

FINDINGS AND ANALYSIS
1. Comparing Migration Exodus from Puerto Rico

Guiding Question #1. How does post-Hurricane Maria exodus compare with that of previous migration waves?

Figure 2 presents the net migration estimates between 1941 and 2017 from Puerto Rico to the U.S. mainland derived by using three traditional measures, population balance equation (PBE), U.S. Census data (American Community Survey/Decennial Census) (ACS), and the Net Movement of Passengers (NMP). As noted in the method and data section, these migration indices are not ideal to estimate Puerto Rican migration in short periods of time such as in the aftermath of Hurricane Maria. As shown in Figure 2, the estimates produced by these measures tend to converge over long periods of times (post-1990s), even though the NMP tends to show more volatility (i.e., wider variation) than the estimates derived from the ACS or the PBE.

Table 1 presents results from the four indicators by decades between 1941 and 2018. The results yield 2 main findings. First, SEMI net migration is comparable to that of traditional net migration indicators over the long term. This is especially seen in the recent two migration waves, the 2006 economic crisis (-630,027) and 2017 post-Hurricane Maria (-223,861). For example, SEMI showed a net migration estimate of -630,027 during the economic crisis period (2006 to 2016) while ACS indicated a net migration of -590,433 and -626,011 for PBE (see table 1). However,

Figure 2. Estimated Migration Flows from Puerto Rico to the U.S., 1941-2017

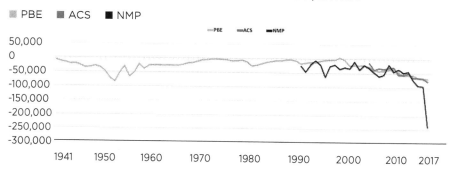

Source: 1941-2017 Department of Health and U.S. Census Bureau Population Estimates; 1991-2016 Bureau of Transportation Statistics; 2005-2017 American Community Survey.

Table 1. Comparing Net Migration Estimates from Puerto Rico to stateside U.S., 1941 through 2018

Year	PBE	ACS	NMP	SEMI
1941-1949	-191,054			
1950-1959	-508,478			
1960-1969	-226,198			
1970-1979	-49,898			
1980-1989	-114,320			
1990-1999	-66,641		-257,557	
2000-2009	-272,381	-144,393	-350,273	-107,715*
2010-2018*	-475,379**	-458,484	-689,009**	-522,312
2006-2016 (Economic crisis)	-626,011	-590,433	-865,497	-630,027
2017-2018 (Post-Hurricane Maria)	-67,500*	-207,169	-239,992*	-223,861

Source: 1941-2017 Department of Health and U.S. Census Bureau Population Estimates; 1991-2018 Bureau of Transportation Statistics; 2005-2018 American Community Survey; 2008-2018 Puerto Rico's Department of Education.
*SEMI net migration estimate is available between 2008 and 2018.
**PBE net migration estimate is not available for 2018, the data reported in this table is for 2017. NMP data does not includes January 2018 through June 2018, the data reported in this table is only for 2017 and 6 months (January 2018 through June 2018) for 2018.

NMP showed higher net migration estimates of -865,497 in the same time period. As previously discussed, NMP net migration(s) tends to be more volatile relative to PBE and ACS. As shown in table 1, Post-Hurricane Maria (2017-2018) net migration yielded higher variations as a result of unavailable data for PBE, since Puerto Rico's Department of Health has not release birth and death rates for 2018 and NMP's data is not available between July 2018 and December 2018. This an example of one of the advantages of using SEMI in the short term until data sources from PBE and NMP become available. In the case of post-Hurricane Maria period (2017-2018), SEMI showed a net migration estimate of -223,861 while ACS net migration estimate was -207,169. On the other hand, net migration estimates for NMP is -239,992 slightly higher relative to ACS and SEMI; however, this is expected to be higher since data for the remaining months of July 2018 through December 2018 is unavailable.

2. Student Enrollment Migration Index
Guiding Question #2: How does the 'Student Enrollment Migration Index' (SEMI) compare to other traditional migration data sources?
In Figure 3, I present data derived from our new estimation method for the Puerto Rican pre- and post-disaster relocation to the U.S. mainland relative to other esti-

Figure 3. Estimated Migration Flows from Puerto to the U.S. 2005-2018

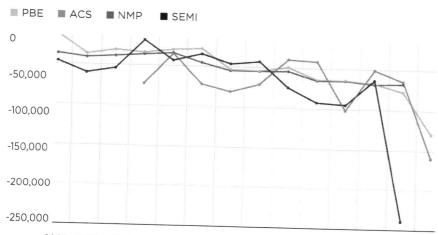

Source: 1941-2017 Department of Health and U.S. Census Bureau Population Estimates; 1991-2017 Bureau of Transportation Statistics; 2005-2018 American Community Survey; 2008-2018 Puerto Rico's Department of Education.

Note: NMP latest data available is September 2018 and PBE's vital statistics is unavailable for 2018.

mation methods currently in use. Figure 3 illustrates the net migration estimates between 2005 and 2018 based on observable available data from the U.S. Census Bureau's American Community Survey and the Puerto Rican Community Survey (2005–2018), the U.S. Bureau of Transportation Statistics (2005–2018), and Puerto Rico Department of Health (2005–2017).

Based on school enrollment data from the Commonwealth of Puerto Rico Department of Education, we estimated a net migration of 159,415 with an upper bound of 176,603 from Puerto Rico to the U.S. mainland in the year since Hurricane Maria made landfall in Puerto Rico. Figure 3 presents SEMI net migration results compared to the other migration indices. SEMI's net migration results relative to the other indices (PBE, ACS, and NMP) produced higher, lower, and/or similar migration estimates between 2008 and 2018. For example, in 2008 SEMI's (-72,575) net migration estimate was higher relative to PBE (-36,349), ACS (-49,194), and NMP (-18,569). As shown in Figure 3, SEMI (-39,563) net migration estimates was somewhat similar to that of other indices (PBE was -34,158; ACS was -29,966; and NMP was -43,460) in 2009. However, between 2010 and 2012 SEMI showed higher net migration estimates relative to other indices. In 2013, SEMI (-39,563) showed similar net migration estimates to that of ACS (-49,194) but lower than PBE (-54,259) and NMP (-74,339). However, SEMI (-41,684), showed net migration estimates that fell between PBE (-65,089), ACS (-64,073), and NMP (-92,310) estimates. In 2015, PBE (-65,089) and ACS (-64,238) showed comparable net migration estimates, while SEMI (-101,575) and NMP (-94,735) had higher outflows. Overall, SEMI (-50,835) showed lower net migration estimates relative to PBE (-68,262), ACS (-67,480), and NMP (-63,508) in 2016. In 2017, ACS reported a net migration estimate of -77,321 while PBE (-67,500) and SEMI (-64,446) showed comparable rates. Again, the 2017 ACS does not account post-Hurricane Maria impacts due to lack of current data availability. However, NMP net migration estimated a total of -239,992, and this accounts more outflow than return migration. SEMI, on the other hand, includes the change of student enrollment in Puerto Rico's Department of Education from 2016 and 2017 academic school year. Lastly, one year after Hurricane-Maria SEMI was able to provide an up to date net migration estimate of -159,415 and this is comparable to the recently released U.S. Census Bureau's out-migration of -129,848. SEMI's release was in September 2018 (Hinojosa and Meléndez 2018), three months prior to U.S. Census Bureau's 2018 Population Estimates.

Lastly, one year after Hurricane Maria SEMI's net migration estimates a total of -159,415 while ACS preliminary population decline estimated a loss of -239,848 between July 1, 2017, and July 1, 2018. Recently released 2018 data from the U.S. Census Bureau estimates a decline of Puerto Rico's population of 129,848 (mostly attributed to out-migration) between July 1 2017, and July 1, 2018, while SEMI measures out-migration between August 2017 and September 2018. As shown in Figure 3, SEMI and ACS out-migration measurements is somewhat close; however, it is important to note the timing is different by two months (SEMI includes August and September of 2018 while U.S. Census Bureau's population estimates includes does not include August and September of 2018). On the other hand, NMP and PBE data is not available to calculate migration estimates for 2018. Using SEMI as an indicator for a short period of time while other data sources become available is an example of migration indicator that can quickly calculate migration estimates from Puerto Rico. As shown in this analysis, SEMI can be used an indicator of migration from Puerto Rico to the U.S. mainland in the short term while other migration sources become available. Using SEMI can provide policymakers and stakeholders with reliable and readily available net migration estimate from Puerto Rico to the U.S. mainland for short-term decision-making in both Puerto Rico and the destination states where migrants are relocating.

3. Post-Hurricane Maria Dispersion
Guiding Question #3: Where did post-Hurricane Maria migrants relocate?
Puerto Rican migration from Puerto Rico due to the recently post-Hurricane Maria exodus has reinforced dispersion in the Puerto Rican diaspora in the United States through the growth or formation of new communities in both old and new areas of settlement. The Puerto Rican population in the United States continues to grow and disperse throughout the U.S., particularly in the southern region. The combination of Puerto Rico's declining economy, which led many Puerto Ricans to flee the island for better economic opportunities in the U.S. mainland, the internal migration of

Table 2. Post-Hurricane Maria Relocation by Regions in February 2018 and August 2018

Region	PBE	ACS	NMP	SEMI
Northeast	26,905	37%	7,641	37%
South	38,300	53%	10,968	53%
Midwest	6,116	8%	1,389	7%
West	1,200	2%	554	3%
Total	**72,521**	**100%**	**20,552**	**100%**

Source: 2017 U.S. Census Bureau, American Community Survey (1-year estimates) and FEMA.

Puerto Ricans from the Northeast and Midwest to the southern states, and general population growth have all resulted in a changing geography for Puerto Ricans in the United States. Thus, new areas of settlement across new and traditional states by the 2006 economic crisis cohort, served as resettlement gateways to post-Hurricane Maria migrants, especially in the southern and northeast regions.

Prior to Hurricane Maria, between 2000 and 2016, notable Puerto Rican population growth was apparent in the following states: North Carolina, Texas, Georgia, Virginia, and Florida, all of which are located in the U.S. South. Puerto Rican population growth was also seen in Pennsylvania and Ohio, both states of traditional settlements for Puerto Ricans. On the other hand, Puerto Rican population declined in the following states: New York, New Jersey, Illinois, and California. Lastly, Puerto Ricans in Connecticut and Massachusetts showed no population growth or decline, instead the population remained steady between 2000 and 2017. However, both states are expected to show population growth as a result of migrants from the 2017 post-Hurricane Maria exodus. The top 15 destination states for Puerto Rican migrants from Puerto Rico during the economic crisis (2006–2017) were: Florida, Pennsylvania, New York, Texas, Massachusetts, New Jersey, Connecticut, Ohio, Georgia, North Carolina, Virginia, Illinois, Michigan, South Carolina, and California. Such states included both traditional (New York, California, Massachusetts, New Jersey, Connecticut, Ohio, Illinois, and Pennsylvania) and new states of settlement (Texas, Georgia, North Carolina, Virginia, Michigan, and South Carolina).

Table 2 shows requested data of FEMA's change of address claims from February 2018 (5 months after post-Hurricane Maria) and August 2018 (11 months post-Hurricane Maria), and settlement location from the 2017 American Community Survey (1-year estimate) at the regional level (U.S. Department of Homeland Security 2018). This data was further used to map the settlement patterns of displaced evacuees from Puerto Rico to the U.S. mainland (see Figure 4). Overall, post-Hurricane Maria migrants showed dispersed settlement patterns throughout the continental U.S., especially in states of traditional settlement and in states in the southern region. As shown in table 2, five months post-Hurricane Maria, a total of 19,271 households from Puerto

Table 3. Post-Hurricane Maria Relocation by Top 15 States in February 2018 and August 2018 (FEMA's Change of Address)

Rank		2017 ACS (1-year estimate)	%	Rank		August 2018 FEMA (Households)	%
1	Florida	21,762	30%	1	Florida	8,873	43%
2	Pennsylvania	7,558	10%	2	New York	2,111	10%
3	Massachusetts	5,414	7%	3	Massachusetts	1,765	9%
4	Texas	4,938	7%	4	Pennsylvania	1,449	7%
5	Connecticut	4,507	6%	5	Connecticut	1,220	6%
6	New York	4,346	6%	6	New Jersey	925	5%
7	New Jersey	3,795	5%	7	Texas	761	4%
8	Ohio	2,187	3%	8	Illinois	665	3%
9	Maryland	1,956	3%	9	Georgia	283	1%
10	Georgia	1,933	3%	10	Ohio	267	1%
11	North Carolina	1,866	3%	11	North Carolina	249	!%
12	Illinois	1,712	2%	12	California	238	1%
13	Virginia	1,168	2%	13	Virginia	166	1%
14	New Hampshire	838	1%	14	Maryland	161	1%
15	California	817	1%	15	Wisconsin	144	1%
	Other States	7,724	11%		Other States	1,275	6%
	Total	**72,521**	**100%**		**Total**	**20,552**	**100%**

Source: 2017 U.S. Census Bureau, American Community Survey (1-year estimates) and FEMA.

Rico changed their home address from Puerto Rico to the U.S. mainland and this figure slightly increased to 20,552 households in August 2018, 11 months post-Hurricane Maria. Table 2 also shows the distribution of incoming Puerto Ricans from Puerto Rico using the 2017 American Community Survey, whereby more than half (53%) settled in the south followed by 37 percent in the northeast, 8 percent in the Midwest, and 2 percent in the west. Regionally, five months after Hurricane Maria, more than half (56%) of the evacuees who changed their home address relocated to the South, followed by 35 percent in the Northeast, 7 percent in the Midwest, and 3 percent in the West (see table 2). FEMA's change of address claims shows similar relocation patterns at the regional level to that of Puerto Rican migrants reported by the 2017 American Community Survey (1-year estimate). For example, the 2017 ACS reported at least 37 percent of the Puerto Rican migrants relocated to the Northeast, however, immediately following the storm, FEMA claims showed that at least 35 percent relocated to the same region 5 months post-Hurricane Maria and then slightly increased to 37 percent, 11 months after the storm. Relocation patterns to the south was also

Figure 4. Evacuees by Households as of August 2018 (Change of Mailing Address)

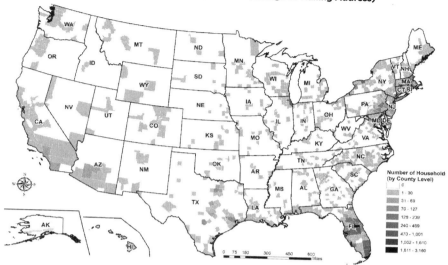

Source: FEMA as of August 2018.
Note: This data reflects self-reported data on any survivor's current mailing address in CONUS. Addresses often change without letting FEMA know, and many survivors may have returned home, or since moved to CONUS, without this data set being updated. Many or most of these addresses have not changed since they first registered with FEMA. Many survivors may have a mailing address with a friend or relative and many not actually moved to CONUS.

similar amongst the 2017 ACS (37%) Puerto Rican migrants and FEMA claims (56% in February 2018 and 53% in August 2018) as well, as both data sources showed more than half relocated to that particular region (see table 2). However, 11 months post-Hurricane Maria, with the exception of the West (7%) and Midwest (3%), the south declined from 56 percent to 53 percent, while the northeast increased from 35% to 37% between February 2018 and August 2018.

Table 3 shows the top 15 states with the most evacuees who changed their mailing address from Puerto Rico to the relocated state and data from the 2017 American Community Survey (1-year estimate). Six states from the south followed by five from the northeast, and four states from the Midwest were the top 15 states most evacuees relocated to (see table 3). Overall, Puerto Rican migration reported by the 2017 ACS showed that the majority of the migrants relocated to Florida (30%) followed by Pennsylvania (10%), Massachusetts (7%), Texas (7%), Connecticut (6%), New York (6%), New Jersey (5%), Ohio (3%), Maryland (3%), and Georgia (3%). FEMA claims revealed similar trends in terms of relocating in states reported by the 2017 ACS, in other words, post-Hurricane Maria evacuees (reported by FEMA claims) relocated in states of traditional and new settlements. Secondly, evacuees reported by FEMA claims who relocated in states of traditional settlement tended to disperse outside central city areas (see figure 4).

According to the 2017 ACS, 30 percent of the Puerto Rican migrants from Puerto Rico relocated to Florida (see table 2), however, during post-Hurricane Maria period, 45 percent of the FEMA claims (8,611 households) relocated to Florida in February 2018 and this slightly decreased (in terms of percent distribution) to 43 percent (8,873 households) in August 2018. This shows Puerto Rican migration to Florida was further exacerbated due to Hurricane Maria. The following Northeastern states such as New York (2,943 in February 2018 and 2,111 in August 2018), Massachusetts (1,501 in February 2018 and 1,765 in August 2018), Pennsylvania (1,296 in February 2018 and 1,449 in August 2018), Connecticut (1,014 in February 2018 and 1,220 in August 2018), and New Jersey (855 in February 2018 and 925 in August 2018).

All in all, settlement relocation and patterns during post-Hurricane Maria period also showed dispersion throughout the U.S. mainland. The FEMA relocation data is an indicator of the dispersion of the Puerto Rican exodus throughout the U.S. As shown in Figures 4 and 5, Florida and other U.S. southern states continue to receive a majority of the Puerto Rican migrants. Yet, traditional states of settlements, such as New York, Pennsylvania, Massachusetts, Connecticut, Illinois, Ohio, and California, are currently experiencing population growth as well, and more importantly dispersed settlement patterns within their respective states when compared to existing Puerto Rican settlements.

Interestingly, in traditional states like New York, post-Hurricane Maria households also showed dispersed settlement patterns in upstate New York besides the New York City region. School enrollment data also show this trend, particularly in New York State, whereby Puerto Rican school-age children showed higher enrollment rates in New York State's upstate region than in school districts located in New York City (Meléndez and Hinojosa 2017). Pennsylvania is another example, whereby the city of Philadelphia was once a large Puerto Rican settlement (Whalen 2001). However, as shown in Figure 4, post-Hurricane Maria showed dispersed settlement patterns, especially in counties outside of the city of Philadelphia. Overall, Puerto Rican evacuees, as measured by those who changed their FEMA-claims address from Puerto Rico to stateside U.S. continue to show patterns of dispersion throughout the continental U.S., a pattern evident in states of traditional settlements as well as in states of new settlement.

4. Post-Maria Demographic Impacts

Demographic Trends

Demographically, the 2006 post-economic crisis exodus and 2017 post-Hurricane Maria exodus, caused an accelerated depopulation in Puerto Rico. Between 2000 and 2005, the population in Puerto Rico was slightly higher or equal to stateside Puerto Ricans. By 2006, stateside Puerto Ricans outnumbered the Puerto Rican population in Puerto Rico, and this demographic trend continues today. In addition to migration, mortality and fertility is also linked to Puerto Rico's depopulation. As

Figure 5. Death and Births in Puerto Rico, 2000-2017

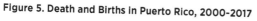

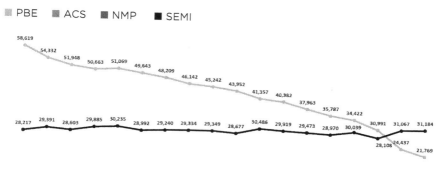

Source: Estadisticas Vitals de Puerto Rico 2000-2016, Department of Health.

shown in Figure 6, the number of births in Puerto Rico declined by half (-52%) from 58,619 in 2000 to 30,991 in 2016. The low number of births in Puerto Rico can be in part attributed to (higher educational attainment among Puerto Rican females). As shown in Figure 6, death rates and birth rates are at almost equilibrium in 2016 and as a result natural growth is not expected to occur in Puerto Rico (Macarrón Larumbe 2014). However, the number of deaths outpaced the number deaths in 2017 and 2018. Puerto Rico's population is expected to further decline as a result of high number of deaths and migration exodus after Hurricane Maria.

Education System

Puerto Rico's Department of Education also faced challenges from the island's post-economic crisis and post-Hurricane Maria, by forcing many school districts to close or merge their schools as a result of the declining student population in their classrooms and government budget cuts. A total of 265 public schools or 24 percent are closed and 855 schools remained open in the 2018–2019 academic year. The majority of school closures were disproportionately located in the island's rural areas (65%) relative to urban areas (35%). According to Puerto Rico's Department of Education, 306,652 students matriculated in pre-kindergarten to 12th grade (prek-12) public schools in the 2018–2019 academic school year, a percent change of -2 percent compared to February 2018 (319,750 matriculated students), six months after Hurricane Maria struck the island. However, between 2007–2008 and 2018–2019 academic school years, student enrollment showed a percent change -40 percent, from 526,565 to 313,724 students. Student enrollment declines is a result of households with children migrating to the U.S. mainland and lower fertility rates, however, the intensity of family migration increased post-Hurricane Maria. This resulted to rapid population declines in *municipios* throughout the island. According to Puerto Rico's Department of Education, between 2018 and 2022, or post-Hurricane Maria, a total of 305 public schools will be closed due to lower student enrollments, which is predicted to decline by 9 percent and government budget cutbacks (López Alicea 2018).

School enrollment declines is mainly attributed to migration, as children are more likely to accompany their parents and/or family members. After the economic crisis period, Puerto Rico's student enrollment declined from 544,076 in 2006 to 319,422 in 2017, a difference of 224,654 of students or a decline of 41 percent. According to Puerto Rico's Department of Education, student enrollment is expected to further decline to 291,846 by 2022 as a result of the post-Hurricane Maria exodus.

In addition to school closures and lower student enrollment, Puerto Rico's public-school teachers and other school administration support staff were also affected by both migration waves. In 2006, there were 40,514 public school teachers and in 2017 it was estimated to decline to 20,915 teachers. However, it is estimated by 2022 there will be a slight increase of 24,776 public school teachers in Puerto Rico. In all, Puerto Rico's education system, which includes both students and teachers/staff, were heavily affected by both the 2006 economic crisis and post-hurricane exodus.

SUMMARY AND CONCLUSIONS

Hurricane Maria has shown the need for timely and reliable data source for policymakers and stakeholders in Puerto Rico and in the U.S. mainland. This paper shows that existing data sources on Puerto Rican migration did not provide such timely needed data due to the unavailability of commonly used data sources. Using the Student Enrollment Migration Index (SEMI) in the short term is superior relative to other migration indices (PBE, NMP, and ACS) in the short-term due to its reliability and availability.

As the number of Puerto Ricans continue to grow in the U.S. mainland, Puerto Rico is depopulating. Puerto Rico's depopulation, initially spurred by the 2006 post-economic crisis exodus combined with lower fertility rates and higher mortality rates, will further have an economic and social impact on Puerto Rico. Puerto Rican population growth in the U.S. mainland is seen beyond states of traditional settlement and this was especially seen amongst post-Hurricane Maria evacuees using FEMA change of address data for two time periods, five months after the storm (February 2018) and 11 months (August 2018).

The implications of the post-Hurricane Maria exodus for Puerto Rico included rapid population declines as a barrier to economic development, exacerbation of school closing, and increased number of vacant housing units. All in all, the magnitude of Puerto Rican migration and the current impacts Puerto Rico is facing is a complex story that has not been seen or experienced in prior migration waves. Economic crisis and post-Hurricane Maria, an accelerated exodus, makes recovery more difficult in Puerto Rico.

NOTES

[1] An additional data source, the Survey of Travelers (or Encuesta Sobre Información del Viajero, in Spanish) was conducted by the Puerto Rico Planning Board (PRPB) from 1982 to the 1988, 1991 to 2002, and 2005–2007. The main objective of the PRPB survey was to collect information about the volume and characteristics of travelers from Puerto Rico to the U.S. The so-called "ramp" survey was based on a sample drawn from all the commercial flights leaving or entering Puerto Rico from the Luis Muñoz Marín International Airport in San Juan, and subsequently from the Rafael Hernández airport in Aguadilla. This study was discontinued for lack of funding.

[2] Demographic balancing equation is defined as P2= P1 + (B – D) + (I – E)], where P2=the number of individuals in a population at time 1; P1= the number of individuals in that population at some later time 2; B= the number of births in the period from time 1 to time 2; D= the number of deaths from time 1 to time 2; I= the number of people entering as immigrants; and E= the number of people leaving as emigrants.

[3] The Puerto Rico Community Survey (PRCS) is an island wide a customized version of the American Community Survey (ACS) designed to provide data every year for Puerto Rico communities.

[4] Data collection took place between January 2017 and mid-September 2017.

[5] The 2017 American Community Survey (1-year estimates) data released on September 13, 2018 used the same total population count (3,337,177) as estimated by the 2017 Population Estimates for Puerto Rico. This does not reflect post-Hurricane Maria population in Puerto Rico (3,337,177) due to data collection postponement as a result of Hurricanes Irma and Maria in September 2017. For further information, see U.S. Census Bureau (2018b).

[6] This data is available at the beginning of each semester and thus offers the opportunity to estimate an early indicator of emigration to the U.S.

REFERENCES

21 Puerto Ricans Here as Domestics. 1948. *The New York Times* 28 February, 17.

Barnes, Sandra L. 2002. Achievement or Ascription Ideology? An Analysis of Attitudes About Future Success for Residents in Poor Urban Neighborhoods. *Sociological Focus* 35(2), 207–25.

Birson, Kurt. 2014. Puerto Rican Migration and the Brain Drain Dilemma. Puerto Rican Economic Resiliency after the Great Recession In. *Puerto Ricans at the Dawn of the New Millennium*, eds. Edwin Meléndez and Carlos Vargas-Ramos. 2–23. New York: Centro Press.

Birson, Kurt and Meléndez, Edwin. 2014. Puerto Rican Economic Resiliency after the Great Recession. In *Puerto Ricans at the Dawn of the New Millennium*, eds. Edwin Meléndez and Carlos Vargas-Ramos. 98–117. New York: Centro Press.

Centro de Estudios Puertorriqueños. History Task Force. 1979. *Labor Migration Under Capitalism: The Puerto Rican Experience*. New York: Monthly Review Press.

Concepción Torres, Ramón Luis. 2008. Puerto Rican Migration, Settlement Patterns, andAssimilation in the Orlando MSA. M.A. thesis, SUNY Binghamton.

Duany, Jorge. 2002. Mobile Livelihoods: The Sociocultural Practices of Circular Migrants between Puerto Rico and the United States. *International Migration Review* 36(2), 355–88.

Delgado, Linda. 2005. Jesus Colon and the Making of a New York City Community, 1917 to 1974. In *The Puerto Rican Diaspora: Historical Perspectives,* eds. Carmen T. Whalen and Víctor Vázquez-Hernández. 68–87. Philadelphia: Temple University Press.

Echenique, Martín and Luis Melgar. 2018. Mapping Puerto Rico's Hurricane Migration With Mobile Phone Data. *CityLab* 11 May. <https://www.citylab.com/environment/2018/05/watch-puerto-ricos-hurricane-migration-via-mobile-phone-data/559889/>.

Enchautegui, María E. 1993. The Value of U.S. Labor Market Experience in the Home Country: The case of Puerto Rican Return Migrants. *Economic Development and Cultural Change* 42(1), 169–91.

Enchautegui, María E. and Richard Freeman. 2005. Why Don't More Puerto Rican Men Work? The Rich Uncle (Sam) Hypothesis. No. 11751. National Bureau of Economic Research.

Fitzpatrick, Joseph P. 1968. Puerto Ricans in Perspective: The Meaning of Migration to the Mainland. *International Migration Review* 2(2), 7–20.

Franqui-Rivera, Harry. 2014. The Well-Being of Puerto Rican Veterans and Service Members and their Place within the Diaspora. In *Puerto Ricans at the Dawn of the New Millennium*, eds. Edwin Meléndez and Carlos Vargas-Ramos. 182–209. New York: Centro Press.

García-Ellín, Juan Carlos. 2014. A Brief Look at Internal Migration of Puerto Ricans in the United States, 1990–2010. In *Puerto Ricans at the Dawn of the New Millennium*, eds. Edwin Meléndez and Carlos Vargas-Ramos. 40–60. New York: Centro Press.

Godoy, Ricardo, Glenn P. Jenkins and Karishma Patel. 2013. Puerto Rican Migration: An Assessment of Quatitative Studies. *CENTRO: Journal of the Center for Puerto Rican Studies* 15(2), 206–231.

Government of Puerto Rico. 2018. New Fiscal Plan for Puerto Rico. <http://www.aafaf.pr.gov/assets/newfiscalplanforpr-01-24-18.pdf/>.

Hinojosa, Jennifer. 2017. Brain Drain, Revisited. In *State of Puerto Ricans 2017*, eds. Edwin Meléndez and Carlos Vargas-Ramos. 25–31 New York: Centro Press.

Hinojosa, Jennifer and Edwin Meléndez. 2018. Puerto Rican Exodus: One Year Since Hurricane Maria. Research Brief. Center for Puerto Rican Studies, Hunter College, CUNY. <https://centropr.hunter.cuny.edu/sites/default/files/RB2018-05_SEPT2018%20%281%29.pdf/>.

Hinojosa, Jennifer, Nashia Román and Edwin Meléndez. 2018. Puerto Rican Post-Maria Relocation by State. Research Brief. Center for Puerto Rican Studies, Hunter College, CUNY. <https://centropr.hunter.cuny.edu/sites/default/files/PDF/Schoolenroll-v2-3-3-2018.pdf/>.

Johnson, Alex, Daniel Arkin, Jason Cumming and Bill Karins. 2017. Hurricane Irma Skirts Puerto Rico, Leaves 1 Million without Power. *NBC News* 7 September.

López, Iris. 2005. Borinkis and Chop Suey: Puerto Rican Identity in Hawaii, 1990 to 2000. In *The Puerto Rican Diaspora: Historical Perspectives,* eds. Carmen T. Whalen and Víctor Vázquez-Hernández. 43–67. Philadelphia: Temple University Press.

López Alicea, Keila. 2018. El Departamento de Educación se ajusta a los recursos que tiene. *El Nuevo Día* 26 January. <https://www.elnuevodia.com/noticias/locales/nota/ eldepartamentodeeducacionseajustaalosrecursosquetiene-2393253/>.

Macarrón Larumbe, Alejandro. 2014. Lessons from the European Demographic Winter for Puerto Rico. In *Puerto Ricans at the Dawn of the New Millennium*, eds. Edwin Meléndez and Carlos Vargas-Ramos. 210–34. New York: Centro Press.

Macisco, John J. 1968. Assimilation of the Puerto Ricans on the Mainland: A Sociodemographic Approach. *International Migration Review* 2(2), 21–39.

Maldonado, Edwin. 1979. Contract Labor and the Origins of Puerto Rican Communities in the United States. *International Migration Review* 13(1), 103–21.

Meléndez, Edgardo. 2015. Puerto Rican Migration, the Colonial State, and Transnationalism. *CENTRO: Journal of the Center for Puerto Rican Studies* 27(1), 50–95.

Meléndez, Edwin. 1994. Puerto Rican Migration and Occupational Selectivity, 1982–1988 *International Migration Review* 28(1), 49–67.

Meléndez, Edwin and Jennifer Hinojosa. 2017. Estimates of Post-Hurricane Maria Exodus from Puerto Rico. Research Brief. Center for Puerto Rican Studies, Hunter College, CUNY. <https://centropr.hunter.cuny.edu/research/data-center/research-briefs/estimates-post-hurricane-maria-exodus-puerto-rico/>.

Meléndez, Edwin, Jennifer Hinojosa and Nashia Román. 2017. Post-Hurricane Maria Exodus from Puerto Rico and School Enrollment in Florida. Research Brief. Center for Puerto Rican Studies, Hunter College, CUNY. <https://centropr.hunter.cuny.edu/research/data-center/research-briefs/post-hurricane-maria-exodus-puerto-rico-and-school-enrollment/>.

Meléndez, Edwin and M. Anne Visser. 2011. Low-Wage Labor, Markets and Skills Selectivity among Puerto Rican Migrants. *CENTRO: Journal of the Center for Puerto Rican Studies* 23(2), 39–62.

Mills, C Wright, Clarence O. Senior and Rose K. Goldsen. 1950. *The Puerto Rican Journey: New York's Newest Migrants*. New York: Harper & Brothers.

Mora, Marie T., Alberto Dávila and Havidan Rodríguez. 2018. *Population, Migration, and Socioeconomic Outcomes among Island and Mainland Puerto Ricans: La Crisis Boricua*. Lanham, MD: Lexington Books.

Perloff, Harvey S. 1975 [1950]. *Puerto Rico's Economic Future*. New York: Arno Press.

Sandis, Eva E. 1970. Characteristics of Puerto Rican Migrants to, and from, the United States. *International Migration Review* 4(2), 22–43.

Silver, Patricia. 2010. Sunshine Politics: Puerto Rican Memory and the Political in New Destinations. *CENTRO: Journal of the Center for Puerto Rican Studies* 26(2), 4–37.

_____. 2014. New Puerto Rican Diasporas in the Southern States. In *Puerto Ricans at the Dawn of the New Millennium*, eds. Edwin Meléndez and Carlos Vargas-Ramos. 82–97. New York: Centro Press.

_____ and William Vélez. 2017. "Let Me Go Check Out Florida": Rethinking Puerto Rican Diaspora. *CENTRO: Journal of the Center for Puerto Rican Studies* 29(3), 98–125.

Tienda, Marta. 1989. Puerto Ricans and the Underclass Debate. *The ANNALS of the American Academy of Political and Social Science* 501(1), 105–19.

U.S. Census Bureau. 2018a. Nevada and Idaho are the Nation's Fastest Growing States. Newsroom 19 September. <https://www.census.gov/newsroom/press-releases/2018/estimates-national-state.html/>.

U.S. Census Bureau. 2018b. Impacts of Hurricanes on Data Collection and Estimate Quality for Puerto Rico, Texas, and Florida. *American Community Survey* September. <https://www.census.gov/programs-surveys/acs/technical-documentation/user-notes/2018-02.html/>.

U.S. Department of Homeland Security. FEMA. 2018. FEMA CONUS February and August. <https://www.fema.gov/>.

Whalen, Carmen Teresa. 2001. *From Puerto Rico to Philadelphia: Puerto Rican Workers and Postwar Economies*. Philadelphia: Temple University Press.

_____. 2005. Colonialism, Citizenship, and the Making of the Puerto Rican Diaspora: An Introduction. In *The Puerto Rican Diaspora: Historical Perspectives*, eds. Carmen T. Whalen and Víctor Váquez-Hernández. 1–42. Philadelphia: Temple University Press.

Whalen, Carmen T. and Víctor Vázquez-Hernández, eds. 2005. *The Puerto Rican Diaspora: Historical Perspectives*. Philadelphia: Temple University Press.

Después del Huracán: Using a Diaspora Framework to Contextualize and Problematize Educational Responses Post-María

JASON G. IRIZARRY, ROSALIE ROLÓN-DOW AND ISAR P. GODREAU

ABSTRACT

Already struggling from the effects of decades of economic recession, failing infrastructure, and the deleterious impact of more than a century of colonial rule by the United States, the devastation caused by Hurricane María further exacerbated the woeful economic conditions of the Island, causing many Puerto Ricans to flee and seek refuge stateside. As Diaspora communities receive hundreds of thousands of new arrivals, we seek to critically analyze how educational institutions, from K-12 schools to institutions of higher education in the States, have responded to meet the needs of displaced Puerto Ricans. In addition to documenting the work of schools in the Diaspora, this article also aims to step back and explore how Diaspora communities can most effectively support the Island's efforts to recover, rebuild, and reopen its own educational institutions. [Keywords: Puerto Rican Education, Diaspora, Hurricane María, Diaspora Framework, School Choice]

Jason G. Irizarry (jason.irizarry@uconn.edu) is an associate professor in the Department of Curriculum and Instruction and faculty associate in El Instituto: Institute for Latino/a, Caribbean and Latin American Studies at the University of Connecticut. He is the author of *The Latinization of U.S. Schools: Successful Teaching and Learning in Shifting Cultural Contexts I* (Paradigm, 2011) and co-editor of *Diaspora Studies in Education: Toward a Framework for Understanding the Experiences of Transnational Communities* (Peter Lang, 2014).

Rosalie Rolón-Dow (rosa@udel.edu) is an associate professor in the School of Education at the University of Delaware. Her teaching and research endeavors aim to address issues of educational (in)equity and seek to promote socially just educational practices and policies that draw on the strengths and cultural resources of families and communities. She is also co-editor of *Diaspora Studies in Education: Toward a Framework for Understanding the Experiences of Transnational Communities* (Peter Lang, 2014).

Early on the morning of September 20, 2017, Hurricane María made landfall in the coastal town of Yabucoa, Puerto Rico. For more than 30 hours, the most powerful storm to hit the Island in a century battered the land and its residents, leaving a path of destruction in its wake. Already struggling from the effects of decades of economic recession, failing infrastructure, and the deleterious impact of more than a century of colonial rule by the United States, the devastation caused by María further exacerbated the woeful economic conditions of the Island. With homes and businesses destroyed, roads unpassable, no electricity or running water for the majority of the Island—a condition that still persists as we write this article months later— and a painfully slow and insufficient aid response from the U.S., many residents have been forced to flee the Island in order to survive. With thousands of Puerto Ricans leaving the Island weekly for the continental United States, and some returning as conditions improve or with resources to help the rebuilding effort, it is hard to pinpoint exactly how many individuals have joined the already more than 4 million of their compatriots in the Diaspora. Prior to the exodus from the Island caused by Hurricane María, Puerto Ricans in the Diaspora already outnumbered those on the Island. Conservative estimates suggest that the population of the Island is expected to decrease by more than 470,000 by 2019 (Meléndez and Hinojosa 2017).

As stateside Diaspora communities prepare to receive hundreds of thousands of new arrivals, we seek to critically analyze how educational institutions, from K-12 schools to institutions of higher education in the states, have responded to meet the needs of displaced Puerto Ricans in the aftermath of Hurricane María. In addition to documenting the work of schools in the Diaspora, this article also aims to step back and explore how Diaspora communities can most effectively support the Island's efforts to recover, rebuild, and reopen its own educational institutions *después del huracán*.

Puerto Rican Diaspora communities have always played a prominent role in shaping the political, social, and economic landscape of the Island. The fight to free Puerto Rico from Spanish colonial rule in the mid 19th century was launched from New York City, where Dr. Ramon Emeterio Betances and others committed to the cause of independence founded the Revolutionary Committee of Puerto Rico (Sánchez-Korrol 1994). Stateside groups dedicated to improving the plight of the Puerto Rican people in the Diaspora, such as the Young Lords, included as part of their mission supporting the Island and advocating for independence (Melendez 2003). And while many non-Puerto Ricans have stepped up to support the Island recover from the devastating impact of Hurricane María, Puerto Ricans in the Diaspora have played a prominent role in not only providing supplies and on the ground

Isar P. Godreau (isar.godreau@upr.edu) is a researcher at and former director of the Institute of Interdisciplinary Research at the University of Puerto Rico at Cayey (2003–2011). She is the author of *Scripts of Blackness: Race, Cultural Nationalism and US Colonialism in Puerto Rico* (University of Illinois Press, 2015) and coauthor of *Arrancando mitos de raíz: guía para la enseñanza antirracista de la herencia africana en Puerto Rico* (Editora Educación Emergente, 2013).

assistance on the Island but also in pressuring U.S. government representatives to increase support for the Island. With each passing day, there seems to be a new story of emerging from Diaspora communities through mainstream or social media, documenting a supply drive with items to be delivered to the Island by local Puerto Ricans with family or connections on the Island. Most recently Diaspora Puerto Ricans organized a "unity march" on the Mall in Washington, DC, to draw increased attention to the insufficient response by the U.S. government to the plight of Puerto Ricans on the Island and call for increased government investment in meeting the immediate basic survival needs of millions of Puerto Ricans in the short term and in a longer-term rebuilding effort that works in the best interests of the Island and its people. Recovery and rebuilding efforts on the Island, as well as initiatives to support Puerto Ricans in the Diaspora, are rooted and must be understood as continuing a long-standing tradition of Puerto Ricans on the Island and in the Diaspora working in unison for the greater good of all. This article, written by three Puerto Rican scholars, also seeks to bridge Island and Diaspora by drawing from the plethora of stories reported in the media as well as personal narratives from Diaspora and Island communities, to answer the following questions: How are educational institutions in the states supporting Puerto Rican students? What are the implications of the migration motivated by Hurricane María for stateside as well as Island schools? How might Puerto Ricans use opportunities to rebuild and improve the educational experiences and outcomes for our youth?

METHODS

To answer these questions, we apply a Diaspora framework, utilized in previous work (see: Rolón-Dow and Irizarry 2014), to address three juxtapositions—associated issues with contrasting effects— that we assert must be contextualized and problematized as we critically examine the education of Puerto Rican students post-María. The juxtapositions reflect tensions emerging in the responses from communities and educational institutions to meet the needs of those who have remained on the Island as well as those who have sought refuge stateside. The first, Welcome Centers/Hostile Communities speaks to the laudable efforts of Diaspora communities to embrace new arrivals from Puerto Rico, including offering support to help ease the transition for students into schools, help families secure housing and other necessary services. It simultaneously unpacks some of the systemic shortcomings of these efforts and the persistence of institutional racism in communities that are receiving Puerto Ricans. The second, Finding Room in New Destinations/What's Left Behind explores the implications of a mass exodus from Puerto Rico on the Island's schools, generally, and the public higher education system, more specifically. It chronicles efforts by stateside colleges and universities to accommodate Puerto Rican students while simultaneously questioning the potential implications on a system of higher education that was already vulnerable as a result of the Island's financial crisis. The final juxtaposition, Privatization/Education for the Public Good, critically examines the tensions and opportunities associated with rebuilding schools on the Island and modifying approaches to educating Puerto Ricans in Diaspora schools.

As we seek to contextualize and problematize educational responses post-María, we draw from a diverse array of recently published periodicals, historical articles, social media posts, and narratives emerging from Island and Diaspora communities to critically examine the current status and potential future directions of Puerto Rican education on the Island and in the Diaspora. As Puerto Rican scholars committed to educational equity and social justice, we seek to call attention to some of the under-examined aspects of supporting Puerto Rico and its people—wherever they might be. We hope that this piece can contribute to an ongoing dialogue and can potentially shape future policies and practices relative to the education of Puerto Ricans.

APPLYING A DIASPORA FRAMEWORK

While the term *diaspora*[1] is often used to describe a quantifiable group of people dispersed away from their homeland, we draw on more dynamic understandings of the term that frame *diaspora* as an active construct helpful for understanding particular stances, claims or projects culturally produced by groups of people typically characterized as Diasporas (Brubaker 2005; Flores 2009). This focus on a dynamic process pays attention to the ways meanings of diaspora are continually produced, negotiated, and/or resisted in relation to other groups, across generations and geographic locations and in and through the sociopolitical, historical, and cultural conditions germane to a particular group (Flores 2009).

The diasporization of Puerto Ricans was precipitated by the United States invasion of Puerto Rico during the Spanish-American war. The colonization of the Island that followed and continues unresolved to this day created political, economic, and cultural entanglements that powerfully shape the lived realities of Puerto Ricans and that led to an ongoing circular migration pattern between the Island and stateside communities (Duany 2007). The dispersal of Puerto Ricans to stateside communities was facilitated by the "granting" of U.S. citizenship to Puerto Ricans shortly before WWI and by policies that hampered economic and political sovereignty for Puerto Rico. The early, most dramatic movement of Puerto Ricans to United States urban centers occurred between the late 1920s and the early 1970s (Acosta-Belen and Santiago 2006; Whalen and Vazquez-Hernandez 2005). Yet beyond this initial dispersal, Puerto Ricans continued to engage in circular migration patterns between the Island and the United States. Recent settlement patterns have gone beyond long-standing, established Diaspora communities in such places as New York City, Chicago, and Philadelphia, for example, and now extends across wider geographic regions into new sunbelt communities in Florida, Texas, and North Carolina (Vargas-Ramos 2006). In the early 2000s, the number of Puerto Ricans living in the United States was roughly equal to the number living on the Island (Falcón 2004), but since that time, the dire unresolved economic crises of the Island led to further exodus of Puerto Ricans from the Island. While early migration from Puerto Rico was marked by its working-class nature; the most recent migrants have included more middle-class professionals who struggle to find gainful employment on the Island.

A diaspora analytic framework pays attention to the ways that identities and dispositions are forged in and through these circular migration phenomena; for Puerto Ricans, ties to the Island as their real or imagined homeland (Anderson 1991; Safran 1991) challenge assimilation models of migration (Rivera and Batiz 1996). The cultural production of the Puerto Rican diaspora project fostered the creation of Puerto Rican homeplaces with networks and allegiances within and across the porous borders between the states and Puerto Rico (Duany 2007). The diaspora framework is helpful in understanding and analyzing post-hurricane educational responses as it locates them in the historical trajectory of an ongoing Puerto Rican circular migration that continually shapes how and where Puerto Ricans are educated. The strength of familial ties across the Island and stateside communities was powerfully evident after the storm as Puerto Ricans struggled desperately to communicate with each other and as they forged resourceful responses to the storm's aftermath. Whether families were making decisions related to sending children to live with relatives so they could attend stateside schools, deciding to leave as a family unit, or attempting to figure out whether any given Island school was a viable option for their children to return to, all these decisions were impacted by the ongoing ties between the U.S. and Puerto Rico, whether at the political, economic level or at the community and familial level.

A focus on the intersection of diaspora processes with education calls attention to the ways that students experience schooling as an institution with the power to influence social rights and social inclusion. Imposed within a colonial context, Puerto Ricans experience a second-class, paternalistic form of citizenship (Benmayor, Toruellas and Juarbe 1997; Flores 2002) that is often evident in their educational experiences where colonial relations and racialization processes have been extended and reproduced (Walsh 1998). News stories and personal social media posts that began to circulate immediately after the storm included needed reminders for many Americans that the Hurricane was indeed a domestic disaster and that Puerto Ricans, whether on the Island or living next door in stateside communities, are fellow American citizens (Astor 2017). How Puerto Rico is perceived in the U.S. imaginary matters; a recent survey conducted by Morning Consult showed that only 54 percent of Americans knew that Puerto Ricans were citizens. Eighty-one percent of citizens who knew this fact supported aid for Puerto Ricans after the hurricane, compared to 44 percent support among those who did not know of the status of Puerto Ricans (Astor 2017). It is evident that despite a century-long, close relationship as a commonwealth of the U.S. the Puerto Rican Diaspora project is characterized by contested and multidimensional belonging, with the associated struggle for full citizenship rights that this belonging engenders. A diaspora framework helps us focus attention on the ways Puerto Ricans exercise agency in their struggle toward educational experiences that reflect and nurture social inclusion and full citizenship participation whether on the Island or in stateside communities.

FINDINGS
Welcome Centers/Hostile Communities

Losing loved ones, having your home damaged or destroyed, limited access to basic resources such as food and potable water needed for survival, all inflict a level of trauma that few schools or educational practitioners are prepared to deal with and support students and families through. Without electricity for many towns, and the damage to homes and buildings across the Island, the overwhelming majority of the more than 1,000 schools were forced to close. Certainly there are important class and racial differences regarding how Puerto Ricans experienced school closures. Private schools reopened at a much faster rate, and the number of private schools that remain closed at this time pales in comparison to public schools. Nevertheless, many parents of school-aged children, like most Island residents, have been in survival mode, trying to locate resources to feed their families and, in many cases, repair or rebuild their homes. Damaged school buildings and a lack of electricity in many towns have left parents with few options for their children. A lack of access to clean drinking water, the scarcity of food, debris from the destruction of the storm, all present significant hazards to young people. Immediately after the storm, schools have reopened in some towns; in others, schools were converted into "survival centers" where residents could come to access services, get food, and in some cases students participate in informal learning opportunities (Balingit and Hernández 2017). With much of the Island still without electricity for months—the longest blackout ever endured by U.S. citizens— and rebuilding efforts moving at a glacial pace, there is uncertainty about when or if many schools will reopen (Johnson 2017).

Cities across the country, from Miami, Florida to Boston, Massachusetts to Chicago, Illinois established "welcome centers," sites where families can access an array of services, including registering students for schools, applying for jobs, and securing housing.

In the wake of the hurricane, teachers on the Island have exerted significant effort to educate students—outdoors when necessary—working tirelessly to minimize the disruption to their students' education. Young people like Luis Enrique, a 16-year old high school student from Guaynabo, Puerto Rico, traveled to his school daily to assist with cleaning up the space and making it habitable (Liautaud and Giraldo 2017). In addition to working to get his school reopened, Luis also felt a need to support his younger schoolmates, recognizing the cognitive impact of the devastation caused by Hurricane María. His schoolmate, Richelle Torres, and others benefit from the community coming together to support each other by meeting for social gatherings at their school buildings, even if they are not inhabitable, noting, "Even though we don't have class, we come here to see each other and communicate" (Liautaud and Giraldo 2017). As demonstrated by these remarkable young Puerto Ricans, even in the most difficult of circumstances, Puerto Ricans have worked tirelessly to educate their children. Nevertheless, discouraged by the pace of recovery efforts and seeking to ensure their basic survival, thousands of families have chosen to relocate to the states and have enrolled their children in schools there. Proactively responding to the new influx of Puerto Ricans, many long-standing, established Puerto Rican Diaspora communities have mobilized quickly to receive and support students and families fleeing the difficult conditions on the Island. Aspects of the response have been swift, effective, and supportive; others have been problematic and disheartening.

The Department of Education in Florida, for example, understood that most students would be arriving without school records or other documentation typically necessary to register for school, these documents having been destroyed or made inaccessible after the hurricane. They temporarily waived the requirement for thirty days and enrolled students expeditiously, trying to accommodate evacuees (Dobrin 2017). Cities across the country, from Miami, Florida to Boston, Massachusetts to Chicago, Illinois established "welcome centers," sites where families can access an array of services, including registering students for schools, applying for jobs, and securing housing. Orange County, Florida school officials set up a welcome center for students and teachers in the Orlando airport, enrolling students and interviewing teachers as soon as they disembarked from the plane (Keierleber 2017).

In New Britain, Connecticut, the school district partnered with a local state university to provide services for displaced students arriving in their community. In addition to helping families enroll their children in school, they are also paying particular attention to the emotional needs of students and establishing scholarships for college tuition (CBS 2017). Chicago has also seen a large influx of evacuees arriving in their schools. Like many of the other communities receiving students escaping the humanitarian crisis, they too are temporarily waiving the documentation, such as immunization and guardianship records, needed to register for school. The commitment to supporting Puerto Rican students and families—evidenced in policy and practice across the Diaspora—is laudable and noteworthy. At a time when there seems to be a systematic attack on Latinxs in the United States, from disparaging remarks coming out of the white house to tax reform policies that will have a disproportionately adverse impact on Latinx communities, these local efforts demonstrate the will, strength, and perseverance of Puerto Ricans and a fervent commitment to educating Puerto Rican youth, despite the most difficult of circumstances.

The racialized differences in responses to the humanitarian crisis on the Island of Puerto Rico and stateside coastal communities in Texas and Florida reeling from similarly devastating effects of hurricanes are stark. Through tweets, the President of the United States has stated an unwavering commitment to stateside communities, noting the government would "stay as long as necessary" to help the people recover and rebuild. Conversely, he has repeatedly lamented the cost of the Puerto Rican recovery effort, disrespected Puerto Rican leaders who have disagreed with his naïve, positive appraisal of recovery efforts on the Island, and noted "we cannot stay in Puerto Rico forever." Few articles have addressed the racial/ethnic differences in the response to catastrophe on the Island compared to stateside communities (see: Negrón-Muntaner 2017). Even fewer have critically analyzed or unpacked the potentially problematic aspects of enrolling Puerto Rican students in schools and districts that have at times been hostile to the inclusion of Puerto Ricans and have historically underserved Puerto Rican communities. That is, the experiences of Puerto Rican students have been and continue to be racialized (Rolón-Dow 2005), with Puerto Ricans, despite their American citizenship, treated as a racialized "other," and this "othering" has had—and continues to have—an adverse effect on Puerto Rican students.

Most Puerto Rican evacuees have come to stateside communities where they have family members, very often settling ethnic-enclave communities with significant Puerto Rican populations. For the most part, wherever we have large populations of Puerto Rican students, we have school systems that underserve them (Nieto 1998; Irizarry and Antrop-González 2007). Springfield, Massachusetts; New York City, New York; Orlando, Florida; Philadelphia, Pennsylvania; Hartford, Connecticut; Chicago, Illinois all have sizeable Puerto Rican populations and chronically underperforming schools. It is important to note that these are also some of the most economically disadvantaged communities in their respective states, and schools are already struggling to secure sufficient resources. What might the impact of adding dozens or hundreds of new students to school systems that already fail to meet the needs of Puerto Rican students and families? What funding, if any, is available to provide services for recent arrivals?

Many stateside communities have also been hostile to the meaningful inclusion of Puerto Rican students. Recent events at Holyoke High School in Massachusetts, for example, have revealed discomfort evident in some White people to a burgeoning Puerto Rican population in their schools. During an assembly dedicated to celebrating Latinx Heritage Month, a Puerto Rican student read an original poem, parts of which spoke to the oppression and marginalization she feels as a Puerto Rican female in that school and community. The performance was videotaped and shared through social media, causing a backlash that reverberated beyond the high school. The student was threatened, and comments on social media reflected a deep-seeded contempt for Puerto Ricans in the area. Hundreds of comments spewed in public forums and in the comments section of the online edition of a local newspaper suggested that Puerto Ricans should "reflect on where they would be without the United States." Puerto Ricans were described as "deadbeats," and it was suggested colonialism is leveraged as a reason for Puerto Ricans to "justify entitlements" (Johnson 2017). While the poem, like any text, can be critiqued, the vitriol in the response to the young woman's performance and other events hosted by the Puerto Rican community in the town, such as a reception for Puerto Rican political prisoner Oscar Lopez, suggest that racism is alive and well. Latinx students and parents are acutely aware of the race-based, deficit views that inform the perspectives of many of their detractors (Irizarry 2011; Quiñones and Kiyama 2014).

Puerto Rican evacuees entering stateside schools are also entering systems that are largely dysfunctional. Chicago, for example, has been engaged in a highly contentious school closing and consolidating effort. Beginning in 2013, the city planned to close fifty schools and provide additional resources and facility upgrades to accommodate the schools receiving students displaced from their neighborhood schools. According to a report from the Chicago Teachers Union, receiving schools remain under-resourced, lacking sufficient personnel and programmatic support (Caref, Hainds, Jankov, and Bordenkircher 2014). As Puerto Rican evacuees arrive in Chicago, the city is now bracing for another round of school closures (Freidman 2017). Teachers have also had to strike to call attention to insufficient school funding and other problematic policies and practices that limit their ability to effectively educate the city's youth. Puerto Rican students with significant need, given the trauma they have recently endured, are entering systems that have major struggles that impede them from working in the best interests of students.

Beyond critique of the sociopolitical contexts Puerto Rican new arrivals have to endure, those conditions evidenced by the examples above and countless others available through a simple internet search, there are also significant pedagogical concerns that have to be addressed systematically for Puerto Rican students to be sufficiently supported. Prior to arriving stateside, many students have been out of school for weeks or, in some cases, months, leaving significant gaps in their learning. The schools in the communities they hail from are typically smaller and more intimate. In many of the cities receiving large numbers of Puerto Rican evacuees, schools can be ten times larger, serving kids from a wider geographic area than community schools on the Island. The drastic differences in setting will be a challenge for many students. Schools can and should do more to ease these transitions.

There are also significant needs in the area of social and emotional support. Puerto Rican students arriving have just endured a significant trauma. Hurricane María was one of the most devastating storms in the Island's history. For many, their homes were damaged or destroyed. Questions about how and when they might be rebuilt abound; also, uncertainty about your family's future undoubtedly causes stress than can impact students' ability to transition smoothly into their new school settings. Moreover, many children came without their parents, who have to remain on the Island to settle family affairs, care for loved ones who do not have the resources, ability, or desire to leave, and work toward rebuilding their homes and lives on the Island. Being separated from loved ones can weigh heavily on students. School counselors already had full caseloads and were working to capacity. What resources are being leveraged to provide support for Puerto Rican students?

According to the Census, less than one-third of the Island's population reported speaking English well (Census 2010). Many students will need language support and opportunities to learn content in their native language while simultaneously working to develop English fluency. Most schools have struggled to educate emergent bilingual students, especially those of Latinx descent, effectively. Adding new

Puerto Rican emergent bilinguals to schools and districts that have historically failed to educate this group effectively presents additional challenges that need to be addressed as quickly as possible.

In short, the ways that Puerto Ricans in the Diaspora and others have rallied to support the Island and its residents is inspiring and noteworthy. These efforts are important and timely. In many stateside communities, schools and community-based organizations have worked tirelessly to meet the needs of Puerto Ricans displaced by the Hurricane. Nevertheless, there are also significant challenges that must be addressed to best serve newly arrived Puerto Rican students. Many of the communities that are receiving students have been fraught with racist policies and practices, and segments of these communities are hostile to the idea of a burgeoning, more empowered Puerto Rican population potentially outnumbering Whites. While there have been some pockets of success, for the most part districts that serve long-standing stateside Puerto Rican communities have failed to provide Latinx students with a quality education that gives them desirable employment or postsecondary options. These schools have fallen short in meeting the needs of Puerto Rican students who come from families that have been here for generations and are ill equipped to meet the needs of new arrivals.

From a diasporic perspective, the influx of new arrivals promises to transform the racial, ethnic and linguistic texture of the communities receiving displaced Puerto Ricans. As U.S. citizens, there is also the potential to put a Puerto Rican imprint on the political landscape in local communities and nationally. Similarly, the experiences Puerto Ricans have in the states will influence their understandings of Puerto Rican identity and through their interactions with the Island and its residents—whether through financial support, political advocacy on behalf of the Island, etc...—will also shape the future trajectory of the Island.

Finding room in new destinations/what's left behind

Yerianne Roldán and Zuleyka Avila were in the midst of their high school senior year, already envisioning their future as freshman university students in Puerto Rico (Sanchez and Nadworny 2017). With the arrival of Hurricane María, their plans drastically changed. Overnight, both found themselves attending Colonial High School in Orlando, Florida, at times thankful for new opportunities, yet anxious about the uncertain path in front of them and longing for the senior high school year they had imagined among friends back in Puerto Rico. Like Yerianne and Zuleyka, numerous educators, parents, and youth suddenly faced countless decisions related to their schooling trajectories. As university students and parents of school-age children and youth pondered what to do after the storm, many were faced with the difficult decision of whether to seek a place to continue attending classes in stateside schools or whether to stay on the Island, hoping for a quick opening of local schools.

While many school districts quickly mobilized to receive Puerto Rican students, they also expressed concerns related to their capacity to find room for displaced Puerto Ricans. Per-pupil expenditures allocated to students in Puerto Rico did not follow them as they transitioned to stateside schools. School districts quickly had to formulate plans for resource allocation without knowing the full extent of migration, which will undoubtedly continue for months. The number of Puerto Ricans enrolling in Connecticut schools doubled from October to November 2017, and district officials reported feeling strained and challenged to accommodate the growing number of students in districts strapped for resources (Megan 2017). As William Clark, a chief operating officer for the New Haven Public Schools, explained, without additional funding, school districts faced difficult decisions in pulling resources used for other purposes to accommodate increasing enrollments (Megan 2017). Furthermore, students from Puerto Rico arrived as many districts were submitting their enrollment surveys for the year; these surveys are crucial in determining state funding appropriations. Just three weeks after the storm, The Florida Department of Education announced conditional plans for distributing additional funds; but these plans stipulated that a 5 percent increase in overall district enrollment or 25 percent increase in the enrollment of individual schools was needed for receiving funds (Clark 2017). This left schools who increased enrollment up to 24 percent with limited funds for addressing the additional needs spurred by the influx of Puerto Rican students. Across states, elected officials were called upon to help secure federal funding. In a letter dated December 1, 2017, thirty Congress members from states, including Florida, New York, New Jersey, Connecticut, Pennsylvania, and Massachusetts, requested increased and swift allocation of funds to school districts most impacted by the displaced students. The letter made a case for increasing funding beyond the $1.235 billion initially allocated by the Office of Management and Budget (OMB) given a projected relocation of close to half a million Puerto Ricans to the United States from 2017 to 2019.

School districts quickly had to formulate plans for resource allocation without knowing the full extent of migration, which will undoubtedly continue for months.

The urgency of addressing questions related to funding for the schooling of new arrivals is acute, given that stateside Puerto Ricans disproportionately attend under-resourced, low-performing schools. Beyond finding a seat for students to occupy and adequately funding per-pupil expenditures for new arrivals, school districts must provide adequate services for children, including meeting their needs as English Language Learners and being prepared to address emotional needs related to living through a natural disaster and being unexpectedly uprooted from their Island homes.

Beyond providing new streams of funding to educate the displaced students, plans must also be made to help displaced students adapt to their new educational communities. Students like Yerianne, Zuleyka, and their incoming Puerto Rican classmates who enrolled in a Florida school benefited from having a critical mass of Puerto Rican faculty and staff at their school, including a principal who reminded the students of his family's prior experiences migrating from the Island. It's important to consider, however, that Puerto Rican students have historically experienced unwelcoming school environments that included discriminatory practices and that sought to assimilate them without value for their Puerto Rican identities. Some school personnel quickly recognized the importance of countering anti-Puerto Rican sentiments and of helping students feel welcome and connected to their home communities. An Orange County superintendent, Barbara Jenkins, reported anti-immigrant sentiments expressed through phone calls but responded with a welcoming message affirming the rights of Puerto Ricans as U.S. citizens and the need to treat them with support and compassion (Sanchez and Nadworny 2017). As school district responses move from short-term efforts to long-term plans, it will be important to consider how to build on previous additive, culturally sustaining models of schooling for Puerto Rican students (Irizarry and Antrop-González 2007) and how to institute educational policies and practices that utilize and build on the Diaspora community wealth available to Puerto Ricans (Rolón-Dow 2014).

The educational trajectories of Yerianne Roldán and Zuleyka Avila were not only impacted by the post-María responses across the K-12 spectrum; just a month and a half after arriving in Florida, they were surprised to find out that Valencia College and the University of Central Florida were committed to providing them scholarship assistance should they decide to enroll in these institutions for their freshman year and beyond (Williams 2017). Dozens of higher education institutions quickly responded to the plight of university students. Some universities made offers of fully funded or partially funded semesters of study for Puerto Rican students from the Island. Three weeks after the storm, Andrés Martínez-Muñiz, a chemistry major at the University of Puerto Rico, opened an email in his inbox from a Brown University professor that he had worked with over the summer (Brown University 2017). This set him on a trajectory to become one of up to 50 UPR students to enroll at Brown University tuition-free and to receive help with housing and travel over the course of the fall and spring semesters.

Other universities including, NYU, Smith, Dartmouth, Cornell, and Tulane,[2] offered admission into their institutions for Fall 2017, Spring 2018, or both semesters. These scholarships usually required a fairly rapid response from students in Puerto Rico, many of whom were without Internet access to receive information, learn about the offers and apply. Another common response implemented by state and community college systems in Connecticut, Florida, and New York was offering in-state tuition to incoming Puerto Rican students. In addition, recognizing that many students depend on their families on the Island for financial support, institutions such as Florida International University granted in-state status for Puerto Rican students already enrolled at its university. At times, these efforts from universities were supplemented by private foundations such as the Heckscher Foundation for Children, which provided funds for tuition for displaced students attending CUNY's system (City University of New York 2017).

Quick responses by stateside institutions to the educational crisis spurred by the storm addressed some short-term concerns and needs of families and students. Concerns about potentially losing an entire semester or even an academic year were alleviated for those who were quickly able to take advantage of the tuition-free or tuition-reduced spots across stateside university campuses. Students' goals and motivations for obtaining degrees were bolstered through these opportunities, allowing some students and their families to sustain hopes for expanded opportunities from obtaining university degrees. Rosamari Palerm, a student planning for a Spring 2018 graduation, took advantage of reduced tuition and room and board at St. Thomas University in Miami. She expressed feeling guilty about leaving the Island but remembered her mother's words, who told her, "This is for your future, this is what we want for you. You don't say no to this kind of opportunity." Furthermore, Rosamari realized that she could alleviate some of the immediate stress on her family unit as she was one less person to feed in her home in Puerto Rico (Beeler 2017).

While stateside responses play an important role in meeting the needs of some displaced university students, the majority of university students remained on the Island and must deal with the uncertainties of what their university experiences will look like as the UPR faces a 50 percent budget cut of public funding and students a 300 percent tuition spike in the next 5 years. Rather than strengthening the institution after the hurricane, these and other austerity measures imposed by the federally elected fiscal oversight board intensified after the hurricane and will have long term effects in terms of increasing social inequalities (Brusi, Bonilla and Godreau 2018). Critics have argued that to understand this attack on the public university, the state of the UPR system pre-storm and its long history of activism against colonialism and neoliberal reform must be understood and taken into account (Brusi, Bonilla and Godreau 2018). In fact, the Spring 2017 semester was marked by disruption as students protested massive budget cuts fueled by the broader financial crisis in Puerto Rico's economy that left the university with diminishing public funds.

For those able to consider it, the choice to stay or leave was not easy and was charged with mixed and complex emotions that may have included sadness and guilt mixed with relief and possible excitement over new opportunities. Those students who were able to enroll in stateside universities also face challenges that need to be addressed, including possible mental health impacts of living through the trauma of the storm, language difficulties, and challenges related to establishing a sense of belonging within higher education contexts that already struggle to create inclusive campus climates for underrepresented, underserved groups.

It's unclear what the outcome will be for students who enrolled in stateside universities post-María. Perhaps some who were close to graduating will complete the credits needed and earn their degrees in the course of one or two semesters. But this process will require coordination between the stateside and Island universities to ensure credit requirements are fulfilled for the home institution (Godreau, Bonilla, and Walicek 2017). Students with intentions to return to the Island after a semester may face new challenges if their families also moved to the states. Will the short-term commitments to offer reduced or free tuition be extended in the long-run to meet the financial needs of these students who will face much higher tuition fees than the usual UPR tuition?

Given the catastrophic impact of the storm on communications infrastructure on the Island, access to information regarding these opportunities was limited and uneven. Students and their families had to access information while also navigating immense hardships and stressors related to meeting basic human needs on the Island in the days, weeks, and months after the storm. Furthermore, given that 46 percent of Puerto Ricans live in poverty, many university students on the Island come from families with limited resources, and even if they knew of these opportunities, were likely unable even to contemplate the costs associated with leaving the Island and resuming their studies at a stateside university. Opportunities, while providing relief for some, thus raised questions related to extant educational opportunity gaps along social class lines in Puerto Rico. It is important to consider how access to these opportunities is marked by or exacerbates social class differences and how it impacts access, opportunity, and equity in Puerto Rican higher education.

One innovative approach that paid attention to the impact on the UPR system was Tulane University's requirement that displaced students receiving a tuition-free semester at their school pay their regular tuition dollars to their home institution.

The exodus of middle-class professionals with degrees from the University of Puerto Rico (UPR) or current UPR students in the months after the storm raises concerns over the loss of human capital resources on the Island, as well as concerns for how the strained UPR system will rebuild and the consequences on the students, faculty, and staff who remain on the Island. By early November, hundreds of students had resettled in various campuses across stateside universities, and more were projected to leave for the spring semester. In Florida alone, there were close to 900 students enrolled across its universities (Korn 2017). Additionally, some graduate students also relocated to universities that offered to help. One innovative approach that paid attention to the impact on the UPR system was Tulane University's requirement that displaced students receiving a tuition-free semester at their school pay their regular tuition dollars to their home institution (Baribeau 2017). This approach, perhaps informed by Tulane's own challenges post Hurricane Katrina, lessened the loss of tuition revenue for UPR and other universities on the Island. This approach of considering stateside help in reference to the existing challenges facing the UPR system prior to the storm and the new daunting challenges post-María needs to be an integral part of ongoing educational responses.

While stateside responses play an important role in meeting the needs of some displaced university students, the majority of university students remained on the

Island and must deal with the uncertainties of what their university experiences will look like as the Island continues its recovery. Furthermore, the state of the UPR system pre-storm must be understood and taken into account. The Spring 2017 semester was marked by disruption as students protested massive budget cuts fueled by the broader financial crisis in Puerto Rico's economy that has left the university with diminishing public funds. Given the dominant role that the UPR's public higher education system has played in spurring educational attainment and social and economic development on the Island, the urgency of addressing the state of higher education on the Island post-storm is magnified.

Despite the daunting task of rebuilding a battered and weakened university system, there is always hope. Creativity and resilience among Puerto Ricans were on full display immediately after the storm. Jeffrey Herlihy-Mera, faculty member at one of the UPR campuses, reported that just two weeks after the storm, he sensed the determination from his department chair, Héctor Huyke, who stated, "Tengo mi machete" ("I have my machete"), as he resolved to clear fallen trees and brush to quickly reopen the university for students (Herlihy-Mera 2017). Other faculty, students, parents, and alumni also took it upon themselves to gather their tools and join clean-up efforts at the university. As Paula Paulino, an art history major at the university, cleaned, she stated that "This college is really the only place I can call home, so it's important to me that it is repaired and starts working again... I think if so many students and others came out to help it's because we want to feel like we're part of putting back together something we love" (LaFranchi 2017).

The intersections of diaspora processes and education are clearly evident in the tensions that emerge when stateside institutions of higher education, seemingly benevolently, offer to take in displaced Puerto Rican college students without considering some of the implications for students and the universities they left behind. For example, differences in the academic calendars between Island and stateside universities all but prevent a seamless transition between institutions. Additionally, which courses taken at stateside universities will transfer and be applicable toward degree programs is still unclear. Declining enrollments at institutions of higher education on the Island, exacerbated by students taking advantage of opportunities to continue their studies in the states, can be used as justification to shrink the university system on the Island, especially at smaller branch campuses that have historically been more vulnerable to shifts in enrollment. The multidimensional belonging that characterizes Puerto Ricans in the Diaspora will continue to be complicated for displaced Puerto Rican college students as they weigh their allegiances to the Island institutions with opportunities available to them in the states.

Privatization/Education for the Public Good
The effects of the storm have made the Island's schools more vulnerable to privatization. Prior to Hurricane María, Puerto Rico's school district served approximately 350,000 students across the Island in approximately 1,100 schools serving small, rural

towns and larger urban communities. When comparing the number of enrolled students in Puerto Rico's schools to stateside districts, the Island's school system ranks as the third largest, only trailing New York City and Los Angeles Public Schools. Large urban districts that have struggled historically to meet the educational needs of students have been vulnerable to privatization efforts, where for-profit companies vie for control of public schools, which they often recast as charter schools. Charter schools are public schools that are funded publicly but most often are exempt from many of the mandates that govern public schools, including the use of unionized teachers, the length of the school day, and adherence to a particular curriculum. There are currently more than 6,900 charter schools in operation in the United States, serving more than 3 million students (National Alliance for Public Charter Schools 2017). The academic outcomes of charter school students, like those of students that attend traditional public schools, are mixed. Some schools have produced stellar results; others have woefully underperformed. Even though, generally speaking, they have not outperformed public schools (Bettinger 1999; Bifulco and Ladd 2006), there is an increasing push to privatize public schools and increase the number of charter schools that are run by private companies but funded with public money.

The current Secretary of Education of the United States, Betsy DeVos, a staunch advocate for charter schools, does not have any educational degrees in the field of education, has never attended or sent her children to public schools, and has never worked in a public school. Nevertheless, she is in charge of shaping the federal government's education policy initiatives. Her ascent to the position of Secretary of Education was predicated on her work to expand charter schools in Detroit, Michigan, and likely influenced by the millions of dollars her family has donated to the Republican party and Trump campaign. The expansion of school choice in the form or charter schools has largely been a failed effort in Detroit (Gonzales and Shields 2014). Nationally school choice has often exacerbated inequality and funneled money away from already struggling school districts (Ravitch 2010). In December 2016, Puerto Rico's Governor, Pedro Rosello, appointed Julia Keleher as the Island's Secretary of Education. Secretary Keleher had never worked as an educator in Puerto Rico, or anywhere else for that matter, and came to the position after a career in business, leaving Puerto Ricans to question: "¿De dónde salió la designada secretaria de Educación?" (¿De dónde salió la designada secretaria de Educación? 2016). Hiring someone with a business management background, as opposed to educational policy or pedagogy, for example, might seem odd on first glance. However, the appointment of Secretary Keleher to lead Puerto Rico's education system follows an increasingly popular stateside trend of trying to apply business principles to improve schools. The notion of school "choice" positions families as consumers of education who can choose to spend their allotted per pupil expenditure—the average amount of money spent to educate students in a particular district—as they choose. The research suggests that, at best, choice has improved opportunities for some select students but has simultaneously had a net negative impact on the system as a whole, further exacerbating existing inequalities (Orfield and Frankenberg 2013). The appointment of Secretary Keleher, combined with extensive damage and destruction of schools across the Island, resulting in an exodus of students and teachers post-María, provides the Island's government with the opportunity to reshape Puerto Rican education. The background of the Secretary, combined with the Island government's neoliberal agenda, where everything, including education, is treated as a commodity, portends a pessimistic fate for Puerto Rican schools.

The seeds of privatization of Puerto Rico's schools was sown prior to Hurricane María making landfall. The control board created and empowered by the U.S. federal government in 2016 to implement PROMESA (Puerto Rico Oversight, Management, and Economic Stability Act) and oversee Puerto Rico's finances called for the closing of 300 schools on the Island and for teachers to be furloughed two days a month for the duration of the school year in an effort to save money and chip away at Puerto Rico's debt (Robles 2017). Secretary of Education Keleher affirmed the control board's plan to close schools, although she suggested that the total will be fewer than 300. Closing schools that are in disrepair or underutilized might have merit, although this premise has been challenged (Bonilla, Brusi, and Bannan 2018). Some of the schools that were closed had not experienced a significant reduction in the number of students. The Department of Education was promoting the widespread adoption of charter schools at the same time that they were closing existing schools, alleging a decrease in the student population. Moreover, because many families live below the poverty line and lack adequate transportation, closing neighborhood schools can become a cause rather than a result of migration. Finally, some of the closed schools, were actually considered "excellent" by the Department itself. We argue that some of the measures imposed to remedy budget shortfalls seem cruel, heavy-handed, and oppressive. For example, in addition to furlough days, the control board has proposed a salary freeze for teachers (Robles 2017), who on average make $21,000 compared to the average salary of over $50,000 in stateside schools, until 2021 (NCES 2013; US News 2017). Teachers' salaries on the Island have not increased since 2008. A decade of stagnant salary growth has not allowed teachers to keep pace with cost of living increases, forcing many to leave the Island, which is, perhaps, not an unintended consequence. Additional teachers who left the Island after Hurricane María were given until January 8th to return and reclaim their jobs (Chávez and Cohen 2017). Underenrollment and staff shortages will undoubtedly be leveraged to shrink an already vulnerable, economically challenged school system under the banner of economic and administrative efficiency.

Actions taken to close schools, freeze teachers' salaries, and the like all underscore an agenda dedicated to defunding public education in favor of privatization. Many Puerto Ricans believe the destruction and displacement caused by Hurricane María will lead to public schools being given to private companies to run. A similar effort was made in 2010 when the Island government considered privatizing the University of Puerto Rico system (Rodríguez 2011). Recent comments from the Secretary Keleher have only fueled speculation that school reform efforts in Puerto Rico will be led by charter schools. On October 26, 2017, she tweeted: "Sharing info on Katrina as a point of reference; we should not underestimate the damage or the opportunity to build better schools." After Hurricane Katrina struck New Orleans in 2005, approximately 90 percent of the schools were converted into charter schools. More than a decade of evidence suggests that charters have not been any more effective in educating Louisiana's youth than the public schools they replaced (Tuzzolo and Hewitt 2006; Akers 2012; Orfield and Frankenburg 2013). In fact, scholars argued that the market-based reforms charter schools represent further marginalized communities of color, such as New Orleans, have "not responded to the needs of racially oppressed communities" and have allowed education entrepreneurs to profit "by obtaining public monies to build and manage charter schools" (Buras 2011, 297). Similarly, the overwhelming majority of New Orleans' 7,000 teachers, many of whom were teachers of color, were let go and replaced primarily with alternatively certified, White teachers, and control of the schools shifted from the local community to the corporations that run the schools (Buras 2011). Puerto Ricans have spoken out against these market-driven, neoliberal reforms. Twenty one teachers, including leaders of the teacher's union on the Island, were arrested after protesting at the Secretary of Education's office in San Juan; their action was in response to what they believed was an unnecessary delay in opening structurally sound schools after the hurricane (Singer 2017). Puerto Rican teachers have been stalwarts of their students and have pushed back against privatization efforts and other measures that they don't believe are in the best interests of students and families. As the numbers of Puerto Rican teachers and students dwindle, the effort to privatize gains strength.

Puerto Rican teachers have been stalwarts of their students and have pushed back against privatization efforts and other measures that they don't believe are in the best interests of students and families.

Applying a diaspora framework that recognizes the sociohistorical context that shapes the current relationship between the Island and the United States government, it is important to note that Puerto Rico's status as a colonial possession of the United States has rendered elected Puerto Rican officials largely powerless in resolving the Island's issues. Puerto Ricans didn't choose to be American citizens; citizenship was imposed with restrictions, including precluding Puerto Ricans on the Island from voting in federal elections and denying the Island a voting representative in Congress. This form of second-class citizenship, which extends a form of citizenship that denies full participation in the democratic process, can be aptly described as "inclusive exclusion" (Venator-Santiago 2013). In short, Puerto Rico lacks the political sovereignty necessary to develop a system that works in the best interest of Puerto Ricans, making Puerto Rico vulnerable to the whims of the U.S. federal government.

To be clear, there have been Puerto Rican elected officials who have also been complicit in these efforts. The so-called[3] "debt crisis" facing the Island, for example, is largely the byproduct of the Jones Act, which was designed to benefit the United States at the expense of Puerto Ricans (Bury 2017). Similarly, communities on the Island lack "educational sovereignty" (Moll and Ruiz 2005), the right to determine to decide how Puerto Ricans on the Island are educated. Education policy historically has sought to advance U.S. aims and exalt American culture over Puerto Rican culture (Fox 1924; Negrón de Montilla 1988). An important and highly significant body of research asserted that U.S. control of Puerto Rican schools sought to advance a linguistic and cultural genocide on the Island (Algren de Guitiérrez 1987; Álvarez 1986; Barreto 1998; Solís-Jordán 1994). Puerto Ricans attending school in the Diaspora have similarly had their cultural identities ignored, at best, and often maligned (Irizarry 2011; Rolón-Dow and Irizarry 2014). As the Island engages in an inevitable process of change, companies seeking to profit off the tragedy facing Island schools will seek to assert their will and offer market-based solutions that have failed to produce increased opportunities and learning gains for students in urban communities across the United States. Moreover, these proposed remedies often fail to honor or even recognize the local cultural idiosyncrasies and "funds of knowledge" (Moll, Amanti, Neff and Gonzalez 1992) that exist in these communities, offering one-size fits all solutions that ignore cultural differences or take into account the sociopolitical contexts that shape school reform. Any effort to improve the Island's schools must meaningfully include the perspectives of Puerto Rican communities and honor their educational sovereignty.

PUERTO RICO SE LEVANTA

As Puerto Ricans go about reconstruction—rebuilding the Island and/or settling into new communities in the Diaspora post-María—there is much uncertainty and questions abound. We are left with more questions than answers. Length and financial support for the Island's recovery efforts remain unclear. Which educational institutions will reopen? How many Puerto Ricans will leave the Island in search of increased opportunities? How many might return? While there are few constants or certainties in these times of significant change, the indomitable spirit of the Puerto Rican people provides hope for a brighter future. While we honor the strength and resiliency demonstrated by Puerto Ricans in the wake of this tragedy, this does not in any way absolve the state, which is now in bankruptcy, from its responsibility to protect people from disasters by passing it onto it onto its citizens and communities—at home and in the Diaspora—who must now make ends meet and desperately organize to survive in the context of an absent state that caters to private investors and hedge-funds creditors who seek to profit from Puerto Rico's debt, especially after the hurricane. The phrase *Puerto Rico se levanta* has been a rallying cry that speaks to the desire and firm commitment among the Puerto Rican people to bounce back from the effects of this tragedy. As we go about creating policy and programs to guide these rebuilding efforts and support students and educational institutions, more specifically, it is imperative that we consider these as embedded within a diaspora framework that acknowledges the exchange of people, culture, and ideas across the porous borders between Puerto Rico and the United States. Puerto Rican identities, like others, are produced in relation to notions of nation(s)—Puerto Rican, American—and while Puerto Rico is not a sovereign country, it is a nation in every way but law. Narratives of Puerto Ricans as Americans have been prominent in stories about and responses to Hurricane María. Puerto Ricans moving to the states do not face the legal citizenship barriers, but do they take up cultural citizenship. New arrivals from the Island are enrolling in U.S. schools that have consistently exalted the value of assimilation over education and consistently underserved Puerto Ricans and other Latinx students (Irizarry 2011; Valenzuela 1999). How might we develop educational responses that build on assets, networks, and relationships across and within communities and facilitate notions of belonging inherent in cultural citizenship, particularly as the U.S. federal government has become increasingly nationalistic, positioning Puerto Rico as a colonial subject and foreign "other"?

As the Island rebuilds, reorganizes, and rises up there are questions regarding who gets to inform the vision for the future of Puerto Rico and Puerto Ricans. We argue that Diaspora citizenship participation must be taken into consideration. Our intent is not to romanticize the relationship between Puerto Ricans in the Diaspora and on the Island. In addition to circular migration and the *va y ven* between the Island and the states, where millions of Puerto Ricans have spent considerable time on the Island and in the states, there have also been tensions and questions of authenticity that also characterize the relationship. The number of Puerto Ricans in the states outnumbers those on the Island, and many of those in the Diaspora have deep connections and commitments to the Island. How might we bring together the Island and the Diaspora to create policies and practices that work in the best interests of Puerto Ricans?

Finally, any attempts to rebuild the Island and its educational institutions, as well as those to embrace and educate Puerto Ricans in the Diaspora, are complicated by the political status of the Island. Educational sovereignty is directly tied to political sovereignty. With the influx of Puerto Ricans into the states after Hurricane María, hundreds of thousands of Puerto Ricans now have the right and ability to participate in the American political process more fully, being able to take part in federal elections and petition their voting representatives in U.S. Congress. Their status as American citizens remains unchanged; however, taking up residency in the states affords rights central to full participation in democracy that are not available to Island residents. The possibilities associated with increased Puerto Rican participation in the electoral process presents significant implications for shaping the trajectory of the United States as well as the political status of the Island. Attending to the education of Puerto Ricans on the Island and in the Diaspora is vital for creating a more promising future—one in which Puerto Ricans inform current policy and shape their own futures.

NOTES

[1] We choose to capitalize the word Diaspora when specifically referencing the Puerto Rican Diaspora and apply the lower case "d" when speaking more generally about diaspora processes.

[2] This is not a comprehensive list of universities who made these types of offers.

[3] We use "so-called" to bring attention to the unidirectional nature of discussions about the economic woes of the Island, including the money owed to hedge funds. Any accurate and robust analysis of Puerto Rico's debt must also address not only what the Island owes its creditors, but also the draconian policies and practices that have resulted in the debt as well as what is owed to the Puerto Rican people who have put more into the coffers of the United States than they have ever taken.

REFERENCES

Akers, Joshua M. 2012. Separate and Unequal: The Consumption of Public Education in Post-Katrina New Orleans. *International Journal of Urban and Regional Research* 36(1), 29–48.

Algren de Guitiérrez, Edith. 1987. *The Movement Against Teaching English in Schools of Puerto Rico.* Lanham, MD: University Press of America.

Álvarez, M. 1986. Americanization in Puerto Rico: A Critical Assessment of the Educational Process. Master's thesis, California State University, Long Beach.

Anderson, Benedict. 1991. *Imagined Communities: Reflections on the Origin and Spread of Nationalism,* revised edition. New York: Verso.

Astor, Maggie. 2017. Puerto Rico: What Other Americans Should Know. *New York Times* 25 September.

Balingit, Moriah, and Arelis R. Hernández. 2017. Puerto Rican Schoolchildren Could Be Out of School for Months. *The Washington Post* 3 October.

Baribeau, Simone. 2017. Hurricane María Blows Gulf Between University of Puerto Rico and its Students. *Forbes* 7 November.

Barreto, Amilcar. 1998. Colonialism: Political Economy, Language and Ideology in Puerto Rico. Ph.D. dissertation, The Union Institute.

Beeler, Carolyn. 2017. Some Puerto Rican College Students Displaced by Hurricane María Have Already Started Classes Again – in Florida. *PRI's The World* 19 October. <https://www.pri.org/stories/2017-10-19/some-puerto-rican-college-students-displaced-hurricane-María-have-already-started/>.

Benmayor, Rina, Rosa M. Torrecilla and Ana L. Juarbe. 1997. Claiming Cultural Citizenship in East Harlem: 'Si Esto Puede Ayudar a la Comunidad Mia. In *Latino Cultural Citizenship: Claiming Identity, Space, and Rights,* eds. William V. Flores and Rina Benmayor. 152–209. Boston: Beacon Press.

Bettinger, Eric P., 1999. The Effects of Charter Schools on Charter Students and Public Schools. Teachers College, Columbia University, National Center for the Study of Privatization in Education Occasional Paper No. 4.

Bifulco, Robert and Helen F. Ladd. 2006. The Impacts of Charter Schools on Student Achievement: Evidence from North Carolina. *Education Finance and Policy* 1(1), 50–90.

Bonilla, Yarimar, Rima Brusi and Natasha Lycia Ora Bannan. 2018. 6 Months After Maria, Puerto Ricans Face a New Threat—Education Reform: Colonialism and disaster capitalism are dismantling Puerto Rico's public-school system. *The Nation*. 21 March. <https://www.thenation.com/article/colonialism-and-disaster-capitalism-are-dismantling-puerto-ricos-public-school-system/>.

Brown University. 2017. Brown Welcomes Displaced University of Puerto Rico Students, Faculty. *News from Brown* 22 October. <https://news.brown.edu/articles/2017/10/puerto-rico/>.

Brubaker, Rogers. 2005. The 'Diaspora' Diaspora. *Ethnic and Racial Studies* 28(1), 1–19.

Brusi, Rima, Yarimar, Bonilla and Isar Godreau. 2018. When Disaster Capitalism Comes for the University of Puerto Rico: The ongoing privatization of Puerto Rico's recovery threatens not only the university's autonomy, but its very existence. *The Nation*. 20 September. <https://www.thenation.com/article/colonialism-and-disaster-capitalism-are-dismantling-puerto-ricos-public-school-system/>.

Bury, Chris. 2015. Is this 1917 Law Suffocating Puerto Rico's Economy? *PBS News Hour* 13 August. <https://www.pbs.org/newshour/economy/jones-act-holding-puerto-rico-back-debt-crisis/>.

Buras, Kristen L. 2011. Race, Charter schools, and Conscious Capitalism: On the Spatial Politics of Whiteness as Property (and the Unconscionable Assault on Black New Orleans). *Harvard Educational Review* 81(2), 296–331.

CBS. 2017. Connecticut Community Welcomes Evacuees from Puerto Rico. *WCAX.com* 20 October. <http://www.wcax.com/content/news/Connecticut-community-welcomes-evacuees-from-Puerto-Rico-451909783.html/>.

Chávez, Aida, and Rachel M. Cohen. 2017. Puerto Ricans Fear Schools Will Be Privatized in the Wake of Hurricane María. *The Intercept* 8 November. <https://theintercept.com/2017/11/08/puerto-rico-schools-system-with-post-katrina-new-orleans-as-the-model/>.

City University of New York. 2017. CUNY Wins Heckscher Grant to Allow Hurricane-Displaced Puerto Ricans and Virgin Islanders to Study Tuition-Free. 19 November. <http://www1.cuny.edu/mu/forum/2017/11/19/cuny-wins-heckscher-grant-to-allow-hurricane-displaced-puerto-ricans-and-virgin-islanders-to-study-tuition-free/>.

Clark, Kristen M. 2017. Give Florida Schools Leeway to Take in Displaced Puerto Ricans, Lawmakers Ask State. *Miami Herald* 2 October.

¿De dónde salió la designada secretaria de Educación? 2016. *PrimeraHora.com* 28 December. <https://www.primerahora.com/noticias/gobierno-politica/nota/dedondesalioladesignadasecretariadeeducacion-1196930/>.

Dobrin, I. 2017. 'Get Us Out of Here': Amid Broken Infrastructure, Puerto Ricans Flee to Florida. *New England Public Radio* 13 October. <https://www.npr.org/2017/10/13/557108484/-get-us-out-of-here-amid-broken-infrastructure-puerto-ricans-flee-to-florida/>.

Duany, Jorge. 2007. Nation and Migration: Rethinking Puerto Rican Identity in a Transnational Context. In *None of the Above: Puerto Ricans in the Global Era*, ed. Frances Negrón-Muntaner. 51–63. New York: Palgrave Macmillan.

Falcón, Angelo. 2004. *Atlas of Stateside Puerto Ricans*. Washington, DC: Puerto Rico Federal Affairs Administration.

Flores, Juan. 2002. Islands and Enclaves: Caribbean Latinos in Historical Perspective. In *Latinos: Remaking America*, eds. Marcelo Suárez-Orozco and Mariela Páez. 59–74. Berkeley: University of California Press.

_____. 2009. *The Diaspora Strikes Back: Caribeño Tales of Learning and Turning*. New York: Routledge.

Fox, A.L. 1924. American Rule in Puerto Rico. Master's Thesis, University of Chicago.

Friedman, Brandis. 2017. New Round of Chicago Public School Closures Looming. *WTTW News* 30 November. <http://chicagotonight.wttw.com/2017/11/30/new-round-chi-cago-public-school-closures-looming/>.

Godreau, Isar, Yarimar Bonilla, and Don E. Walicek. 2017. How to Help the University of Puerto Rico — and How Not To. *The Chronicle of Higher Education* 27 November.

Gonzales, Sandra. M., and Carolyn M. Shields. 2014. Education "Reform" in Latino Detroit: Achievement Gap or Colonial Legacy? *Race Ethnicity and Education* 18(3), 321–40.

Herlihy-Mera, Jeffrey. 2017. At the U. of Puerto Rico After María. *The Chronicle of Higher Education* 9 October.

Irizarry, Jason G. 2011. *The Latinization of U.S. Schools: Successful Teaching and Learning in Shifting Cultural Contexts*. Boulder, CO: Paradigm Publishing.

Irizarry, Jason G. and René Antrop-González. 2007. RicanStructing the Discourse and Promoting School Success: Extending a Theory of Culturally Responsive Pedagogy for DiaspoRicans. *CENTRO: Journal of the Center for Puerto Rican Studies* 19(2), 36–59.

Johnson, Patrick. 2017. Holyoke Schools Respond to Turmoil, Threats in Fallout from Latino Heritage Month Event. *Springfield Republican* 9 October. <http://www.masslive.com/news/index.ssf/2017/10/holyoke_schools_respond_to_tur.html/>.

Johnson, Tim. 2017. In Puerto Rico, Frustrated Parents Wonder When Schools Will Reopen. It May Be A While. *Chicago Tribune* 1 October.

Keierleber, Mark. 2017. Puerto Rico Teachers Fleeing Hurricane María Arrived at Orlando's Airport With Nothing. They Left With Jobs. *The 74million.org* 10 October. <https://www.the74million.org/article/puerto-rico-teachers-fleeing-hurricane-María-arrived-at-orlandos-airport-with-nothing-they-left-with-jobs/>.

Korn, Melissa. 2017. Puerto Rico Sees Hundreds of College Students Leave in Hurricane's Aftermath. *Wall Street Journal* 8 November.

LaFranchi, Howard. 2017. San Juan Residents Pitch in with Cleanup, Lifting Their Own Spirits. *Christian Science Monitor* 6 October. <https://www.csmonitor.com/USA/Society/2017/1006/San-Juan-residents-pitch-in-with-cleanup-lifting-their-own-spirits/>.

Liautaud, Alexa and Cassandra Giraldo. 2017. These Puerto Rican Kids Are Fighting to Reopen Their Schools. *Vice News* 2 November. <https://news.vice.com/en_us/article/3kp5gv/these-puerto-rican-kids-are-fighting-to-reopen-their-school-after-María/>.

Megan, Kathleen. 2017. School Districts Strained by Increasing Numbers of Students from Puerto Rico. *Hartford Courant* 20 November. <http://www.courant.com/education/hc-news-puerto-rico-school-kids-hurricane-20171115-story.html/>.

Meléndez, Edwin, and Jennifer Hinojosa. 2017. Estimates of Post-Hurricane María Exodus from Puerto Rico. Center for Puerto Rican Studies. Centro RB2017-01, October. <https://centropr.hunter.cuny.edu/sites/default/files/RB2017-01-POST-MARIA%20 EXODUS_V3.pdf/>.

Melendez, Miguel. 2003. *We Took the Streets: Fighting for Latino Rights with the Young Lords.* New York: St. Martin's.

Moll, Luis and Richard Ruiz. 2005. The Educational Sovereignty of Latina/o Students in the United States. In *Latino Education: An Agenda for Community Action Research,* eds. Pedro Pedraza and Melissa Rivera. 295–320. Mahwah, NJ: Erlbaum.

Moll, Luis. Cathy Amanti, Deborah Neff and Norma Gonzalez. 1992. Funds of Knowledge for Teaching: Using a Qualitative Approach to Connect Homes and Classrooms. *Theory into Practice* 31(2), 132–41.

Murphy, Stephanie and Carlos Curbelo. 2017. Letter to House and Senate Appropriators Regarding Funding for Schools that Enroll Displaced Students. 1 December.

Negrón de Montilla, Aida. 1990. *La americanización de Puerto Rico y el sistema de instrucción pública, 1900-1930,* 2nd ed. Río Piedras: Editorial de la Universidad de Puerto Rico.

Negrón-Muntaner, Frances. 2017. The Crisis in Puerto Rico is a Racial Issue. Here's Why. *The Root* 12 October. <https://www.theroot.com/the-crisis-in-puerto-rico-is-a-racial-issue-here-s-why-1819380372/>.

Nieto, Sonia. 1998. Symposium: Fact and Fiction: Stories of Puerto Ricans in U.S. Schools. *Harvard Educational Review* 68(2), 133–64.

Orfield, Gary and Erica Frankenberg. 2013. *Educational Delusions? Why Choice Can Deepen Inequality and How to Make It Fair.* Berkeley: University of California Press.

Quiñones, Sandra and Judith M. Kiyama. 2014. Contra la Corriente (Against the Current): The Role of Latino Fathers in Family–School Engagement. *School Community Journal* 24(1), 149–76.

Ravitch, Diane. 2010. *The Death and Life of the Great American School District: How Testing and Choice Are Undermining Education.* New York: Basic Books.

Rivera-Batiz, Francisco and Carlos E. Santiago. 1996. *Island Paradox: Puerto Rico in the 1990s.* New York: Russell Sage Foundation.

Rodríguez, Víctor M. 2011. Social Protest and the Future of Higher Education in Puerto Rico. *American Association of University Professors* July-August. <https://www.aaup.org/ article/social-protest-and-future-higher-education-puerto-rico#.WlQgDmXap-U/>.

Rolón-Dow, Rosalie. 2010. Taking a Diasporic Stance: Puerto Rican Mothers Educating Children in a Racially Integrated Neighborhood. *Diaspora, Indigenous, and Minority Education* 4(4), 268–84.

_____. 2014. Finding Community Cultural Wealth in Diaspora: A LatCrit Analysis. In *Diaspora Studies in Education: Towards a Framework for Understanding the Experiences of Transnational Communities,* eds. Rosalie Rolón Dow and Jason G. Irizarry. 83–104. New York: Peter Lang.

Rolón-Dow, Rosalie and Jason G. Irizarry, eds. 2014. *Diaspora Studies in Education: Toward a Framework for Understanding the Experiences of Transnational Communities.* New York: Peter Lang.

Safran, William. 1991. Diasporas in Modern Societies: Myths of Homeland and Return. *Diaspora: A Journal of Transnational Studies* 1(1), 83–99.

Sanchez, Claudio and Elissa Nadworny. 2017. For Many Puerto Ricans, College Plans Washed Away with Hurricane María. *NPR Ed* 20 November. <https://www.npr.org/sections/ed/2017/11/20/564059885/when-college-plans-washed-away-with-hurricane-María/>.

Sánchez-Korrol, Virginia. 1994. *From Colonia to Community: The History of Puerto Ricans in New York City.* Berkeley: University of California Press.

Singer, Steven. 2017. Making Puerto Rico the New New Orleans – Steal the Schools and Give Them to Big Business to Run For Profit. *Common Dreams* 10 November. <https://www.commondreams.org/views/2017/11/10/making-puerto-rico-new-new-orleans-steal-schools-and-give-them-big-business-run/>.

Solís-Jordán, J. 1994. *Public School Reform in Puerto Rico.* Westport, CT: Greenwood.

Suárez-Orozco, M. and Mariela Páez, eds. 2008. *Latinos: Remaking America.* Berkeley: University of California Press, 2008.

Tuzzolo, Ellen and Damon T. Hewitt. 2006/2007. Rebuilding Inequity: The Re-emergence of the School-to-Prison Pipeline in New Orleans. *High School Journal* 90(2), 59–68.

Vargas-Ramos, Carlos. 2006. Settlement Patterns and Residential Segregation of Puerto Ricans in the United States. Policy Report 1(2). Centro de Estudios Puertorriqueños, Hunter College (CUNY). < https://centropr.hunter.cuny.edu/sites/default/files/working_papers/ACF65EF.pdf/>.

Walsh, Catherine. 1998. Symposium: "Staging Encounters": The Educational Decline of US Puerto Ricans in [Post]-Colonial Perspective. *Harvard Educational Review* 68(2), 218–44.

Williams, Rachel. 2017. Valencia, UCF Surprise Two Displaced Students from Puerto Rico with Scholarships. *Valencia Today* 3 November. <http://news.valenciacollege.edu/valencia-today/valencia-ucf-surprise-two-displaced-students-from-puerto-rico-with-scholarships/>.

Valenzuela, Angela. 1999. *Subtractive Schooling: US.-Mexican Youth and the Politics of Caring.* Albany: State University of New York Press.

Venator-Santiago, Charles, R. 2013. Extending Citizenship to Puerto Rico: Three Traditions of Inclusive Exclusion. *CENTRO: Journal of the Center for Puerto Rican Studies* 25(1), 50–75.

Political Crisis, Migration and Electoral Behavior in Puerto Rico

CARLOS VARGAS-RAMOS

ABSTRACT

Puerto Rico is in political crisis. Evidence of this crisis is the precipitous drop in voter turnout in the 2016 elections after more than three decades of small but steady decline. Some political observers and practitioners have attributed this decline to the emigration from the island, a product itself of an enduring economic crisis engulfing Puerto Rico. However, emigration is not a factor in the decline of electoral participation in Puerto Rico. Based on statistical analyses of aggregate voting and population data, results show that Puerto Rico's decline in voter participation is not attributable to emigration. Rather, an extant legitimacy crisis of the political system and its political class might be a more proximate and likely explanation for the drop in electoral participation in 2016. [Key words: Puerto Rico, voting, migration, crisis, political participation, elections]

The author (cvargasr@hunter.cuny.edu) is a political scientist based at the Center for Puerto Rican Studies, who works on the impact of migration on Puerto Rican political behavior, political attitudes and orientations, as well as on issues of racial identity. Among other recent works, he is editor of *Race, Front and Center: Perspectives on Race among Puerto Ricans* (Centro Press, 2017), and co-editor of *Puerto Ricans at the Dawn of the New Millennium* (Centro Press, 2014).

Puerto Rico is in crisis. The crisis is political in nature. Puerto Ricans are not satisfied with the political system they live in and the political class that governs them locally. A sign of this dissatisfaction with the political system is evident in the precipitous drop in the level of participation at election time that happened in the elections held in 2016. Dissatisfaction may also be reflected in the level of emigration from the island. Emigration is not a new phenomenon, but rather a historical trend. The collapse in the exercise of the franchise in Puerto Rico, however, is a new phenomenon, and it requires explanation.

It has been proposed that emigration from the island is the underlying reason for the decline in turnout in the 2016 elections. However, the analysis I present in this paper shows that emigration does not account for the decline in the rate of participation in those elections. A decline in population driven by emigration may have resulted in fewer votes being cast at election time in 2016, but it does not explain why fewer registered voters turned out to vote. The decline in voter participation rate in 2016 was much larger than any decline in population could account for. Emigration cannot, and in fact does not, account for the decline in turnout, as I demonstrate in this analysis. Instead, to account for such a decline in participation, I suggest and propose alternatively that recent as well as secular changes in the political system are the likely explanation for why a sizable segment of the Puerto Rican electorate disengaged from the political process.

Voting as a legitimizing factor

The focus on turnout at election time is crucial given its significance in practical as well as symbolic terms for the political system in Puerto Rico. Historically, Puerto Rico has exhibited high rates of electoral participation by any measure. Since the middle of the twentieth century through its end, the average turnout rate in general elections on the island every four years has ranged between 73 percent and 89 percent of duly registered voters (see Table 1) (Bayrón Toro 2000). Even when measuring turnout by a more stringent standard —the citizen, voting-age population[1]—turnout during the last four decades of the twentieth century had not been below 64, and often hovered around 80 percent (see Table 2) (Cámara Fuertes 2004). However, the 2016 elections yielded only a 55 percent rate of participation of registered voters; a level of participation never experienced in the previous 68 years in Puerto Rico. I propose that this turnout rate, meager by Puerto Rico's standards, may be an indication of the disenchantment and disappointment of Puerto Rico's electorate in its political class and its political system. I suggest further that very limited political alternatives to manage life in Puerto Rico may have turned off the electorate in a manner never witnessed before, indicating a likely crisis in the existing political system.

As Robert Anderson has argued, "[t]he electoral system is the keystone of legitimization in the Puerto Rican political system... So the party system in Puerto Rico is intimately tied into the mass-participation electoral system, which in turn is one of the bulwarks of a larger political system characterized by a relation of direct dependence upon (or increasing integration with) the metropolitan United States" (Anderson 1983, 6). Moreover, while voting is not the only way the inhabitants of the island can convey their political preferences and goals to government officials, it is by and large the most common form of political participation and one that characterizes in singular fashion Puerto Rican political behavior (Cámara Fuertes 200; Ramírez 1977; Rivera et al. 1991). The precipitous drop in the turnout rate in the 2016 may serve as an indicator of a growing disaffection with the political system and the regime the electoral system sustains.

All political regimes need a modicum of political support from those ruled by the political authorities. While the level of political support for governmental authorities and the broader political regime does not have to be constant (Easton 1975), as it may fluctuate within a band of tolerance for the regime. This is because "in spite of shortcomings and failures, the existing political institutions are better than any others that might be established, and that they therefore can demand obedience," particularly in governments that attain power through a democratic process of free elections (Linz 1978, 16). Yet a regime cannot sustain itself over the long run without political support. Bruce Gilley has established good governance (i.e., the rule of law, control of corruption and government effectiveness), along with democratic right and welfare gains as broad determinants of state legitimacy (Gilley 206). Juan Linz himself has described how both governmental efficacy (i.e., "the capacity of a regime to find solutions to the basic problem facing any political system") and effectiveness (i.e., "the capacity to actually implement the policies formulated, with the desired results") "can strengthen, reinforce, maintain or weaken the belief in legitimacy" (Linz 1978, 18, 20, 22). The profound economic crisis affecting the Commonwealth regime, under the administration of either the New Progressive Party or the Popular Democratic Party, may be nurturing the disaffection in the political system given the incapacity of the governmental apparatus to provide relief from the decade-long economic decline, and the increasing cynicism involving ministerial malfeasance; in other words, due to impaired governance.

If Robert Anderson is correct in describing voting in Puerto Rico as a cornerstone on which the legitimacy of the Commonwealth regime rests, then an erosion in participation in this process of regime support may be seen as an indicator of receding legitimacy for it. The steady but gradual erosion in electoral participation witnessed on the island since the 1990s may indicate that disaffection with the political system may have been brewing for a few electoral cycles (see Table 1). Turnout in Puerto Rico peaked in 1984, when 89 percent of registered voters turned out to vote. Since that time, there has been a steady decline in the turnout of registered voters, particularly after 1992, when turnout of registered voters reached 85 percent. By 2012, turnout was 78 percent of registered voters. By a different measure—the total number of votes cast in an election—voting had reached its peak in 2000, when more than 2 million votes were cast. By 2012, only 1.8 million voters had cast their vote. In 2016, only 1.5 million voters went to the polls.

Table 1. Registered voter turnout for governor in Puerto Rico, 1948-2016

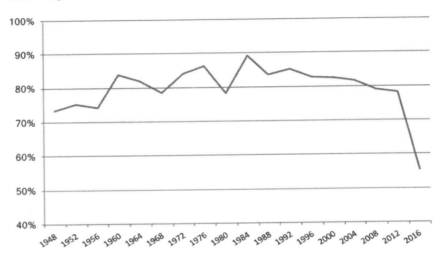

Source: Comisión Estatal de Elecciones de Puerto Rico.

Table 2. Turnout in elections for governor in Puerto Rico by the citizen, voting-age population, 2000-2016

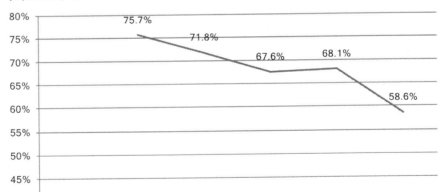

Source: Comisión Estatal de Elecciones de Puerto Rico; U.S. Census Bureau.

Political and governmental leaders and commentaries in the popular press have pointed to migration as a reason for the decline in electoral participation (Cortés Chico 2016; Ruiz Kuilan 2017). While "exit" as an individual strategy to deal with individual consequences of the economic crisis might possibly account for *some* of the decline in voting in the past two elections, it does not in fact account for much of the very large decline in voting. Migration may be understood as a direct repercussion of the economic crisis, leading to individual-level responses as a solution to the larger social and political problems. In that sense, then, the impact of migration on the decline of voting in Puerto Rico might be characterized as an indirect consequence of the economic crisis on the political system. However, this is not what appears to be taking place in Puerto Rico at present. Rather, the extent of "loyalty" in the political system appears to be declining (Hirschman 1970). Yet, instead of resorting to "voice" to address the political implications of the economic crisis, Puerto Ricans may be muting their voices in situ.

In the space that follows I will address how population change as a result of migration does not account for the large decline in electoral participation in Puerto Rico between 2012 and 2016; that is, in the drop in the percentage of registered voters who turned out to vote from one election to the next. Population change might have an effect on a different measure of voting —the number of votes cast between elections— but, while that impact may be statistically significant, its full effect is not enough to account for the unprecedented drop in electoral participation. I then infer from these results and alternatively propose for further study that the increasing abstention in the Puerto Rican electorate in 2016 may actually be a response to their declining faith in the political system, its political institutions and political class in their ability to respond to the needs and wants of Puerto Ricans.

Accounting for decreasing turnout: migration as an exit strategy?

Explanations in the popular press to account for the decline in electoral participation in the general elections of 2016 and the plebiscite on the status of Puerto Rico in 2017 have included emigration from Puerto Rico (Cortés Chico 2016; Ruiz Kuilan 2017). Undoubtedly, the general decline in population in Puerto Rico, given primarily by migration, has had a depressive effect on levels of turnout at election time, as I will explain in greater detail below. However, this is an insufficient explanation to account for such a profound decline in voting in Puerto Rico.

The proposition that population change in a jurisdiction as a result of the movement of people into or out of that jurisdiction may affect its voting levels is a reasonable one considering what we know about voting at the aggregate level. The literature on the analysis of voter turnout, when the level of analysis is not the individual but rather some geographic jurisdiction (e.g., district, precinct, municipality, state, nation), indicates that population change affects the level of turnout at election time because population change affects a jurisdictions' size, density and stability, among other things. It has been observed that the size of a jurisdiction affects voting levels because jurisdictions with larger size populations tend to have lower rates of participation in elections (Geys 2006; Frandsen 2002, cf. Carr and Tavares 2014; Tavares and Carr 2013). The hypothesized reasons for this effect are that jurisdictions with greater population increase the information costs involved in political activity and participation (e.g., knowledge about the different issues and actors affecting governance and politics), as well as the calculation an individual may make about the difference her vote may make at election time in relation to the costs of voting (Geys 2006). Jurisdictions with smaller populations may increase turnout by providing a context in which social pressure to vote allows for the identification of non-compliant members of the community. Population density, often measured by the number of people by square mile of territory, may increase the likelihood of voting since more dense jurisdictions tend to enlarge social networks an individual may have, networks that reduce information and participation costs. Population stability is related to higher rates of participation than in jurisdictions with greater movement of their population because of the reduced information costs in stable jurisdictions. Stability is measured often by a number of indicators, for instance, whether the population has lived in the same residence for a given number of years, the overall length of residence in a given jurisdiction, or the level of residents who own the homes they live in. Length of residence in a particular jurisdiction is related to the level of knowledge an individual has about that jurisdiction and its politics. It is argued that homeownership increases stability by anchoring residents in the same location over a longer period of time than renters. It is also argued that homeowners may have a greater stake in the jurisdictions they reside, making them prone to pay more attention to and become involved in the political system.

Jurisdictions with smaller populations may increase turnout by providing a context in which social pressure to vote allows for the identification of non-compliant members of the community.

Population movement as a result of migration from a jurisdiction captures in and of itself the level of that jurisdiction's population stability. The more people move in or out of a jurisdiction, the less population stability it experiences. In addition, migration contributes directly to a jurisdiction's population size, by increasing it or decreasing it (along with its natural rate of growth, measured by the number of birth minus the number of deaths). As with population size, migration also affects a jurisdiction's population density. A jurisdiction's territory tends to be fairly stable over time, though it may be affected by erosion, orographical events or politico-administrative action. Given a jurisdiction's stable territorial extension, emigration reduces a jurisdiction's population density, while immigration increases it.

Given these effects of migration on a jurisdiction's population size, density and stability, it is reasonable to expect that migration will affect its level of electoral participation. Yet, little research has been conducted on the effects of population change in Puerto Rico's electoral process. Existing research provides contradictory results on the effect of migration on level of voting by analyzing the levels of participation of migrants returning to Puerto Rico after a sojourn abroad. While some findings show voting decreasing among return migrants (Cámara Fuertes 2004), others show no such decreasing effect on voting among Puerto Rican return migrants after their sojourn (Vargas-Ramos 2005, 2013). This work seeks to expand our knowledge of the effect of population change on electoral participation by examining the dramatic drop in voter turnout in the 2016 elections relative to the previous election cycles in the context of extensive emigration from Puerto Rico.

Puerto Rico's population had a notable decline first noted in the 2010 census, when Puerto Rico lost 2 percent of its population (3,725,789) compared to the 2000 figures (3,808,610); the first time in more than two centuries that the island had lost population. This change in population is evident in Table 3, which shows increases between 2000 and 2004, and between 2004 and 2008. Thereafter, the data show declines in the island's overall population between 2008 and 2012 and between 2012 and 2016. This pattern is also evident when comparing the change in the citizen, voting-age population. However, the data show that between 2000 and 2008 this segment of the population nevertheless grew faster than the population as a whole. Moreover, between 2008 and 2016, the citizen, voting-age population declined at slower rate than the population as a whole. The data on voting, however, showed declines since 2000, in contrast to the changes in population overall or the citizen, voting-age population in particular. What is notable is the large decline in total votes cast in the 2016 relative to those cast in 2012, as well as the turnout between those two election cycles calculated using the citizen, voting-age population. Whereas the decline in population between 2012 and 2016 was about 5 percent, the decline in votes cast was 15 percent for the same period. Moreover, turnout among the citizen, voting-age population declined nearly 14 percent. These changes in participation were greater than the declines in population, including that segment eligible to register to vote and turnout to do so (i.e., CVAP). The recent decline in population in Puerto Rico has been the result of emigration, not a decrease in the natural rate of population growth. For instance, between 2010 and 2016, the balance between birth and deaths in the island was a positive number of 45,000 people. During the same period, however, more than 360,000 people left the country.[2] Yet this population decrease as a result of migration (about 10 percent) is still lower than the decrease in turnout.

Explaining the declining in voting: Methodological considerations

Political science explains voting on largely individual-level as well as systemic factors (Blais 2006). Powerful predictors of voting are the level of socioeconomic status (e.g., income, education, work status), demographic variables (e.g., age, gender), political orientations and attitudes (e.g., interest, knowledge, efficacy, trust) as well as the extent and intensity of associational involvement. Therefore, those individuals with more schooling, higher incomes, more prestigious occupations, those in older age cohorts as well as those more interested in politics, more knowledgeable about politics and the political system, and with a greater sense of efficacy are more likely to engage in political activity as are those who are more engaged in associational activity (Verba and Nie 1972; Verba et al. 1995). However, these predictors do not always operate consistently in Puerto Rico (Cámara Fuertes 2004; cf. Vargas-Ramos 2005, 2013). There are also systemic variables that incentivize participation in politics; for instance, the receptiveness of the system to popular input, the competitiveness of the party system, the level of patronage and government employment (Rosenstone and Hansen 1993; Cámara Fuertes 2004). Then, there are contextual factors that influence how individuals engage in political activity, for instance, population size and density, residential stability, among others (Huckfeldt 1979; Cho and Rudolph 2008; Darmofal 2006; Geys 2006).

Methodologically, the type of analysis of political activity is limited by the availability of data to subject to analysis. For voting, the ideal source of data would come from those who, being eligible to vote, actually turned out to vote and survey them about their voting behavior and other relevant characteristics that may explain their actions, and compare those responses with those of people who are also registered to vote but did not do so. However, this type of study is not common. Rather, a very large number of studies on voter behavior rely on survey research from a sample of the population at large, not exclusively actual voters, and basing their analysis on the accuracy of the statements respondents provide, without further validation. Alternatively, research also relies on analysis of aggregate voting data. The nature of such analysis depends on the questions under research, but attempts to attribute individual behavior on the bases of aggregate data may lead to ecological fallacies. These fallacies can be avoided with proper methodological specifications, but such research highlights the limitation of needed data.

Table 3: Changes in population and votes

	Change in population	Change in total cast	CVAP	CVAP Turnout
2000		2.2%		
2004	2.3%	-1.3%	4.1%	-5.1%
2008	1.2%	-2.4%	3.8%	-5.9%
2012	-5.7%	-3.3%	-4.0%	0.8%
2016	-5.0%	-15.4%	-1.7%	-13.9%

Source: Comisión Estatal de Elecciones de Puerto Rico; U.S. Census Bureau.

The analysis of political behavior in Puerto Rico is often hampered by the limited availability of data. There is a dearth of surveys that may be used for such analysis, and many of the extant surveys are proprietary and unavailable for general use. Moreover, there are no validated surveys available for general use; that is, surveys that verify with the local elections board whether a person who reported they voted in a particular election did in fact do so. Consequently, analysts may have to resort to the analysis of aggregate data to draw inferences and conclusions. One great advantage of using aggregate data is that it is evidence of actual behavior, not simply an unverified response by an individual in a survey who may be responding influenced by social desirability. Moreover, for a number of questions, such as the one posed in this paper, it may be not simply sufficient, but the appropriate level of analysis as well. In fact, for an analysis of changes in demographic characteristics in a political system, an analysis of aggregate voting is rather appropriate. Voting is an individual act, but it is an individual act bounded in a larger system of individuals and institutions. Moreover, the analysis of turnout is the analysis of a system based on the aggregation of individual acts bounded institutionally. Turnout is the characteristic of the system, not of an individual, even if it is a characteristic based on the cumulative activities of individuals.

An analysis at the municipal level also provides 78 observations, rather than simply one.

To establish the extent to which population decline given by migration may have contributed to the decline in turnout I resort to an analysis of turnout at the municipal level. An analysis of registered voter turnout or of votes casts at a general election in Puerto Rico at the municipal level—the dependent variables in this analysis—captures variability in those activities, which allows the measurement of the extent to which variables of interests (such as population movement in and out of the municipio) affect voting. An analysis at the municipal level also provides 78 observations, rather than simply one. For these analyses, I rely on electoral data from Puerto Rico's Board of Election (Comisión Estatal de Elecciones de Puerto Rico) for 2012, 2016 and all other elections going back to 1948. I also rely on population data from the U.S. Census Bureau, using data from the American Community Surveys (5-year estimates) for 2011 and 2016, as the case may be.

Puerto Rico has 78 *municipios*, political and administrative units into which the island is divided. They are the primary sub-state unit, one that may be equivalent of U.S. counties. They fluctuate in geographical extension and size between five square miles and 125 square miles. Their population in 2016 ranged between 1,500 people and more than 363,000. Islandwide, there was a decline in voter turnout between the elections of 2012 and 2016 of more than 22 percentage points, from 78.2 percent to 55.4 percent of registered voters. At the municipio level, the decrease in registered voter turnout between those elections ranged between 19 percentage points and 35 percentage points. Thus, in 2012, turnout at the municipio level ranged between 68 percent at the low end and 87 percent at the high end. In 2016, turnout ranged between 45 percent and 71 percent. Turnout between 2012 and 2016 decreased because there was a decline of nearly 289,000 votes, even though there had been an increase of more than 464,000 people in the number of registered voters (see Table 4). The average decline in vote cast between the last two elections was 15 percent, ranging between 21 percent and 8 percent at the municipal level. In other words, voting decreased in *all* municipios in Puerto Rico between 2012 and 2016, whether measured by registered voter turnout rate or the number of votes cast.

FINDINGS
A bivariate analysis

As indicated above, there were declines in both the general population as well as in the citizen, voting-age population in Puerto Rico between 2011 and 2016. These proportions might suggest that in fact the drop in overall population as well as the decline in the population eligible to register to vote because they are U.S. citizens, 18 years of age or older, went hand in hand with the decline in both the registered voter turnout rate. as well as the number of votes cast in Puerto Rico between 2012 and 2016. However, this was not necessarily the case when analyzing closely the data at the municipal level. Just as the data for the elections between 2012 and 2016 at the state level (i.e., encompassing the entire territorial jurisdiction of the Commonwealth of Puerto Rico) show that there was a decrease in the overall population as a whole and in the population that is eligible to register to vote, as well as a decline in the level of registered voters who turned out to vote and the total number of votes cast between those elections, the proportion in the decrease in population or in the citizen voting-age population at the municipal level was much smaller overall than the decrease in the proportion of registered voters that turned out to vote or the total number of votes cast in that election.

This reduced impact of a municipio's population change or the change in a municipio's citizen, voting-age population observed between 2011 and 2016 on the (percent) difference in votes cast between the elections of 2012 and 2016 was confirmed by a simple regression model. As shown in table 5, the regression coefficients for change in the municipio's population (model 3) and change in the municipio's citizen, voting-age population (model 4) are positive and statistically significant, indicating that an increase in the municipio's population or its citizen, voting-age population would result in an increase in votes cast between elections. A reduction in votes cast would take place if there was a decrease in the municipio's population or in its citizen, voting-age population. However, while these results would indicate a statistically significant impact of population change on voting, in fact, the effect is substantively minimal. This is the case because, even as the population increases, the net effect on votes cast would remain negative. This is illustrated more clearly in Figure 1 and in Figure 2, which provide graphic representation of the effect of population change on votes cast.

Table 4a: Election data for Puerto Rico and municipios, 2012 and 2016

	2012	2016	Difference	Percent change
Islandwide				
Registered voters in PR	2,402,941	2,867,557	464,616	19.3%
Total votes cast in PR	1,878,969	1,589,991	-288,978	-15.4%
Votes cast for governor in PR	1,877,179	1,580,184	-296,995	-15.8%
Registered voter turnout rate in PR	78.2%	55.4%		-29.1%
At municipio level				
Average number of votes cast for governor	24,066	20,258	3,807	-15.4%
High end in range of votes cast for governor	177,602	151,349	-262	-8.0%
Low end in range of votes cast for governor	1,495	1,233	-26,253	-21.0%
Average turnout in election for governor	79.4%	56.7%	-22.6%	-28.6%
High end in range of turnout for governor	87.0%	71.0%	-16.0%	-19.0%
Low end in range of turnout for governor	68.0%	45.0%	-23.0%	-35.0%

Source: Comisión Estatal de Elecciones de Puerto Rico.

Table 4b: Population data for Puerto Rico and municipios, 2011 and 2016

	2011	2016	Difference	Percent change
Islandwide				
Total population	3,742,586	3,529,385	-213,201	-5.7%
Total citizen, voting-age population	2,759,510	2,712,072	-47,438	-1.7%
At municipio level				
Average population	47,981	45,248		-5.7%
High end in range of municipio's population	399,474	363,744		-8.9%
Low end in range of municipio's population	1,831	1,508		-17.6%
Average citizen, voting-age population	35,378	34,770		-1.7%
High end in range of municipio's CVAP	282,231	267,312		-5.3%
Low end in range of municipio's CVAP	1,450	1,120		-22.8%

Source: U.S. Census Bureau, American Community Survey (5-yr. estimates), 2011 and 2016.

As can be appreciated, in municipios where there was no growth in their population between 2011 and 2016, votes casts between 2012 and 2016 decreased by 14.2 percent (see Figure 1). In municipios whose population grew at 5 percent—the maximum growth observed between 2011 and 2016—the proportion of votes cast declined 13 percent. In municipios whose population declined by 18 percent—the most it declined during the period under analysis—the proportion of votes cast declined by 18.6 percent. A similar effect is seen in municipios without any growth in their citizen, voting age population. Such municipios experienced a decline of a 15.2 percent in votes cast (see Figure 2). Even for municipios whose citizen, voting-age population increased by the maximum observed between 2011 and 2016 (9%), the proportion of votes cast still declined by 13.2 percent. In municipios with a 23 percent decline in the citizen, voting-age population—the maximum decline experienced—votes cast declined by 20.2 percent. In other words, irrespective of the volume in the increase or decline in population, the number of votes cast declined between election years by a margin that exceeded any population change.

While change in a municipio's overall population or its citizen, voting-age population had a positive and statistically significant effect on the proportion of votes cast between 2012 and 2016, albeit not in a way that overdetermined the magnitude of the decline in votes cast, the effect of population change on the turnout rate of registered voters had not statistically significant impact whatsoever (see models 1 and 2 in Table 5).

Multiple variable analyses

The effect that an independent variable may hold in a bivariate analysis may include effects of other factors not included in a model. To account for the possible effect(s) of such omitted variable(s), I specify a more complete model. I include the following predictors of participation highlighted in the literature based on their theoretical importance, relevance or empirical impact: the size of the population, as greater size has been established by analysis of aggregate data to lower the electoral participation, given the greater impersonality of the political participation system for those who live in highly populated jurisdiction, is likely to produce as well as the calculus that one single person's vote is less likely to make an large impact in the final electoral outcome (Carr and Tavares 2014; Tavares and Carr 2013; Frandsen 2002; Geys 2006); a higher density of the population on the other hand is observed to increase voting as it promotes density of networks and informational exchanges as well as mobilization efforts (Carr and Tavares 2014; Tavares and Carr 2013; Cho et al. 2006); the stability of a jurisdiction, measured by the percentage of homeowners in a jurisdiction as well as the percentage of residents who resided in the same residence the year before, has been empirically demonstrated to increase turnout as permanence imbues voters with more information about the electoral field and homeowners appear to have a higher stake in electoral outcomes (Geys 2006; Kohfeld and Sprague 2002); heterogeneity in a community is also argued to promote participation, and social inequality is one such form heterogeneity (Oliver 2000), measured in terms of income inequality captured by the

Table 5: Effect of population change on change in voter turnout and change in vote cast, 2012-2016 (unstandardized OLS regression coefficients; standard error in parenthesis)

	Percent change in voter turnout		Percent change in vote cast	
	Model 1	Model 2	Model 3	Model 4
Constant	-.281*** (.006)	-.286*** (.004)	-.142*** (.006)	-.152*** (.003)
Population percent change, 2011-2016	.101 (.103)	-	.243** (.094)	-
Change in pct of CVAP, 2011-2016	-	.062 (.085)	-	.217** (.076)
R-square	0.013	0.007	0.081	0.096
Adjusted R-square	0	-0.006	.069**	.084***
F-ratio	0.967	0.543	6.665	8.059
Degrees of freedom	77	77	77	77

*=p<.1; **=p<.05; ***=p<.01.

GINI index as well as the percent of the population in the labor force as well as the municipalities median household income; in Puerto Rico patronage is theorized to impact the motivation to participate at election time (Barreto and Eagles 2000; Cámara Fuertes 2004), and it is measured in this model with the percentage of the population employed in government; partisanship is very important mobilizational variable as is the closeness of an election (Barreto and Eagles 2000; Cámara Fuertes 2004; Geys 2006; Blais 2006). The more closely contested an election is, the more incentive a voter has to turnout out to vote; and mobilization agents such as political parties also have a greater incentive to turn out both loyal followers as well as inconstant voters to support their cause. Moreover, voters with a partisan attachment have a greater motivation to participate at election time. Such partisanship and closeness of an election is measured by a moving average in which difference in support for the PNP candidate for governor (over the PPD candidate for governor) at the municipal level is compared with the support islandwide for this PNP candidate over four consecutive elections (2000–2012). This index, therefore, captures two important components: partisanship in a municipality over four election cycles prior to the 2016 elections, as well as the closeness of the elections in those cycles.

A multiple variable regression analysis of registered voter turnout at the aggregate level shows that the main independent variable of interest—the percent change in a municipio's population—had a statistically significant impact on the percent change in turnout between the 2012 and 2016 elections at the municipio level in Puerto Rico, but only at a lower level of significance (p=.077) than is customarily ac-

Figure 1. Effect of municipal population change on votes cast for governor, 2012-2016

Percent change in municpal population 2011-2016.

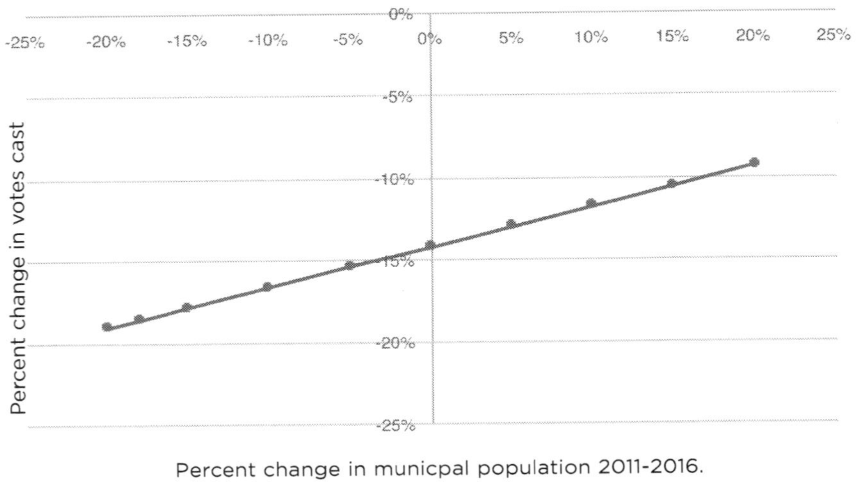

Figure 2. Effect of percent change of citizen, voting-age population on votes cast for governor, 2012-2016

Percent change in municipios citizen, voting-age population 2011-2016.

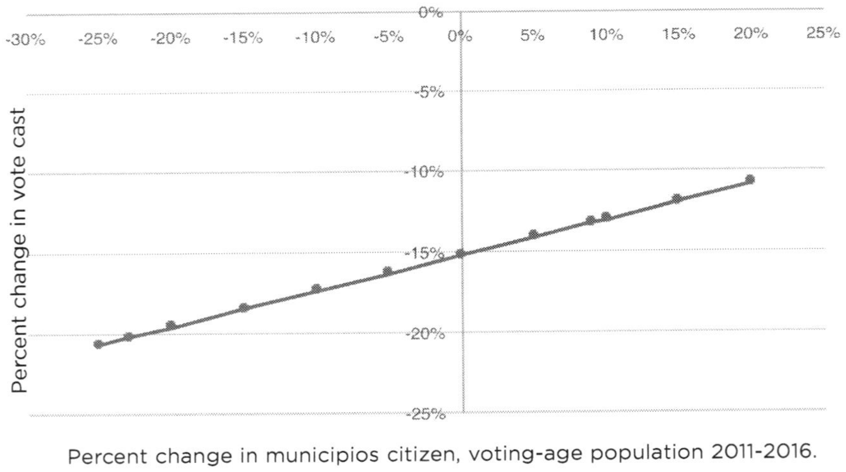

cepted (p= 0.05 or smaller) (see model 1 in Table A1 in the Appendix). Moreover, the results also indicate that even an increase in a municipio's overall population, say, the maximum 5 percent growth, would still result in a 24.7 percent decline in registered voter turnout, other variables held constant. (A maximum decrease in municipal population of 18% would result in a 28.7% decrease in turnout.) On the other hand, the change in a municipio's citizen, voting-age population did not even register a significant effect on the change in registered voter turnout between elections at even a lower level of statistical significance (see model 2 in Table A1). Therefore, these variables that might indicate directly a relationship between migration and electoral participation, given by the fact that between 2011 and 2016 population changes over-all were driven by migration and not natural growth, do not appear to have any discernable independent impact on the turnout of registered voters. In these cases, the multivariate results for the effect of population change on registered voter turnout mirror those of the bivariate regression analysis.

The turnout of registered voters at election time may not be affected by population changes or changes in the citizen, voting-age population. However, these variables do have a statistically significant impact on another measure of voting—the number of votes cast at election time. An increase in a municipio's population between 2011 and 2016 resulted in a lower decrease in the percentage of vote casts between 2012 and 2016, while a decrease in population resulted in greater decline in votes cast, all other factors held constant (see model 3 in Table A1). On average, the municipal population declined 5.1 percent between 2011 and 2016, and at that rate of population decline, the percentage of vote cast declined 15.5 percent. In municipios with a population increase of 5 percent, the maximum noted, the decline in votes cast was 12.6 percent. On the other hand, in municipios with a decrease of 18 percent in population, the largest decline in the analysis, the decline in votes cast was 19.2 percent.

Similarly, when assessing the impact in the change in the citizen, voting-age population, municipios with increases in this variable experienced a lower decline in votes cast than municipios with a decrease in the CVAP (see model 4 in Table A1). On average, there was a decline of 1.03 percent in the citizen, voting-age population at the municipal between 2011 and 2016. In municipios that saw this rate of decline, the proportion of votes cast decreased by 16.1 percent. Where the voting-eligible population increased, say, by 9 percent, the largest increase experienced, the percent decline in votes cast was 13.8 percent; while a 23 percent decline in the CVAP, the largest experienced in a municipio, the percent of votes cast declined 21.2 percent.

It is in this measure of participation (i.e., votes cast) over time that one can appreciate the effect of population change on voting between 2012 and 2016, providing some evidence of the demographic effect of the economic crisis on the political system. These effects of change of population in general and the population that is eligible to vote on the vote are statistically significant and independent of other factors considered in the analysis. Yet, they are still not large enough to account for the large drop in votes between the 2012 elections and those held in 2016.

Additional findings

Other statistically significant results from the multiple variable regression equations indicate that the effects of population size on registered voter turnout and votes cast between elections operated in a manner described by the literature on voting—the larger the population size of a municipio, the lower the turnout rate, or more specifically in this analysis, the greater the decline in the change of voter turnout or votes cast between 2012 and 2016. The density of the municipio's population also behaves in the manner observed in other research, although only as measured by votes casts, not turnout by registered voting: the greater the density, the higher the change in votes casts (or, effectively, the lower the decline in the change of votes cast).

Separately and independently from the change in the municipio's population or its citizen, voting-age population is the effect on voting of the change in stability as measured by the change in the percentage of the municipio's population that resided in the same home the year before. Contrary to what would be expected, greater stability in a municipio's population actually led to a greater drop in votes cast between elections. On average, the proportion of a municipio's residents who remained in their home relative to the previous year increased slightly—by 0.74 percent. In those municipios the percent change in votes casts between 2012 and 2016 decreased by 15.5 percent, while holding all other factors constant and including in the equation a measure of total population change (see model 3 in Table A1). But in municipios in which the percentage of residents lived in the same home the year before decreased by 15 percent, the percent of votes cast decreased by 11.7 percent. Moreover, in municipios in which residents remained in the same home from the previous year increased by 15 percent, the percent change in votes cast decreased by 19 percent! Results are very similar when including a municipio's change in its citizen, voting-age population instead of its population change (see model 4 in Table A1). This finding is not just contrary to expectations but it is also intriguing. Instead of serving to ameliorate the precipitous drop in votes cast between elections, stability in a municipio's population appears to be driving the downward trend in voting between 2012 and 2016. This finding raises the question of whether it is precisely the most stable elements of a municipio's population that are most dissatisfied with the political system.

One additional result is the effect of sustained support for the PNP in elections prior to 2016. This measure of partisanship and closeness of elections, captured in the four elections moving average (2000–2012), however, is inconsistent. It has a statistically significant effect on the change in votes cast between elections, when including in the equation a municipio's population change (see model 3 in Table A1). The effect is positive, indicating that a municipio's steady support for PNP candidates over four elections cycles between 2000 and 2012, increases the number of votes cast between 2012 and 2016. This is a dampening effect, since, as noticed throughout, the drop in votes casts has been precipitous. Therefore, municipios with the most constant support for the PNP experienced a large drop in the number of votes casts, but lower than municipios with less support for the PNP, with all other factors held constant.

The exhaustion of the participatory political regime: unsatisfactory political choices

The results presented above reveal firmly how population change in Puerto Rico did not substantively affect electoral participation between 2012 and 2016, if at all. Emigration from the island is not what accounts for the steep and unprecedented decline in turnout in the 2016 elections relative to previous electoral contests. If this is the case, then, what explains the sharp drop in electoral participation among the Puerto Rican electorate? In the space that follows, I outline an argument to serve as a hypothesis to test in future research to account for steep decline in voter turnout in Puerto Rico. This hypothesis centers on the exhaustion of the participatory regime in Puerto Rico as a result of the declining efficacy and effectiveness of the political apparatus to solve basic issues of economic growth.

The deep link between an electoral system based on extensive mass participation and the legitimization of the political system was the work of one of the leading political parties in Puerto Rico during the past eighty years: the Popular Democratic Party (PPD).

As stated above, voting in general and high rates of electoral participation (i.e., turn-out at election time) in particular are highly significant in terms of both procedural capacity of the political system as well as symbolically. The deep link between an electoral system based on extensive mass participation and the legitimization of the political system was the work of one of the leading political parties in Puerto Rico during the past eighty years: the Popular Democratic Party (PPD). This party was the political force that gave life to and shaped the present political regime that governs the relations between Puerto Rico and the United States: the Commonwealth. A populist mass-based party, the PPD sought in large electoral mobilization the consolidation and legitimization of a political project that sought for Puerto Rico greater political autonomy and self-government from the United States as well as its economic development. Moreover, once the electoral arena became a highly contested two-party system, with the PPD and the New Progressive Party (PNP) alternating in power since 1968, there was an even greater incentive for both political forces to mobilize their bases at election time.

[Initially the highest leadership of the PPD saw the Commonwealth regime as a way station to independence, as Puerto Rico achieved a level of economic development that would allow it to become a self-sustaining nation-state. However, the economic development projects faltered. The Puerto Rican government under the leadership of the PPD did achieve a profound transformation of the economy from an eminently agricultural one to one based on manufacturing to the present one based mostly on services and retail trade (Dietz 1986; Pantojas-García 1990), with significant government sector involvement throughout. However, the PPD-led government was never fully able to address structural imbalances in its budgets as it attempted to maintain economic growth that addressed issues of extensive poverty throughout the island.]

The pillars of the PPD governing project were therefore political autonomy from the United States and economic growth. Political autonomy for Puerto Rico was boosted in the historical context it emerged: the Cold War and the decolonization process throughout the world after the Second World War. Economic development projects also received a boost from the international context in which Puerto Rico sought to expand its economic growth through export-led industrialization based on extensive tax incentives and subsidies for "foreign" investors.

The pillars of the PPD platform, however, are crumbling. Its formula for economic growth has been exhausted. The growth of bilateral and multilateral trade agreements (NAFTA, CAFTA, WTO) has reduced significantly one of the comparative advantages of Puerto Rico in economic terms: unrestricted entry of goods and services into the U.S. market (Castañer and Ruiz 1997). As a result, Puerto Rico-based producers have to compete more aggressively in the United States with producers from other economies for the goods and services they produce. As a result of that increasing competition, some of those producers have left the Puerto Rican market for other locations that make them more competitive. The elimination of the federal fiscal exemptions under section 936 of the Internal Revenue Code by 2006, which triggered the present economic crisis, eliminated the other comparative advantage that Puerto Rico had around direct "foreign" investments, which subsidized the export-led model of economic development. As a result, direct investment in Puerto Rico from abroad has declined, factories have closed or retrenched, and the economy is still unable to provide jobs for all those who want one as well as unable to entice people outside of the labor force to venture into it. The PPD therefore does not appear to have a viable model of economic development that it can present to the electorate in a convincing manner.

Politically, the PPD suffered a major setback as a result of two salient U.S. Supreme Court decisions (i.e., *Puerto Rico v. Sanchez-Valle* [15-108] and *Puerto Rico v. Franklin California Tax Free Trust* [15-233]). In essence, these two rulings underscored the complete subordination of Puerto Rico to the Congress of the United States, according to the territory clause of the U.S. constitution. As a result, these decisions undercut the argument that the PPD had advanced for decades that, upon the enactment of Public Law 600 in the United States in 1950, the ratification of this law by the Puerto Rican electorate in a plebiscite in 1951, and the ratification of Puerto Rico's constitution by the U.S. Congress in 1952, Puerto Rico and the United States had entered into a "compact," whereby changes to the political relationship between the two of them had to be negotiated bilaterally (Trías Monge 1997; Thornburgh 2001). Such position had already been questioned administratively by two separate Presidential task forces on the status of Puerto Rico (2005 and 2011), which, in response to claims for further autonomy for Puerto Rico, had already underscored that one Congress could not bind permanently another by submitting itself to mutual-consent provisions involving a territory.

A less critical, yet still very significant political development undermining the political project of the PPD is the result of a non-binding plebiscite in 2012, in which, for the first time, a majority of eligible voters in Puerto Rico (53.97%) indicated they did not want to maintain the current territorial status. These results were significant not because they departed notably from the actual preference of most voters over the last three decades. They did not. Previous non-binding plebiscites in Puerto Rico (in 1993 and 1998) indicated that a simple majority (50.7%) or near majority (49.3%) of voters wanted non-territorial alternatives to the political relationship with the United States (see Table 6). (It must be noted that the wording of those plebiscites did not include explicitly the concept or terminology of territory, but rather competing political status options.) The 2012 plebiscite, however, was the first time that Puerto Rican voters explicitly voted against a territorial option for Puerto Rico in explicit terms. As a political force that has advocated for nearly four decades a "permanent" relation with the United States, but not by joining the United States as a constituent member on equal standing as other states, the PPD is witnessing a narrowing set of options to its political project and an electorate that is decreasingly supportive of those options.

But the political crisis in Puerto Rico is not limited to narrowing options for political and economic projects for the Popular Democratic Party. Other political forces face similar pressures. This is most notably the case for the Puerto Rican Independence Party (PIP) and the larger Puerto Rican independence movement. The electoral outcomes for the last half a century, whether in regular government elections or plebiscites on the status question, have shown that the overwhelming majority of Puerto Rican voters do not want independence for Puerto Rico. Rather, most Puerto Rican voters want a permanent relationship with the United States whether as a territory with autonomy or as a state of the Union. Certainly, the repression the pro-independence movement has suffered under U.S. colonialism has contributed to its diminished political and mobilizing capacity (Bosque-Pérez and Colón Morera 1997). Nevertheless, the PIP has not been able to articulate a convincing economic program for the broad electorate. There is fear in Puerto Rico that independence would bring decreasing economic capacity and more widespread poverty, so that the island's economy would come to resemble those of surrounding Caribbean and Central American countries—a prospect that does not appear to be appealing to working and middles classes in Puerto Rico. A permanent relationship with the United States as a territory or as a state of the United States would forestall the possibility of further immiseration. Moreover, the PIP and other pro-independence forces have not been able to project the capacity to govern under the current system. A handful of legislators from the PIP has been elected at the municipal level and to the island's legislature over the decades, but these political figures have not been in position to lead an executive branch of government, municipal or otherwise, that may show the electorate a governing capacity from this segment of the political class.

While the diminished prospects for the advocates of autonomy or independence might suggest a rosy picture for advocates of statehood for Puerto Rico, this is not necessarily the case. Advocacy for statehood does have the advantage that statehood for Puerto Rico may appear to the electorate as a possibility that is open and available.

While Commonwealth-style autonomy may be running out of steam, statehood is still a feasible possibility that has not been realized, and as such it remains a goal for which to strive, toward which the electorate may turn. Therefore, statehood is a political option that may enjoy the potential to generate enthusiasm around which to mobilize an electorate; more so as other alternatives appear diminished. As a result, statehood may appear as a viable and credible future political prospect. Whether this possibility is in fact achievable is not a forgone conclusion, nor, for reasons provided below, very likely.

Moreover, proponents of statehood have yet to articulate a concrete and convincing project for the economic development of the island that goes beyond parity with other states in federal funding. The principle of equality between states will make Puerto Rico eligible for parity in funding from the U.S. government, but that same principle will preclude Puerto Rico from being given preferential treatment, for instance, in the issuance of federal tax incentives, such as those that until recently had sustained economic development in Puerto Rico. Moreover, parity will also subject Puerto Ricans to U.S. federal income taxes, from which they have been largely exempt given its territorial status. Admittedly, the number of potential taxpayers subject to income taxes will be reduced in an island in which presently only 45 percent of the population 16 years and older is in the labor force, 45 percent of all persons lives under the federal poverty level and 38 percent receives food assistance through a program similar to the food stamps program/SNAP. While statehood may increase the resources for the social safety net a large segment of the Puerto Rican population relies on, this political status does not provide in and of itself an evident economic comparative advantage for Puerto Rico in relation to the other fifty states of the American union or the counties of the circum-Caribbean region. More importantly, advocates for statehood have not developed or presented to the electorate such an economic development plan under statehood, and implicitly and explicitly are relying instead on a presumed windfall of federal funding under that political status to address not only the economic crisis Puerto Rico is undergoing, but its ongoing economic development as well.

A reliance on the principle of parity, on the one hand, and, on the other, of political equality and equal treatment for U.S. citizens in Puerto Rico, are also what is driving advocacy for statehood in Puerto Rico, particularly as it respects prodding the U.S. Congress to address the island's status question. This approach based on self-righteous demands for equal treatment by granting the U.S. citizens of the territory statehood may play well among a large segment of the electorate in Puerto Rico, but it neglects the political dimensions of admission to the Union as they play out in Washington, DC. There is no actual interest in the Congress of the United States to address the issue of Puerto Rico's status. There is no impending crisis affecting the United States that will force the United States government to address the issue of Puerto Rico's status as there may have existed after the Second World War with the advent of the push for decolonization worldwide and the deepening Cold War. Moreover, there is little incentive to respond to a petition from Puerto Rico for admission to the union as a state, and there are substantial political reasons why such a petition would not be taken up. If Puerto Rico were to become a state, it would have more representation in the U.S. House of Representatives than twenty-one states of the Union, with all the attendant political weight such representation may bring to the island in Congress, particularly as it may respect funding. Moreover, of the approximately five members of the House of Representatives Puerto Rico who may be entitled based on population, at minimum four, and possibly all five prospective representatives are likely to be Democrats, eliciting Republican opposition to admit such an overwhelming Democratic state. Underscoring this point is the fact there is no other territory that might be admitted along with Puerto Rico that might balance its Democratic predominance. The population in Washington DC, the U.S. Virgin Islands, Guam or American Samoa numbers in the hundreds of thousands, too small compared to the 3.1 million inhabitants of Puerto Rico at present. Furthermore, these territories are also either solidly Democratic or lean in that direction. Republican opposition to admitting Puerto Rico is very likely. In addition, there will be little appetite among Republicans in Congress to admit a territory that is so reliant on federal funding for its population's well-being as the Republican current political project entails reducing the size of government and furthering the role of states in the administration of government. Puerto Rico's current fiscal crisis underscores the point that the Government of Puerto Rico is incapable of sustaining itself (i.e., meeting its financial obligations), undermining one of the practical principles of incorporation of a territory as a state. Puerto Rico's historical and current situation does not make it a very attractive candidate for statehood under these circumstances.

Domestically, the PNP still has to contend with the political reality that there is sustained opposition in the electorate to statehood for Puerto Rico. This opposition springs from the advocates of independence as well as the advocates of autonomy. Support for statehood, as established in non-binding plebiscites, has shown increasing support. Since 1967, when that status option obtained 39 percent of the vote, it increased to 46 percent in 1993 and 1998, and then to 61 percent in 2012 and 97 percent in 2017 (see Table 6a). These summary numbers, however, require explanation. The 1967 plebiscite was boycotted by the leading pro-statehood party—the defunct Partido Estadista Republicano (PER)—as well as the PIP. This boycott therefore obscures the actual level of support for those status options. Similarly, the plebiscite in 2012 saw a roll-off in the number of voters who turned to the polls to cast a vote but did not vote for the status option choices provided. As mentioned above, this is the plebiscite that established that a majority of voters opposed the present territorial status. The number of voters who cast a vote on that question was 1,798,987.[3] Those who then cast a vote for one of three status options offered on the ballot numbered 1,363,854 (see Table 6b). Using this figure as denominator, the percentage for the 834,191 votes the statehood option received was 61 percent. Using as denominator the total number of voters who cast a ballot in that election but abstained from choosing a status option would yield statehood a level of support of 46.3 percent. Then there is the 2017 plebiscite, which showed a 97 percent level of support for statehood. However, that status option only received 508,862 votes in 2017 compared to the 834,191 it had received five years before, in an election that saw 523,891 voters turn out to the polls. While supporters of statehood may correctly claim that their status option received 97 percent of the votes cast, it may not be able hold that the elections represented a victory when there was a very active boycott to the process and they were able to bring to the polls fewer supporters to their cause in 2017 than in 2012.

A public opinion poll conducted six months before the 2016 general elections found an extraordinary lack of trust in Puerto Rican governmental institutions across the board.

Both leading political parties—the PPD and PNP—which have alternated in heading the insular government as many times since 1968, have proven incapable of addressing effectively the present economic crisis which began in Puerto Rico in 2006. They have both been blamed for contributing to the practice of borrowing money to cover deficits in the government's operation budget (Federal Reserve Bank of New York 2014). They have also shared in profligate spending to, among other things, sustain patronage support. Indeed, the island's real GNP has declined in 9 of the last 13 years and has actually had negative growth (contracted) in 9 of those 13 years (Marxuach 2015), a period during which both parties alternated in holding the reins of power. Moreover, since 1998, Puerto Rico's governments has run budget deficits on 15 of the 16 fiscal years. As the cost of borrowing to cover these budget deficits increased, the percentage of the budget dedicated to debt services has increased at twice the rate of growth of the overall governmental expenditures (Marxuach 2015). The fiscal crisis in Puerto Rico had reached such a point that the government was on the verge of insolvency, unable to fulfill its debt obligations, and had sought to restructure its debt, but unable to do so under extant federal law. Consequently, in exercise of its constitutional authority and as the institution that holds sovereignty over Puerto Rico, the Congress of the United States authorized the creation of the Financial Oversight and Management Board for Puerto Rico in 2016 "to achieve fiscal responsibility and access to the capital markets."

These actions, I argue, have led to a loss of faith in Puerto Rican governmental institutions and its political class. A public opinion poll conducted six months before the 2016 general elections found an extraordinary lack of trust in Puerto Rican governmental institutions across the board. Ten percent of those polled trusted the incumbent governor, 36 percent had trust in an unnamed future governor, 11 percent trusted the local House of Representatives, 12 percent trusted the local Senate and 19 percent trusted the local judicial branch (López Cabán 2016). By way of contrast, federal institutions, such as the Federal Bureau of Investigations and the U.S. Supreme Court, received levels of trust upward of 80 percent; and even the Financial Oversight Board enjoyed a 79 percent level of trust among Puerto Rican respondents.

Table 6a: Support for statehood for Puerto Rico in plebiscites (percentage)

	1967	1993	1998	2012	2017
Statehood	39	46.3	46.5	61.16	97.13
Commonwealth	60.4	48.6	-	-	-
Current territorial status	-	-	0.1	-	1.35
Sovereign ELA (Free Association)	-	-	-	33.34	-
Free Association	-	-	0.3	-	-
Independence	0.6	4.4	2.5	5.49	-
Independence/Free Association	-	-	-	-	1.52
None of the Above	-	-	50.3	-	-

Source: Comisión Estatal de Elecciones de Puerto Rico.

Table 6b: Support for status options for Puerto Rico in plebiscites (votes cast)

	1967	1993	1998	2012	2017
Statehood	274,312	788,296	728,157	834,191	508,862
Commonwealth	425,132	826,326	-	-	-
Current territorial status	-	-	993	-	7,048
Sovereign ELA (Free Association)	-	-	-	454,768	-
Free Association	-	-	4,536	-	-
Independence	4,248	75,620	39,838	74,895	-
Independence/Free Association	-	-	-	-	7,981
None of the Above	-	-	787,900	-	7,981
Total number of votes cast	703,692	1,690,242	1,560,431	1,363,854	523,891
Total registered number of voters	1,067,349	2,312,912	2,197,825	2,402,941	2,260,804

Source: Comisión Estatal de Elecciones de Puerto Rico.

Even just before the 2016 general elections *la Junta* enjoyed a 62 percent favorability rating among respondents (López Alicea 2016). Furthermore, as one of the reviewers of a previous version of this paper has suggested, the creation of the Financial Oversight Board may have undermined local political elites and institutions, diminishing the need among the electorate to participate in the election of a government whose political autonomy and fiscal authority have been compromised.

Whether low level of support for local political institutions and government leaders increases or erodes further as a result of the insufficient response to the crisis created by hurricanes Irma and Maria is yet to be determined. Moreover, the poor response by federal agencies (e.g., Federal Emergency Management Administration, U.S. Army Corps of Engineers) may reverse the greater level of trust in U.S. government institutions and agencies among people in Puerto Rico, perhaps further disheartening Puerto Rican voters and undermining even more their diminishing faith in any type of governmental institution on the island. In fact, this is evident in recent public opinion polls. The assessment of leading governmental figures and institutions among the people of Puerto Rico in the aftermath of hurricanes Irma and Maria indicate that the incumbent governor had a favorability rating (i.e., good or very good) of 37 percent; FEMA, 36 percent; local electric power utility (PREPA), 28 percent; the U.S. Congress, 25 percent; the Financial Oversight Board, 23 percent; and the President of the United States, 17 percent (*El Nuevo Día* 2018a). The job approval for the incumbent governor, however, experience a marked decline between June 2017 (39%) and November 2018 (25%) (*El Nuevo Día* 2018b). The disenchantment with all government institutions on the island, whether federal or Commonwealth is palpable.

This diminishing faith in governmental institutions appears to be setting the stage for a legitimacy crisis in governmental institutions. This seemingly increasing lack of faith, I propose, is a leading explanation to the extraordinary decrease in the turnout rate in Puerto Rico. Between 1948, the first time Puerto Ricans were able to elect a governor, and 2012 the turnout rate ranged between 73 percent and 89 percent of registered voters (see table 1). In 2016, however, only 55 percent of registered voters turned out to vote in the elections, an unprecedented proportion of the electorate. Even when using the citizen voting-age population (CVAP) as a reference category, the level of participation between 1972 and 2000 ranged between 74 percent and 82 percent. Between 2000 and 2016, using the more stringent reference category of the citizen voting-age population to calculate electoral participation, turnout ranged between 75 percent and 59 percent, with the lowest level of turnout taking place in 2016 (see Table 2). Voters in Puerto Rico are not turning out to vote seemingly because political parties and candidates are not offering them credible alternatives to solve the serious economic problems facing the island. Moreover, the unconvincing performance of the two leading political parties at the helm of the government seems to be undermining the electorate's confidence in their ability to provide good governance to the island. These assertions, however, need to be tested empirically. The results from public opinion surveys referenced immediately above provide some evidence for these statements, but are insufficient unless tied to action (i.e., voting or abstention). It would have been ideal if there had been public opinion polls conducted at election time (i.e., exit polls) or shortly thereafter; particularly polls that surveyed both registered voters who turned out to vote and registered voters who did not turn out to vote. Lacking this evidence, we may need to wait until the next electoral cycle in 2020; at which time opinion polls may be conducted in panel form prior to the elections and then, in their wake, to establish whether voters' attitudes toward the government and the political parties and candidates contesting the elections influenced their actions at the voting booth. Moreover, the elections in 2020 would provide additional evidence of whether the results in 2016 were idiosyncratic and unique or whether they represented an inflection point in the political trajectory of Puerto Rico.

The role of independent candidacies on turnout

Reviewers of a previous version of this paper have indicated the importance of assessing the impact of the seemingly increased number of independent candidacies for governor as an indicator of the displeasure with the choices provided by political parties among the electorate, but an indicator nevertheless of support for the political participation system. Certainly, the fact that voters were presented with alternatives to those provided by established political parties and that those voters responded positively by providing unprecedented support for those independent candidates would be indication of continued support for the extant electoral system. In fact, the 2016 elections were unusual also in the high number of independent candidacies for governor and the support they received. In fact, they were the highest of any elections held in Puerto Rico since 1972 (see Table 7). While the level of support for independent candidacies before 2016 ranged between 3.3 percent in 2004 and 7.6 percent in 1984, independent candidates for governor collectively garnered 19 percent of the total vote for governor. This fact notwithstanding, it remains the case that even with this level of support for independent candidacies, and by extension the electoral regime, the turnout rate in those elections was nearly 23 percentage points lower. It might be argued that without independent candidacies the turnout rate might have been even lower than the historically low 55 percent of registered voters to turned to the polls.

The proposition that independent candidacies for governor might have had an effect on turnout is nevertheless a fair one and worthy of testing. I therefore specified another multiple variable regression model to test the independent effect voting for independent candidates for governor might have had on the turnout of registered voters or votes cast between 2012 and 2016. To that effect, I constructed a variable that averaged the difference in the rate of voting for independent candidates for governor at the municipal level from what that rate was islandwide between 1972 and 2012 to capture the regional strength of support for independent candidacies over time. The results indicate that introducing support for independent candidacies does not have a statistically significant impact on percent change in votes cast for governor between 2012 and 2016, nor does it affect the effects that change in population at the municipal level nor change in the citizen, voting-age populationthe percent change in votes casts between those elections (see model 3 and 4 in Table A2 in the Appendix). Independent candidacies do have a statistically significant impact on the percent change in voter turnout between 2012 and 2016 (see model 1 and model 2 in Table A2). However, the effect is negative. That is, the greater the percentage of the vote for independent candidates for governor at the municipal level, the lower the turnout rate in 2016. It appears that it is in municipalities whose voters were already inclined to move away from the candidates presented by political parties in previous election that the greatest decline occurred. Might this be an indication that it is among those voters that the greatest dissatisfaction existed? Further research awaits a fuller answer to this question. Aside from this finding, it is pertinent to note that in spite of the statistically significant effect that independent candidacies have on the turnout of registered voters, the effect of population change on turnout and of change in the citizen, voting-age population on turnout remain essentially unaltered. The effects of those other variables of interest remain insignificant statistically. Overall, these results indicate that even when introducing another variable into the equation, the effect of population change on voting between 2012 and 2016 remains unaltered: migration did not affect voting meaningfully.

Conclusion

Puerto Rico had been experiencing slight but steady declines in its high level of electoral participation, in the order of one to three percentage points per election, for two decades. In 1992, the turnout rate was 85.2 percent. In 2012, it was 78.2 percent. However, between 2012 and 2016, participation fell by 29 percent to an unprecedented low rate of 55.4 percent of registered voters. The accompanying population decline that has been taking place in Puerto Rico since the 2000s, however, has not been the reason for the decline in turnout at election time between 2012 and 2016. Rather, it appears that there is widespread disaffection with a political regime that is unable to address very basic economic, political and social demands. Moreover, alternatives to the extant regime appear equally unpalatable. As a result, the electorate is turning off.

Emigration may appear correlated, but it is not a cause of the decline in electoral turnout in Puerto Rico.

Emigration may appear correlated, but it is not a cause of the decline in electoral turnout in Puerto Rico. This depressing effect of emigration on voting in Puerto Rico is more evident only in the amount of votes cast in elections. Since 2000 the total number of votes for governor has declined at a rate between one and three percent from election. The exception again was the decline between 2012 and 2016 elections, when the total number of votes cast declined by 15 percent. Yet, while statistically

Table 7. Rate of Voting for Governor from Smaller Parties or Independent Candidacies

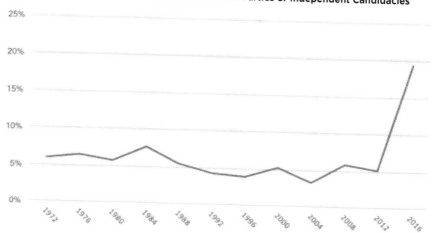

Source: Comisión Estatal de Elecciones de Puerto Rico.

significant, the effect of change in population or in the citizen, voting-age population between 2011 and 2016 on the percent change of votes casts at the municipio level do not change the overwhelming decline in votes casts in the 2016 elections. It declined 15.4 percent on average, and it declined in every single municipio in Puerto Rico in the range of 8 percent to 21 percent.

The causes for the large decline in voting in Puerto Rico are elsewhere, not in the demographic change taking place on the island over the previous five years. These findings are robust and consistent. This analysis suggests that the cause of the political crisis in Puerto Rico may be the disaffection with the political parties in the system and the political class that leads them. But further research is needed for substantiate this proposition.

NOTES

[1] Electoral participation can be measured by the proportion of registered voters to turn out to vote at any given election. This is generally the rate of participation reported by election boards when releasing reports. However, registered voters are a subset of the larger population that resides in a particular jurisdiction. The citizen, voting-age population (CVAP) is another of the population that resides in a jurisdiction, but it is larger than the number of registered voters, since not every person that is eligible to vote, by virtue of the fact that they are citizens and eighteen years of age or older, does in fact register to vote. Consequently, the proportions of electoral participation based on the CVAP tend to be lower than those using registered voters as the denominator. The CVAP is useful when comparing participation over the long term since it captures what percentage of those potentially eligible to vote does turn out, whereas the turnout rate based only on registered voters may be affected by whether the local board of elections are more or less diligent or aggressive in purging voter rolls from election to election.

[2] U.S. Census Bureau.

[3] Turnout for the 2012 elections in which questions on the status of Puerto Rico were asked included not only those for the plebiscite, but also for the general elections for governor, legislature, mayors and municipal councils for that electoral cycle. For the 2012 elections, the Elections Board (i.e., Comisión Estatal de Elecciones) reported a total of 2,402,941 registered voters. According to the actual results provided after the canvass of votes (i.e., escrutinio de votos), the Elections Board accounted for 1,878,969 registered voters turning out to vote (78.19%). Of these 1,878,969 voters who turned out on election day, 1,877,179 voted for candidates for governor (78.12% turnout), while 1,798,987 voters (74.87%) voted on the first plebiscite question (i.e., "Do you agree that Puerto Rico should have its present form of territorial status?" [Yes/No]). The number of registered voters who then answered the question on non-territorial options ("Please, mark which of the following non-territorial option would you prefer: Statehood, Independence, Free Associated State") was 1,363,854 (56.76%). The number of votes obtained by the Statehood option was 834,191; Independence, 74,895; and Free Associated State, 454,768. If the turnout rate for each preferred status option were to be divided by the total number of duly registered voters (2,402,941), then 34.72 percent supported Statehood; 18.92 percent preferred Free Associated States; and 3.11 percent favored Independence. If the denominator used to determine turnout for this status option questions were based on the total number of voters who voted on this question (1,363,854), then Statehood received 61.16 percent support; Free Associated States received 33.34 percent; and Independence, 5.49 percent. If the total number of voters accounted for the Board of Elections as having voted in those elections overall (1,878,969) were used as denominator, then the level of support for Statehood would be 43.96 percent; Free Associated State, 24.2 percent; and Independence, 3.98 percent.

REFERENCES

Anderson, Robert W. 1983. The Party System: Change and Stagnation. In *Time for Decision: The United States and Puerto Rico*, ed. Jorgen Hein. 3–25. Lanham, MD: The North-South Publishing Co.

Barreto, Amílcar A. and D. Munroe Eagles. 2000. Modelos ecológicos de apoyo partidista en Puerto Rico, 1980-1992. *Revista de Ciencias Sociales* 9, 135–65.

Bayrón Toro, Fernando. 2000. *Elecciones y partidos plíticos de Puerto Rico, 1809-2000*. Mayagüez, PR: Editorial Isla.

Blais, Andre. 2006. What affects voter turnout? *Annual Review of Political Science* 9, 111–25.

Bosque-Pérez, Ramón and José Javier Colón Morera. 1997. *Las carpetas: persecución política y derechos civiles en Puerto Rico*. Río Piedras, PR: Centro para la Investigación y Promoción de los Derechos Civiles, Inc.

Cámara Fuertes, Luis R. 2004. *The Phenomenon of Puerto Rican Voting*. Gainesville: University Press of Florida.

Carr, Jered B. and Antonio Tavares. 2014. City Size and Political Participation in Local Government: Reassessing the Contingent Effect of Residential Location Decisions within Urban Regions. *Urban Affairs Review* 50(2), 269–302.

Castañer, Juan A. and Ángel Ruiz. 1997. The Importance of Trade to an Export-led Economy in the Present Context of Free Agreements in the Western Hemisphere: A Quantitative Analysis for the Puerto Rican Economy. Rio Piedras, PR: Unidad de Investigaciones Económicas, Departamento de Economías, Universidad de Puerto Rico de Río Piedras.

Cho, Wendy K.T., James G. Gimpel and Joshua J. Dyck. 2006. Residential Concentration, Political Socialization, and Voter Turnout. *Journal of Politics* 68(1), 156–67.

Cho, Wendy K.T. and Thomas J. Rudolph. 2008. Emanating Political Participation: Untangling the Spatial Structure Behind Participation. *British Journal of Political Science* 38, 273–89.

Cortés Chico, Ricardo. 2016. Más incritos que electores. *El Nuevo Día* 25 September. Accessed 28 August 2017. <https://www.elnuevodia.com/noticias/politica/nota/masincritosqueelectores-2244589/>.

Darmofal, David. 2006. The Political Geography of Macro-Level Turnout in American Political Development. *Political Geography* 25, 123–50.

Dietz, James L. 1986. *Economic History of Puerto Rico: Institutional Change and Capitalist Development*. Princeton, NJ: Princeton University Press.

Easton, David. 1975. A Re-Assessment of the Concept of Political Support. *British Journal of Political Science* 5(4), 435–57.

El Nuevo Día. 2018a. La encuesta: Evaluación de líderes, agencias, utilidades, e instituciones por su labor luego del huracán María hasta hoy. 14 November, 9.

El Nuevo Día. 2018b. La encuesta: Rosselló internalize resultados. 15 November, 4–5.

Federal Reserve Bank of New York. 2014. An Update on the Competitiveness of Puerto Rico's Economy. New York: Federal Reserve Bank.

Frandsen, Annie G. 2002. Size and Electoral Participation in Local Elections. *Environment and Planning C: Government and Policy* 20(6), 853–69.

Geys, Benny. 2006. Explaining Voter Turnout: A Review of Aggregate-Level Research. *Electoral Studies* 25(4), 637–63.

Gilley, Bruce. 2006. The Determinants of State Legitimacy: Results from 72 Countries. *International Political Science Review* 27(1), 47–71.

Hirschman, Albert O. 1970. *Exit, Voice, and Loyalty: Responses to Decline in Firms, Organizations, and States*. Cambridge, MA: Harvard University Press.

Huckfeldt, R. Robert. 1979. Political Participation and the Neighborhood Social Context. *American Journal Political Science* 23(3), 579–92.

Kohfeld, Carol W. and John Sprague. 2002. Race, Space, and Turnout. *Political Geography* 21(2), 175–93.

Linz, Juan J. 1978. *The Breakdown of Democratic Regimes: Crisis, Breakdown and Reequilibration*. Baltimore: The Johns Hopkins University Press.

López Alicea, Keila. 2016. Intriga el apoyo a la Junta de Control Fiscal. *El Nuevo Día* 19 August. Accessed 28 August 2017. <https://www.elnuevodia.com/noticias/politica/nota/intrigaelapoyoalajuntadecontrolfiscal-2232357/>.

López Cabán, Cynthia. 2016. Desconfía los boricuas en sus instituciones *El Nuevo Día* 22 May. Accessed 28 August 2017. <https://www.elnuevodia.com/noticias/politica/nota/desconfianlosboricuasensusinstituciones-2201574/>.

Marxuach, Sergio M. 2015. Analysis of Puerto Rico's Current Economic and Fiscal Situation. San Juan, Puerto Rico: Center for A New Economy. October

Oliver, J. Eric. 2000. City Size and Civic Involvement in Metropolitan America. *American Political Science Review* 94(2), 361–73.

Pantojas-García, Emilio. 1990. *Development Strategies as Ideology: Puerto Rico's Export-led Industrialization Experience*. Boulder, CO: Lynne Reinner Publishers.

President's Task Force on Puerto Rico's Status. 2005. Report by President's Task Force on Puerto Rico's Status. Washington, DC, December.

_____. 2011. Report by the President's Task Force on Puerto Rico's Status. Washington, DC, March.

Ramírez, Rafael. 1977. *El arrabal y la política*. Río Piedras: Editorial Universitaria, Universidad de Puerto Rico.

Rivera, Ángel I., Ana I. Seijo and Jaime W. Colón. 1991. La cultura política y la estabilidad del sistema de partidos de Puerto Rico. *Caribbean Studies* 24(3-4), 175–220.

Rosario, Frances. 2016. Baja la participación electoral de la Isla. *El Nuevo Día* 9 November. Accessed 28 August 2017. <https://www.elnuevodia.com/noticias/politica/nota/bajalaparticipacion electoraldelaisla-2260595/>.

Rosenstone, Steven J. and John H. Hansen. 1993. *Mobilization, Participation and Democracy in America*. New York: MacMillan Publishing Co.

Ruiz Kuilan, Gloria. 2017. Hay controveria por la baja participación plebiscitaria en municipios PNP. *El Nuevo Día* 13 June. Accessed 28 August 2017. <https://www.elnuevodia.com/noticias/politica/nota/controversiaporlabajaparticipacion plebiscitariaenmunicipiospnp-2330630/>.

Tavares, Antonio F. and Jered B. Carr. 2013. So Close, Yet So Far Away? The Effects of City Size, Density and Growth on Local Civic Participation. *Journal of Urban Affairs* 35(3), 283–302.

Thornburgh, Richard. 2001. Puerto Rican Separatism and United States Federalism. In *Foreign in a Domestic Sense: Puerto Rico, American Exceptionalism and the Constitution*, eds. Christina Duffy Burnett and Marshall Burke. 349–72, Durham, NC: Duke University Press.

Trías Monges, José. 1997. *Puerto Rico: The Trials of the Oldest Colony in the World*. New Haven, CT: Yale University Press.

Vargas-Ramos, Carlos. 2013. Puerto Ricans: Citizens and Migrants —A Cautionary Tale. *Identities: Global Studies in Culture and Power* 20(6), 665–88.

————. 2005. El género y la participación política en Puerto Rico. *Caribbean Studies* 33(1), 205–48.

Verba, Sidney and Nie, Norman. 1972. *Participation in America*. Chicago: University of Chicago Press.

Verba, Sidney, Schlozman, Kay L., and Brady, Henry E., 1995. *Voice and Equality: Civic Voluntarism in American Politics*. Cambridge, MA: Harvard University Press.

APPENDIX

Table A1: Effect of population change on change in voter turnout and change in vote cast, 2012-2016 (unstandardized OLS regression coefficients; standard error in parenthesis)

	Percent change in voter turnout		Percent change in vote cast	
	Model 1	Model 2	Model 3	Model 4
Constant	-.059 (.047)	-.064 (.046)	-.033 (.043)	-.041 (.043)
Population density 2016 (natural log)	.006 (.006)	.007 (.006)	.013** (.006)	.013** (.006)
Total population 2016 (natural log)	-.025*** (.006)	-.026*** (.006)	-.019*** (.006)	-.02*** (.006)
Population percent change, 2011-2016	.175* (.098)	-	.286*** (.09)	-
Change in percent employed in gov't, 2011-2016	.004 (.031)	.001 (.031)	.012 (.028)	.008 (.028)
Change in labor force participation, 2011-2016	.01 (.035)	.012 (.036)	-.034 (.033)	-.031 (0.33)
Change in median HH income, 2011-2016	-.034 (.042)	-.03 (.042)	-.077* (.039)	-.07* (.039)
Change in percent home occupied by owner, 2011-2016	-.067 (.053)	-.071 (.054)	-.05 (.049)	-.058 (.05)
Change in percent residing same home year before, 2011-2016	-.221 (.118)	-.208* (.118)	-.243** (.109)	-.223** (.109)
Change in Gini index, 2011-2016	.01 (.067)	.009 (.067)	-.054 (.062)	-.055 (.062)
Four elections moving average (2000-2012)	.047 (.088)	.028 (.088)	.169** (.081)	.137* (.081)
Change in pct of CVAP, 2000-2012	-	.134 (.081)	-	.231*** (.075)
R-square	0.293	.288	0.326	.321
Adjusted R-square	0.187***	0.181***	.225***	.22***
F-ratio	2.772	2.704	3.236	3.166
Degrees of freedom	77	77	77	77

$*=p<.1$; $**=p<.05$; $***=p<.01$.

Figure A1. Effect of municipal population change on votes cast for governor, 2012-2016

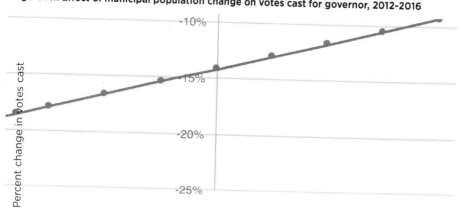

Percent change in municipal population from 2011 to 2016.

Figure A2. Effect of percent change of citizen, voting age population on votes cast for governor, 2012-2016

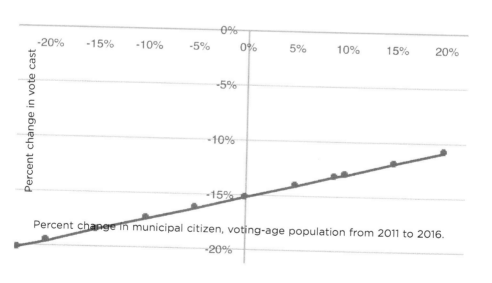

Percent change in municipal citizen, voting-age population from 2011 to 2016.

Table A2: Effect of population change on change in voter turnout and change in vote cast, 2012-2016 (unstandardized OLS regression coefficients; standard error in parenthesis)

	Percent change in voter turnout		Percent change in vote cast	
	Model 1	Model 2	Model 3	Model 4
Constant	-.094* (.049)	-.099** (.049)	-.047 (.047)	-.054 (.046)
Population density 2016 (natural log)	.011* (.007)	.012* (.007)	.015** (.006)	.015** (.006)
Total population 2016 (natural log)	-.026*** (.006)	-.026*** (.006)	-.019*** (.006)	-.02*** (.006)
Population percent change, 2011-2016	.091 (.106)	-	.252** (.099)	-
Change in percent employed in gov't, 2011-2016	.-.00001 (.03)	-.002 (.03)	.01 (.028)	.007 (.028)
Change in labor force participation, 2011-2016	.006 (.035)	.007 (.035)	-.036 (.033)	-.033 (0.33)
Change in median HH income, 2011-2016	-.04 (.041)	-.038 (.041)	-.079** (.039)	-.073* (.039)
Change in percent home occupied by owner, 2011-2016	-.09* (.054)	-.091* (.054)	-.059 (.051)	-.066 (.051)
Change in percent residing same home year before, 2011-2016	-.178 (.118)	-.17 (.118)	-.226** (.111)	-.208* (.111)
Change in Gini index, 2011-2016	.018 (.067)	.02 (.068)	-.065 (.064)	-.065 (.064)
Four elections moving average (2000-2012)	-.596* (.311)	-.618* (.316)	.-.238 (.293)	-.23 (.298)
Average rate of third party/independent candidates	-.034 (.096)	-.045 (.094)	.137 (.09)	.109 (.089)
Change in pct of CVAP, 2011-2012	-	.057 (.089)	-	.203** (.084)
R-square	0.33	.327	0.332	.327
Adjusted R-square	.218***	.214***	.221***	.215***
F-ratio	2.953	2.909	2.986	2.914
Degrees of freedom	77	77	77	77

*=p<.1; **=p<.05; ***=p<.01.

A Note on the Territorial Government and Incorporation Bills for Puerto Rico Introduced in Congress, 1898–2018

CHARLES R. VENATOR-SANTIAGO

ABSTRACT

Following the Spanish-American War of 1898, the United States invented a new tradition of territorial expansionism with a corresponding constitutional doctrine to rule Puerto Rico and other unincorporated territories. For more than a century, the United States has relied on this racist constitutional interpretation to legitimate the separate and unequal rule of Puerto Rico. Drawing on an analysis of the Congressional Research Index for all legislative sessions between 1898 and 2018, this note describes all the territorial government and incorporation bills introduced in Congress throughout this period. Although upward of 134 status bills for Puerto Rico were introduced, and in some cases debated, in Congress, only eleven provide for the creation of a territorial government or the incorporation of Puerto Rico. All but one of these bills were introduced prior to the enactment of the Puerto Rican Constitution of 1952. For more than a century, Congress has refused to enact territorial legislation that expressly incorporates Puerto Rico and repudiates the racist doctrine of territorial incorporation. [Key Words: Puerto Rico, U.S. Congress, Territorial Incorporation, Puerto Rico Status]

The author (charles.venator@uconn.edu) is an Associate Professor with a joint appointment in the Department of Political Science and El Instituto at the University of Connecticut. He is also the Secretariat and Vice-President/President Elect (2021-2022) of the Puerto Rican Studies Association. He is the coordinator of the Puerto Rico Citizenship Archives Project and the American Samoa Nationality and Citizenship Archives Project, and the author of *Puerto Rico and the Origins of U.S. Global Empire: The Disembodied Shade* (Routledge, 2015)..

In recent years, Puerto Rico's territorial status has received some renewed, albeit ephemeral attention in the mainland United States and around the world. The island's fiscal crisis and the plethora of political responses, including Congress's reliance on a fiscal oversight board to manage local partisan clientelism received worldwide attention. Likewise, the federal government's response to the devastation created by Hurricane Maria left some wondering if Puerto Rico was just another island in the middle of the ocean. Central to these debates is Puerto Rico's unincorporated territorial status and the implications of this status for Puerto Ricans and other United States citizens residing in the island. Under prevailing Supreme Court interpretations, because Puerto Rico is an unincorporated territory, it is constitutional to enact discriminatory legislation for the island (*Harris v. Santiago-Rosario* 1980, 446 U.S. 651). Stated differently, it is constitutional for Congress, and the federal government more generally, to rule Puerto Rico as a separate and unequal possession of the United States empire so long as the island remains an unincorporated territory.

Following the Spanish-American War of 1898, the United States invented a new territorial law and policy to rule annexed territories primarily inhabited by non-Anglo-Saxon populations. Central to the new expansionist tradition was the invention of the unincorporated territorial status with a corresponding constitutional doctrine, also known as the doctrine of territorial incorporation. The doctrine of territorial incorporation enabled the federal government to rule unincorporated territories as separate and unequal possessions belonging to the United States. Unincorporated territories retained their status until Congress enacted legislation that either explicitly incorporated or made the territory a part of the United States or changed the territories status. The United States has government Puerto Rico as an unincorporated territory for more than a century. Throughout this period, Congress has refused to debate and/or enact any territorial incorporation legislation.

This note provides an overview of all federal territorial government and incorporation bills introduced in Congress between 1898 and 2018. With the exception of one bill introduced in the House of Representatives in 1993 at the behest of the United Nations, calling for a consultation on whether Puerto Rico should be incorporated, all bills providing for either the creation of a territorial government for Puerto Rico or the territorial incorporation of the island were introduced prior to 1952. This note is limited to providing an overview or description of the doctrine of territorial incorporation used to govern Puerto Rico and the territorial government and incorporation bills introduced in Congress between 1898 and 2018. This note is divided into three parts. Part I provides an basic overview of the prevailing U.S. territorial acquisition laws and policies in 1898. Part II explains the legal arguments defining the contours of the doctrine of territorial incorporation. Part III provides a description of all territorial government and incorporation bills introduced in Congress between the annexation of Puerto Rico and the 2018.

Part I: Prevailing Territorial Doctrines in 1898

Scholars generally agree that in 1898, debates over the acquisition of territories were divided in two camps, namely the anti-imperialist or colonialist and the imperialist (Torruella 1988, 24–32; Sparrow 2006, 44–55). Initial legal and political debates over the annexation of the Spanish ultramarine colonies in the aftermath of the War of 1898 were framed on whether past precedents would be applied to annexed territories, which were primarily populated by non-Anglo-Saxon populations. As I have explained in more detail elsewhere (Venator-Santiago 2015), proponents of the anti-imperialist interpretation argued that established constitutional precedents bound the United States to colonize the new territories and eventually admit them as new states of the Union. In contrasts, imperialists argued for the mere strategic occupation of the new territories. Although the debates among advocates of each camp were fairly plural, it is possible to identify a consensus on several questions that can help establish a clearer distinction between both camps, including opinions about the intent of the acquisition, the constitutional source of power, and the status of the acquired territory.[1]

However, as most scholars who have studied this history will note, while the U.S. Constitution contains a Statehood Admissions Clause (Art. IV, §3, cl. 1), it does not spell out any process whereby a territory will be organized into a state that could be admitted into the Union

---

My contention is that United States colonialism was premised on the *annexation* of territories that could be settled by citizens and subsequently organized into future states that could be admitted into the Union on an equal footing with the founding thirteen states.[2] All territories annexed prior to 1898 were subsequently organized and admitted into thirty-seven states (Farrand 1896; Grupo 1984; Sheridan 1985). However, as most scholars who have studied this history will note, while the U.S. Constitution contains a Statehood Admissions Clause (Art. IV, §3, cl. 1), it does not spell out any process whereby a territory will be organized into a state that could be admitted into the Union. Notwithstanding, Congress originally enacted the *Northwest Ordinance of 1789* (1 Stat. 50), spelling out a procedure whereby a territory could undergo various stages of political organization and once sufficiently populated (60,000 inhabitants), it could petition for statehood. Yet, as Max Farrand argued, Congress began to abandon this procedure in 1836 (1896, 38). Alternatively, it is possible to argue that while early territories followed some the *Northwest Ordinance's* plan of organization, the actual admissions process was more complex and political. To be sure, as Peter B. Sheridan notes, different territories followed different procedures for admission to statehood:

Seventeen territories, for example, gained statehood without enabling acts. Four other states (Kentucky, Maine, Vermont, and West Virginia) were admitted by simple congressional acts of admission without undergoing a preliminary stage of territorial organization; all four areas had been parts of thither States before admission. California and Texas similarly were not organized territories before admission. California had been administered by the American Army, and Texas had been an independent republic before it was annexed. In seven cases (Tennessee, Michigan, Iowa, California, Oregon, Kansas, and Alaska), the United States Congress was presented by the respective "States" with "Senators" and "Representatives" from these areas before statehood was granted. This procedure, known as the "Tennessee Plan," was first adopted in 1796, when a constitution was drafted and representatives were elected, all without any authorization from Congress. (1985, 2–3)

The reason for this mixed experience, Barry R. Weingast (1998) argues, is that historically, the statehood admissions process has been fraught with a wide array of ideological, partisan, and political interests in Congress. Decisions to admit new states have been guided by a range of other political debates over the impact of adding a new state on the apportionment of congressional seats as well as policy debates of the period. However, the points that I want to emphasize are simple. However, the point that I want to emphasize is that nowhere in this procedural histories is there a qualification distinguishing between incorporated and unincorporated territories.

United States colonialism is primarily anchored on three constitutional sources. Following the annexation of a territory, Congress is empowered to govern the territory under the terms of the so-called Territories or Property Clause (U.S. Const. art. IV, §3, cl. 2). The Admissions Clause (U.S. Const. art. IV, §3, cl. 1) authorizes Congress to admit a new state. A pre-condition for admission, however, is that a future state must possess a Republican form of government (U.S. Const. art. IV, §4). Although the federal government can draw from other constitutional sources of power during the initial acquisition of the territory, once it has been annexed, the Constitution establishes that territories are essentially congressional constructs governed under the authority of the latter clauses. Moreover, while the constitutional text recognizes three types of spaces, namely states, districts, and territories, it does not highlight any difference between incorporated or unincorporated territories.

Prior to 1898, the colonialist tradition treated territories as a constitutional part of the United States. Chief Justice John Marshall summarized the key premise of U.S. colonialism in *Loughborough v. Blake*:

Does the term designate the whole, or any particular portion of the American empire? Certainly, this question can admit but one answer. It is the name given to our great republic, which is composed of States *and territories*. The district of Columbia, or the territory west of Missouri, is not less within the United States, than Maryland or Pennsylvania; and it is not less necessary, on the principles of our constitution, that uniformity in the imposition of imposts, duties, and excises, should be observed in the one, than in the other. (1820, 18 U.S. 317, 319—emphasis added)

The latter passage affirms two key points. First, the Court did not recognize a substantive difference in the status of districts and territories. Second, all annexed territories were treated as a part of the United States for constitutional purposes (*American Insurance v. Canter* 1828, 542).

In contrast, the imperialist tradition was premised on the occupation of territories for economic or military strategic interests. For example, the legal history of the Guano Islands unequivocally demonstrates the how Congress visualized the occupation of territories for the sole purpose of commercial gain (*Jones v. United States* 1890, 137 U.S. 202; Skaggs 1994). Likewise, the history of U.S. military campaigns contains ample evidence of how the federal government sought to occupy territory for strategic purposes. Yet, what is important to emphasize is that with the one possible exemption of the acquisition of the Kingdom of Hawai'i, creating new states was not a driving impetus in the occupation of territories.

Alternatively, imperialists drew on various constitutional sources of power. For example, rather than invoking the Territories Clause, imperialists could draw on the Commerce Clause (U.S. Const., art. I, §8, cl. 3) as a constitutional source of authority to legitimate commercial expansionism. Likewise, imperialists often situated their power on the Commander-in-Chief Clause (U.S. Const. art. II, §2, cl. 1), a clause that empowered the president to use military force to occupy a sovereign territory or a part thereof. The point is that the federal government did not invoke the Territories Clause as a source of power to legitimate imperialist occupations.

Historically, occupied territories have been treated as sovereign places located outside of the United States. For example, following the British occupation of Maine, the in *U.S. v. Rice* the Court established that the port of Castine remained a foreign territory for tariff purposes while under the British occupation (1819, 17 U.S. 246, 254). Likewise, in *Fleming v. Page* the Court affirmed the power of the U.S. government to treat the Port of Tampico, while under U.S. occupation during the Mexican-American War of 1848 as a foreign port for domestic or constitutional purposes (1850, 50 U.S. 603). And in the case of the North's occupation of the South, the Court also affirmed in *New Orleans v. The Steamship Company* the principle that the Port of New Orleans could be ruled as an occupied territory, even after the end of the Civil War (1874, 87 U.S. 387). Again, the main point is that the United States treated occupied territories as foreign possessions located outside of the United States.

Although the case of Native Americans requires a separate discussion beyond the scope of this note, and may be an example of a different type of expansionism, I treat the relevant U.S. law and policy as a form of imperialism. To be sure, unlike the colonial territories, historically the federal government has recognized degrees or semblances of tribal sovereignty (*Cherokee Nation v. Georgia* 1831, 30 U.S. 1; Aleinikoff 2002). Likewise, the federal government has never invoked the Territories Clause as a source of authority over tribes of Native American nations. Instead, it has invoked a wide array of constitutional sources, including the Commerce Clause, to legitimate the occupation of tribal lands. More importantly, although the federal government has treated tribal lands as a "geographical" part of the United States, it has never described tribal lands as a constitutional part of the nation (Deloria Jr. and Wilkins 1999).

In sum, it is possible to discern three clear contrasts between United States co-lonialist and imperialist traditions of territorial expansionism. First, while the intent of colonialist expansionism was to annex new territories that could be organized into new states of the Union, the imperialist tradition sought to occupy territories for strategic interests. Second, whereas the colonialist tradition anchored its source of constitutional power on the Federalist provisions of the Constitution, namely the Third and Fourth Sections of Article 4, imperialists looked to other sources of ex-ecutive power and congressional power. To be sure, the federal government did not invoke the Territories Clause to legitimate any laws and policies addressing the oc-cupation of sovereign territories. Third, whereas annexed territories were treated as a constitutional part of the United States empire, occupied territories were situated outside of the polity. The question for many was what to do with annexed territories that were primarily inhabited by those who believed in the white supremacist ide-ologies of the period's Anglo-American exceptionalism. The solution was to invent a new or "Third View" (Lowell 1899) of territorial expansionism that enabled the federal government to cherry-pick, reject, or combine past precedents that could be used to rule the newly annexed territories. The corresponding constitutional inter-pretation has since been described as the doctrine of territorial incorporation.

Part II: Contemporary Theories of Territorial Incorporation: Three Views

Presently, it is possible to discern three theories of territorial incorporation. The prevailing theory can be described as a legal doctrine or body of opinions whose substance and contours were defined by the Supreme Court's rulings in the *Insular Cases*. The Court's interpretation argues that Congress has never enacted explicit legislation providing for the territorial incorporation of Puerto Rico; and therefore, the island has remained an unincorporated territory since 1901. In recent years, Judge Gustavo A. Gelpí (2017) has argued that, over time, both the Supreme Court and Congress have treated Puerto Rico like a state. This theory suggests that, over time, both the Court and Congress have implicitly or tacitly incorporated Puerto Rico. More recently, I have argued that while Puerto Rico remains an unincorporated territory, Congress has consistently enacted legislation that selectively treats the is-land as an incorporated territory. My argument, however, is different to that of Judge Gelpí because I argue that Congress' actions are part of an antinomy that informs prevailing U.S. territorial law and policy. Let me explain.

Between 1898 and 1901, United States law and policymakers invented the third tradition of territorial expansionism, sometimes described as the doctrine of territo-rial incorporation (Burnett and Marshall 2001; Rivera-Ramos 2007; Sparrow 2006), or the doctrine of separate and unequal (Torruella 1988), to govern Puerto Rico and the other Spanish ultramarine territories annexed by the United States in the after-math of the Spanish-American War. As I suggested before, the new territorial tradition of expansionism and corresponding constitutional doctrine both selectively departed and combined elements from the colonialist and anti-imperialist precedents. My contention is that the contours of the new territorial doctrine were introduced during the initial annexation process, normalized by Congress with the *Foraker Act of 1900* (31 Stat. 77), and institutionalized by the Supreme Court in the *Insular Cases of 1901*. The Supreme Court subsequently modified the doctrine of territorial incorporation in *Balzac v. People of Porto Rico* (1922, 258 U.S. 298). In order to understand the relevance of the territorial incorporation legislation, it is important to understand the parameters established by these legal debates.

Unlike prior treaties of territorial annexation, the Treaty of Paris did not provide for or promised to collectively naturalize the inhabitants of Puerto Rico.

The United States military formally occupied Puerto Rico on July 25, 1898, and subsequently annexed Puerto Rico, Guam and the Philippines on April 11, 1899 under the terms of the *Treaty of Paris of 1898* (1899, 30 Stat. 1754). Whereas Spain declared Cuba's independence, it ceded Puerto Rico and Guam and sold the Philippines to the United States. However, Article 9 established the core parameters of the subsequent status of the inhabitants of Puerto Rico. Unlike prior treaties of territorial annexation, the *Treaty of Paris* did not provide for or promised to collectively naturalize the inhabitants of Puerto Rico (Van Dyne 1904, 143; Gettys 1934, 145; López Baralt 1991, 108–10). Instead, the first clause of Article 9 invented a local nationality that barred island-born Spanish citizens residing in Puerto Rico from either retaining their citizenship or acquiring a U.S. citizenship. Puerto Ricans were ascribed an anomalous legal status. The second clause of Article 9 established that Congress would be responsible for defining the future civil and political rights of Puerto Ricans. The exclusion of the inhabitants of Puerto Rico enabled subsequent law and policymakers to invent a new territorial status.

Simultaneously, the President established a two-year military dictatorship tasked with establishing local public institutions that would facilitate the island's control (Trias Monge 1991). There is a general consensus that Brigadier General George V. Davis, the last of the U.S. military dictators appointed to rule the island, was responsible for creating the core public institutions to govern Puerto Rico. In his last report as governor of Puerto Rico, Brigadier-General Davis summarized the military's role in shaping the new territorial status within the emerging U.S. global empire:

The scope of these orders was very wide. Almost every branch of administration-political, civil, financial, and judicial-was affected by their provisions. It may be that the military governors exceeded their authority when they changed the codes, the provisions of which were not in conflict with the political character, institutions, and Constitution of the United States; but in the absence of instructions to the contrary, it was conceived to be the privilege and duty of the military commanders to make use of such means with a view to adapting the system of local laws and administration to the one which, judging from precedents, Congress might be expected to enact for the island, thus preparing the latter for a territorial régime when Congress should be ready to authorize it. *It has been pointed out that the course adopted is understood to have been, tacitly at least, approved by Congress, for with two slight exceptions, specified in the [Foraker Act of 1900], every order promulgated by the military governors has been confirmed by Congressional enactment, has become part of the supreme law of the land, and will so remain until abrogated or changed by Congress or by the legislative assembly of the island.* (H.R. 1902, Doc. No. 56-2, 47—emphasis added)

General Davis also noted that unlike prior cases of territorial annexation, Congress had not enacted legislation changing Puerto Rico's territorial status since the United States acquired Puerto Rico. Until Congress enacted legislation providing for the territorial "incorporation" of Puerto Rico within "the American Union," General Davis concluded, the island should be governed as a "dependency" of the United States (1900, 75–6). Governing Puerto Rico as a "dependency" would enable Congress to selectively rule Puerto Rico as a foreign possession for the purposes of collecting import duties on merchandize trafficked in and out of the island (1900, 73). In sum, General Davis recommended treating Puerto Rico as a foreign possession or dependency under the United States sovereignty.

A year later, Congress created a civil government for Puerto Rico under the terms of the *Foraker Act of 1900*. Unlike prior organic or territorial legislation, the *Foraker Act* selectively treated Puerto Rico as a foreign territorial possession for domestic and constitutional purposes. Specifically, the Third Section of the act extended the *Dingley Tariff of 1897* (30 Stat. 151) and imposed a temporary 15 percent tariff on merchandize trafficked between the island and the mainland. The intent of the *Foraker* tariff, Representative Sereno E. Payne (R-NY) argued during the corresponding congressional debates, was to generate local revenues to subsidize the construction of local infrastructure projects proposed by General Davis (i.e.. schools, roads, etc.) (33 Cong. Rec. 1908, 1942). These revenues were especially important because Hurricane San Ciriaco had recently devastated the island's infrastructure. In the corresponding congressional debates, Senator John C. Spooner (R-WI) defended this provision by arguing that "Territory belonging to the United States, as I think Puerto Rico and the Philippine Archipelago do, becomes a part of the United States in the international sense, while not being a part of the United States in the *constitutional sense*" (33 Cong. Rec. 3608, 3629). This interpretation was especially important because the prevailing interpretation of the Uniformity Clause of the Constitution (U.S. Const., art. 1, §8, cl. 1) barred the imposition of a tariff on U.S. soil. Both the tariff and the corresponding interpretation became the foundation of the subsequent Supreme Court's doctrine of territorial incorporation.

As I noted before, soon thereafter, in a series of rulings generally known as the *Insular Cases*, the Supreme Court developed a new constitutional interpretation or doctrine of the status of territories that affirmed the emerging insular or territorial law and policy. The ensuing interpretation departed from prior colonialist and imperialist precedents. To be sure, whereas annexed colonial territories were treated as a part of the U.S. polity, occupied territories were generally situated outside of the United States. The core elements of the new doctrine of territorial incorporation were first outlined by Justice Edward D. White's concurring opinion in *Downes v. Bidwell* (1901, 182 U.S. 244). In *Downes* a plural majority of the Court (5-4) affirmed the constitutionality of the *Foraker* tariff and the power of Congress to enact legislation that applied or withheld constitutional provisions to Puerto Rico. Central to Justice White's interpretation is the legal construction of a distinction between incorporated and unincorporated territories. Incorporated territories, Justice White argued, were those destined to become states of the Union or "part of the American family" (1901, 339). In contrast, unincorporated territories did not possess "the privilege of statehood" (1901, 336). It followed, Justice White further reasoned, unincorporated territories could be ruled as "foreign to the United States in a domestic sense" (1901, 341). Stated differently, unincorporated territories could be treated as possessions that belonged to, but were not a part of, the United States *until* they were incorporated. Again, disregarding a serious analysis of the colonialist history, Justice White concluded that only incorporated territories could become states of the Union.

In addition, Justice White adopted a new interpretation of the applicability of the Constitution to the territories. Again, whereas by 1898 both the Court and Congress had concluded that annexed colonial territories were a part of the United States for constitutional purposes and therefore the constitutional provisions not locally inapplicable extended *ex propio vigore* or on their own force, occupied territories were outside of the U.S. and therefore constitutional provisions did not apply or Congress could enact legislation extending some constitutional provisions not locally inapplicable. Justice White's doctrine argued that only fundamental rights applied to Puerto Rico. Additional rights and constitutional provisions not locally inapplicable could be applied or withheld to the island via jurisprudence or in some instances through legislation. Justice White rejected the notions that either the Constitution applied *ex propio vigore* or not at all to unincorporated territories like Puerto Rico.

It is important to note, however, that the Supreme Court continued to shape the contours of the ensuing doctrine of territorial incorporation over the years. In 1922, the Court modified a key premise of Justice White's interpretation in *Balzac v. People of Porto Rico*. In *Downes*, Justice White argued that Congress possessed the power to enact legislation that expressly or *implicitly* incorporated Puerto Rico and other unincorporated territories more generally (182 U.S. 244, 312). Presumably, Congress could enact legislation expressly incorporating or changing Puerto Rico's territorial status or it could enact legislation that implicitly treated Puerto Rico as an incorporated territory. To be sure, as Efrén Rivera Ramos has noted, writing for the majority, Chief Justice White, established in 1905 in Rasmussen v. United States (197 U.S. 51) that Congress' enactment of legislation providing for the collective naturalization of the inhabitants of a territory could be interpreted as an implicit form of territorial incorporation (84). Drawing on the precedent established in *Rasmussen*, following the collective naturalization of Puerto Ricans under the terms of the *Jones Act of 1917* (39 Stat. 951), local judges assumed that Puerto Rico had been implicitly incorporated. A year later, the Supreme Court, however, rejected this interpretation *People of Porto Rico v. Muratti* and *People of Porto Rico v. Tapia* (1918, 245 U.S. 639) without providing any explanation. In *Balzac*, Chief Justice William H. Taft modified Chief Justice White's interpretation by establishing that "incorporation is not to be assumed without express declaration, *or an implication so strong as to exclude any other view*"(258 U.S. 298, 306). Chief Justice Taft's modification required a clear declaration by Congress that Puerto Rico was incorporated. Again, as noted before, Congress has never enacted legislation providing for the explicit incorporation of Puerto Rico. To this extent, Puerto Rico remains an unincorporated territory.

As I noted above, a second interpretation offered by Judge Gelpí and Gregorio Igartúa (Lloréns Vélez 2017) contends that for all intents and purposes the United States has incorporated Puerto Rico. In Judge Gelpí's words:

...over the years, Congress has chiseled Puerto Rico into a de facto state. From a judicial perspective, both at the local and federal levels, today Puerto Rico is identical to every State in that it has its local system of trial and appellate courts, and at the same time a parallel system of federal courts. (2017, 139)

Elsewhere he argues that most federal laws, civil and criminal, apply to Puerto Rico just as if the island were a state (2017, 189). Because Puerto Rico has, at times, been treated like a state, it follows that the island has been implicitly or tacitly incorporated. Of course, in recent years both Congress and the Supreme Court have respectively rejected this argument with the PROMESA legislation and rulings such as *Puerto Rico v. Sanchez Valle* (2016, 579 U.S.). Instead, both Congress and the Supreme Court have reaffirmed Puerto Rico's unincorporated territorial status.

Like Judge Gelpí, I agree that overtime Congress has selectively enacted legislation that treats Puerto Rico as a state and as an incorporated territory and the Supreme Court has applied most constitutional provisions not locally inapplicable. However, I also argue that Congress' enactment of laws that treat Puerto Rico as a state and/or an incorporated territory, without explicitly enacting legislation that incorporates the island, is an example of the antinomies that inform U.S. territorial law and policy. I use the term antinomy to describe two competing and coexisting legal logics. On the one hand, as I noted before, the Supreme Court has established that Puerto Rico is an unincorporated territory until Congress enacts legislation that explicitly incorporates the island. To this extent Puerto Rico remains a foreign territorial possession in a domestic or constitutional sense. On the other hand, Congress, invoking its constitutionally enumerated power under the Territories Clause, has also enacted birthright legislation that treats Puerto Rico as a part of the United

States for the sole purpose of extending birthright or *jus soli* citizenship to the island (Venator-Santiago 2018). In a sense, both the Court and Congress have corresponding constitutional powers to rule and enact relevant, albeit contradictory, legislation. My contention, however, is that the prevailing U.S. territorial law and policy tolerates this and other types of contradictions or antinomies. Just because Congress enacts legislation that selectively treats the island as an incorporated territory does not mean that Puerto Rico's territorial status has changed.

Just because Congress enacts legislation that selectively treats the island as an incorporated territory does not mean that Puerto Rico's territorial status has changed.

To sum up, between 1898 and 1901, the U.S. government established that Puerto Rico was an unincorporated territory and has not changed the island's constitutional status since. Unlike, incorporated territories, unincorporated territories are not meant to become states of the Union. Although Congress has enacted legislation that treats Puerto Rico like a state and/or an incorporated territory, Congress has never enacted legislation that explicitly changed Puerto Rico's territorial status. Nor has the Supreme Court ruled that Puerto Rico is an incorporated territory. To this extent, Puerto Rico remains an unincorporated territory at the time of this writing.

Part III: Puerto Rico's Territorial Incorporation Legislation

Drawing on a reading of the Congressional Record Index, I have identified upward of 134 status and plebiscitary bills for Puerto Rico introduced, and in some cases debated, in Congress between 1898 and 2018. These bills included an array of status options for Puerto Rico, as well as an array of procedures to change the island's political status. Yet, only ten bills sought to provide a territorial government for Puerto Rico and one sought to discuss the question of the island's territorial status. Ten of these bills were introduced in Congress prior to Puerto Rico's adoption of a local constitution in 1952. Only one bill was introduced after 1952 and before 2018. More importantly, only five bills provided for the territorial incorporation of Puerto Rico. None of the eleven bills were debated outside of their respective committees.

Federal lawmakers introduced two bills addressing the question of Puerto Rico's territorial status during the *Foraker Act's* debates or during the 56th Congress. The first bill, *H.R. 5466*, was introduced in the House Committee on Insular Affairs by Representative John Fletcher Lacey (R-IA) on January 8, 1900. Although this bill was part of a broader debate over the *Foraker Act*, there is no evidence that it received much support. Unlike other bills, *H.R. 5466* treated Puerto Rico as a district rather than a territory. Central to Representative Lacey's bill was a continuation of the military's local laws and public policies (§11). This bill created a barebones civil government for Puerto Rico subordinated to the federal government. However, this bill provided for a territorial delegate (§21) with the same powers as other territorial delegates. Likewise, the bill contained a provision (§22) that extended all United States tariff and internal revenue laws to Puerto Rico, effectively treating the island as a part of the United States.

It is interesting to note that Representative Lacey's bill was more consistent with the Supreme Court's opinion in *Loughborough* than with the prevailing academic interpretations of the period. As I noted above, in *Loughborough* the Supreme Court established that districts (e.g., Washington, D.C.) were equivalent to territories for constitutional purposes. To this extent, describing Puerto Rico as a district would have been tantamount to treating Puerto Rico as a colonial territory. Representative Lacey's bill also treated Puerto Rico as a "dependency" until Congress enacted legislation changing the status of the island (§11). Here Farrand's argument is helpful. Farrand, a well-known legal historian at the time, invoked a historical reading of the notion of the district to describe a territorial status located somewhere in-between a foreign possession and an incorporated territory. Drawing on a reading of the history of the districts of Louisiana and Alaska, Farrand argued that the *Foraker Act* created a different and inferior status for Puerto Rico (1900, 681). The question is whether Representative Lacey understood or was even familiar with Farrand's argument. At present I can only highlight the tension present in the language of Representative Lacey's bill, which at the end of the day did not receive significant support.

On January 22, 1900, Representative Robert Lee Henry (D-TX) introduced a second bill via the House Committee of Insular Affairs, *H.R. 7020,* expressly treating Puerto Rico as a territory. The bill sought to create an organized "territorial government" with corresponding institutions in Puerto Rico (§2). Like virtually all other territorial bills, *H.R. 7020* also extended all parts of the constitution that were not locally inapplicable. This bill was introduced in the House, but died in Committee. Representative Henry was a progressive Democrat, and this bill represented an anti-imperialist or colonialist alternative to the *Foraker Act*. In other words, Representative Henry's bill sought to treat Puerto Rico as a territorial part of the United States in line with established colonialist precedents.

On December 2, 1901, during the 57th Congress, following the Supreme Court's rulings in the *Insular Cases*, Representative Edgar D. Crumpacker (R-IN) introduced a joint resolution in the House Committee on Insular Affairs providing for the territorial incorporation of Puerto Rico into the United States. This is the first bill explicitly providing for the territorial incorporation of Puerto Rico. Representative Crumpacker's resolution, *H.J. Res. 5,* provided "(t)hat the island of Porto Rico [sic] be, and is hereby, incorporated into and made a part of the United States; and all laws locally applicable and not in conflict with Acts passed for the special government thereof are hereby extended to said island." For Representative Crumpacker, territorial incorporation meant treating Puerto Rico as a constitutional part of the United States.

Almost a decade later, during the 63rd Congress, Senator Willard Saulsbury Jr. (D-DE) introduced *S. 5845* in the Senate Committee on Pacific Islands, providing for the creation of a territorial government for Puerto Rico. The bill did not contain lan-

Table 1: Federal Territorial Incorporation Legislation for Puerto Rico, 1898-2018

Congress	Year	Bill/Law	Sponsor	Sponsoring Political Party	Committee	Congressional Action	Type of Legislation	Status
56th	8 January 1900	H.R. 5466	Representative John F. Lacey (R-IA)	Republican	House Committee on Insular Affairs	Introduced in the House Died in Committee	Organic Act	District
	22 January 1900	H.R. 7020	Representative Robert L. Henry (D-TX)	Democrat	House Committee on Insular Affairs	Introduced in the House Died in Committee	Organic Act	Territorial Government
57th	2 December 1901	H.J. Res. 5	Representative Edgar D. Crumpacker (R-IN)	Republican	House Committee on Insular Affairs	Introduced in the House Died in Committee	Joint Resolution	Territorial Incorporation Act
63rd	13 June 1914	S. 5845	Senator Willard Saulsbury Jr. (D-DE)	Democrat	Senate Committee on Pacific Islands and Puerto Rico	Introduced in the House Died in Committee	Organic Act	Territorial Government (§4)
64th	7 December 1915	S. 26	Senator Willard Saulsbury Jr. (D-DE)	Democrat	Senate Committee on Pacific Islands and Puerto Rico	Introduced in the House Died in Committee	Organic Act	Territorial Government (§4)
66th	10 July 1919	H.J. Res. 144	Representative Leonidas C. Dyer (R-MO)	Republican	House Committee on Insular Affairs	Introduced in the House Died in Committee	Join Resolution/ Referendum	1. Independence; 2. Territorial Government; 3. Status quo.
67th	16 January 1922	H.R. 9934	Representative John I. Nolan (R-CA)	Republican	Senate Committee on Pacific Islands and Puerto Rico	Introduced in the House Died in Committee	Organic Act	Territorial Incorporation Act (§2)
75th	6 January 1937	H.R. 1992	Resident Commissioner Santiago Iglesias-Pantin (PR-S/C)	Socialist/ Coalition	House Committee on Insular Affairs	Introduced in the House	Organic Act	Territorial Incorporation Act (§2)
76th	3 January 1939	H.R. 147	Resident Commissioner Santiago Iglesias-Pantin (PR-S/C)	Socialist/ Coalition	House Committee on Insular Affairs	Introduced in the House Died in Committee	Organic Act	Territorial Incorporation Act (§2)
76th	12 January 1940	H.R. 9361	Resident Commissioner Bolivar Pagán (PR-S/C)	Socialist/ Coalition	House Committee on Insular Affairs	Introduced in the House Died in Committee	Organic Act	Territorial Incorporation Act (§2)
103th	22 November 1993	H.R. 3715	Representative Don E. Young (R-AK)	Republican	House Committee on Natural Resources	Referred to Committee on Natural Resources Died in Committee	Organic Act	Recognized Puerto Rico as a Territory and requested a greater degree of home rule prior to statehood Territorial Incorporation Act

guage providing for the "incorporation" of Puerto Rico. Instead, *S. 5845* sought to create a territorial government along the lines of the pre-1898 colonial territories. The bill provided for the extension of all constitutional provisions not locally inapplicable (§5) and treated the Puerto Rican territory as a part of the United States for internal revenue laws (§7), as well as for tariffs and duties (§8). Senator Saulsbury's bill treated Puerto Rico as a part of the United States and like an incorporated territory. A year later, on December 7, 1915, and during the 64th Congress, Senator Saulsbury introduced *S. 26*, another version of the latter bill in the Senate Committee on Pacific Islands and Porto Rico [sic]. Both bills died in committee.

On July 10, 1919, during the 66th Congress, Representative Leonidas C. Dyer (R-MO) introduced *H. J. Res.* 144 in the House Committee on Insular Affairs, providing for an island- wide referendum or plebiscite on the political status of Puerto Rico. Unlike prior bills, Representative Dyer's resolution called for an electoral event that gave local voters a choice among three status options, namely independence, a territorial form of government, or the status quo. It is interesting to emphasize that the resolution/referendum did not contain a statehood option or any reference to a future statehood for Puerto Rico.

On January 16, 1922, during the 67th Congress, Representative John I. Nolan (R-CA) introduced *H. R. 9934*, a territorial incorporation bill, in the House Committee on Insular Affairs. This bill was designed to amend the *Jones Act of 1917* by incorporating the island into the United States. The bill contained two core provisions. The first established an "incorporated Territorial government" in Puerto Rico (§2). The second recognized that the Constitution and other U.S. laws that were not locally inapplicable would "have the same force and effect within" Puerto Rico (§4). Again, territorial incorporation meant that Puerto Rico would become a part of the United States for constitutional purposes.

On January 6, 1937, during the 75th Congress, Puerto Rican Resident Commissioner Santiago Iglesias-Pantín (C-PR) introduced *H.R. 1992*, also a territorial incorporation bill, in the House Committee on Insular Affairs. Like *H. R. 9934*, Resident Commissioner Iglesias-Pantín's territorial incorporation bill, *H. R. 1992* sought to amend the *Jones Act of 1917* and contained two fundamental provisions, one creating an incorporated territorial government for Puerto Rico, (§2) and another extending constitutional provisions not locally inapplicable to the island (§4). This was the first territorial incorporation bill introduced by a Puerto Rican Resident Commissioner. Although the legislative record on this bill is fairly scant, Resident Commissioner Iglesias-Pantín advocated statehood for Puerto Rico, and based on legislative record of other bills he introduced in Congress, it is safe to state that the intent of *H.R. 1992* was to cement a pathway for Puerto Rico to achieve statehood. On January 3, 1939, during the 76th Congress, Resident Commissioner Iglesias-Pantín introduced in the House *H.R. 147*, another version of his previous territorial incorporation bill. Both of his bills died in committee.

On April 12, 1940, during the 76th Congress, Puerto Rican Resident Commissioner Bolívar Pagán Lucca (C-PR) introduced *H. R. 9361* in the House Committee on Insular Affairs. Unlike all prior territorial bills, *H. R. 9361* recognized Puerto Rico as a territory and requested a greater degree of "home rule" that could enable Puerto Ricans to develop a statehood constitution (Preamble). The text of the bill consisted on a series of amendments, primarily of the *Jones Act of 1917*, that sought to treat Puerto Rico as a constitutional part of the United States. The bill was conceived as a bridge to the future statehood of Puerto Rico.

First, between 1898 and 2018, it is possible to identify upward of 134 political status bills introduced, and in some cases debated, in Congress.

Although Congress has debated an array of status bills for Puerto Rico since the enactment of the 1952 Puerto Rican Constitution, between 1952 and 2018, federal lawmakers only discussed one territorial incorporation bill. To be sure, on November 22, 1993, during the 103rd Congress, Representative Don Young (R-AK) introduced *H.R. 3715* in the House Committee on Natural Resources, a measure that authorized consultations for the development of Articles of Incorporation for territories in the United States. Representative Young's bill responded to the United Nations' call for the eradication of colonialism through a process of self-determination. According to the bill, "a territory may be considered decolonized once incorporated into an administering power consistent with a freely expressed act of self-determination of the of the territory" [Sec. 1(a)(1)(C)]. Unlike prior bills of territorial incorporation, which were designed to address Puerto Rico's constitutional status, Representative Young's bill sought to allay the U.N. demands to decolonize Puerto Rico and the other U.S. territorial possessions.[4]

To sum up, I want to highlight seven possible findings. First, between 1898 and 2018, it is possible to identify upward of 134 political status bills introduced, and in some cases debated, in Congress. Of these bills, only eleven contain language explicitly addressing the territorial status of Puerto Rico and only four (five if counting *H.R. 3715*) explicitly call for the territorial incorporation of Puerto Rico. Most bills introduced and/or debated in Congress call for the resolution of Puerto Rico's political status beyond a territorial stage. Second, only the bills introduced by Puerto Rican Resident Commissioners explicitly describe the island's territorial incorporation as a precursor to statehood. Third, with the exception of *H.R. 3715*, which calls for "consultations," all bills were introduced prior to 1952 or the creation of the Puerto Rican Constitution, which conferred a greater degree of local administrative autonomy on the island's residents. Fourth, all bills died in committee, suggesting that Congress has never taken seriously the possibility of "incorporating" Puerto Rico. Fifth, more (5) Republican lawmakers supported some sort of territorial status for Puerto Rico than Democrats (3). Sixth, with the exception of two bills, all bills were introduced in the House of Representatives. Of course, Puerto Rico does not have a seat in the Senate, and it is more likely that the island's Resident Commissioner, who is seated in the House, can influence more members of the House of Representatives. Finally, central to most of the territorial bills discussed above was a concern with extending all constitutional provisions that are not locally inapplicable to Puerto Rico, including the tariff, duties, and internal revenue provisions of the Constitution. For most lawmakers, treating Puerto Rico as a territory meant making the island a part of the United States.

Conclusion

In sum, I want to offer two concluding remarks and a suggestion for further research. As I repeatedly note above, Puerto Rico's separate and unequal status is contingent on its unincorporated territorial status. Clearly, Congress has no intention of incorporating Puerto Rico or changing its territorial status. If anything, it is possible to argue that Congress prefers to retain the flexibility to rule Puerto Rico without being bound or limited by a more democratic application of the Constitution. Likewise, while incorporating Puerto Rico would address the anti-democratic relationship between Puerto Rico and the U.S., there appears to be a consensus interpretation suggesting that incorporating Puerto Rico would bind Congress to eventually grant Puerto Rico statehood. Likewise, the prevailing consensus argues that once Puerto Rico is incorporated, it becomes a permanent part of the United States and Congress would not be able to grant Puerto Ricans independence should they prefer this status option in the future. Unfortunately, for more than a century, Congress has refused to enact binding legislation, enabling Puerto Ricans to choose a status option.

In addition, a common feature of all territorial government bills is a recognition that constitutional provisions that are not locally inapplicable should be extended to Puerto Rico. Stated differently, territorial government and incorporation bills addressed the inequalities created by the island's unincorporated territorial status and the corresponding doctrine of territorial incorporation. For more than a century, progressive/liberals, conservatives, libertarians and socialists, as well as democrats and republicans, have refused to extend the constitution to Puerto Rico in a democratic and egalitarian manner. Simultaneously, the Supreme Court continues to find ways to defer to Congress. If, after more than a century, Congress continues to worry about the question of a permanent relationship between the island and the States, perhaps a simpler solution would be to enact legislation extending all constitutional provisions that are not locally inapplicable to Puerto Rico. At least this type of legislation could begin to repudiated the racist doctrine of territorial incorporation that has defined the separate and unequal status of Puerto Rico within the U.S. empire.

Finally, this note is meant to provide an overview of the legislative initiatives seeking to address the question of Congress' efforts, or lack thereof, to enact legislation that explicitly incorporates Puerto Rico into the U.S. empire. I am interested in providing a structural overview of the problem. A more interesting project could focus on the available papers of the authors of the bills discussed in this note and provide substantive explanations of why they chose the political positions that they did. Perhaps a more histobiographical interpretation of the territorial government and incorporation bills for Puerto Rico could reveal some new insight about the logics of U.S. empire.

NOTES

[1] My analysis of the differences between the colonialist, imperialist and global empire (Third View) traditions of territorial expansionism include other categories of comparison such as the questions of the extension of citizenship and civil rights to acquired territories. However, for purposes of this note, I will limit my discussion to the three issues raised above.

[2] Although I see some continuities in my argument with prevailing settler colonialist research, my focus is on the structural dimensions of colonialism and the role that constitutional law plays in shaping he contours of the U.S. nation-state building process, here understood as an expression of global expansionism. For a discussion of differences between the settler colonialism and the colonialism scholarship, see generally Lorenzo Veracini's text titled *Settler Colonialism* (2010).

[3] It is important to note that Hawai'i was a sovereign monarchy when annexed by the United States in 1899.

[4] It is important to note that Representative Young was an active participant in the 1989-1991 failed plebiscitary debates for Puerto Rico. To this extent, *H.R. 3715* should also be read against this backdrop.

REFERENCES

Aleinikoff, T. Alexander. 2002. *Semblances of Sovereignty, The Constitution, the State, and American Citizenship*. Cambridge, MA: Harvard University Press.

American Insurance v. Canter. 1828. 26 U.S. 511.

Balzac v. People of Porto Rico. 1922. 258 U.S. 298.

Burnett, Christina Duffy and Burke Marshall, eds. 2001. *Foreign in a Domestic Sense: Puerto Rico, American Expansion, and the Constitution*. Durham, NC: Duke University Press.

Coudert, Frederic R. 1926. The Evolution of the Doctrine of Territorial Incorporation. *Columbia Law Review* 26, 823–50.

Deloria Jr., Vine and David E. Wilkins. 1999. *Tribes, Treaties & Constitutional Tribulations*. Austin: University of Texas Press.

Dingley Act. 1897. Ch. 11, 30 Stat. 151.

Downes v. Bidwell. 1901. 182 U.S. 244.

Farrand, Max. 1896 *The Legislation of Congress for the Government of the Organized Territories of the United States, 1789-1895*. Newark: Wm. A. Baker.

———. 1900. Territory and District. *The American Historical Review* 5(4), 676–81.

Fleming v. Page. 1850. 50 U.S. 603.

Foraker Act. 1900. Ch. 191, 31 Stat. 77.

Gelpí, Gustavo A. 2017. *The Constitutional Evolution of Puerto Rico and Other U.S. Territories (1898-Present)*. San Juan: Inter American University of Puerto Rico.

Gettys, Luella. 1934. *The Law of Citizenship in the United States*. Chicago: The University of Chicago Press.

Grupo de Investigadores Puertorriqueños. 1984. *Breakthrough From Colonialism: An Interdisciplinary Study of Statehood*. 2 vols. Río Piedras: Editorial de la Universidad de Puerto Rico.

Incorporating Porto Rico into the United States. 1901. H. J. Res. 5, 57th Cong.

Jones v. United States. 1890. 137 U.S. 202.

Jones Act. 1917. Pub. L. No. 64-368, 39 Stat. 951.

Lloréns Vélez, Eva. 2017. Is Puerto Rico on a Path to Incorporation? *Caribbean Business* 13

February. Accessed 20 January 2018. <http://caribbeanbusiness.com/is-puerto-rico-on-a-path-to-incorporation/>.

López Baralt, José. 1999. *The Policy of the United States Towards its Territories with Special Reference to Puerto Rico.* Río Piedras: Editorial de la Universidad de Puerto Rico.

Loughborough v. Blake. 1820. 18 U.S. 317.

Lowell, Abbott Lawrence. 1899. The Status of Our New Possessions – A Third View. *Harvard law Review* 13, 155–76.

Nationality Act. 1940. Pub. L. No. 76-853, 54 Stat. 1137.

New Orleans v. The Steamship Company. 1874. 87 U.S. 387.

Northwest Ordinance. 1789. Ch. 8, 1 Stat. 50.

People of Porto Rico v. Muratti and People of Porto Rico v. Tapia. 1918. 235 U.S. 639.

Providing for an Advisory Referendum by the People of Porto Rico as to the Form of Government They Desire. 1919. H.J.Res. 144, 66th Cong.

Puerto Rico v. Sanchez Valle. 2016. 579 U.S. ___.

Puerto Rico Oversight, Management, and Economic Stability Act (PROMESA). 2016. Pub. L. No. 114-187, 130 Stat. 549.

Remarks by Representative Payne of New York. 1900. Speaking on behalf of the *Foraker Act,* on 19 February, 33 Cong. Rec. 1908, 1942.

Remarks by Senator Spooner of Wisconsin. 1900. Speaking on behalf of the *Foraker Act,* on 2 April, 33 Cong. Rec. 3608, 3629.

Rivera Ramos, Efrén. 2007. *American Colonialism in Puerto Rico: The Judicial and Social Legacy.* Princeton, NJ: Markus Wiener Publishers.

Sheridan, Peter B. 1985. Admission of States Into the Union After the Original Thirteen: A Brief History and Analysis of the Statehood Process. CRS 85-765Gov. Washington, DC: Government Printing Office.

Skaggs, Jimmy M. 1994. *The Great Guano Rush, Entrepreneurs and American Oversees Expansion.* New York: St. Martin's Press.

Sparrow, Bartholomew H. 2006. *The Insular Cases and the Emergence of the American Empire.* Lawrence: University Press of Kansas.

To Improve the Form of Government of Puerto Rico, Granting a Greater Degree of Home Rule Under the Jurisdiction an Sovereignty of the United States of America; To Amend to that effect an Act entitled "An Act to Provide a Civil Government for Puerto Rico, and for Other Purposes." 1940. Approved 2 March 1917, H.R. 9361, 76th Cong.

To Make Porto Rico an Incorporated Territory of the United States. 1922. H.R. 9934, 67th Cong.

To Make Porto Rico an Incorporated Territory of the United States. 1937. H.R. 1992, 75th Cong.

To Make Porto Rico an Incorporated Territory of the United States. 1939. H.R. 147, 76th Cong.

To Provide a Civil Government for the District of Puerto Rico, and for Other Purposes. 1900. H.R. 5486, 56th Cong.

To Provide Consultations for the Development of Articles of Incorporation for Territories of The United States. 1993. H.R. 3715, 103rd Cong.

To Provide a Government for the Territory of Puerto Rico. 1900. H.R. 7020, 56th Cong.

To Provide a Government for the Territory of Porto Rico. 1914. S. 5845, 63th Cong.

To Provide a Government for the Territory of Porto Rico. 1915. S. 26, 64th Cong.

Torruella, Juan R. 1988. *The Supreme Court and Puerto Rico: The Doctrine of Separate and Unequal.* Río Piedras: Editorial de la Universidad de Puerto Rico.

Treaty of Paris. 1899. 30 Stat. 1754.

Trías Monge, José. 1991. *El choque de dos culturas jurídicas en Puerto Rico, el caso de la responsabilidad civil extracontractual.* Austin, TX: Equity Publishing Company.

UNITED STATES CONGRESS. HOUSE OF REPRESENTATIVES. 1902. ANNUAL REPORTS OF THE WAR DEPARTMENT FOR THE FISCAL YEAR ENDED JUNE 30, 1900, PART 13: REPORT OF THE MILITARY GOVERNOR OF PORTO RICO ON CIVIL AFFAIRS, H.R. Doc. No. 56-2 (2nd Sess.).

UNITED STATES WAR DEPARTMENT, BUREAU OF INSULAR AFFAIRS. 1900. REPORT OF BRIG. GEN. GEO. W. DAVIS, U.S.V. ON CIVIL AFFAIRS OF PUERTO RICO, 1899. WASHINGTON: GOVERNMENT PRINTING OFFICE.

U.S. v. Rice. 1819. 17 U.S. 246.

Van Dyne, Frederick. 1904. *Citizenship of the United States.* New York: The Lawyer's Cooperative Publishing Co.

Venator-Santiago, Charles R. 2015. *Puerto Rico and the Origins of U.S. Global Empire: The Disembodied Shade.* London: Routledge.

————. 2018. Puerto Rico y las antinomias de la ciudadanía de Estados Unidos *80grados* 31 May. Accessed 19 January 2019. <http://www.80grados.net/puerto-rico-y-las-antinomias-de-la-ciudadania-de-estados-unidos/>.

Veracini, Lorenzo. 2010. *Settler Colonialism: A Theoretical Overview.* New York: Palgrave/McMillan.

Weingast, Barry R. 1998. Political Stability and Civil War: Institutions, Commitments and American Democracy. In *Analytic Narratives,* eds. Robert H. Bates et al. 148–93. Princeton, NJ: Princeton University Press.

ACKNOWLEDGEMENTS

CENTRO: Journal of the Center for Puerto Rican Studies recognizes the following reviewers for their work evaluating manuscripts during this calendar year (2018). The names listed did not necessarily review essays included in this number.

Luz del Alba Acevedo, *Universidad de Puerto Rico—Río Piedras*

René Antrop-González, *Metropolitan State University*

Elizabeth Aranda, *University of South Florida*

César J. Ayala, *University of California—Los Angeles*

Efraín Barradas, *University of Florida*

Amilcar Barreto, *Northeastern University*

Ramón Borges-Méndez, *Clark University*

Peter Carlo Becerra, *Universidad de Puerto Rico—Río Piedras*

Tania Carrasquillo Hernández, *Linfield College*

José G. Conde Santiago, *Universidad de Puerto Rico—Ciencias Médicas*

Jason Cortés, *Rutgers, The State University of New Jersey—Newark*

Dinorah Cortés-Vélez, *Marquette University*

José E. Cruz, *State University of New York—University at Albany*

Marie Cruz-Soto, *New York University*

Alberto Dávila, *Southeast Missouri State University*

Carmelo Esterrich, *Columbia College*

Harry Franqui-Rivera, *Bloomfield College*

Ana María García, *Instituto Nueva Escuela*

Ivis García, *University of Utah*

Myrna García, *Syracuse University*

Luis Gautier, *University of Texas—Tyler*

Carlos Gorrin Peralta, *Universidad Interamericana de Puerto Rico—Recinto Metropolitano*

Martin Guzman, *Columbia University*

Ylce Irizarry, *University of South Florida*

Thomas Herndon, *Loyola Marymount University*

Caél Keegan, *Grand Valley State University*

Lawrence La Fountain-Stokes, *University of Michigan—Ann Arbor*

Scott Larson, *University of Michigan—Ann Arbor*

Aldo Lauria-Santiago, *Rutgers, The State University of New Jersey—New Brunswick*

André Lecours, *University of Ottawa*

Benjamin Lemoine, *Dauphine Université Paris*

Nancy López, *University of New Mexico*

Pablo J. López, *Universidad Nacional de José C. Paz*

Carmen Lugo-Lugo, *Washington State University*

Arthur MacEwan, *University of Massachusetts—Boston*
Yolanda Martínez-San Miguel, *University of Miami*
Edgardo Meléndez, *City University of New York—Hunter College*
Edwin Meléndez, *City University of New York—Hunter College*
Marie T. Mora, *University of Texas—Rio Grand Valley*
Enrique Morales-Díaz, *Westfield State University*
Francis Daniel Nina Estrella, *Universidad de Puerto Rico—Río Piedras*
Anaida Pascual Morán, *Universidad de Puerto Rico—Río Piedras*
María Pérrez-Lugo, *Universidad de Puerto Rico—Mayagüez*
Margaret Power, *Illinois Institute of Technology*
Sandra Pujals, *Universidad de Puerto Rico—Río Piedras*
Sandra Quiñones, *Duquesne University*
Carlos Ríos-Bedoya, *Michigan State University*
Ángel Rivera, *Worcester Polythecnic Institute*
Ángel Israel Rivera, *Universidad de Puerto Rico—Río Piedras*
Carmen Haydée Rivera, *Universidad de Puerto Rico—Río Piedras*
Fernando I. Rivera, *University of Central Florida*
Rosario Rivera Negrón, *Universidad de Puerto Rico—Cayey*
Magaly Roy-Féquière, *Knox College*
Betsy Sandlin, *Sewanee: The University of the South*
Ruth Santiago, *Independent Scholar*
Brad W. Setser, *Council on Foreign Relations*
Maritza Stanchich, *Universidad de Puerto Rico—Río Piedras*
Galvin Stevenson, *Pratt Institute*
William Súarez, *City University of New York—Hostos Community College*
Wilfredo Toledo, *Universidad de Puerto Rico—Río Piedras*
Maura Toro-Morn, *Northern Illinois State University*
Wilson Valentín-Escobar, *Hampshire College*
William Vélez, *University of Wisconsin—Milwaukee*
Charles R. Venator-Santiago, *University of Connecticut—Storrs*
Valery Vézina, *Memorial University of Newfoundland*
Antonio Weiss, *Harvard University*
Micah Wright, *Boise State University*

BOOKS FROM THE CENTRO PUBLICATIONS

State of Puerto Ricans 2017

Edited by Edwin Meléndez and Carlos Vargas-Ramos

This book provides an updated overview of some of the most salient subjects and themes about the Puerto Rican population in the United States at present. It highlights the continued mobility and expansion of the Puerto Rican population throughout the country, including state-to-state migration, migration from Puerto Rico in light of the economic crisis in the island, as well as the role of service in the armed forces in anchoring new areas of settlement. ISBN 978-1-945662-12-6; 2017, $20 (pbk)

Almanac of Puerto Ricans in the United States, 2016

Jennifer Hinojosa and Carlos Vargas-Ramos

This almanac is a compendium of demographic, economic and social data about the Puerto Rican population in the United States. It compares conditions among Puerto Ricans in selected states with those of Puerto Ricans nationally and Puerto Rico, using aggregate data from the United States Census Bureau's American Community Survey for 2014, one-year estimates. The information presented spans the range from educational attainment, language proficiency, labor force participation, earnings and income, purchasing power, poverty and housing. The almanac further provides visual representation of Puerto Rican settlement by mapping their spatial location nationally and selected states. ISBN 978-1-945662-07-2; 2016, $15 (pbk)

FORTHCOMMING BOOKS

Liberalism and Identity Politics: Puerto Rican Community Organizations and Community Action in New York City
Jose E Cruz

PATRIA: Puerto Rican Revolutionaries in Nineteenth Century New York
Edgardo Meléndez

Before the Wave: Puerto Ricans in Philadelphia, 1910–1945

Víctor Hernández-Vázquez

This book recounts the genesis of the Puerto Rican community in Philadelphia during the interwar years (1917-1945). It connects the origins of this community to the mass migration of the post-WW II (1945-1985) years when Puerto Ricans consolidated their presence in Philadelphia. This study compares the experiences of Puerto Ricans with that of the Italians, the Polish, and African Americans in Philadelphia during the early twentieth century. The scholarship on Puerto Ricans outside of New York has been, by and large, limited to the postwar period and a closer examination of the interwar years provides us a more complete picture of how the postwar migrants were established and developed over a much longer period than previously believed. ISBN: 9781945662027 (pbk) 2017 129 pages, $19.99 (pbk)

The Bodega: A Cornerstone of Puerto Rican Barrios (The Justo Martí Collection)

Carlos Sanbria

From the 1940s to the 1970s bodegas, those ubiquitous corner-stores, in New York City's barrios were more than places where Puerto Rican recent immigrants bought their groceries. As the photographs in this photo-essay book demonstrates, they were also anchors for the social and cultural life of neighborhoods. This photo book is based on a selection of bodega pictures taken by the well-known photographer of New York's Latino life Justo Martí. ISBN: 978-1-945662-06-5 (pbk) 2017 43 pages, $15.00

Puerto Ricans at the Dawn of the New Millennium

Edited by Edwin Meléndez and Carlos Vargas-Ramos

A new millennium, with new realities! The demographic and socioeconomic profile of Puerto Ricans has changed dramatically. The depictions that emerge from this book are tales of resiliency amid declining opportunity and the enduring challenges faced by those still caught in the trough of the recession. The book is also a story about those who left the island for the mainland United States in search of economic opportunities and about the social contexts of the new communities throughout the United States in which they have settled. ISBN 978-1-878483-79-9 (pbk); 2014; 319 pages; Price: $24.99 (pbk)

The AmeRícan Poet: Essays on the Works of Tato Laviera

Edited by Stephanie Alvarez and William Luis

The AmeRícan Poet is a collection of thirteen essays, an intro-duction and a foreword by fifteen established and emerging scholars. Known as a Nuyorican poet, Laviera is more appropriately celebrated as an AmeRícan writer of national and international prominence. As a whole, the essays discuss diverse aspects of Laviera's life and substan-tial body of work that includes five published collections of poetry, twelve written and staged plays, and many years of political, social, liter-ary and healthcare activism. As the AmeRícan poet, the collection confirms Tato Laviera's much deserved reputation as a major poet in any language. ISBN: 978-1-878483-66-9 (pbk); 2014; 418 pages, Price: $24.99 (pbk)

Gilberto Gerena Valentín: My Life as a Community Activist, Labor Organizer, and Progressive Politician in New York City

Gilberto Gerena Valentín
Edited by Carlos Rodríguez Fraticelli; Translated by Andrew Hurley with an Introduction by José E. Cruz

Gilberto Gerena Valentín is a key figure in the development of the Puerto Rican community in the United States, espe-cially from the forties through the seventies. He was a union organizer, community leader, political activist and general in the war for the civil-rights recognition of his community. In his memoirs, Gilberto Ger ena Valentín takes us into the center of the fierce labor, political, civil-rights, social and cultural struggles waged by Puerto Ricans in New York from the 1940s through the 1970s. ISBN 978-1-878483-74-4 (pbk); 2013; 315 pages, Price: $20 (pbk)

Soy Gilberto Gerena Valentín: memorias de un puertorriqueño en Nueva York

Gilberto Gerena Valentín
Edición de Carlos Rodríguez Fraticelli

Gilberto Gerena Valentín es uno de los personajes claves en el desarrollo de la comunidad puertorriqueña en Nueva York. En sus memorias, Gilberto Gerena Valentín nos lleva al centro de las continuas luchas sindicales, políticas, sociales y culturales que los puertorriqueños fraguaron en Nueva York durante el periodo de la Gran Migración hasta los años setenta. ISBN: 978-1-878483-64-5 (pbk)—ISBN: 978-1-878483-45-4 (ebook); 2013; 302 pages, Price: $20 (pbk); $6 (ebook)

The State of Puerto Ricans 2013

Edited by Edwin Meléndez and Carlos Vargas-Ramos

The State of Puerto Ricans 2013 collects in a single report the most current data on social, economic and civic conditions of the Puerto Rican population in the United States available from governmental sources, mostly the U.S. census Bureau. ISBN: 978-1-878483-72-0 (pbk); 2013; 91 pages, Price: $15 (pbk)

The Stories I Read to the Children: The Life and Writing of Pura Belpré, the Legendary Storyteller, Children's Book Author, and New York Public Librarian

Edited and Biographical Introduction by Lisa Sánchez González

The Stories I Read to the Children documents, for the very first time, Pura Belpré's contributions to North American, Caribbean, and Latin American literary and library history. Thoroughly researched but clearly written, this study is scholarship that is also accessible to general readers, students, and teachers. Lisa Sánchez González has collected, edited, and annotated over 40 of Belpré's stories and essays, most of which have never been published. Her introduction to the volume is the most extensive study to date of Belpré's life and writing. ISBN: 978-1-878483-80-5 (pbk)—ISBN: 978-1-878483-45-4 (ebook); 2013; 286 pages; Price: $20 (pbk); $7.99 (ebook from Amazon)

To purchase these publications, and to subscribe to CENTRO Journal, visit Centro Store (http://www.centropr-store.com)

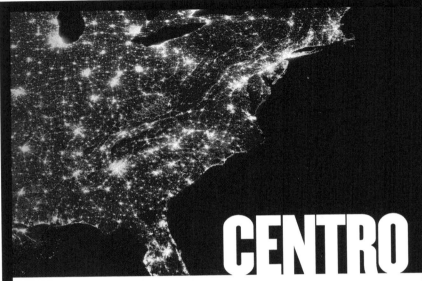

CARIBBEAN STUDIES

A journal published twice a year

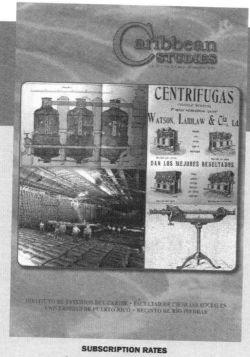

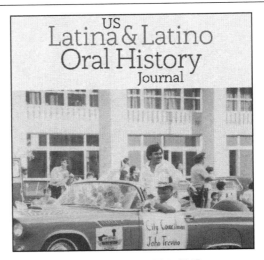

US
Latina & Latino
Oral History
Journal

CONTENTS, VOLUME 1, 2017:

The Origins of the 1975 Expansion of the Voting Rights Act:
Linking Language, Race, and Political Influence
LUIS RICARDO FRAGA

Raza Unida Party Women in Texas: Oral History, Pedagogy, and Historical Interpretation
EMILIO ZAMORA

"We are Asking for Equal Education":
Mexican Americans and the Quest for Educational Equity in Arizona
MARITZA DE LA TRINIDAD

The 1960s Chicano Movement for Educational Reform and the Rise of
Student Protest Activism on San Antonio's Westside
JAMES B. BARRERA

Pathways to Political Office:
Maria Cárdenas and the Creation of Single-Member Districts in San Angelo, Texas
TIFFANY J. GONZÁLEZ

INDIVIDUALS $43 / VOLUME | INSTITUTIONS $130 / VOLUME
CANADIAN SUBSCRIBERS ADD $20 POSTAGE. ALL OTHER INTERNATIONAL SUBSCRIBERS ADD $27.

UNIVERSITY OF TEXAS PRESS

Post Office Box 7819, Austin, Texas 78713-7819
P: 512.471.7233 | F: 512.232.7178 | journals@utpress.utexas.edu
UTPRESS.UTEXAS.EDU

S T U D I E S I N

LATIN AMERICAN

POPULAR CULTURE

MELISSA A. FITCH, EDITOR
UNIVERSITY OF ARIZONA

INDIVIDUALS $43 / VOLUME | INSTITUTIONS $130 / VOLUME
CANADIAN SUBSCRIBERS ADD $20 POSTAGE. ALL OTHER INTERNATIONAL SUBSCRIBERS ADD $27.

UNIVERSITY OF TEXAS PRESS

Post Office Box 7819, Austin, Texas 78713-7819
P: 512.471.7233 | F: 512.232.7178 | journals@utpress.utexas.edu
UTPRESS.UTEXAS.EDU

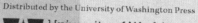
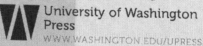

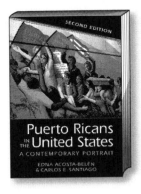
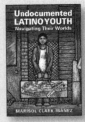

39889109R00192